JESUS,
DIVINE MESSIAH

JESUS, DIVINE MESSIAH

THE NEW TESTAMENT WITNESS

ROBERT L. REYMOND

Presbyterian and Reformed Publishing Company
Phillipsburg, New Jersey

Copyright © 1990 by Robert L. Reymond

Scripture quotations are from the New International Version or the author's own translation.

Manufactured in the United States of America

Library of Congress Cataloging-in-Publication Data

Reymond, Robert L.
    Jesus, divine Messiah : the New Testament witness / Robert L. Reymond.
        p.   cm.
    Bibliography: p.
    Includes indexes.
    ISBN 0-87552-402-8
    1. Jesus Christ—Divinity—Biblical teaching.   2. Jesus Christ—History of doctrines—
Early church, ca. 30–600.   3. Bible. N.T.—Theology.   I. Title.
BT216.R49   1990
232'.8'09015—dc20   89–35362
                                                                                          CIP

CONTENTS

PREFACE

"What do you think of the Christ? Whose Son is He?" Jesus asked the Pharisees (Matt. 22:42). In this book I have attempted to answer Jesus' questions by expounding the key christological passages of the New Testament. I have tried to allow the very voice of Scripture (*ipsissima vox Scripturae*) to supply its answer to these questions. Central, of course, to any scriptural answer is what Jesus Himself believed and taught. Therefore, I set forth first His self-witness as accurately as I could. I also tried to listen carefully to the New Testament writers—to the Synoptic Evangelists no less than to John, to James no less than to Paul, to Jude no less than to Peter or to the writer of Hebrews. I trust that I have listened to them as they intended to be heard. The reader must judge, of course, whether or not I have.

I also have written as a systematic theologian. Professional New Testament scholars, even evangelical New Testament scholars, may judge that I have read the New Testament, particularly the Gospels, "too flatly" at times, that I have left no room for genuine differences between the Christ of the Synoptics, the Christ of Paul's witness, and the Christ of John's Gospel. They may conclude that I have failed to give sufficient place to the role that "functional Christology" played in the "development" of New Testament Christology as a whole. They may also think that I have read the Gospels "too historically" because I have not entered in any significant way into genre criticism—a major interest in current New Testament research—in my exegesis of some relevant Gospel pericopes.

In response, let me assure my colleagues in the New Testament field that I have no brief against any "functional christological insights" or any results of genre study that can be *exegetically* sustained. On the other hand, if some New Testament scholars become troubled because, in their opinion, I have read the Gospels "too flatly" here or "too historically" there, I must say that I too am troubled by what I see as the willingness of at least some New

Testament scholars to postulate differences between and to impose "functional" christological categories upon New Testament statements where frankly I, as a systematic theologian, who also have an interest in good exegesis, find no exegetical warrant for doing so. It will be apparent where I think this has been done. I respectfully suggest that modern New Testament scholarship may read the New Testament writers too developmentally and functionally at times. I also suggest that New Testament scholarship, as the result of form criticism, redaction criticism, and genre criticism, may read the Gospels today too much as mere forms of ancient secular literature and lose sight of the fact that their authors, after all is said and done, intended their accounts as the *historical* record of those aspects of the person and ministry of Jesus that were central to the apostolic proclamation of the gospel.

Of course, no knowledgeable person will deny that the New Testament writers expressed their theological convictions in a variety of ways. And to the degree that their expressions and vocabularies vary, there will be different nuances in some of their perceptions. In my opinion, when they are compared, the resulting composite picture only makes for a richer New Testament representation of the apostolic voice. This is what lies, for example, behind the fact that we have four canonical portrayals of Jesus' ministry and Passion. But however much or little the New Testament writers differed in their nuanced perceptions of other things—such as the way they represented Christ's salvific work (ransom, propitiation, etc.)—it is my conviction that they did not differ essentially in their basic perception of Jesus. I suggest that they all came to believe that He is in fact the Messiah and that He is God in the same sense that Christians today would say that God the Father is God, and that they wrote with this basic perception of Him. If I am wrong in this conviction, I want to be shown by exegesis. Such an interdisciplinary dialogue can only result in a better, deeper, and truer understanding of Jesus.

I want to express my appreciation to the Board of Trustees of Covenant Theological Seminary for granting me sabbatical leave to research this study. I also want to express my gratitude to the Board of Tyndale House, Cambridge, and the Board of Rutherford House, Edinburgh, for the privilege of studying in their library facilities. It was a special privilege to present some of this material as the Lecturer at the latter study center during Rutherford House Week in May of 1986. The courteous and constructive reception those lectures received on that occasion encouraged me to "finish the race."

Words of appreciation must also be expressed to the publisher and the editor of Presbyterian and Reformed Publishing Company. The commitment of Mr. Bryce Craig to the project was always reassuring, and the many helpful suggestions of Mr. Thom Notaro and his staff improved the book immensely.

I will be forever indebted to my wife, Shirley, who is also my greatest encourager, who made our little "flats" in Cambridge and Edinburgh seem so much like home, and to our children—Stephanie, Robert, Jr., and Jeffrey— who were willing to let their parents be away from them for several months to get the research done.

To all these special people, as well as to so many others that it is impossible to name them all, I simply say: "Thank you. I have labored, but you have entered into my labors. You too will have your reward."

PRESENT DENIALS OF
THE DEITY OF JESUS

What's the Problem?

The Christian church, it would seem, has always been embroiled in controversy, not always of its own making, true enough, but controversy nonetheless. And it has often been the case that the controversy has been "within the family," as variant doctrines were developed and espoused. For example, in the Nicene and Post-Nicene periods of the church, roughly A.D. 300–600, the Greek church, centered mainly in the Catechetical Schools of Alexandria and Antioch, was engaged in heated dispute regarding the trinitarian/christological controversies dealing respectively (1) with the related issues of the deity of Christ (and the Holy Spirit) and the implications of that teaching for the doctrine of the triune nature of God, and (2) with the manner in which the divine and human natures are to be related to each other and to the one person of Christ. The Latin (Western) church, on the other hand, found itself in the fifth century involved in the soteriological controversy[1] precipitated by the great conflict between Pelagius and Augustine (A.D. 411–31). In sum, this controversy centered in the question of whether God saves man or a man can and must save himself. The church, of course, determined rightly at that time (at the Sixteenth Council of Carthage in A.D. 418–31 and the Council at Ephesus in A.D.431) that Christianity was to remain "a religion of rescue" and not rot down into "a religion of self-help."[2]

The soteriological controversy has again and again engaged the church's interest and energies—for instance, in the Gottschalk controversy in the

---

1. Philip Schaff (*Nicene and Post-Nicene Christianity*, A.D. 311-600, vol. 3, *History of the Christian Church*, 5th ed. rev. [Grand Rapids: Eerdmans, 1960], p 783), speaks of these as "Anthropological Controversies," in that they raise the question of the degree to which men are involved in their own salvation.

2. Cf. ibid., pp. 785-815, and Benjamin B. Warfield, *The Plan of Salvation* (Grand Rapids: Eerdmans, 1955), pp. 35-36, for more detail.

ninth century, in the doctrinal struggles of the Reformation period in the sixteenth century, in the Calvinist-Arminian debates within the Reformed church in the seventeenth century, and in our own day in the church's opposition to secular humanism's contention that men must save themselves from whatever ills beset them. But once the church settled the doctrines of the two-natured person of Christ and the Trinity in the intense struggle at Nicaea in A.D. 325 and in the debates culminating at Chalcedon in A.D. 451, these doctrines saw virtually no further challenge. (The monophysite and monothelite controversies, mainly in the Eastern church in the succeeding two centuries, entailed "relapses" into contradictions that Chalcedon had already substantially overcome.) Church leaders refined the doctrines—for example, Leontius of Byzantium (or Leontius of Jerusalem) contributed the *enhypostasis,* and Calvin insisted upon the autotheotic character of the Son—but not until the so-called European Enlightenment (the *Aufklärung*) of the eighteenth century, which encouraged a rationalistic criticism of the Bible and opposition to all supernatural religion, did any substantial opposition form. The creeds of Nicaea and Chalcedon, in other words, became the touchstone of christological orthodoxy for catholic Christendom for the next fifteen hundred years, even through the turbulent divisions of the church into Eastern church and Western church in A.D. 1054 and then of Western Christendom itself into Roman Catholic Church and Protestant Church in the sixteenth century. Indeed, to this very day, if not in men's minds at least still in the church's creeds and confessions, we find both the doctrine and the language of the Nicene Creed and the Definition of Chalcedon.[3]

But for the last two centuries, beginning with Schleiermacher's *The Christian Faith* (cf. sections 95-96) and continuing in our day particularly, the conciliar formulations of Nicaea and Chalcedon espousing a two-natured Christ have fallen upon hard times. Today, one can find evidence virtually everywhere—on every continent, in both Protestant and Roman Catholic circles—that the theologically "in thing" is to contend for a Jesus who was only a man by nature and for a Bible that is virtually silent regarding the classical incarnational Christology of a two-natured Christ—true God and true man in the one person of Jesus Christ.[4] It is very much in vogue to

---

3. Cf. Augsburg Confession (1530), Article III; First Helvetic Confession (1536), Article XI; Second Helvetic Confession (1566), Article XI; Heidelberg Catechism (1563), Question 35; Belgic Confession (1561), Articles X, XVIII, and XIX; First Scotch Confession (1560), Article VI; Thirty-Nine Articles of the Church of England (1563, 1571), Article II; and Westminster Confession of Faith (1647), Article VIII, ii.

4. Throughout this book I may refer, for the sake of variation in style, to this doctrine of Christ's

believe that the better case can be made for understanding Jesus as only a man—a very unusual man, of course, with a special mission from God—and to explain the biblical ascriptions of divine qualities to Him in other than ontological terms.[5] Illustrations of this trend abound virtually without end, but four will suffice to make my point.

1. In his lecture on "The Christological Confession of the World Council of Churches" that Jesus Christ is "God and Saviour" (the confession of the WCC meeting in 1948), Rudolf Bultmann raised the question of whether this confession accords with the New Testament. It all depends, he responded, on what is meant by the word "God." "Is Christ's nature intended to be designated in the designation of him as 'God'—his metaphysical nature or his significance? Does the pronouncement have soteriological or cosmological character or both?"[6] "Neither in the Synoptic Gospels nor in the Pauline Epistles," he declared, "is Jesus called God."[7] Any significance that one might attach to his concession with regard to the one "certain passage" in John 20:28 (Thomas's confession) is immediately blunted by his remark that everywhere else Jesus is always spoken of as subordinate to God.[8] His conclusion is that "the formula 'Christ is God' is false in every sense in which God is understood as an entity which can be objectified. . . . It is correct, if 'God' is understood here as the event of God's acting."[9] We will have many occasions to refer to Bultmann's views later, but even here it is clear that, for Bultmann, Jesus in Himself (*in se*) was only a man.

2. In 1977 a symposium of seven British theologians published *The Myth of God Incarnate* in which they called upon the church to recognize "that Jesus was . . . 'a man approved by God' for a special role within the divine

two natures in a variety of ways: for example, classical Christology, incarnational Christology, and so on; but I will always have the doctrine of His two natures in mind.

5. I recognize that there are those who, while they fully accept the *biblical* doctrine of incarnational Christology, believe that the *classical* formulations of Nicaea and Chalcedon, the latter particularly, in one way or another distort the biblical portrayal of Christ. A. N. S. Lane, Lecturer in Historical Theology at London Bible College, may be cited as a representative of this group. He faults the Chalcedon statement for asserting the impassibility of the eternal Son, thereby leading to a "dualistic Christ," a Christ who can suffer and a Christ who cannot suffer, which is "foreign to the New Testament portrait of Christ." Lane also believes that the Chalcedonian Christ is docetic, that is, He is in some sense something other than true man (a further result of the "unabashedly dualist" tendency in the Chalcedonian definition of Christ), this docetism, Lane contends, evidencing itself in the Definition's "practical denial" of human limitations in Christ. Cf. his article, "Christology Beyond Chalcedon," in *Christ the Lord*, ed. Harold H. Rowdon (Leicester: Inter-Varsity Press, 1982), pp. 257-81.

6. Rudolf Bultmann, *Essays Philosophical and Theological*, trans. James C. G. Greig (New York: Macmillan, 1955), p. 275.

7. Ibid.

8. Ibid., p. 276.

9. Ibid., p. 287.

purpose, and that the later conception of him as God incarnate, the Second Person of the Holy Trinity living a human life, is a mythological or poetic way of expressing his significance for us."[10] John Hick summarized how he thinks it happened that Jesus, though only a man, came to be regarded also as God:

> It was natural and intelligible both that Jesus, through whom men had found a decisive encounter with God and a new and better life, should come to be hailed as son of God, and that later this poetry should have hardened into prose and escalated from a metaphorical son of God to a metaphysical God the Son.[11]

Maurice Wiles, another contributor, categorically declared, "Incarnation, in its full and proper sense, is not something directly presented in scripture."[12]

3. In his review of I. Howard Marshall's commentary on the Johannine letters in the NICNT series, the American Roman Catholic scholar Raymond E. Brown on two accounts criticized Marshall's suggestion that the Johannine letters can be profitably read as an introduction to the theology of the New Testament as a whole since they stress a "real Christianity" that is "based on the incarnation and sacrificial death of the Son of God." Marshall implies "a continuity in NT thought" that Brown believes never existed, and, while "incarnation is truly characteristic of Johannine Christology," it is "quite uncharacteristic of about 90% of the rest of the NT."[13] Brown's remarks simply mean, if he is right, that by far the major portion of the New Testament does not espouse an incarnational Christology, but reflects rather "other forms of NT theology."

4. James D. G. Dunn asserts in his *Christology in the Making,*

> If we are to submit our speculations to the text and build our theology only with the bricks provided by careful exegesis we cannot say with any confidence that Jesus knew himself to be divine, the pre-existent Son of God.[14]

Of the three Synoptic passages that, according to Dunn, might offer some basis for classical incarnational Christology (Mark 12:6; Mark 13:32; and Matt. 11:27 with its parallel in Luke 10:22), the contrast between "servants" and the "Son" in the first passage

---

10. John Hick, ed., *The Myth of God Incarnate* (Philadelphia: Westminster Press, 1977), p. ix.

11. Ibid., p. 176.

12. Maurice Wiles, "Christianity Without Incarnation?" in Hick, *Myth of God Incarnate,* p. 3.

13. Raymond E. Brown, *The Catholic Biblical Quarterly,* 42, no. 3 (July 1980): 413.

14. James D. G. Dunn, *Christology in the Making: A New Testament Inquiry Into the Origins of the Doctrine of the Incarnation* (London: SCM Press, 1980), p. 32.

provides no sure foundation since the contrast can be fully explained as part of the dramatic climax of the parable. As for the other two, it is precisely in Jesus' reference to himself as "the Son" that most scholars detect evidence of earliest Christians adding to or shaping an original saying of less christological weight.[15]

Dunn, in fact, can find an explicit statement of incarnation in *only one* passage in the New Testament—the so-called "Logos Poem" of John 1![16] But even this "poem" reflects not Jesus' own self-understanding but the theology of subsequent Christian reflection.[17]

Dunn believes that incarnational Christology began to emerge in Christian thought when Paul pressed into service both pre-Christian Jewish Wisdom language to express what for him was the "cosmic significance of the Christ-event" and "mystery" language to express the conviction that Christ was the eschatological fulfillment of God's purpose from the beginning. But the idea never occurred to Paul, according to Dunn, to think of Christ "as a heavenly being who had pre-existed with God from the beginning."[18] It was when these language forms, found particularly in Colossians and Ephesians, were later read apart from their original contexts that pre-existence and a role in creation began to be ascribed to Christ. Here, Dunn declares, "we see the most immediate antecedent to the doctrine of the incarnation, the womb from which incarnational christology emerged."[19] Then when a second-generation Christianity in the last decades of the first century extended the "Son of God" language "backward"—from resurrection, to death and resurrection, then to the beginning of Jesus' ministry, then to His conception and birth, and finally to a timeless eternity—the Christian mind was ready for the full-blown Logos Christology of John's prologue in which degrees or stages of His sonship are left behind and a divine sonship of unchanging timelessness is reached.[20]

Dunn claims to demonstrate the development of the Christ-idea from "Christ-event" in which *God acted for men* in Jesus to "incarnation" in which

15. Ibid., p. 28.
16. Ibid., p. 241.
17. Ibid., p. 30. Dunn believes, because the style of the Fourth Gospel is "so consistent" and "so consistently different" from the Synoptics, "that it can hardly be other than a Johannine literary product . . . elaborated in the language and theology of subsequent Christian reflection" (ibid.). Again, because of the "complete lack of real parallel in the earlier tradition: no other Gospel speaks of Jesus coming down from heaven and the like," Dunn writes, ". . . it would be verging on the irresponsible to use the Johannine testimony on Jesus' divine sonship in our attempt to uncover the self-consciousness of Jesus himself" (ibid., p. 31).
18. Ibid., p. 255.
19. Ibid., p. 256.
20. Ibid.

Christ as preexistent Son of God became flesh and *acted for God among men*. Of course, if all this is so, then the formulations of Nicaea and Chalcedon have, at best, enshrined only one christological model of the New Testament—the latest to develop—and their value as descriptions of the person of Christ is reduced virtually to zero since they now can command only that degree of appreciation which one is willing to yield to the last among several other New Testament christological models.

Clearly, if these four examples are representative expressions across the spectrum of enlightened New Testament scholarship today, classical incarnational Christology—that of a two-natured Christ as defined by Nicaea and Chalcedon—is no longer held in the high esteem it once enjoyed. In short, both Nicaea and Chalcedon are in trouble.

What's Behind It All?

Even though a significant portion of modern New Testament scholarship has urged major modifications in the church's understanding of Christology, the average Christian can hardly be blamed if he expresses some hesitancy about a theological shift that discards the central feature (one person, two natures) of a doctrinal formulation that virtually all of Christendom for fifteen centuries has adjudged the doctrinal reflection of the teaching of Holy Scripture itself. I think all will agree that this is no light matter. It is no small matter either that an outright rejection of incarnational Christology as such would require radical revision not only in Christology (which would become a variant of anthropology if Bultmann is to be believed), but also throughout the entirety of Christian dogmatics, because of the interrelatedness of the doctrines of the Christian system one with the other. (For example, Trinitarianism would give way to Unitarianism; salvation would become a variant of philosophical existentialism or socio-religious humanism.) In fact, unless there are uncommonly sound reasons approaching the level of unimpeachability for such a shift, the average Christian is justified if he concludes that such a departure from the established faith of the centuries is grossly irresponsible. Are there such reasons, and if there are, what are they? What precisely is behind this present ferment in Christology?

In this chapter I will present seven modern objections raised against the classical doctrine of a two-natured Christ. Although there are others, I believe that they will be found, upon analysis, to be only variations of one of these seven. I will also offer some general responses to them along the way, not as my final word on them, since I will necessarily interact with them directly or indirectly, explicitly or implicitly, throughout the book. But my responses may persuade the reader, whether evangelical or not, that it is not a waste of time or energy to continue with me as I consider again the biblical material concerning a Christ who is very God and very man.

"It Is a Christology 'From Above' "

The first objection against classical Christology is the charge that it begins "from above" rather than "from below." This means that the classical formulation begins from God, more specifically, from the triune God and from a Christ whose deity is already a given, who is already God the Son, who as the preexistent Son of God, as the eternal Logos, became man, rather than with the human Jesus, the Jesus of history. As a result, such questions thrust themselves to the fore: How is it that God can also be a man? What does it mean that the Son of God became a man? What does it mean to say that Jesus is a man in such a construction? Indeed, is Jesus truly a man under such conditions? And finally, is the Christ of faith really the earthly historical Jesus? A Christology "from above," many modern scholars maintain, always threatens the genuinely human existence of Jesus. Maurice Wiles puts the matter thus:

> Throughout the long history of attempts to present a reasoned account of Christ as both fully human and fully divine, the church has never succeeded in offering a consistent or convincing picture. Most commonly it has been the humanity of Christ that has suffered; the picture presented has been of a figure who cannot by our standards of judgment . . . be regarded as recognizably human.[21]

Raymond E. Brown even speaks of "the perils created by [the] brilliant insights" of John's Gospel and says,

> The Gospel Prologue opens up the possibility of neglecting the human career of Jesus: if one stresses the incarnation as the unique moment of contact with God, what difference does it make what the Word did once the Word had become flesh?[22]

Gerald O'Collins, another Roman Catholic scholar, though not espousing it himself, characterizes this concern in this fashion:

> The figure in the manger may cry like any baby. He may grow up seemingly just another boy playing on the streets of Nazareth. He may

---

21. Wiles, in Hick, *Myth of God Incarnate*, p. 4.
22. Brown, p. 414.

preach in the style of a wandering rabbi. The Roman forces of occupation can put him to death by that hideous combination of empalement and display which they call crucifixion. But all the same we know he is really God and this injects an element of make-believe into the whole life-story from Bethlehem on. He looks like a man, speaks like a man, suffers and dies like a man. But underneath he is divine, and this makes his genuine humanity suspect. . . . Along lines suggested by Christmas pantomimes, Daisy looks something like a cow and moos better than most cows. But all through the act we know she is no real cow at all. Right from the manger does Jesus simply play at the role of being a man?[23]

There are several things that need to be said in response to this objection. First, I think evangelicals must heed its implicit warning and admit that it is altogether possible in their theologizing so to concentrate both their own and the church's attention on the deity of Christ that His humanness suffers eclipse in the church's witness and proclamation. The church must say "Enough!" to docetism wherever it appears and recognize anew the attraction in the *human* face of our sympathizing heavenly High Priest (cf. *Belgic Confession*, chap. 26).

It is also true that the evangelical witness may have been unduly hasty at times in "beating the world over the head" with biblical "proof texts" for the deity of Christ. Evangelicals must reclaim lost high ground here by recognizing that there is something tremendously compelling and powerfully winsome about the *man* Jesus Christ,[24] His ethical teaching, His conflicts with temptation, His attitude toward the pain and felt alienation of other human beings, and His sensitive views on life in this world in general as set forth in the Gospel narratives. This is doubtless one reason that such men as Mahatma Gandhi found Him so fascinating. The church surely can use Jesus' humanity to real apologetic advantage to define what true humanness is in a day when men feel "dehumanized" in so many ways. Indeed, it should not be overlooked that in the days of our Lord's earthly ministry men first encountered Him and perceived Him as a man (Phil. 2:8; Heb. 2:14-17). So certainly something can be said for a biblically oriented Christology "from below" as long as it does not lose sight of everything else that the New Testament says about Him.

But beyond this, we must question the character of any Christology "from below" that claims to be the key for unlocking the real meaning of Jesus for

23. Gerald O'Collins, *What Are They Saying About Jesus?* (New York: Paulist Press, 1977), p. 2.

24. We must be careful here to recall, if classical Christology is correct, that we never have to do just with the man Christ Jesus at any point in His career.

us. We must ask, What are its underlying presuppositions? What philosophical, sociological, psychological, and psychoanalytic theories control it in its effort to isolate out of the whole biblical picture of Jesus the "truly human" elements of Jesus in order to build a scientific Christology "from below" that will also address the real needs of men? After all, in the modern world, where thought-forms are so thoroughly shaped by the human social sciences, can one afford to neglect Freud, Jung, and Erikson in his attempt to erect a Christology "from below"? Do any of the diverse portraits of the Christ "from below" proposed to date deserve our allegiance? Are we to follow Bultmann's "demythologized" Jesus to "authentic existence"? Or J. A. T. Robinson's Jesus as God's "representative to man"? Or Tillich's Jesus as the "Bearer of the New Being"? Or Pannenberg's Jesus as "the man of the future"? Or Küng's Jesus as the "Advocate and Deputy of God"? What about Rahner's Jesus as the "unique, supreme case of the total actualization of human destiny"? Or Schoonenberg's Jesus as "the embodiment of God's presence"? Or Schillebeeckx's Jesus as "the revelation of the eschatological face of all humanity"? Or Goulder's Jesus as "the man of universal destiny"? Or Lampe's Jesus as the "supreme exemplar of perfect and unbroken response to the Father"? And are we to pinpoint the uniqueness of His humanity in His "being for others," His "being for God," His "sinlessness," or what?

Whatever one's answer here, every humanist Christology "from below," while it may safeguard the genuine humanness of Jesus (I personally do not think it will inasmuch as it must "mythologize" the human Jesus by some existential vision, if He is to be unique and final for men, into a "superman" in order to accredit to Him the universal human esteem it deems He deserves), must still face this problem: Does it say enough to justify the church's calling Him, in its worship and in its confessions, "true God and true man"? Every Christology "from below" presupposes that there is some kind of continuity, which can be displayed by the theologizing process, between the human and the divine in Jesus that makes it possible to ascend in thought from reflecting upon Jesus' humanity to a "divinity" that requires the ascription of "Godness" to Jesus. The results thus far, however, have been disappointing.[25] Such "divinity," whether represented in terms of "being open to God" or "being for God" or "being open for others" or being even "sinless," does not push us that far. Even His being the *supreme* revelation of God to man does not require that we believe, when we reflect upon Jesus, that we are considering God Himself. For as O'Collins rightly

25. Cf. Colin E. Gunton, *Yesterday and Today: A Study of Continuities in Christology* (Grand Rapids: Eerdmans, 1983), chaps. 2 and 3.

observes, "The agent of divine revelation cannot automatically be assumed to be identical with God."[26] Not even a historical resurrection from the dead, derived simply from the evidence of the empty tomb and subsequent postcrucifixion appearances, in and of itself, necessarily requires that one ascribe ontological deity to Him as some evangelicals mistakenly maintain. Pinchas Lapide, for example, declares that Jesus was really raised from the dead, but he remains an orthodox Jewish theologian! He understands Jesus' resurrection simply as part of God's providential purpose to spread the knowlege of the God of Israel throughout the world.[27] Herein resides the fundamental problem that every Christology "from below" must honestly face: Does its construction compel us to move beyond Jesus' humanness to Thomas's great confession? Or does it offer to the church and to men a Jesus whose "deity," in the final analysis, is only His total dedication to God or to a special mission from God or to a fullness of Spirit within Him? The church must seriously inquire whether such Christologies "from below" do not rule out at the outset, by their very methodologies, one alternative, namely, the ascription of deity to Him in the classical sense, inasmuch as one cannot by induction (Paul would say "by [human] wisdom" [1 Cor. 1:21]) ascend from the finite to the infinite, Thomas Aquinas's famous (but logically flawed) theistic arguments notwithstanding.

The church must clearly understand what is at stake when asked to grant legitimacy to these modern efforts to explain Jesus "from below." If He is only a man in these Christologies, and their advocates urge on grounds they have discovered that we should "worship" Him, that act of devotion constitutes *idolatry* and stands under biblical anathema. But if He is not only a man but also God in the classical sense, and we either refuse to acknowledge Him as such or fail to recognize Him as such, that refusal or that failure constitutes either apostasy or unbelief respectively. The Scripture informs us that only divine judgment awaits such recalcitrance (John 8:24).

While they may argue that classical Christology has insurmountable, inherent tensions and difficulties within it, "christologists from below" should be willing to face the fact that their Christologies also have their own set of tensions and problems. They would do well to heed and to work within the constraints of the following feature that Gunton observes in the New Testament's depiction of Jesus:

> Amidst all the diversity of [the New Testament's] Christology one thing remains constant, and that is the refusal to abstract the historical events

---

26. O'Collins, *What Are They Saying About Jesus*, p. 2.
27. Cf. Lapide, *The Resurrection of Jesus* (London: SPCK, 1984).

from their overall theological meaning. The historical man Jesus is never construed apart from his meaning as the presence of the eternal God in time. The New Testament . . . will not allow us to choose between time and eternity, immanence and transcendence, in our talk about Jesus. The two are always given together.[28]

The reader will have to decide as he continues this study which set of problems he prefers—those of classical Christology (which are not, as charged, insurmountable) or those of the new christologists.

"It Is an Ontological Christology"

A second objection to classical Christology charges that its depiction of Jesus is exegetically insensitive to the intention of Scripture, that it depicts Christ in *ontological* terms rather than along New Testament *functional* lines. This simply means that the Definition of Chalcedon is charged with being concerned to set forth who Christ is *in Himself (in se)* rather than to represent Him, as does the New Testament, in terms of what He is *for us (pro nobis)*. So conclude many biblical scholars, notably Oscar Cullmann, who writes, "When it is asked in the New Testament 'Who is Christ?', the question never means exclusively, or even primarily, 'What is his nature?', but first of all, 'What is his function?' "[29]

The Nicene and Post-Nicene church, it seems, child that it was of its own time and influenced by the Aristotelianism of the Antiochene Catechetical School and (mainly) the Platonism of the Alexandrian Catechetical School, in its conciliar descriptions of Christ against heretics was imbued with a philosophical metaphysic that compelled it unwittingly to conceptualize the person of Christ in terms of "natures." As a result, it viewed Him in so-called ontological categories rather than in the rich functional language of the "theologies" of the New Testament. Even though Cullmann concedes that the Fathers were concentrating their attention upon the person of Christ because of the "necessity of combating the heretics," he still contends that their emphases were misplaced, with the ensuing discussion of "natures" being "ultimately a Greek, not a Jewish or biblical problem."[30] Their emphases, as a result, injected an unrelievable tension into the church's creedal portrayal of Christ, which either has threatened to rend asunder the unity of

---

28. Gunton, *Yesterday and Today*, p. 207.
29. Oscar Cullmann, *The Christology of the New Testament*, trans. Shirley C. Guthrie and Charles A. M. Hall (London: SCM Press, 1959), pp. 3-4.
30. Ibid., p. 17.

His person or has placed His essential manhood in jeopardy. The resultant Christ of the Definition of Chalcedon is neither descriptive of the Christ of the Gospels nor relevant in a modern world where men no longer think in ontological categories but rather in functional categories. In short, for men today, it is argued, classical Christology is unreal and unintelligible because of its ontological conceptualization of Jesus.

It is difficult not to grow a bit impatient with twentieth-century theologians who think they would have reacted differently or done better than the fifth-century Fathers in combating the heresies that faced them, particularly when they fail to make clear how they would have responded differently to the specific views of the person of Christ circulating at that time. The issues before the Councils of Nicaea and Chalcedon, as Cullmann acknowledges, were not primarily, "What is Christ's function? What has He done for us?" but "Was the Logos created or uncreated, and if the latter, how is the divine Logos to be related to Jesus' manness so that justice is done to both Christ's deity and His humanity." A. N. S. Lane, pointing out that Chalcedon was not disinterested in the soteriological (functional) question, as is evident from the words, "for us men and for our salvation," which appear in the Definition, also rightly observes that Chalcedon simply did not set out to present an all-embracing, totally comprehensive Christology:

> Its essential task was to protect Christology against heresy in four particular forms, and to expound the essential points which those heresies undermined. With such a limited, albeit important, aim there [was] no need to represent the full range of New Testament teaching about Christ.[31]

Furthermore, for Cullmann to contend that such ontological considerations were "Greek" and foreign to Hebraic thought is simply not so. The Jews of Christ's day had a good grasp of their God's ontological distinctiveness from all that He had created. It was precisely this conviction of the Creator-creature distinction that underlay their horror that a man standing in their midst would claim God as His Father in such a unique and essential sense as to make Himself equal with God (John 5:17-18; cf. 8:58-59; 10:33; 19:7). This was for them clearly a blasphemous claim. And, I suggest, the blasphemy for them was that Jesus claimed *ontological* continuity between Himself as God's Son and the Creator God as His Father.

I would also insist that it is really rather superficial to suggest that men can forever concentrate on what Jesus did for them and never address the ontological question of who He is. Indeed, *it is as psychologically impossible for*

31. Lane, in *Christ the Lord*, p. 264.

modern men as it was for the men of New Testament times to be satisfied with an interest only in Jesus' functional significance and never question or address the ontological issue that His functional significance forces upon them. Let us not forget that while often it was what those first men saw Him do that drew them to Him, they were also quick to speculate who He might be. We are informed that, upon beholding His miracle of stilling the storm, both His disciples and the men in the other boats were driven by the absolutely staggering character of the miracle to ask themselves, not "What has He done here? And what does it all mean for us?," but "Who is this, that even the wind and sea obey Him!" (Mark 4:41). Even more pointed, if that is possible, is Matthew's report of their question on the same occasion: "What kind of person [Ποταπός] is this that even the wind and the sea obey Him?" (8:27). The force of their question can only be fully appreciated when one recalls that for them as Jews there could only be one proper response to this question (cf. Pss. 93:3-4; 104:7-8; 107:23-32), though admittedly to apply this conclusion to Jesus soon proved unsettling to their view of the monadic nature of God. And to respond to the question at all intelligently would certainly have required them to enter deeply into "ontological considerations."

Even more significant for our present point is that Jesus Himself was not content to allow men to bask only in the brilliance of His teachings and the wonder of His deeds and to concern themselves solely with the functional significance of His mission. At the appropriate moment in the process of educating His disciples, Jesus Himself raised the ontological question, "Who do people say I am?" And after hearing their report concerning what others had been saying about Him, He drew His disciples still more deeply into the ontological issue with His question: "But what about you? Who do you say I am?" (Matt. 16:13-15). Now if He hoped to receive only a functional response, we can only conclude that He was disappointed, since Peter responded with both a functional and an ontological answer: "You are the Christ [functional], the Son of the living God [ontological]" (Matt. 16:16). We can be assured that the second part of Peter's response was ontological in its intent because Jesus declared that Peter, by saying this, gave evidence that he was the blessed beneficiary of the Father's revelatory activity (Matt. 16:17; cf. 11:25), a pronouncement hardly necessary if Peter were only confessing Jesus to be the Messiah, since many other people were also entertaining this perception about Him (John 7:31). It is also noteworthy that not until He was satisfied that His disciples understood *who* He was (the ontological question) did He begin to indoctrinate them regarding His saving mission by the way of the cross (Matt. 16:21-23).

Germane also to this same point is that Jesus forced the religious authori-

ties of His day to face the very "metaphysical" issue that the Council of
Nicaea addressed in A.D. 325: "What do you think about the Messiah? [Note:
He is already talking about the Messiah, admittedly a functional title.] *Whose
Son is He?"* (Matt. 22:41-42). And when the response of these religious
leaders seemed to limit the Messiah's origin only to His human ancestry
("the son of David," and therefore of human descent), Jesus asked them:

> How is it then that David, speaking by the Spirit, calls Him "Lord"? For
> he says, "The Lord [Heb, יהוה] said to my Lord [Heb, אדני]: 'Sit at My
> right hand until I put Your enemies under Your feet.'" If then David
> called Him "Lord," *how can He be his Son?* (Matt. 22:43-45).

How indeed! If ever a question was designed to compel a consideration of
"natures," this is it! For not only is the Messiah David's lineal descendant
but, according to Psalm 110, He is also David's Lord and the "Son of God" in
a sense that entitles Him to sit on God's throne and to exercise universal and
everlasting dominion (cf. the psalm in its entirety and Heb. 1:5-13). The
church of the fourth and fifth centuries, confronted by what it determined
were heresies and doctrinal aberrations concerning Jesus, gathered together
periodically in ecumenical councils to sort out this very quandary, which
Jesus forced the Pharisees to face.

So whatever one may say about the concerns and interests of the New
Testament witness to Jesus, the one thing he should not say is that the New
Testament does not raise "ontological" questions concerning Christ's per-
son. Reginald H. Fuller and others have also argued as much,[32] G. C.
Berkouwer even calling into question the academic integrity of a theology
that would dismiss the ontological aspects of New Testament Christology:

> Certainly theology is in bad form when, in discussing [Christ's utter-
> ances pointing to the mystery of His origin], it reaches for such de-
> preciatory words as "speculation" and "ontology." For in order to
> eclipse *this* origin, *this* miraculous being, *this* gracious reality, it has to
> set aside the whole gospel.[33]

Walter Kasper, in fact, dismisses the choice between functional and ontological Christologies as "illusory and a position into which theology must

---

32. Reginald H. Fuller, *The Foundations of New Testament Christology* (New York: Charles Scribner's Sons, 1965), pp. 247-50; cf. also, Reginald H. Fuller and Pheme Perkins, *Who Is This Christ?*
(Philadelphia: Fortress Press, 1983), pp. 9-10, and Gerald Bray, "Can We Dispense With Chalcedon?" *Themelios* 3, no. 2 (Jan. 1978): pp. 2-9.

33. G. C. Berkouwer, *The Person of Christ,* trans. John Vriend (Grand Rapids: Eerdmans, 1954),
p. 165.

not allow itself to be maneuvered."[34] And the New Testament even goes beyond these somewhat mild statements recognizing the legitimacy of the ontological questions concerning the person of Christ in the Gospels. So far does the New Testament press the importance of the ontological issue that it reports that Jesus grounded a man's eternal destiny in a right view of who He is: "If you do not believe that I am, you will die in your sins" (John 8:23-24). It bears saying again, in light of Jesus' solemn warning here, that whatever else one may say about the concerns of the New Testament witness to Christ, he should not say that its interests are purely functional and never ontological. Neither should he say, I hope to show, that the church was in error when it depicted Christ as "perfect in deity and perfect in manhood, truly God and truly man, . . . of the same essence with the Father according to deity and of the same essence with us according to manhood."

In my emphasis on ontological considerations in this section, I do not intend in any sense to suggest that one should concern himself only with ontological considerations concerning Christ. This would be tantamount to reducing soteriology to a narrowly conceived Christology. But I do intend to erect a hedge against the other extreme, which, by means of a functional Christology, virtually reduces Christology to soteriology. A balance must be struck and always maintained between the two.

"It Is an Incarnation-centered Christology"

A third objection to classical Christology—closely related to the preceding objection but one that I am treating separately because of the somewhat different manner in which its concern is represented—is that it makes the event of the incarnation rather than the cross and resurrection of Christ the central doctrine about Him. Both Wolfhart Pannenberg and Walter Kasper oppose a classical Christology for this reason. Kasper writes:

> If the divine-human person Jesus is constituted through the Incarnation once and for all, the history and activity of Jesus, and above all the cross and the Resurrection, no longer have any constitutive meaning whatsoever. Then the death of Jesus would be only the completion of the Incarnation. The Resurrection would be no more than the confirmation of his divine nature. That would mean a diminution of the whole biblical testimony. According to Scripture, Christology has its centre in the cross and the Resurrection.[35]

34. Walter Kasper, *Jesus the Christ*, trans. V. Green (London: Burns and Coates, 1976), p. 24.
35. Ibid., p. 37.

Now there is no question that a Christology that makes the event of the incarnation the virtual "be-all and end-all" of the New Testament statements about Jesus must be faulted for its insensitivity to the equally strong emphasis it places on the significance of His death and resurrection. It is not by accident that the four Evangelists devote a major portion of their respective Gospels to the *last week* of Jesus' life. Clearly, they intend for Christ's cross work and His resurrection to be kept at the center of any Christology that would lay claim to a sensitive reading of their story. For one to concentrate primarily if not exclusively on the event of the incarnation is clearly unbiblical. But who, in fact, does this? The Nicene and Post-Nicene Fathers may have done so to a degree. Medieval theology did do so to a certain degree. But certainly since the Reformation few evangelical Protestant scholars could be faulted for doing so. Evangelical Protestantism has made the cross and resurrection central to its theological interests and to church proclamation. But it also recognizes, as did the early Fathers, that for the New Testament writers it is because Christ is who He is that His death and resurrection have the transcendent value they have in behalf of men's salvation. For this reason evangelical Protestants have held tenaciously to the ontological deity of Jesus.

The one Protestant theologian who can be faulted for making the incarnation *the* reconciling event is the Swiss theologian Karl Barth. And it is against Barth's Christology, most directly, that Pannenberg and others have erected their Christologies "from below" as antidotes. Barth views the incarnation as the really crucial event in man's reconciliation to God:

> The being of Jesus Christ, the unity of the living God and this living man, takes place in the event of the concrete existence of this man. It is a being, but a being in history. The gracious God is in this history, so is reconciled man, so both are in their unity. And what takes place in this history, and therefore in the being of Jesus Christ as such, is atonement. Jesus Christ is not what He is—very God, very man, very God-man—in order as such to mean and do and accomplish something else which is atonement. But His being as God and man and God-man consists in the completed act of the reconciliation of man with God.[36]

Clearly, for Barth the incarnation as such is the reconciling act! Jesus' death on the cross does little more than reveal the depth of the humiliation resulting from God turning Himself into His opposite, namely, man. The

---

36. Karl Barth, *Church Dogmatics*, trans. G. W. Bromiley, vol. 4, pt. 1 (Edinburgh: T. & T. Clark, 1956), pp. 126ff.

resurrection essentially reveals the exaltation of man that takes place in the being of Jesus Christ.

This construction of the significance of the incarnation, however, does not do justice to the biblical doctrine of reconciliation, which sees the reconciliation of God to the world as effected by Christ's work on the cross. Again and again during His earthly ministry, Jesus Himself declared, "My hour has not yet come." Then, standing in the shadow of the cross, He exclaimed, "The hour has come . . . and what shall I say? 'Father, save Me from this hour?' No, it was for this very reason I came to this hour" (John 12:23-27). The New Testament nowhere speaks of our being reconciled by the event of the incarnation *per se*, but rather insists that our reconciliation to God is through the death of His Son (Rom. 5:10; Col. 1:22). It affirms that Christ effected peace between God and men through the blood of His cross (Col. 1:20; Eph. 2:16). Barth cannot square the emphasis of these passages with his christological construction. As a result, despite his claims to the contrary, he does not stand in the mainstream of Reformation thought when by his christological reconstruction he interprets the person of Christ in terms of His work and His work in terms of His person. The Reformed faith, with Paul, has uniformly and consistently proclaimed the centrality of the cross (1 Cor. 1:17, 18, 23; 2:2). Of course, the Reformed faith has also recognized that the value of the cross as God's saving instrument resides in the fact that at the cross it was the *Lord of glory* who was crucified (1 Cor. 2:8), who thereby rendered up to God, because of His intrinsic personal worth, a propitiatory sacrifice of infinite value to satisfy the offended holiness and divine justice of God registered against man's sin. So it is important to the New Testament— indeed, critically so—that one never lose sight of who did the cross work, namely, the Lord of glory. While Barth's Christology diminishes the glory of the cross, placing the event of the incarnation as such at the center of his theology, it has never been characteristic of evangelical Christianity or, for that matter, of classical Christology to do so. Consequently, this objection is not really against classical Christology as much as it is against Barth's modern christological reconstruction.

"It Is a Hellenized Christology"

A fourth accusation is that the Christ of Nicaea and of Chalcedon is "the philosopher's Christ," so thoroughly Hellenized by both the language and metaphysical garb of Greek philosophy that He bears little if any resemblance to the Christ of Scripture, the very human Jesus of Nazareth. The point is sometimes facetiously put, "Can one really imagine Jesus responding to a seeker's inquiry concerning who He was with, 'I am truly God and truly man, consubstantial with the Father according to My deity and consubstantial with you according to My manness, having two natures which are not confused, which do not change, which are not divided, but which are not separated either, the difference of My natures being by no means removed by their union in Me but the properties of each nature being preserved and coalescing in My one person and one subsistence, not parted or divided into two persons but still one and the same Son and only-begotten God, Word, the Lord Jesus Christ'?"

What can one say in response? Resisting the impulse to say, "Yes, had He lived in the fifth century and given the circumstances of the fifth-century situation, I can imagine Him responding precisely in this fashion," let me be the first to admit that the Fathers did employ terminology derived from the Greek philosophical tradition, such as the Greek words, οὐσια, ὁμοούσια, φύσις, and ὑπόστασις ("essence," "same essence," "nature," and "subsistence") and the Latin words, substantia, consubstantia, natura, and persona ("substance," "same substance," "nature," and "person") in their efforts to define as precisely as they knew how just who Jesus Christ is. I readily admit that these words had as their background the thought-form of Greek philosophy. But are they to be faulted for this? Is this really the pertinent issue?

Consider the following facts. The Greek autograph of the Definition of Chalcedon (there was also a Latin translation), although philosophical in appearance, can be translated almost in its entirety by any second-year Greek student with the aid of a standard Greek New Testament lexicon. It is not difficult Greek syntax. And as I said, with only a few exceptions every word can be located in a standard lexicon for the Κοινή ("common") Greek of the New Testament. What is truly striking about the Definition, when one takes into account how difficult the Fathers could have made it, is its brevity, its simple phrasing, and its common Greek vocabulary. As for its Hellenistic cast, can we of all people—we who live at a time when as never before there is the steady, strident call for "contextualizing" the biblical message—fault them for speaking to their age and culture in such fashion? "Hellenize" the New Testament portrayal of Christ they certainly did; compromise or distort the New Testament portrayal—that needs yet to be demonstrated. Reginald Fuller writes in this regard:

> If the church was to preserve and to proclaim the gospel in the Graeco-Roman world, it had to answer [the ontological questions, How can the Son share the same being as the Father and yet be distinguishable? How can Jesus be God and man at the same time? etc.] in terms of an

ontology which was intelligible to that world. Its answer to these questions was the doctrine of the Trinity and the Incarnation. . . .

We must recognize the validity of this achievement of the church of the first five centuries within the terms in which it operated. It is sheer biblicism to maintain that the church should merely repeat "what the Bible says"—about Christology as about anything else. The church has to proclaim the gospel into the contemporary situation. And that is precisely what the Nicene Creed and the Chalcedon formula were trying to do. [As Montefiore says,] "The Definition of Chalcedon was the only way in which the fifth-century fathers, in their day, and with their conceptual apparatus, could have faithfully creedalized the New Testament witness to Christ."[37]

I totally agree. The question that should be asked is not, Did they "Hellenize" Christ, that is, describe the Christ of the New Testament with philosophical language? Of course, they did. *Any historical fact of transcendent significance such as the event of the incarnation must inevitably require the language of metaphysics if men are to explain it theologically.* Serious theological discussion of Jesus Christ—and this is true for every Christology "from below" and every "functional Christology" as well—will necessarily invoke the aid of philosophical language and concepts to address the final and ultimate meaning of reality. As a case in point, Pannenberg's *Jesus—God and Man* is a sustained attempt to write a Christology "from below," but when Pannenberg teaches that "Jesus' essence is established retroactively . . . from his resurrection . . . in its being,"[38] he has entered deeply into metaphysics by the claim that Jesus' resurrection has ontic retroactive significance for the essence of Jesus. Pannenberg would be the first, in fact, to acknowledge as much. So the question of "Hellenization" is not really to the point.

The much more critical question is: In their attempt to describe for their own time precisely who Jesus Christ is, did the Fathers deviate from the intention of the New Testament data in any way? Is the New Testament portrayal of Christ's person in some way falsified? These questions are, of course, what the remainder of this book will address. But I think it can be said even at this juncture that, whatever one may finally think of their end product, their Christology is anything but "Greek" in theological content. As Lane says, it was "profoundly un-Greek" in content, "challenging Greek culture at a fundamental point."[39] This challenge may be seen first in their "un-Hellenistic" willingness to accept something (the incarnation) as true

37. Fuller, *Foundations of New Testament Christology*, pp. 249-50.
38. Wolfhart Pannenberg, *Jesus—God and Man*, trans. Lewis L. Wilkins and Duane A. Priebe (London: SCM Press, 1968), p. 136.
39. Lane, in *Christ the Lord*, pp. 263, 264.

that they could not entirely comprehend. This submitting of their minds to an authority external to themselves can be traced to their conviction that they, possessing the New Testament, possessed the very revelation of God, the only proper response to which is human submission. It is this attitude of submission that explains their employment of γνωριζομένον ("being made known") in the middle of their Christological definition, indicating that "the Chalcedonian Fathers were accepting, and giving conciliar authority to, what had had its distinct place in the Church's Christological thought from earliest days."[40] The "un-Greek" character of their Definition is discernible also in their perception of the nature of the incarnation itself as the uniting of God and man in one person so that it is both appropriate and necessary to say that Christ is "very God and very man." It is not that in the Greek philosophical strain of the period there were no mediators between God and man; to the contrary, there were mediators galore, usually represented as "emanations" of God between God and man. But, on the one hand, all such mediators were created, and thus subordinate to the "One," the utterly transcendent God. On the other hand, the world, with which the lowest mediator came in contact, was viewed as intrinsically evil. It was because of this latter condition, the evil nature of matter, that levels of mediators had been posited between the world of men and the transcendent God in the first place. Consequently, a mediator who was in Himself both the uncreated God and a sinless man was totally unlike anything in the Greek (and Gnostic) scheme of things.

All of this means that, in fairness to these Fathers, we must conclude that, while their words had for their background the history of Greek metaphysics, this factor was not the decisive, controlling influence in their thinking. Rather, as they themselves would have certainly insisted, simple fidelity to the New Testament witness concerning Jesus was their primary concern.

"It Is a Prescientific Christology"

A fifth objection to classical Christology is that it is "prescientific" in its understanding of the relationship between the "other world" and the "this world" order of things. It presupposed the literalness of both the "unseen" and the "seen" worlds and, along with the culture of its time, accepted the literal penetration of the former into the latter in the form that biblical supernaturalism assumes. The incarnation, in "the word became flesh"

---

40. R. V. Sellers, *The Council of Chalcedon* (London: SPCK, 1953), p. 217.

motif, was literally comprehended. This perception of the incarnation is said to be part and parcel of the widespread inclination of that age to grant wholesale legitimacy to the occurrence of miracles. But that was before man "came of age" through the Enlightenment and the ensuing modern scientific revolution. Now, according to Bultmann and his followers, modern man knows better. Today, the world, as the totality of the spatio-temporal phenomena and the only legitimate object of human knowledge, may be approached both externally and objectively (the physical sciences) and internally and subjectively (the social sciences). But regardless of one's approach, the world must be understood as a closed system of cause and effect. Every this-world effect has a this-world cause. God can no longer be introduced as the *Deus ex machina* device to explain this-world phenomena or events. Bultmann avers, "Modern man acknowledges as reality only such phenomena or events as are comprehensible within the framework of the rational order of the universe."[41] He also states,"Modern men take it for granted that the course of nature and of history like their own inner life and their practical life, is nowhere interrupted by the intervention of supernatural powers."[42] And again he declares, "Modern science does not believe that the course of nature can be interrupted or, so to speak, perforated by supernatural powers."[43] The classical doctrine of the incarnation, for Bultmann, is consequently the result of the later conciliar failure to recognize in the New Testament the presence of the influence of Jewish Apocalyptic and Gnostic mythology. The New Testament, according to Bultmann:

> proclaims in the language of mythology that the last time has now come. "In the fulness of time" God sent forth his Son, a pre-existent divine Being, who appears on earth as a man. . . . All this is the language of mythology, and the origin of the various themes can be easily traced to the contemporary mythology of Jewish Apocalyptic and in the redemption myths of Gnosticism.[44]

"What a primitive mythology it is," he continues, "that a divine Being should become incarnate, and atone for the sins of man through his own blood!"[45] Bultmann concludes that "man's knowledge and mastery of the world have advanced to such an extent through science and technology that it is no longer possible for anyone seriously to hold to the New Testament

---

41. Rudolf Bultmann, *Jesus Christ and Mythology* (New York: Charles Scribner's Sons, 1958), p. 37.
42. Ibid., p. 16.
43. Ibid., p. 15.
44. Bultmann, "New Testament and Mythology," in *Kerygma and Myth*, ed. Hans Bartsch (New York: Harper and Brothers, 1961), pp. 2, 3.
45. Ibid., p. 7

view of the world."[46] Where it is so held, as in the case of classical Christology
and the beliefs of evangelical Christianity in general, it simply indicates, as far
as Bultmann is concerned, the regrettable fact that some, "ostrich-like," are
still living as "prescientific" men.

Does this conclusion necessarily follow? Is it true that modern science has
necessarily relegated all present-day belief in the supernatural and miraculous
to the category of "baggage from the prescientific age of man"? There is no
question that this opinion is widely held today. But if there is a *modern* myth
(and I recognize that I am using the word in a different sense than Bultmann), this is it. I must ask, over against Bultmann et al.: Is it so that modern
science compels both the necessity of "demythologizing" classical Christology and its reinterpretation along Heideggerian existentialist lines? Is the
mindset of modern man really such that he is incapable of believing anything not scientifically demonstrable? What I find truly amazing is just how
many *unscientific* things modern man does believe, such as the modern
"scientific" view that this present physical universe with all of its interrelatedness, interdependency, complexity, and awe-inspiring beauty is the
result of impersonal forces evolving through aeons of times by chance
mutations, catastrophic interruptions of nature, and so on; or that man is the
result solely of these same impersonal forces latent in nature; or that man is
essentially good and morally perfectible through education and social
manipulation; or that universal morals need not be grounded in ethico-
religious absolutes.

In fact, Bultmann's view of the implications of modern science for the
historical understanding of the cardinal doctrines of the Christian faith is not
scientifically established at all but rather reflects an *a priori* secular or positivistic "scientism" that many scientists reject today. He ascribes an infalli-
bility, a finality, and powers to modern science that in fact it simply does not,
cannot, and never will have. No scientific fact, in and of itself, can prove that
this universe is a closed system of cause and effect; the scientific method
cannot demonstrate that the supernatural has never before intruded and
will never in the future intrude itself into the world or that the miraculous
has never occurred before and will never occur in the future. The most astute
philosophers of science among us would never claim that science can so
demonstrate, nor would they try so to demonstrate. They recognize that to
believe modern science has demonstrated that the miraculous (in the New
Testament sense) cannot occur is blind dogmatism. This explains why
literally thousands of scientists today, at work in every field of the pure

46. Ibid., p. 4.

sciences, are quite comfortable as both men of science and men of faith, standing without apology in the historic tradition of the church's teaching and submitting to the full, sweeping supernaturalism of the Scriptures. I refer, for example, to the memberships of the American Scientific Affiliation and the Creation Research Society. These scientists adamantly oppose any suggestion that this world is a closed system of cause and effect. Still further, they recognize that even from the standpoint of logic such a position as Bultmann espouses, since it involves a universal negation, cannot be proved empirically.

Bultmann's "modern man," the man who has "come of age," who can no longer tolerate the "mythical" idea of a real incarnation, had his counterpart, in fact, in the days of the New Testament. Doubtless for other reasons but just as certainly, there were men who could not believe some aspect or other of the Christian proclamation. Thomas, for example, declared that he would not believe in Jesus' resurrection until he saw the nail marks (John 20:25). Second-century Gnostics could not reconcile Christianity's insistence that "the Word became flesh and dwelt among us" with their philosophical view regarding matter as evil. So they refused to believe in the incarnation. Unbelief is not a phenomenon new to the church in this age—the result of modern man's newly learned sophistication—and unknown to the apostles. Unbelief is simply *man's* problem, and it has ever been the case that some have mocked at the supernaturalism of the Bible, others have said, "We want to hear you again on this subject," and some have believed (Acts 17:32-34).

The upshot of all this is that while it will always be opposed as unscientific or prescientific by a positivistic scientism, which is not real science at all, New Testament incarnationalism has nothing to fear from true science.

"It Is a Triumphalist Christology"

The next objection has to do with the implications in classical incarnational Christology for the truth character of the other religions of the world as well as the world's political states.

If God in a unique and final way became incarnate in Jesus of Nazareth and in no other, then it follows, according to this objection, that Christianity lays claim not only to the exclusive possession of religious truth but also to monarchical transcendence over the other world religions. This precludes any ultimate peaceful commerce within the "brotherhood" of world religions. Furthermore, this "triumphalist" vision—traceable, it is alleged, to the doctrine of the incarnation—has controlled Christian theology all too long and has led inevitably to Western Christendom's absolutist and authoritarian claims in the political arena as well, with Christ Himself as the theological basis of the Christian Empire and of political and ecclesiastical power in the present age. This world—the ever-shrinking "global village" that it is and faced with all kinds of political and economic forces working at cross-purposes with one another—it is urged, can ill afford the unbecoming triumphalist exclusivism implicit in the church's incarnational Christology.

None to my knowledge has voiced this concern more fervently of late than some of the contributors to *The Myth of God Incarnate*. Maurice Wiles, for example, writes:

> Where the categorical and absolute character of the religious demand as it impinges on the Christian, is tied to the historical person of Jesus in a strict metaphysical way (as in traditional incarnation doctrine), that does involve a prejudgment of the potential significance of other religious faiths . . . of a kind that is very hard to justify from our standpoint within one particular stream of religious and cultural development.[47]

Wiles goes on to call for the abandonment, not of Christian religious demand as such, but of its linkage "in its absoluteness" to the figure of Jesus set forth in traditional incarnational Christology.[48] John Hick, editor of *The Myth of God Incarnate*, also writes:

> Understood literally the Son of God, God the Son, God-incarnate language implies that God can be adequately known and responded to *only* through Jesus; and the whole religious life of mankind, beyond the stream of Judaic-Christian faith is thus by implication excluded as lying outside the sphere of salvation. This implication did little positive harm so long as Christendom was a largely autonomous civilization with only relatively marginal interaction with the rest of mankind. But with the clash between the Christian and Muslim worlds, and then on an ever broadening front with European colonization throughout the earth, the literal understanding of the mythological language of Christian discipleship has had a divisive effect upon the relations between that minority of human beings who live within the borders of the Christian tradition and that majority who live outside it and within other streams of religious life. . . .
> If Jesus was literally God incarnate, and if it is by his death alone that men can be saved, and by their response to him alone that they can

47. Maurice Wiles, *Incarnation and Myth: the Debate Continued*, ed. M. Goulder (Grand Rapids: Eerdmans, 1979), pp. 10-11.
48. Ibid., p. 11.

appropriate that salvation, then the only doorway to eternal life is Christian faith. It would follow from this that the large majority of the human race so far has not been saved. . . . Is not such an idea excessively parochial presenting God in effect as the tribal deity of the predominantly Christian West? . . .

It seems clear that we are being called today to attain a global religious vision which is aware of the unity of all mankind before God . . . we must affirm God's equal love for all men and not only for Christians. . . . If, selecting from our Christian language, we call God-acting-towards-man the Logos, then we must say that *all* salvation, within all religions, is the work of the Logos. . . . But what we cannot say is that all who are saved are saved by Jesus of Nazareth. The life of Jesus was one point at which the Logos—that is, God-in-relation-to-man—has acted. . . . From now onwards . . . we have to present Jesus . . . in a way compatible with our new recognition of the validity of the other great world faiths as being also, at their best, ways of salvation. We must therefore not insist upon Jesus being always portrayed within the interpretative framework built around him by centuries of Western thought.[49]

Don Cupitt, yet another contributor, traces the roots of early and medieval concepts of the Christian Empire with all of its absolutism and authoritarianism in the political and ecclesiastical spheres, by an unmitigated inevitability, to the dogma of the incarnation, which makes Christ "the manifest Absolute in history."[50] If the church is to reestablish Jesus' moral (and eschatological) lordship in the world as a guide for the world's improvement, it must abandon the dogma at the root of Jesus' temporal lordship, namely, the doctrine of the incarnation.[51]

To Wiles's and Hick's calls for the church to abandon its "exclusivist" doctrine of incarnational Christology in favor of a religious pluralism that sees the Logos "savingly" at work in all of the world's great religions, we would respond that undoubtedly every Christian should normally support *legal* tolerance toward other religions, as John Stott writes. That is to say, Christians should actively support laws that adequately protect the rights of the individual to profess, practice, and propagate his religious views, with due allowance, of course, for the protection of the rest of the citizenry from excesses of religious fanaticism that would inflict bodily harm upon others. Furthermore, every Christian should cultivate in himself and encourage in others *social* tolerance toward other religions. In other words, the Christian

---

49. Hick, *Myth of God Incarnate*, pp. 179, 180, 181, 182.
50. Don Cupitt, in Hick, *Myth of God Incarnate*, pp. 140-41.
51. Ibid.

should respect the religious views others hold and should seek to understand them and to encourage the same in others toward his own faith. But when it comes to *intellectual* tolerance, that is to say, the cultivation of "a mind so broad that it can tolerate every opinion, without ever detecting anything in it to reject"—this "is not a virtue; it is the vice of the feeble-minded."[52] Of course, neither Wiles nor Hick can be charged with such feeble-mindedness, for they have reference to the "other great world faiths" such as Islam and Judaism when they speak of the Logos as being at work in other faiths. They do not attribute to the work of the Logos the superstitious and demonic elements that loom large, for example, in so many of today's third-world primitive cultures. Stott himself recognizes that such intellectual tolerance is rare, the more popular expression of it being the demand for a religious syncretism in which the *best* of the differing religious beliefs are harmonized into a single system.[53] It is this "inter-faith dialogue" of religious pluralism that Wiles and Hick are calling for, to which incarnational Christology is said to be a major stumbling block. The *Myth* contributors sincerely believe that the religious syncretism they envision will aid in bringing about a badly needed universal brotherhood of men.

But this entire argument begs the question of truth. *If* Jesus is in fact God incarnate (and this book will examine the New Testament testimony), Christians cannot accept this rationale for an intellectual religious pluralism. And if Jesus is in fact God incarnate, and if the church would be governed by truth, it must continue to insist that Jesus is *unique*, finally and transcendentally so. Historically, this uniqueness resides in His birth; His obedient life and sacrificial death; His resurrection, ascension, and present session at the Father's right hand; and His eschatological return as the Judge and Savior of men. Theologically, it resides in the incarnation, the Atonement, and the several (including the cosmically final) aspects of His exaltation. *If* Jesus Christ is in fact God incarnate, Jesus must continue to be proclaimed as the *only saving way* to the Father, as He said (John 14:6), His the *only saving name* among men, as Peter said (Acts 4:12), and His the *only saving mediation* between God and man, as Paul said (1 Tim. 2:5). Furthermore, the church must declare that the goal the religious pluralist so devoutly seeks—a universal religious brotherhood binding all men everywhere joyously together in one world of common humanity—is, on his grounds, unobtainable—not only because such pluralism does not transform the human heart, but also because *only the genuinely and transcendentally unique has such universal*

52. John Stott, *The Authentic Christ* (Basingstoke: Marshalls Paperbacks, 1985), p. 70.
53. Ibid.

significance that it deserves to be universally proclaimed and universally received.
Without such transcendent finality—displayed, for example, in the New
Testament witness to Jesus—directing and energizing the innate and explicit religious demands of the community of men, there can be no universal
significance or power in such an appeal. And any religious commerce, if it is
achieved, will finally have to be imposed upon men against their will (cf.
Rev. 13:11-17).

If Brian Hebblethwaite's assessment that Cupitt's opinion reflects "sheer
perversity in moral judgment"[54] should seem too strong, then his related
insight—that what has ever given Christianity its characteristic moral and
religious power is its "conviction that its Lord has humbled himself and
taken the form of a servant"[55]—is right on target! The un-Christ-like political triumphalism of the organized church in the West during certain periods
can be traced to any number of other forces and influences, not the least of
which is man's hubris ("pride"), but to charge it to the church's doctrine of
the incarnation is a glaring piece of theological "reaching" for the sake of a
highly individualistic and questionable religious vision.

To abandon biblical incarnationalism in favor of a religious pluralism, *if*
Christ is indeed God incarnate, is tantamount to the gravest breach of the
First Commandment, and it would involve one in unspeakable infidelity to
the Lord of Glory who wears a diadem out-rivaling all the diadems of all the
world's religious and political leaders. In a word, to do so would mean that
the church had simply ceased to be *Christian!* The Christian church can
afford to follow the modern call for religious pluralism only at the greatest
costs both to itself and to the world to which it has been sent. Moreover, to
follow this call would be to set the church on a course that can only lead to
disappointment and judgment in the end.

"It Is a Precritical Christology"

The last and probably most significant objection—because it directly or
indirectly accounts for all the other modern objections—contends that the
Nicene and Chalcedonian formulations were drawn up prior to the rise of
the critical analyses of the Gospels and Epistles that dominate the field of
New Testament research today.

In the nineteenth century, a negative biblical criticism, assuming the
evolutionary development of religious thought, began to dominate in the

---

54. Brian Hebblethwaite, "The Moral and Religious Value of the Incarnation," in Goulder,
Incarnation and Myth, p. 89.
55. Ibid.

great centers of learning, particularly in Europe and England. This attitude surfaced in Old Testament studies under the direction of such notable scholars as Graf, Keunen, Wellhausen, Cornill, Driver, and Briggs, and rapidly spread to New Testament studies through such scholars as Strauss, Wrede, Weiss, Schmiedel, and Bousset. Form criticism dominated Gospel studies in this century through the influence of Dibelius and Bultmann, and then redaction criticism arose through the influence of Marxsen, Bornkamm, and Conzelmann. Any remaining significant knowledge of the historical Jesus of the Gospel records was pushed so far back into the dark recesses of first-century church tradition that today the more skeptical practitioners of these methods generally argue that reliable knowledge of Jesus is illusory. And while there is a noticeable reaction today among the so-called "new questers for the historical Jesus" away from the agnostic stance captured in Bultmann's famous judgment, "I do indeed think that we can know almost nothing concerning the life and personality of Jesus,"[56] Maurice Wiles still felt it appropriate to say in his 1973 Hulsean Lectures at Cambridge, "It is essential that the doctrinal theologian recognizes that the kind of information about Jesus that theology has so often looked to New Testament scholars to provide is not available."[57] And John Bowden concludes his article entitled "Jesus" in *A New Dictionary of Christian Theology* with these words:

> There is a good deal that we probably do know about Jesus; the trouble is that we cannot always be sure precisely what it is. Because of the very nature of historical research, discussions about Jesus always contain countless approximations, and one of the most confident recent studies (A. E. Harvey, *Jesus and the Constraints of History*, 1982) concedes that "it can still be argued that we can have no reliable historical knowledge about Jesus with regard to anything that really matters" (p. 6). This being so, it is remarkable that attempts to restate the significance of Jesus without the doctrine of Incarnation can be based on what amounts to an interpretation of the character of Jesus which is actually based on very little historical evidence. However christology may be worked out, there is no escaping our considerable ignorance about actual facts.[58]

Why, we may legitimately ask, is there such skepticism regarding the acquisition of significant factual information about the Jesus of history? Why

---

56. Rudolf Bultmann, *Jesus and the Word*, trans. Louise Pettibone Smith and Erminie Huntress Lanters (New York: Charles Scribner and Sons, 1934), p. 8.

57. Maurice Wiles, *The Remaking of Christian Doctrine* (London: SCM Press, 1974), p. 48.

58. John Bowden, "Jesus," in *A New Dictionary of Christian Theology*, ed. Alan Richardson and John Bowden (London: SCM Press, 1983), p. 312.

does one so often hear it said today that the only Jesus we can now recover by New Testament research is the nonhistorical "created" Jesus of the early church's κήρυγμα ("proclamation")? To understand all of this, it is necessary to give a brief overview of the methods dominating twentieth-century New Testament Gospel research.

Source Criticism

Virtually from the time the Gospels were originally composed, for all their similarities (particularly between the Synoptic ["look alike"] Gospels—Matthew, Mark, and Luke), their dissimilarities have attracted the special attention of New Testament students. For example, the sequence of events occasionally varies from Gospel to Gospel. Where Matthew, for instance, gives the sequence of Jesus' temptations one way (4:3-10), Luke reverses the order of the second and third temptations (4:3-12). Then there are the frequent variations from Gospel to Gospel in reporting Jesus' sayings and parables. For example, where Matthew reports that Jesus concludes His lesson on prayer with the words, ". . . how much more will your Father in heaven give *good gifts* to those who ask Him!" (7:11), Luke reports His words this way: ". . . how much more will your Father in heaven give the *Holy Spirit* to those who ask Him!" (11:13). Then the words of others are variously reported. Where Matthew, for example, reports Peter's confession as "You are the Christ, the Son of the living God" (16:16), Mark reports his confession more simply as "You are the Christ" (8:29). How do we explain these differences?

No doubt there is merit in the suggestion that many of the variations can be explained by the fact that Jesus repeated His sermons and parables on more than one occasion and in different contexts. The Evangelists could then be reporting sermons and parables similar in substance but different in detail, because they were given on different occasions.[59] But this suggestion will not explain every variation, for example, the variation in the sequence of Jesus' temptations or in the form of the question Jesus put to His disciples at Caesarea Philippi. Where Matthew reports Jesus asking, "Who do people say the *Son of Man* is?" (16:13), Mark records His question this way: "Who do people say that *I* am?" (8:27). Here is clearly the same occasion and the same question. Why does Matthew use the title "Son of Man" while Mark employs the first person pronoun? Could it be that underlying our present canonical Gospels at a more primitive level of Gospel tradition were earlier literary sources upon which the Synoptic Evangelists relied and in which the

---

59. Cf. Everett F. Harrison, "*Gemeindetheologie:* The Bane of Gospel Criticism," in *Jesus of Nazareth: Saviour and Lord*, ed. Carl F. H. Henry (London: Tyndale, 1966), p. 162.

variations occurred? If so, why did these more primitive literary sources vary? Could it be, if these "aboriginal Gospels" could be isolated one from the other through minute analysis, that the scholarly world could gain not only answers to these questions but also a portrait of the Jesus of this primitive Gospel tradition that is more historically accurate than (perhaps even different from) that given in the canonical Gospels?

To find the answers to these questions, during the first two decades of this century, such scholars as Robinson, Burton, and Streeter engaged in a method known as "source criticism," which sought to discover the supposed literary sources underlying the first three Gospels. Different proposals were put forth. The "two-document theory" (Mark, or Ur-Markus—a written tradition thought to be so close to the canonical Gospel of Mark that for all intents and purposes we actually possess it in Mark's Gospel—and "Q," standing for the German Quelle meaning "source," referring to the non-Markan material used by Matthew and Luke) and the "four-document theory" (Mark [or Ur-Markus], Q, M [the special material found only in Matthew], and L [the special material found only in Luke]) gained the widest general acceptance.

Did these "sources," now "isolated," present a Christ different in kind from the canonical Gospels? Benjamin B. Warfield, in his magnificent study of Jesus' titles in the New Testament, for the sake of argument demonstrated that the so-called "primitive Mark," even if its contents are confined only to the matter common to all three synoptic Gospels, still portrays a Christ in whom deity is "ineffaceably imbedded."[60] All the more so is this true if one adds the fragments peculiar to Mark and M,[61] or Mark and L.[62] The same conclusion holds true, he demonstrated, for Q.[63] (A. T. Robertson demonstrated the same thing in his 1924 work, The Christ of the Logia).[64] In addition, Warfield pointed out, if we grant for the sake of argument that the canonical Gospels are "second generation" documents and that behind them lie these still more primitive documents, "we have simply pushed back [from the seventh decade of the first century] ten, fifteen, or twenty years our literary testimony to the deity of Christ: and how can we suppose that the determinative expression of the Church's faith in A.D. 50 or A.D. 40 differed radically from the Church's faith in A.D. 30—the year in which Jesus died?"[65]

60. Benjamin B. Warfield, The Lord of Glory (reprint, Grand Rapids: Baker, 1974), p. 149.
61. Ibid., pp. 152-53.
62. Ibid., p. 153.
63. Ibid., pp. 153-55. Q is, of course, purely hypothetical and almost certainly never existed as a document. See Martin H. Franzmann, The Word of the Lord Grows (St. Louis: Concordia, 1961), pp. 214-15.
64. A. T. Robinson, The Christ of the Logia (New York: G. H. Doran, 1924).
65. Warfield, Lord of Glory, pp. 147-48.

Historical Criticism

In the face of these undeniable conclusions, those biblical scholars—and there were many—who were predisposed philosophically and theologically against the doctrine of a two-natured Christ placed their confidence in another critical approach to the Gospels known as "historical criticism," in which the critic attempted by the most searching critical analysis to get back to the Jesus "that really was" behind the Jesus of the Evangelists who, it was assumed, had read their own ideas about Him into His teachings and who had attributed much to Jesus that He never said. Scholars such as Bousset, Schmiedel, Pfleiderer, and S. Matthews worked with the assumption that the Evangelists, because they were men of faith, that is, because they revered Jesus and wrote out of a commitment to Him, were incapable of writing objectively about Him. As a result, they have given us not a portrait of Jesus as He really was but as they, in their devotion as spokesmen of the believing community, envisioned Him to be. Warfield states the historical critics' working thesis in these words:

> Faith [was] the foe of fact: and in the enthusiasm of their devotion to Jesus it was inevitable that His followers should clothe Him in their thought of Him with attributes which He did not possess and never dreamed of claiming: and it was equally inevitable that they should imagine that He must have claimed them and have ended by representing Him as claiming them.[66]

The results of their labors were radical indeed. After "the utmost sharpness of inquisition," Schmiedel, for example, concluded that there were only nine "absolutely credible passages" in the Gospels that could serve as "the foundation pillars for a truly scientific life of Jesus,"[67] these nine incidentally proving to Schmiedel that the real Jesus was only a man like other men. All else that the Evangelists report had been so retouched from the standpoint of faith, maintained Schmiedel, that it should be discarded insofar as aiding in the discovery of the real Jesus. Otto Pfleiderer even concluded that the real Jesus was irretrievably hidden under the devotional layer with which faith had enveloped Him.[68]

This eviscerated picture of Jesus, however, was simply incapable of ex-

66. Ibid., pp. 157-58.

67. Schmiedel, "Gospels," *Encyclopaedia Biblica*, ed. T. K. Cheyne and J. Sutherland Black (New York: Macmillan, 1914), p. 1881. The nine passages are Matthew 12:31ff.; 27:46 (and its Markan parallel); Mark 3:21; 10:17ff.; and 13:32; to which he added Matthew 11:5 (and its Lukan parallel); Mark 6:5ff.; 8:12; and 8:14-21. Cf. Warfield's response in his "Concerning Schmiedel's Pillar-Passages," *Christology and Criticism* (New York: Oxford University Press, 1929), pp. 181-255.

68. Otto Pfleiderer, *The Early Christian Conception of Jesus*, cited by Warfield, *Lord of Glory*, p. 162.

plaining the supernatural Christianity that sprang from Him. Moreover, the assumption with which the historical critics worked—that faith is the foe of fact, the enemy of real historical reporting—was defective beyond redemption. That the Evangelists wrote as men of faith, of course, is not to be doubted. Two of them admit as much. Luke acknowledges that his Gospel stood in the train of other Christians' efforts before his (does he include Mark and Matthew among them?) to "set in order a narrative of those things which have been fulfilled among us . . . that [his reader] may know the certainty of the things you have been taught" (1:1-4). And John forthrightly declares that he wrote with the aim of bringing his readers to faith in Jesus as the Christ, the Son of God (19:35; 20:31). Sympathetic they undoubtedly were to Christ and His cause—beyond any question. But "are we to lay it down as the primary canon of criticism that no sympathetic report of a master's teaching is trustworthy; that only inimical reporters are credible reporters"[69]—in spite of the fact that Luke and John expressly state respectively that their concern was to testify "carefully" (ἀκριβῶς, 1:3) and "truthfully" (ἀληθινή, ἀληθής, 19:35; 21:24). Surely, Warfield was right when he declared:

> The procedure we are here invited to adopt is a prescription for historical investigation which must always issue in reversing the portraiture of the historical characters to the records of whose lives it is applied. The result of its universal application would be . . . the writing of all history backwards . . . every historical character [being] the exact opposite to what each was thought to be by all who knew and esteemed him.[70]

Warfield may be guilty in the eyes of some of resorting to the *argumentum reductio ad absurdum* here, but the fact that the historical critic's canon is so vulnerable to the argument indicates its weakness. As James Denney cautioned, the historical critic's canon that insists on only *uninterpreted* facts about Jesus—divested of any and all personal views about Him, theological or otherwise—calls for facts that stand out of relation to everything in the universe, that have no connection with any part of our experience, and that are a blank unintelligibility, a mere irrelevance in the mind of men.[71] C. H. Dodd also has pointed out that events "can take their true place in an historical record only as they are interpreted,"[72] while Leon Morris urges that the historian who is content with a "factual" account of what takes place

69. Warfield, *Lord of Glory*, p. 159.

70. Ibid., p. 161.

71. James Denney, *Studies in Theology* (London: Hodder and Stoughton, 1895), p. 106; cf. also A. M. Hunter, *Interpreting the New Testament 1900-1950* (London: SCM Press, 1951), pp. 46-47.

72. C. H. Dodd, *History and the Gospel* (London: Nisbet, 1938), p. 104.

fails as a historian.[73] Even A. E. Harvey, who is no friend of the teaching of a two-natured Christ, acknowledges that

> it is a mistake to contrast the admittedly heavily interpreted gospel record with an imaginary ideal of objective, completely uninterpreted "history." Such history is never in fact written. Bare objective facts exist only, if at all, in archives and account books. History is what makes sense out of the raw material by a complex process of selection, arrangement, and interpretation.[74]

For these reasons then—first, its inability to explain the existence of the supernatural Christianity that sprang from Jesus on the basis of the minimal amount of "trustworthy" material it recovered about Him from its labors, and second, the defective canon that governed it—the historical-critical movement was adjudged a failure.

Form Criticism

For the last sixty years a third method of New Testament research, form criticism, has increasingly dominated the field. Though there had been predecessors of the form critics, such as Herder, Overbeck, Wendland, and Nordern, it was really Martin Dibelius and Rudolf Bultmann who perfected the form-critical method. The method, technically known as the *Formgeschichtliche* ("form-historical") method, signalizes the effort to penetrate behind the written Gospels and even behind the presumed more primitive literary sources underlying them (*Ur-Markus*, Q, M, L) to the even more primitive *oral* Gospel tradition, and to classify and examine the various "forms" or types of material present in that oral tradition. These "oral forms," form critics presumed, provided material for the aboriginal literary sources of the Gospels, but they also argued that the oral forms were so thoroughly shaped by the racial and socio-cultural character and needs of the several early Christian communities in which they originated that they preclude any real historical basis for the events recorded in the Gospels. The error of the historical-critical method, according to these form critics, was the assumption that there was real historical data, however scant, still to be obtained about Jesus in the Gospels, data that could portray a Jesus who could still be a moral guide to the Enlightenment, if only the historical-critical method could remove the layers of theological encrustation encasing Him. What

---

73. Leon Morris, "The Fourth Gospel and History," in *Jesus of Nazareth: Saviour and Lord*, p. 124.

74. A. E. Harvey, "Christology and the Evidence of the New Testament," in *God Incarnate: Story and Belief*, ed. A. E. Harvey (London: SPCK, 1981), p. 46.

these earlier practitioners of the art had failed to realize, the first form critics maintained, is that the Gospel material had already been so thoroughly reshaped ("mythologized") at the level of oral tradition, as the post-Easter church[75] sought to meet its evangelistic and apologetic needs, that there is virtually nothing remaining of the historical Jesus in the Gospels beyond His mere "thatness." Bultmann declares, for example, in the opening paragraph of his *Theology of the New Testament* that the post-Easter church "frequently introduced into its account of Jesus' message, motifs of its own proclamation."[76] According to Bultmann's analysis of the *Sitze im Leben* ("settings in life") of the isolated forms of tradition (which had been "form-critically" categorized into prophetic sayings, wisdom sayings, legal sayings, parables, "I" sayings, and narrative units of paradigm, conflict stories, miracle stories, Passion stories, and so on), the church was also clearly influenced by Jewish Apocalyptic and Gnostic mythology.

Developments in the method have, of course, occurred. For example, Reginald H. Fuller, both refining and reacting to the views originating with W. Bousset (*Kyrios Christos*) and developed by Bultmann (*Theology of the New Testament*) and F. Hahn (*The Titles of Jesus in Christology*), submits the christological statements of the New Testament to a critical analysis in accordance with the particular *Sitze im Leben* which they occupy in their assigned first-century milieu.[77] Accordingly, he argues that Jesus Himself understood His earthly mission entirely in functional terms, seeing His task as the announcement of the future coming of the Son of Man. After His death, the earliest Aramaic-speaking Christians of Palestine thought of Jesus in a functional-prophetic manner, but they also identified Him with the eschatological Son of Man, which identification Jesus Himself had never made. (The teachings of Peter in Acts and James are often thought to reflect this christological stage.) As the gospel spread to the Jews of the Diaspora, these Hellenistic (Greek-speaking, "Grecianized") Jewish Christians combined with the functional categories certain ontological categories, heightening the representation of Jesus' person during His earthly ministry and adding the thought of His present reign as exalted "Lord." (Paul and the writer of Hebrews would reflect this stage of development.) Finally, in the

---

75. The reader should bear in mind that when the anti-incarnational form critic uses the phrase "post-Easter church," he does not mean to suggest that he believes that Jesus rose from the dead. Rather, he refers to the church that grew out of the "dawning" upon His disciples after His death that Jesus still "lived" among them in a spiritual or "existential" sense in order to transform them.

76. Rudolf Bultmann, *Theology of the New Testament*, trans. Kendrick Grobel (London: SCM Press, 1971), p. 3.

77. Reginald H. Fuller, *The Foundations of New Testament Christology* (New York: Charles Scribner's Sons, 1965).

church's mission to Hellenistic Gentiles, still more ontological categories were added, resulting in the preexistent, incarnational, "divine man" Christology reflected by the Johannine corpus.[78]

Of course, such a christological construction, if true, would mean the end to anything truly transcendentally significant in classical incarnational Christology since it both precludes any real, knowable, historical basis for the events recorded in the canonical Gospels and contends that there never was *one* recognized Christology in the first century but rather that there was a variety of Christologies—a "Synoptic" Christology, a "Pauline" Christology, a "Johannine" Christology, and so on—which in substantive detail differ from each other. Without realizing it, the church simply creedalized that christological form that had taken shape during the church's Hellenistic Gentile mission. But W. D. Davies' *Paul and Rabbinic Judaism* and Martin Hengel's *Judaism and Hellenism* both have demonstrated that the alleged distinctions that Fuller draws between Palestinian and Hellenistic Judaism cannot be asserted, in that no part of Judaism had escaped the influence of Hellenization by 150 B.C. I. Howard Marshall has argued similarly that no significant differences can be drawn between a Jewish and a Gentile Christianity[79] because of (1) the short span of time (some twenty years) that transpired between the death of Jesus and the writing of the earliest Pauline letters, in which a fully developed Christology is already present, and (2) the improbability that a special Jerusalem theology developed independently of a special theology in Antioch (which latter church was deeply involved in the Gentile mission) because of the many contacts that existed between these two Christian centers. He concludes that the three-stage scheme of development is "an inexact means of plotting Christological thought" because the boundaries between the three areas of thought were simply "too fluid."[80]

Redaction Criticism

Other form-critical scholars, beginning with Willi Marxsen, have now added a fourth critical method, redaction criticism, which asserts that allowances have to be made in the final appearance the Gospels assumed, not only for the mythologized oral strata of the tradition, but also for the

78. James Dunn (*Christology in the Making*) reflects a similar vision of the development of New Testament Christology from a nonincarnational to an incarnational kind.

79. I. Howard Marshall, "Palestinian and Hellenistic Christianity: Some Critical Comments," *New Testament Studies* 19 (1972–73): 271-87; cf. also his *The Origins of New Testament Christology* (Downers Grove, Ill.. Inter-Varsity Press, 1976), pp. 32-34.

80. Marshall, *Origins of New Testament Christology*, p. 40.

theological and literary preferences of the Gospel writers themselves who in their selecting and arranging of the material for their respective Gospels did not hesitate, as they "redacted" or edited their material, to *create* a new story in order to meet the needs of their respective communities of belief.

A careful exegetical study of the early sermons of Peter in Acts and the sixty occurrences of εὐαγγέλιον (usually translated "gospel": literally "good news") in Paul's writings discloses, however, that the *apostolic* gospel was (1) the proclamation (κήρυγμα) of the *historical facts* of the death, resurrection, and exaltation of Jesus, together with (2) the apostolic explication of the significance of these events for God and for man, followed by (3) the summons to repent and the invitation to receive forgiveness through faith in Christ's work.[81] And while the church has historically been satisfied that it possesses in the four canonical Gospels the literary "fleshing out" of the essential facts of the life and ministry of that One who is central to the apostolic proclamation—this "fleshing out" itself described by Mark as "the gospel of Jesus Christ" (1:1)—redaction criticism has given rise to scholars' efforts to discern which *genre* a given Gospel writer was patterning his account after as he "created" it: was it (1) the history format genre form comprising ancient memoirs and biography segments, (2) the Semitic model genre form, such as apocalypse, the legend of Achikar, Exodus, the book of Jonah, a Passover Haggadah, Midrashim, and the Mishnah, (3) the kerygma-history genre form, (4) the Greco-Roman biography genre form, (5) the aretalogy genre form in which the miraculous deeds of a "god or hero" are narrated, (6) the Christian novel genre form, (7) the dramatic history genre form, (8) the Greek tragicomic genre form, (9) a combination of these, or (10) the cult of Christ-kerygma genre—unique among genre forms? Whatever genre a given scholar finally approved, these genre scholars generally agree that "it is not the construing of what Jesus did and said that determined the genre, but the genre that determined how what he did and said was construed."

It should now be evident to anyone who has followed this brief overview of the history of twentieth-century New Testament research why Wiles and Bowden, whom we quoted earlier, express such skepticism about ever knowing anything really significant about the historical Jesus. And it should not be surprising that other scholars, faced with the specter of total skepticism in the field of New Testament studies, have reacted—some only mildly, some more vigorously—against the conclusions of the form-critical/ redaction-critical methods, which have shifted the object of faith away

---

81. Cf. Robert H. Mounce, "Gospel," in *Evangelical Dictionary of Theology*, ed. Walter A. Elwell (Grand Rapids: Baker, 1984), pp. 472-74.

from the Jesus of the canonical Gospels to the "demythologized" Christ of the church's proclamation. Though still committed to the form-critical method itself, they began to search for ways to isolate out of the Gospel tradition at least some, if not all, of the authentic sayings of Jesus (assuming there might be some) in order to lay hold upon something of the historical Jesus to justify the church's continuing interest in Him.

J. Jeremias, for example, argued for years that the presence of certain patterns in the reported speeches and sayings of Jesus can only be explained on the ground that we have in them, if not the *ipsissima verba Jesu* ("very words of Jesus") very likely the *ipsissima vox Jesu* ("very voice of Jesus"). He advanced such characteristic patterns as Jesus' reported use of Αββα (Greek transliteration of the Aramaic אבא "Father") without a suffix as an address to God in prayer, of ἀμήν ("in truth") to introduce and to authenticate His own words, of antithetic parallelism, of parables, and of circumlocutions (for example, the passive verbs in the Matthean Beatitudes) to avoid the use of the divine name.[82] Jeremias concluded as a result of his detailed study:

> The linguistic and stylistic evidence . . . shows so much faithfulness and such respect towards the tradition of the sayings of Jesus that we are justified in drawing up the following principle of method: In the synoptic tradition it is the inauthenticity and not the authenticity of the sayings of Jesus that must be demonstrated.[83]

C. H. Dodd echoed Jeremias's conclusion, saying that after full allowance has been made for all the possible limiting factors—changes in oral transmission, the effects of translating Jesus' Aramaic into Greek, and the "redactional" intent of the Evangelists—

> it remains that the first three gospels offer a body of sayings on the whole so consistent, so coherent, and withal so distinctive in manner, style, [and] content, that no reasonable critic should doubt, whatever reservations he may have about individual sayings, that we find reflected here the thought of a single, unique teacher—[even Jesus Christ].[84]

But such optimistic conclusions have not gone unchallenged by a good many form critics, such as V. Hasler, K. Berger, and H. Conzelmann. And Norman Perrin declares, contrary to Jeremias's conclusion,

---

82. Joachim Jeremias, *New Testament Theology, I: The Proclamation of Jesus*, trans. J. Bowden (London: SCM Press, 1971), pp. 8-37.

83. Ibid., p. 37.

84. C. H. Dodd, *The Founder of Christianity* (New York: Macmillan, 1970), pp. 21-22.

Clearly, we have to ask ourselves the question as to whether [Jesus' sayings] should now be attributed to the early Church or to the historical Jesus, and *the nature of the synoptic tradition is such that the burden of proof will be upon the claim to authenticity.*[85]

Faced with the need then to authenticate a historical Jesus who will stir even minimal interest of faith in Him, in their "new quest for the historical Jesus" form-critical scholars, such as Käsemann, Conzelmann, Perrin, and Fuller, among others, have resorted to three criteria—dissimilarity, coherence, and frequency—for isolating the authentic sayings of Jesus and thus for establishing a historical base sufficiently broad for the grounding of faith in Jesus. The *criterion of dissimilarity* is applied as follows: If a saying has no obvious source in contemporary Judaism and if it is not the sort of thing the early church is likely to have formulated, then it is likely that the saying originated with Jesus.[86] By this principle a pool of authentic teaching is isolated. Then the *criterion of coherence* is applied to increase the number of sayings. This is done by noting those other sayings that, although they do not fit into the previous category, nonetheless cohere with those that do. Finally, the *criterion of frequency* of occurrence in the so-called sources of synoptic tradition (Ur-Markus, Q, M, L) comes into play. It assumes that a saying found in two or three sources is more likely to be authentic than a saying found in only one source unless the latter meets the criterion of dissimilarity.

As with Jeremias's proposals, these criteria have not gone unchallenged, and quite properly so. M. D. Hooker, for example,[87] points out that the criterion of dissimilarity eliminates from the teaching of Jesus those areas in which He would have been in agreement with Judaism and the church. That is to say, if the church is, in fact, the outcome of His ministry, it is utterly improbable that no continuity would obtain between His teaching and the post-Easter faith of the church. But on the basis of the criterion of dissimilarity, if Jesus, for example, actually claimed to be the Messiah, we would

85. Norman Perrin, *Rediscovering the Teaching of Jesus* (London: SCM Press, 1967), p. 39, emphasis original.

86. Cf. Ernst Käsemann ("The Problem of the Historical Jesus," *Essays on New Testament Themes*, trans. W. J. Montague [London: SCM Press, 1964], pp. 15-47) for his programmatic argument for the validity of the criterion of dissimilarity.

87. M. D. Hooker, "On Using the Wrong Tool," *Theology* 75, no. 629 (November 1972): 570-81; cf. also her article, "Christology and Methodology," *New Testament Studies* 17 (1970-71): 480-87. R. T. France ("The Authenticity of the Sayings of Jesus," in *History, Criticism, and Faith*, ed. Colin Brown [Downers Grove, Ill.: Inter-Varsity Press, 1976], pp. 101-43) also provides a very helpful treatment of the issue. For I. Howard Marshall's critical analysis of the criterion of dissimilarity, cf. his *Origins of New Testament Christology*, pp. 54-58.

have to disallow it because the church makes that claim on His behalf. Hooker notes:

> This particular criterion . . . *may* perhaps be able to give us a collection of sayings concerning whose authority we may be reasonably confident, but those sayings will not represent the kernel of Jesus' teaching, or be his most characteristic thought. Indeed, they would seem to offer us those sayings which the church treated as peripheral.[88]

She also notes that the criterion of dissimilarity is faulty because it assumes that our knowledge of pre-Christian and first-century Judaism and early Christianity is sufficient to serve as a control of what is unique in Jesus' teaching. But the discovery of the Qumran community and its library (not to mention materials found since Hooker wrote) illustrates that New Testament scholars still have much to learn about New Testament times. "It could be," she writes, "that if we knew the whole truth about Judaism and the early Church, our small quantity of 'distinctive' teaching would wither away altogether."[89]

The criterion of coherence is also suspect because what may seem incoherent to us in our twentieth-century milieu may have been quite coherent in first-century Palestine—and vice versa. And all the more is it difficult to assess coherency if Jesus intended some of His sayings to contain an element of paradox.

Hooker also faults the form-critical scholar for applying these criteria with a degree of subjectivity. To illustrate, she points out that the term "Kingdom of God" is often used by both Jesus and the early church while, with rare exception (once in Acts and twice in the Revelation), the "Son of Man" title is used exclusively by Jesus. On the principle of dissimilarity the form critics should conclude that Jesus never spoke of the Kingdom of God but spoke often about the Son of Man. But what have the form critics concluded? They all regard the Kingdom of God as the very core of Jesus' teaching, but many have reduced the authentic references in Jesus' teachings to the Son of Man to (at most), a mere handful—those dealing with, say, the future coming of the Son of Man! She concludes by stating the obvious: "In the end, the answers which the New Testament scholar gives are not the result of applying objective tests and using precision tools; they are very largely the result of his own presuppositions and prejudices."[90]

This much is plain from Hooker's penetrating analysis of the "tools" of

---

88. Hooker, "On Using the Wrong Tool," p. 575.
89. Ibid.
90. Ibid., p. 581.

form criticism: although these criteria were supposed to deliver the form-critical scholar from skepticism about the historical Jesus, its specter still hovers over all his labors, and the prospect is still frighteningly real that, on form-critical grounds, nothing for sure can ever be said about the historical Jesus.

But granted for the sake of argument that on form-critical grounds some things can be said about Jesus for certain, does even the reduced amount of new material with which the form critic will allow himself to work portray a Jesus different in kind from the Jesus of the canonical Gospels? If the Jesus of history is in fact the incarnate God-man, as classical Christology has insisted, it should come as no surprise that, even in the highly circumscribed "authenticated" material of the form critic, the divine Christ still presides. Royce Gruenler has attempted to meet the form critic on his own ground in this regard. Choosing Norman Perrin's book, *Rediscovering the Teaching of Jesus*, because it is "still the best compendium of 'authentic' sayings of Jesus arrived at by the most radical application of the criterion of dissimilarity,"[91] Gruenler examines Perrin's pool of authentic sayings, using as the criterion of his analysis the later Wittgenstein's theory of the intentionality of language. He shows that, even on the basis of Perrin's highly circumscribed pool of authentic sayings, the Jesus portrayed by them believed Himself to have the divine prerogative to forgive sins, stood in such a relationship to God that the Kingdom (authority) of God was present in His person, and stood in the very place of God Himself, and through Him men can be received back into fellowship with God. Here, Gruenler concludes, is an implicit, if not explicit, high Christology indeed![92]

Is there nothing that can be said positively about the form-critical method and the redaction-critical method as tools for doing New Testament research? Regarding the former, as long as the New Testament scholar seeks to determine the "form" (genre) of a given pericope—for example, whether it is narrative, poetry, parable, hymn, or Passion account—for the benefit such knowledge will yield as he does exegesis, since he will apply different rules when interpreting predictive prophecy from those he will apply when interpreting historical narrative and still other rules when interpreting poetry from those he applies when interpreting a parable, no harm is done so long as the *meaning* of the passage is still finally derived from biblical-theological and grammatical-historical hermeneutics.

Regarding redaction criticism, the church has long recognized and hap-

91. Royce Gordon Gruenler, *New Approaches to Jesus and the Gospels* (Grand Rapids: Baker, 1982), p. 34.

92. Ibid., chaps. 2 and 3, passim.

pily acknowledged that the four Evangelists carefully selected and arranged their material (derived from whatever sources—other Gospels, eyewitnesses, etc.) in order to highlight their respective portrayals of Jesus. This recognition lies behind the oft-drawn generalization that Matthew portrays Jesus as the Messianic King, that Mark portrays Him as the Lord's active Servant, that Luke portrays Him as the man concerned for others, and that John portrays Him as God's Son. This is not only harmless redaction criticism, it is actually quite helpful, inasmuch as the composite picture they give of Jesus is richer than any single Gospel portrayal could have achieved.

But the redaction critic further assumes that the Gospels and Epistles have undergone a warping away from the actual history of the event and the actual teaching of Jesus through an earlier process of theologizing by the early church and the Evangelists, so that they no longer portray Jesus as He really was and are no longer historically reliable. But when he does so, I submit that the redaction critic is being governed more by dogmatic prejudice than by what the facts of the case will allow. What actual textual evidence we have takes us in precisely the opposite direction!

For example, there are indications in the New Testament that the apostles jealously preserved the teachings of Jesus by maintaining the distinction between what Jesus had said and what they themselves were saying to the church. Twice in 1 Corinthians 7, Paul distinguishes Jesus' earlier teaching on marriage and divorce from his later teaching (cf. 7:10: "To the married I give this command, not I, but the Lord"; 7:12: "To the rest I say this, I, not the Lord"). And even though the Gospels were written either after some portions of the New Testament or contemporaneously with other New Testament material, a clear line of demarcation is maintained throughout between Jesus' most common self-designation in the Gospels prior to His death (Son of Man) and the church's most common designation for Him in light of His resurrection and ascension (Lord). "Son of Man" as a postresurrection title of Jesus is found only in Acts 7:56 and Revelation 1:13 and 14:14. If the church had no commitment regarding the preservation of Jesus' precise words, as the form critic implies, it is most unlikely that the Son of Man title would be found almost exclusively in the Gospels. Finally, if the church, as the form critic alleges, freely molded the original sayings of Jesus and actually created others to meet its emerging evangelistic and apologetic needs, it missed some golden opportunities for so doing, indeed, it went about it in a rather clumsy fashion. One would think, if the church were accustomed to doing so, that "Jesus' teaching" on the issue of Gentile circumcision would have been brought into the debate at the Jerusalem council in Acts 15 or on other issues in scores of places in the New Testament material where vital "life and death" matters were being debated. But in the most unnecessary places, as far as the vitals of the faith are concerned, they are brought in. Paul, for example, quotes Jesus in a charge to fellow believers: "It is more blessed to give than to receive" (Acts 20:35), a saying that admittedly does not appear as such in any Gospel, although certainly the spirit of it is evident in other recorded sayings (Matt. 10:8; John 13:34). For another example, compare Luke 10:7 with 1 Timothy 5:18, where Paul instructs the church to provide for the faithful elder. Thus, the *New Testament text itself* shows that form critics are unwarranted in concluding that the life and teaching of Jesus were so completely reconstructed by early church oral tradition that the Gospels contain very little real historical information about Him. David Well's observation on this whole issue is right on the mark:

> Why is it that only now, two thousand years after the event, we are at last beginning to understand what Christianity is all about? But, of course, by the word *we* what is in view is only an elite coterie of scholars. There are masses of Christians, all over the world, who have no ability to pick their way through the layers of literary tradition in Scripture. . . . Are we to suppose that the real interpretation of Jesus is alone accessible only to a tiny minority in the church—its learned scholars— and that the remainder of Christian believers is excluded from such knowledge? To suppose such a thing is to subject the meaning of Scripture to a far more restrictive "tradition" than anything proposed by Rome in the sixteenth century and to invest our new magisterium— the coterie of learned scholars—with an authority more stifling and far-reaching than the Roman Catholic magisterium ever exercised.[93]

And we must not lose sight of the fact that even this tiny minority of scholars in the church cannot agree on what is authentic in the New Testament portrayal of Jesus.

I am convinced that the New Testament material records reliable history and sober truth. Of course, when examining the teachings of Jesus with regard to His self-witness, because the precise wording of a saying can vary from Gospel to Gospel and because what Jesus is reported as saying in Greek He may have said originally in Aramaic, we must be aware that we are probably not working for the most part with the *ipsissima verba Jesu* ("very words of Jesus"). But for the reasons already given, I believe that we still possess at every point, accurately and substantively as the dynamic equivalent of the *ipsissima verba Jesu*, the *ipsissima vox Jesu* ("very voice of Jesus"),

---

93. David F. Wells, *The Person of Christ* (Westchester, Ill.: Crossway Books, 1984), pp. 35-36.

with the words employed by the Gospel writers representing truthfully and reliably the content of Jesus' sayings.

As we have seen from our survey of objections raised against the classical doctrine of a two-natured Christ, many modern scholars prefer a strictly human Jesus who is the "man for others" or the "man for God" (or any number of other perceptions of Him). Some scholars do so from a sincere missiological concern for a Christian witness that avoids all claim to an "achieved transcendence" for itself over the other world religions. Others skeptically claim that it is simply impossible to obtain any information that is really significant and at the same time historically reliable about Jesus. I have offered rebuttals to these objections.

Although among those who have advanced these objections are scholars of great breadth of learning and recognized literary achievement, I am convinced that the New Testament portrayal of Jesus is still sound and offers the basis for an intellectually satisfying faith. When one takes into account the alternative—the utter confusion in modern christological research in both the exegetical and dogmatic fields—the proof is abundant that something has gone dreadfully awry. That is all the more reason for the reader to continue in this present study with me. As I will urge at the end of our study, I believe something far more vital than an intellectually satisfying faith is at stake.

JESUS' SELF-WITNESS

In his brilliant 1926 study on "the modern debate about Jesus' Messianic consciousness" entitled *The Self-Disclosure of Jesus*, Geerhardus Vos analyzed the content of the Old Testament Messianic vision over against the liberal historico-critical distortion of it in his day. He isolated five essential elements: (1) the imposition from above of a *rule over men* that requires of them absolute submission (Gen. 49:10; Num. 24:17-19); (2) the element of the *eschatological*, reflected in the idea that the Messiah will be "the great final King, who stands at the close of the present world order and ushers in the coming world," this new world appearing not in the natural course of events but catastrophically through a divine interposition and, when once attained, bearing the stamp of eternity, with the Messiah Himself standing at the center of this eschatological complex (Pss. 2:8-12; 45:6; 110:1, 5-6; Isa. 9:2-7; Dan. 2:44; 7:13-14; Mal. 3:2-3; 4:1-5); (3) inseparable from the second, the *supernatural* ingredient pervading the whole vision, as it portends the creation of a new world order different in nature from the present one, in which a return to the paradisaical state that existed at the beginning of history is brought about (Isa. 11:1-9; 32:15; 65:17-25); (4) the component of the *soteric* in which both a spiritual and a martial salvation is accomplished by the Lord through His Messiah who delivers His people from divine judgment and introduces them into the blessedness of the new world to come (Isa. 9:4-5; 11:1-16; Mic. 5:4-5a; Zech. 9:9-10); and (5) interwoven through it all, *the specifically religious position that the Messiah Himself occupies* between God and man, entailing basically both His right to receive worship and His identification with God.[1]

In this chapter I intend to show that Jesus believed that He was the Messiah of just such an Old Testament vision by setting forth precisely what

---

1. Geerhardus Vos, *The Self-Disclosure of Jesus* (1926; reprint, Phillipsburg, N.J.: Presbyterian and Reformed, 1978), pp. 17-31.

He thought about both Himself and His mission, ascribing to Him neither more nor less than what He claimed for Himself. More specifically, as we consider the testimony before us in the Evangelists' reported teachings of Jesus, we will attempt to answer two questions: Did Jesus believe and teach that He was the promised Messiah? And did Jesus believe and teach that He was the divine Messiah?

The first New Testament datum that gives us any insight into His self-understanding is found in Luke 2:49 when Jesus, at twelve years of age, expressed an awareness of a special relationship to God as "My Father," which He intimated transcended in significance that familial relationship existing between Himself and His earthly parents. Though it would have been with a child's comprehension, apparently Jesus had already felt His Father's pull toward the holy work He would someday accomplish. We must resist the impulse to say more concerning the character of His self-understanding during the private years preceding His public ministry since we simply have no trustworthy data to say more. Only from data stemming from His public ministry may we deduce His self-understanding.

Jesus' Major Messianic Titles
"Christ" ("Anointed One")

Contrary to what one might assume in light of the very frequent occurrence of the term "Christ" throughout the apostolic writings of the New Testament and in later popular Christian discourse, the title "Messiah" (מָשִׁיחַ—"anointed one") occurs very infrequently in the Old Testament as a reference to the future Davidic Deliverer of the people of God—only three times to be exact (Ps. 2:2; Dan. 9:25, 26).[2] It may also come as a surprise to some to learn that on only three clear occasions did Jesus Himself directly claim in so many words to be the "Christ" (Χριστός), the Greek equivalent of the Hebrew and Aramaic "Messiah."

John 4:25-26. The first of these instances occurred early in His ministry in His conversation with the Samaritan woman at the well. In response to her

---

2. In the Old Testament, priests (Exod. 29:7; 30:30-33; Lev. 4:3; 6:22; 8:12, 30), and kings (1 Sam. 10:1; 16:13; 24:10; 2 Sam. 19:21; cf. 1 Sam. 2:10 and Ps. 89:20) were installed in their respective offices to perform their specific functions through an "anointing" ritual. And in 1 Kings 19:10 and Ps. 105:15 prophets, being organs of revelation, are designated "anointed ones" by virtue of the spirit's "anointing" visitation upon them as they prophesied. Consequently, "Messiah" or "Anointed One" came to be the most popular designation of the future Davidic Ruler who would usher in the promised eschatological Kingdom of God and represent the people before God and God before the people in that Kingdom.

statement "I know that Messiah is coming. . . . When He comes, He will explain everything to us," Jesus declared to her, "I who speak to you am He" (Ἐγώ εἰμι, ὁ λαλῶν σοι).

John 17:3. The second instance is found in His high priestly prayer where He refers to Himself in the third person as "Jesus Christ, whom You sent."

Mark 14:62. The third occurrence came at the very end of His earthly ministry during His trial before the Sanhedrin when, in response to the high priest's adjuration, "I charge you under oath by the living God: Tell us if you are the Christ, the Son of God" (Matt. 26:63; cf. also Mark 14:61: "Are you the Christ, the Son of the Blessed One"; Luke 22:67: "If you are the Christ, tell us"), Jesus declared unequivocally, "I am [Ἐγώ εἰμι], and you will see the Son of Man sitting at the right hand of the Mighty One [cf. Ps. 110:1] and coming with the clouds of heaven [cf. Dan. 7:13]" (Mark 14:62; cf. Matt. 26:64; Luke 22:67-69).

To these three direct claims to messiahship we must add the two following instances when someone *in Jesus' presence* and *to His face* confessed Him to be the "Christ" and He accepted, either expressly or tacitly, the assessment as correct.

Matthew 16:16 (Mark 8:29; Luke 9:20). First, of course, is Peter's famous confession in response to Jesus' inquiry concerning His disciples' understanding of Him: "You are the Christ," he acclaimed (so Mark; Matt.: "You are the Christ, the Son of the living God"; Luke: "the Christ of God"). While according to all three Synoptic Evangelists He would admonish His disciples not to spread this perception of Him abroad, according to Matthew, Jesus first responded with His benediction: "Blessed are you, Simon bar-Jonah, for flesh and blood has not revealed this to you, but My Father who is in heaven" (Matt. 16:17). Clearly, Jesus accepted Peter's assessment of Him as true.

John 11:25-27. Second is Martha's striking declaration in response to Jesus' words: "I am the resurrection and the life. He who believes in Me, even though he should die, shall live, and everyone who lives and believes in Me shall never die. Do you believe this?" Martha unhesitatingly replied, "Yes, Lord; I believe that You are the Christ, the Son of God, who was to come into the world." The absence of any correction by Jesus plainly indicates His acceptance of her description.

Beyond these five instances (John 4:26; 17:3; Mark 14:62; Matt. 16:16; and

John 11:27), nowhere else does Jesus explicitly claim the Messianic investiture through the title "Christ."[3] He used the term sparingly, no doubt because the Messianic idea had become distorted in one way or another away from the balanced vision of Old Testament Messianism. "In circles where a quietistic priestly emphasis was strong, the Levitical character of the Messiah dominated. Where Pharisaic influence was felt, legal and prophetic elements were stressed,"[4] while for the popular imagination Messianism had come one-sidedly to have strong nationalistic, racial, political, and materialistic associations. As a result, Jews of the first century regarded the Messiah primarily as Israel's national deliverer from the yoke of Gentile oppression. Such spiritual elements in the Messianic task as those delineated by Vos had been pushed far to the rear in general Jewish thought. Had Jesus employed uncritically the current popular term as a description of Himself and His mission before divesting it of its one-sided associations and infusing it with its richer, full-orbed Old Testament meaning, which included the work of the Messiah as the Suffering Servant of Isaiah, His mission would have been gravely misunderstood and His efforts to instruct the people even more difficult. Consequently, the evidence suggests that He acknowledged He was the "Christ" only where there was little or no danger of His claim being politicized—as in the case of the Samaritan woman, in private conversation with His disciples (at the same time, demanding that they tell no one that He was the Messiah), in semi-private prayer, or before the Sanhedrin when silence no longer mattered or served His purpose (since He had already publicly ridden into Jerusalem on a donkey in fulfillment of Zech. 9:9 and cleansed the temple in fulfillment of Mal. 3:1-4, claiming by these acts to be Israel's Messiah, and since the Sanhedrin had already determined to execute Him for what they regarded as His blasphemies).

But these five instances are enough, found as they are in all four Gospels (and in the case of His claim under oath at His trial, being made under the most solemn of circumstances), to satisfy most Bible students that Jesus believed Himself to be and in fact explicitly claimed to be the Messiah.

This would end the matter if many form-critical scholars did not believe

---

3. In my opinion, Matt. 22:42-45; 23:10; 24:5 (cf. Mark 13:6; Luke 21:8); 23-24; Mark 9:41; 12:35-37; 13:21-22; Luke 24:44-46; and John 10:24-25 also recount instances in which Jesus implicitly claimed to be the "Christ." But because of the somewhat "oblique" character of the claims, that is, because they are not as direct as the five I have mentioned, I will not lay stress on them at this time in showing that Jesus did claim to be the Messiah.

4. Richard N. Longenecker, *The Christology of Early Jewish Christianity* (London: SCM Press, 1970), p. 65; cf. also M. de Jonge, "The Use of the Word 'Anointed' in the Time of Jesus," *Novum Testamentum* 8 (1966): 132-48; Lohse, "υἱὸς Δαυίδ," *Theological Dictionary of the New Testament*, ed. G. Friedrich, 8 (Grand Rapids: Eerdmans, 1972), 478-82.

that the very infrequency of the term as a self-designation and as an address accepted by Him renders suspect the authenticity of even these five. Accordingly, all five have been explained away by one scholar or another as fabrications (or modifications of other sayings of Jesus) by the early church.

Jesus' claim in John 4:26, for example, supposedly reflects a situation in which the Evangelist saw an opportunity to enhance his own declared purpose in 20:31; consequently he read into the woman's declared "Messianic expectation" his own developed Christology and thus attributed to Jesus the claim to messiahship in this later and developed sense.[5] But there is nothing forced or unnatural in Jesus' claim to be the Messiah at this time and under these circumstances. It is true that John wrote his Gospel from the mature perspective of an aged apostle (John 2:18-22; 7:37-39; 12:16; 21:18-23), and he doubtless intended that his reader should understand Jesus' claim in the maturest sense of the term. But it is not at all inappropriate to insist, if Jesus in fact made the claim, that this is what He intended as well. All the more is it appropriate to think that Jesus could make this claim to the Samaritan woman since there was little or no danger of purely political overtones being read into it, inasmuch as it is well-established that "the Samaritans did not expect a Messiah in the sense of an anointed king of the Davidic house" but saw Him as One who would be a teacher and lawgiver rather than a king.[6]

Regarding Martha's confession of Jesus' messiahship (which we suggest Jesus tacitly approved), Bultmann believed that Wellhausen "may well be right" when he eliminated John 11:18-32 as a later addition from the original form of the narrative.[7] At any rate, Bultmann believed that "it is probable that originally the sisters . . . were anonymous, and that their identification with Martha and Mary is secondary [that is, was made after the fact]," with verses 20-32 being the Evangelist's own composition and reflecting "the theological ideas of the Evangelist."[8] But such a major revision of the narrative is unnecessary and has nothing really to commend it but the form critic's own biased assessment of the data. C. H. Dodd contests outright the legitimacy of a literary-critical analysis of John 11. He writes:

In ch. xi. 1-44 we have a compact *pericope* which has the aspect of a single

5. Oscar Cullmann, *The Christology of the New Testament*, trans. Shirley C. Guthrie and Charles A. M. Hall (London: SCM Press, 1959), p. 125 n. 4.

6. Raymond E. Brown, *The Gospel According to John I-XII*, Anchor Bible Series (Garden City, N.Y.: Doubleday, 1966), pp. 172-73.

7. Rudolf Bultmann, *The Gospel of John: A Commentary*, trans. G. R. Beasley-Murray (Oxford: Basil Blackwell, 1971), p. 401 n. 3.

8. Ibid., p. 396 n. 4.

continuous narrative—the longest in this gospel outside the Passion-narrative. . . . Most significant . . . are the two relatively self-contained dialogues contained in xi. 7-16 and xi. 21-7 respectively, both of which deal with important theological themes. . . . Any attempt to isolate a piece of pure narrative which may have served as nucleus soon becomes arbitrary in its treatment of the text. *There is no story of the Raising of Lazarus . . . separable from the pregnant dialogues of Jesus with His disciples and with Martha. On the other hand, these dialogues could not stand by themselves.* They need the situation in order to be intelligible, and they not only discuss the high themes of Johannine theology, but also promote and explain the action of the narrative.[9]

Surely Dodd's conclusion is more sober and objective than an approach that eliminates entire blocks of Gospel material as compositions reflecting the later theological ideas of the "post-Easter" church or the Evangelist.

Against the occurrence of "Jesus Christ" as a self-designation in Jesus' high priestly prayer, it has been urged, in favor of construing the phrase as a Johannine redaction and thus the reflection of a later christological vision, that there is a certain anachronistic incongruity in Jesus' reference to Himself in the third person by a compound title that seems only later to have acquired the character of a proper name. But there is nothing strange in our Lord's speaking of Himself titularly in the third person. Indeed, it seems characteristic of Jesus' manner of speaking, not only in His general use of the titles "Son of Man" and "Son [of God]" as self-designations but also in His specific employment of third-person self-designations in this very context (cf. "Your Son" in 17:1-2 and "Him whom You sent" in 17:3).

While the title itself is a *hapax* (one occurrence) on Jesus' lips, it is just as possible that Jesus' solemn employment of it on this occasion "gives us the point of departure for its apostolic use from Pentecost on" (Warfield) as that it is a redaction reflecting a later fixed apostolic usage. After all, this compound title as a proper name had to be employed by someone for the first time, and there is no reason why Jesus could not have been the first to employ it as a self-designation and thereby to provide the justification for the later church to develop several other similar compounds.

Finally, the symmetry in 17:3 between the explanatory clauses, "the only true God" and "[even] Jesus Christ" is lost if the compound name is eliminated from Jesus' prayer. Recognizing this, and to offset this loss of balance between the two phrases, many scholars, including Westcott and

---

9. C. H. Dodd, *The Interpretation of the Fourth Gospel* (Cambridge: University Press, 1954), p. 363, emphasis added; cf. also Leon Morris, *The Gospel According to John* (Grand Rapids: Eerdmans, 1971), pp. 532-36, for a full and skillful defense of the historicity of the story as a whole.

Plummer, propose that the former phrase should also be eliminated, with the clause in its most original form now reading: "that they may know You and Him whom You sent." But there is no reason for such a critical revision of the verse. Admittedly, symmetry would suggest that the two explanatory phrases stand or fall together; but precisely because there is nothing incongruous about the former expression in this place, the latter appears to be called for as well in order to preserve the striking balance. Consequently, for these reasons, I urge that the explanatory phrases be left intact and that "Jesus Christ" in John 17:3 be regarded as an explicit self-designation by Jesus of His messiahship.

As for the Petrine confession to which Jesus gives tacit approval in Mark and Luke and explicit approval in Matthew's account, Bultmann treated the pericope as legend created by the "post-Easter" church, by which faith in Jesus' messiahship was antedated to His lifetime. But his reasons are not convincing.[10] That Jesus took the initiative in the questioning (unlike in rabbinic discussions) is no sign that the narrative is a later creation. "One cannot argue from rabbinic practice to the practice of Jesus in this kind of way; had the initiative been taken by the disciples, one suspects that Bultmann would have claimed that the likeness of the narrative to rabbinic discussions was a sign of its artificiality."[11] As for his contention that Jesus would not have asked for information concerning a matter on which He was doubtless already as well informed as His disciples were, one is strongly tempted to judge this argument puerile. Clearly, Jesus intended to force the disciples to come to grips decisively with the nature of His person and work and to face squarely whether their understanding of Him had progressed beyond popular opinion, an essential advance if their faith was to survive His escalating emphasis on His forthcoming execution by the leaders of *religious* Israel.

R. H. Fuller also handles the Matthean pericope form-critically. Since Mark for him represents the more primitive tradition, Fuller declares Jesus' express approval of Peter's confession in Matthew 16:17-19 to be a "Matthean expansion" upon the historical situation and "clearly secondary . . . in its present position."[12] Then he argues that Mark 8:30 (the command to silence)

10. Cf. R. Bultmann, *The History of the Synoptic Tradition*, trans. John Marsh (New York: Harper and Row, 1963), pp. 275-78.

11. I. Howard Marshall, *Gospel of Luke—Commentary on the Greek Text* (Exeter: Paternoster Press, 1978), p. 365.

12. Reginald H. Fuller, *The Foundations of New Testament Christology* (London: Lutterworth Press, 1965), p. 134 n. 32.

is a typical Marcan theme [the so-called "Messianic secret"], and must be eliminated as a Marcan redaction. The passion prediction [8:31-32a] . . . did not belong originally to the scene. For it belongs to the same layer of tradition as the other passion predictions in Mark and is therefore detachable. [The Petrine rebuke in 8:32b] is clearly constructed as a link between the passion prediction and Jesus' rebuke of Peter [and should be eliminated].[13]

By this reconstruction of the narrative, Fuller neatly eliminates 8:30-32 from the original form of the tradition. Jesus' rebuke of Peter comes now as His direct response to Peter's confession of Him as the Messiah! Fuller's revision of the account actually represents Jesus as *rejecting* any and all claims to messiahship "as a merely human and even diabolical temptation."[14] But again, not only is this revision of the narrative unnecessary and "improbable, to say the least,"[15] but W. G. Kümmel brands it positively "untenable, because the first Christian community, which confessed Jesus as the Messiah, would never have transmitted unaltered an account in which Jesus rejected this confession as satanic."[16]

What about Jesus' clear affirmation of messiahship in Mark 14:61-62? This passage as well has "felt the knife" of the form critic. In Fuller's mind, "in view of Jesus' reaction at Caesarea Philippi," this affirmation "is unlikely to be authentic."[17] Fuller prefers to believe that at His trial Jesus in actuality either remained silent in response to the high priest's question, as at Mark 14:61a and 15:5, or responded in the Matthean form: "You have said so" (Σὺ εἶπας), which Fuller interprets "either as a non-committal answer or as an outright denial. And in view of Caesarea Philippi it would have to be a denial."[18] Now it is indeed true that the other Synoptic Evangelists report Jesus' response to the high priest's question in words different from Mark. But the question we must ask ourselves is, Does either Matthew or Luke contradict Mark's reported "I am"? I insist that neither does on the following grounds: Since we have argued above that Fuller's understanding of Peter's confession at Caesarea Philippi is highly untenable, we have eliminated his appeal to that incident (as revised by him) as a reason to question the

13. Ibid., p. 109.
14. Ibid. Ernst Käsemann is also convinced that Jesus did not understand Himself to be the Messiah. Cf. his *Essays on New Testament Themes* (London: SCM Press, 1964), pp. 38, 43.
15. I. Howard Marshall, *The Origins of New Testament Christology* (Downers Grove, Ill.: Inter-Varsity Press, 1976), p. 87.
16. Werner Georg Kümmel, *The Theology of the New Testament*, trans. John E. Steely (London: SCM Press, 1974), pp. 69-70.
17. Fuller, *Foundations of New Testament Christology*, p. 110.
18. Ibid.

authenticity of Jesus' affirmation at His trial. Furthermore, Jesus uses these very words (Σὺ εἶπας) earlier (Matt. 26:25) to answer Judas in the affirmative (cf. 26:14-16, 21-24). Cullmann acknowledges this when he writes, "On the basis of the Greek these words [Σὺ εἶπας] would also signify an affirmative answer."[19] In his definitive study of Jesus' answer to Caiaphas, D. R. Catchpole has shown that the phrase Σὺ εἶπας, though "circumlocutory in formula," is "affirmative in content."[20]

We have seen, then, that both Mark and Matthew (when properly understood) report an affirmative reply by Jesus to Caiaphas's question. The Lukan "If I tell you, you will not believe Me, and if I asked you, you would not answer," need not, as Cullmann thinks, be interpreted as a noncommittal response. It could, perhaps, have immediately preceded the affirmative response Matthew and Mark report. In fact, when Caiaphas asked Jesus, "Are you then the Son of God?" Luke reports that Jesus replied in the affirmative (22:70-71). Certainly Jesus included in *that* reply a claim to messiahship.

There is no convincing reason then for questioning the authenticity of any one of the five passages under present scrutiny; there is equally no sound reason to doubt that Jesus did, in fact, on at least these five occasions, either directly or tacitly, claim to be the "Christ," that is, the Messiah.

Though He did not regularly employ the title, commonly used by the people, to describe Himself and His mission, He did, however, employ another Messianic title as His favorite self-designation, thus revealing His self-understanding and underscoring His claim to be the Messiah. This brings us to a discussion of the title "Son of Man."

"Son of Man" definition

Anyone who attempts the formidable task of mastering the vast literature that has grown up around the "Son of Man" title in the Gospels will feel something of the awe that a mountain-climber experiences when standing at the foot of Mont Blanc or the Matterhorn: the sheer amount of material "to scale" is truly staggering. The student interested in researching the title

---

19. Oscar Cullmann, *Christology of the New Testament*, p. 118.

20. D. R. Catchpole, "The Answer of Jesus to Caiaphas (Matt. XXVI. 64)," *New Testament Studies* 17 (1970–71): 226. D. A. Carson expresses Jesus' intent:

Jesus speaks in this way . . . because Caiaphas's understanding of "Messiah" and "Son of God" is fundamentally inadequate. Jesus is indeed the Messiah and so must answer affirmatively [it is this nuance that Mark's Gospel records]. But He is not quite the Messiah Caiaphas has in mind; so he must answer cautiously and with some explanation (*Matthew*, in *The Expositor's Bible Commentary* [Grand Rapids: Zondervan, 1984], p. 555).

should consult the bibliographies in the surveys by A. J. B. Higgins and I. Howard Marshall.[21] Space limitations preclude a comprehensive treatment; therefore, we will have to content ourselves with what I regard to be the most pertinent data.

The title itself (ὁ υἱὸς τοῦ ἀνθρώπου; anarthrous only in John 5:27, but this anomaly is accounted for in terms of Colwell's observation[22]) occurs sixty-nine times in the Synoptic Gospels, appearing in all four of the so-called earlier documentary sources (Ur-Markus, Q, M, L),[23] and thirteen times in the Fourth Gospel,[24] for a total of eighty-two occurrences in the Gospels.

Their Authenticity. All of these "Son of Man" sayings occur in Jesus' own speeches, with the exception of three occurrences in John 12:34 (twice) and Luke 24:7. In the former two the crowd uses the title when asking Jesus about His use of it (cf. John 3:14; 8:28; 12:32), while in the latter, the angel is quoting Jesus. Traditio-critical scholarship has questioned many if not all of the Son of Man sayings. P. Vielhauer and E. Käsemann, for example, maintain that all of them are later creations of the early church. R. Bultmann, G. Bornkamm, F. Hahn, A. J. B. Higgins, and R. H. Fuller (on the basis of Luke 12:8 and similar sayings) accept only those which refer to a future

21. Cf. A. J. B. Higgins, "Son of Man—*Forschung* Since 'The Teaching of Jesus,' " in *New Testament Essays: Studies in Memory of T. W. Manson*, ed. A. J. B. Higgins (Manchester: University Press, 1959), pp. 119-35; I. Howard Marshall, "The Synoptic Son of Man Sayings in Recent Discussion," *New Testament Studies* 12 (1965–66); 327-51; cf. also Marshall, "The Son of Man in Contemporary Debate," *The Evangelical Quarterly* 62 (1970): 67-87, and his *Origins of New Testament Christology*, 79-80 n. 6. For the reader who desires a brief treatment of the title, three I would recommend are Richard N. Longenecker, *Christology of Early Jewish Christianity*, pp. 82-93: Marshall, *Origins of New Testament Christology*, pp. 63-82; and Royce G. Gruenler, "Son of Man," in *Evangelical Dictionary of Theology*, ed. Walter A. Elwell (Grand Rapids: Baker, 1984), pp. 1034-36.

22. Cf. E. C. Colwell, "A Definite Rule for the Use of the Article in the Greek New Testament," *Journal of Biblical Literature* 52 (1933): 12-21. I am fully aware of the reserve some New Testament scholars (for example, Nigel Turner, D. A. Carson) have expressed concerning the Colwell "rule," and I am aware of their reasons for that reserve. On the other hand, Bruce M. Metzger endorses its *general* validity in his "On the Translation of John 1:1," *The Expository Times* 63 (1951–52): 125-26, and in his "The Jehovah's Witnesses and Jesus Christ," *Theology Today* (April 1953): 75. Leon Morris (*Gospel According to John*, p. 77 n. 15) appeals to it as well to explain the anarthrous θεός in John 1:1c. C. F. D. Moule (*An Idiom Book of New Testament Greek* [Cambridge: University Press, 1953], pp. 115-16) also seems to endorse its general validity.

23. *Mark:* 2:10 (Matt. 9:6; Luke 5:24); 2:28 (Matt. 12:8; Luke 6:5); 8:31 (Luke 9:22; 24:7); 8:38 (Luke 9:26); 9:9 (Matt. 17:9), 12 (Matt 17:12), 31 (Matt. 17:22); 10:33 (Matt. 20:18; Luke 18:31), 45 (Matt. 20:28); 13:26 (Matt. 24:30b; Luke 21:27); 14:21a (Matt. 26:24a; Luke 22:22); 14:21b (Matt. 26:24b); 14:41 (Matt. 26:45); 14:62 (Matt. 26:64; Luke 22:69);

Q *(the so-called "sayings-source")*: Matt. 8:20 (Luke 9:58); Matt. 11:19 (Luke 7:34); Matt. 12:32 (Luke 12:10); Matt. 24:27 (Luke 17:24); Matt. 24:37 (Luke 17:26); Matt. 24:44 (Luke 12:40);

M: 10:23; 12:40; 13:37, 41; 16:13, 27, 28; 19:28; 24:30a, 39; 25:31; 26:2;

L: 6:22; 9:44; 11:30; 12:8; 17:22, 30; 18:8; 19:10; 21:36; 22:48.

24. *John:* 1:51; 3:13, 14; 5:27; 6:27, 53, 62; 8:28; 9:35; 12:23, 34 (twice); 13:31.

coming Son of Man understood as an apocalyptic figure distinct from Jesus. And E. Schweizer accepts as most likely authentic only the sayings having to do with Jesus' earthly ministry. But on the grounds of the form-critical scholar's own "criterion of dissimilarity," their claim to authenticity is virtually unimpeachable! This follows from the correlative facts that (1) "there is no evidence of a well-defined Son of man Christology in Judaism before the time of Jesus,"[25] the appearances of the term in 4 Ezra 13 and 1 Enoch 37-71 (the so-called Similitudes of Enoch) being most probably late first-century A.D. and thus "post-Jesus," and (2) apart from the Gospels, nothing to speak of is made of the Son of Man title in the sermons and writings of the first-century church.[26] F. F. Bruce writes:

> [The "Son of Man"] is a locution unparalleled in the Judaism of the period and one which, outside the Gospel tradition, was not current in the early church. Its claim to be recognized as an authentic *vox Christi* is thus remarkably strong.[27]

Royce G. Gruenler concurs:

> Since nothing in Judaism corresponds precisely to the nuances of meaning Jesus gives to them, and as the early church makes no use of it in its own theology, attempts by radical critics to discount Jesus' originality in applying the title to himself run counter to the fact that it satisfies especially well their own criterion of dissimilarity as the basic test of authentic sayings of Jesus. Rejection of the title . . . may thus be seen to rest on presuppositional, not exegetical, grounds.[28]

We may safely conclude that behind the earliest so-called "layer of literary

---

25. Gruenler, in *Evangelical Dictionary of Theology*, p. 1034.

26. The one occurrence in Stephen's defense before the Sanhedrin (Acts 7:56), the one further occurrence in Heb. 2:6 in the quotation of Ps. 8:4, and the two allusions in Rev. 1:13 and 14:14 to Christ as the Danielic Son of Man can hardly be advanced as the reflection of a major interest in a Son of Man Christology in the early church.

27. F. F. Bruce, "The Background to the Son of Man Sayings," in *Christ the Lord*, ed. Harold H. Rowdon (Leicester: Inter-Varsity Press, 1982), p. 52.

28. Gruenler, in *Evangelical Dictionary of Theology*, p. 1034. Cf. also R. H. Stein:

> Many attempts have been made to deny the authenticity of some or all of the Son of man sayings, but such attempts founder on the fact that this title is found in all the Gospel strata (Mark, Q, M, L, and John) and satisfies perfectly the "criterion of dissimilarity," which states that if a saying or title like this could not have arisen out of Judaism or out of the early church, it must be authentic. The denial of the authenticity of this title is therefore based not so much on exegetical issues as upon [*a priori*] rationalistic presuppositions ("Jesus Christ," in *Evangelical Dictionary of Theology*, p. 584).

Cf. also G. M. Burge, "Sayings of Jesus," in *Evangelical Dictionary of Theology*, pp. 977-78.

sources" in the still earlier so-called "layer of oral tradition" (which surely falls within the period immediately after Jesus' resurrection), the church found itself in immediate possession of a fully developed Son of Man Christology, not of its own creation, but rather one created by Jesus Himself!

Their Referent. The Son of Man sayings depict the Son of Man figure in three distinct situations: His then current ministry, His suffering at the hands of men (maltreated, betrayed, executed, and buried),[29] and His rising and appearing in glory on the clouds of heaven.[30] Who is this Son of Man, or are these situations so disparate that we must more accurately speak of more than one Son of Man?

The church has traditionally understood these sayings as the *ipsissima vox Jesu* and the phrase "Son of Man" as Jesus' foremost *self*-designation, chosen precisely because the title, although assuredly Messianic (cf. following discussion of Dan. 7:13), was ambiguous. Its "mysterious" character enabled Him to reveal as well as conceal His Messianic identity, to claim to be the Messiah with little danger of then-current erroneous perceptions of the office being read into it before He could infuse it with the full-orbed content of the Messianic task foreshadowed in and predicted by the Old Testament.

Furthermore, according to the church's traditional understanding, Jesus spelled out His Messianic task as the Son of Man precisely in terms of the above situations: His then current serving, His suffering (S), and His future glory (G). He applied all three situations to Himself. With His first advent, He fulfilled the first two; the third He fulfilled in the "lesser (typical) coming

29. *Mark:* 8:31 (Luke 9:22; 24:7); 9:12 (Matt. 17:12), 31 (Matt. 17:22-23); 10:33-34 (Matt. 20:18-19; Luke 18:31-33), 45 (Matt. 20:28); 14:21 (Matt. 26:24; Luke 22:22); 14:41 (Matt. 26:45);

Q: Matt. 8:20 (Luke 9:58); Matt. 11:19 (Luke 7:34);

M: 12:40; 26:2;

L: 9:44; 22:48;

John: 3:14; 8:28.

Ever since W. Wrede denied the dominical origin of Jesus' Passion predictions in his *The Messianic Secret* (1940), this denial has continued to have its proponents. Bultmann, for example, declares that the Passion sayings "have long been recognized as secondary constructions of the Church" (*History of the Synoptic Tradition,* p. 152). But masterful defenses have been registered in behalf of the dominical origin of the Passion sayings by W. Manson, *Jesus the Messiah* (London: Hodder and Stoughton, 1956), pp. 125-31; Vincent Taylor, "The Origin of the Markan Passion Sayings," *New Testament Essays* (London: Epworth Press, 1970), pp. 60-71; W. Zimmerli and J. Jeremias, *The Servant of God* (London: SCM Press, 1957), pp. 98-104; J. A. Baird, *The Justice of God in the Teaching of Jesus* (London: SCM Press, 1963), pp. 249-51; and I. Howard Marshall, *Eschatology and the Parables* (Leicester: Theological Students Fellowship, n.d.), p. 16.

30. *Mark:* 8:38 (Luke 9:26); 13:26 (Matt. 24:30b; Luke 21:27); 14:62 (Matt. 26:64; Luke 22:69);

Q: Matt. 24:27 (Luke 17:24); Matt. 24:37 (Luke 17:26); Matt. 24:44 (Luke 12:40);

M: 10:23; 13:31; 16:27, 28; 19:28; 24:30a, 39; 25:31;

L: 12:8; 17:30; 18:8; 21:26;

John: 5:27; 6:27.

in judgment" in the destruction of Jerusalem in A.D. 70. (to which most probably Matt. 10:23; 24:27, 30 and perhaps others refer), and will fulfill completely in His grand and final apocalyptic revelation in eschatological glory.

That the church was correct when it understood the title as Jesus' self-designation and when it applied the three situations of the Son of Man to Jesus is evident from the following four lines of evidence: *First*, where Matthew (5:11) reads "on account of Me," Luke (6:22) reads "for the sake of the Son of Man"; where Matthew (10:30—G) has "I," Luke (12:8—G) has "Son of Man." Where Mark (8:27) and Luke (9:18) have "I," Matthew (16:13) reads "Son of Man," but where Mark (8:31—S and 8:38—G) and Luke (9:22—S and 9:26—G) have "Son of Man," Matthew (16:21—S and 10:33—G) correspondingly reads "He" and "I." Clearly the title, at least at times, was simply a periphrasis for "I" or "me," demonstrating that Jesus intended Himself as its referent, although even here, as Carson notes, "always lurking in the background was the eschatological figure of Daniel 7."[31] *Second*, when Judas kissed Jesus, according to Luke 22:48 (cf. also Matt. 26:23-24, 45), Jesus asked, "Judas, are you betraying the Son of Man with a kiss?" *Third*, as Gruenler trenchantly argues:

> Matt. 19:28 is especially instructive on the matter of who the glorified Son of man is, for Jesus promises his disciples with the authoritative "Truly, I say to you" that "in the new world when the Son of man shall sit on his glorious throne, you who have followed me will also sit on twelve thrones judging the twelve tribes of Israel." Surely Jesus, whom they followed and in terms of whom they shall reign, will not be excluded from reigning with them. Are there then to be two enthroned central figures? The sense of the passage exegetically would imply that only one central person is assumed, namely, Jesus the Son of man.[32]

He argues further:

> It is likely that non-supernaturalist assumptions lie behind the refusal to allow that these sayings [which portray the Son of Man as a glorified divine being] are Jesus' own prophetic vision of his vindication and glorification in the coming judgment. Certainly there is no suggestion elsewhere in the Gospels that he anticipated any other figure to appear after him. In fact, among the Marcan sayings . . . 9:9 [Matt. 17:9; cf.

31. D. A. Carson, "Christological Ambiguities in the Gospel of Matthew," in *Christ the Lord*, p. 113.

32. Gruenler, in *Evangelical Dictionary of Theology*, pp. 1035-36.

also Mark 8:31 (Luke 9:22: 24:7); 9:31 (Matt. 17:22-23); Mark 10:33-34 (Matt. 20:18-19; Luke 18:31-33)] clearly refers to his own rising as the Son of man from the dead, and 14:62, the scene before the high priest, couples his "I am" confession that he is the Christ, the Son of the Blessed, with the surrogate for "I," the Son of man, "sitting at the right hand of Power, and coming with the clouds of heaven."[33]

Fourth, Jesus asked the man born blind, whom He had just healed, "Do you believe in the Son of Man?,"[34] and in response to the man's query "Who is He, Lord? Tell me, that I may believe in Him," Jesus replied, "You have now seen Him; in fact, He is the One speaking with you [ὁ λαλῶν μετὰ σοῦ ἐκεῖνός ἐστιν]" (John 9:35-37).

There can be no legitimate doubt, then, that all four Evangelists, when interpreted correctly, intend their readers to understand that Jesus is the Son of Man in the roles both of suffering Servant, who came "to seek and to save that which was lost" (Luke 19:10) and "not to be served, but to serve and to give His life a ransom for many" (Mark 10:45; Matt. 20:28), and of coming Judge and eschatological King. The exegesis of Luke 12:8; Mark 14:62; and Matthew 19:28 by Bultmann and others, who accept the apocalyptic Son of Man sayings as authentic but only by first distinguishing between Jesus and a future apocalyptic Son of Man, does not impress me. Longenecker quite properly asks:

> Why should the church have been so careful to insert the title Son of Man into the words of Jesus alone, when (as the Bultmannians assert) it really represented their christology and not his? And further, why were Christians so circumspect as to preserve such a saying as that of Luke 12:8 (where Jesus supposedly distinguishes between himself and the coming Son of Man) when for them (as the Bultmannians acknowledge) there was no such distinction between Jesus and the Son of Man?[35]

Marshall also declares:

> The evidence that [Jesus] was really speaking about somebody else

33. Ibid., p. 1035. On Jesus' view of His own uniqueness and finality as the apocalyptic Son of Man, cf. also I. H. Marshall, *Origins of New Testament Christology*, pp. 50-51.

34. There is a textual variant in John 9:35 ("the Son of God") but Metzger notes that "the external support for ἀνθρώπου . . . is so weighty, and the improbability of θεοῦ being altered to ἀνθρώπου is so great, that the Committee regarded the reading adopted for the text [ἀνθρώπου] as virtually certain." Cf. Bruce M. Metzger, *A Textual Commentary on the Greek New Testament* (New York: United Bible Societies, 1971), pp. 228-29.

35. Longenecker, *Christology of Early Jewish Christianity*, p. 89; cf. also Marshall, *Origins of New Testament Christology*, p. 73.

rests solely on the alleged distinction found in Luke 12:8f. (*cf*. Mk. 8:38), Mark 14:62 and Matthew 19:28. None of these texts demands to be interpreted in this way, and it is clear that the early church did not think that they referred to somebody else, nor did it find them sufficiently ambiguous to need reformulation. Nor again is it conceivable that Jesus would place so much emphasis on the significance of a comparatively unknown figure in Jewish apocalyptic, when at other times he makes human destiny rest on men's response to himself. The defenders of this view have the utmost difficulty in explaining how Jesus visualized the relationship between himself and this shadowy figure, and they are compelled to reject the authenticity of the vast bulk of the Son of man sayings.[36]

And Cullmann concludes,

Anyone who accepts these [apocalyptic] sayings as genuine but tries to explain them by the theory that Jesus designates someone other than himself as the coming Son of Man, raises more problems than he solves.[37]

An unprejudiced reading of the Gospel narratives will lead most fair-minded people to two conclusions: first, that Jesus employed the title as a self-designation and, second, that every occurrence of the title, whether describing the suffering Son of Man or the eschatological Son of Man, refers to Jesus Himself.[38]

36. Marshall, *Origins of New Testament Christology*, 73.
37. Cullmann, *Christology of the New Testament*, p. 156.
38. Even though it means that I fall into the category of what I. Howard Marshall terms the "conservative extreme" (*Origins of New Testament Christology*, p. 70), I see no reason why all of the Son of Man sayings in the Gospels should not be attributed to Jesus, even the exegetically difficult one in Matt. 12:32 (Luke 12:10). I must demur here from Geerhardus Vos's admission of the possibility that Jesus, speaking Aramaic as He probably did, may actually have spoken of man generically: He may have said "son of man" and meant simply "man," "and that through misunderstanding in the process of translation into the Greek the title Son of Man slipped in" (*Self-Disclosure of Jesus*, pp. 50, 231). Such a misunderstanding could only have occurred in the so-called "oral layer of tradition," in "Q" (the "sayings-source"), or on the part of the Evangelists themselves. But in any case, an error is injected into the inspired autographs of Matthew and Luke! Though Vos may regard it as "too unnatural" to commend itself, I believe the suggestion of Dalman (shared by Warfield) is valid that "Son of Man" here designates the Messiah in His humiliation, against whom blasphemy is forgivable, in distinction from a word spoken against the glorified Messiah (ibid., p. 51). Warfield's opinion bears quoting:

We cannot say . . . that the difference in the treatment of blasphemy against the Son of Man and against the Holy Spirit is rooted in an intrinsic difference between the two persons. It must rest on some other ground, and those seem to be led by a right instinct who seek it in the humiliation of the Son of Man in His servant-form on earth, and the culminating manifestation of the holiness of God in the Holy Spirit,—though these things rather

Their Background. There remains at this juncture of our study only the matter of considering the source of Jesus' favorite self-designation. There is no need to assume that Jesus coined a totally new term or used an extra-biblical source. (C. Colpe and F. H. Borsch, for example, trace its roots back to ancient mythology; others have postulated, as we have noted earlier, 4 Ezra 13 and 1 Enoch 37-41 as likely sources.) For not only was the heavenly "man-like figure" of Daniel 7:13-14—personal, individual, and Messianic[39]— readily available to Him, but also there can be no legitimate doubt that the *apocalyptic* Son of Man sayings in Mark 13:26 (Matt. 24:30b; Luke 21:27) and 14:62 (Matt. 26:64) are based on the Danielic Son of Man. Only the most radical exegesis, governed by extra-biblical presuppositions, would advance another source for this title. There is a growing consensus—if not among the form-critical scholars on the Continent, certainly among evangelical scholars in Britain and the United States—that Daniel 7 is the primary source.[40]

underlie the compressed statements before us than find expression in it. It is abundantly clear at all events that there is no depreciation of the dignity of the person of Jesus in the contrast that is drawn between blasphemy against Him as forgivable and blasphemy against the Holy Spirit as unforgivable. That it is possible to blaspheme the Son of Man, itself means that the Son of Man is divine (*Biblical and Theological Studies* [Philadelphia: Presbyterian and Reformed, 1952], p. 225).

39. There is virtually universal accord among Old and New Testament scholars on two points: (1) the Aramaic phrase בַּר אֱנָשׁ ("a son of man") is a Semitic idiom for "a man," so that Daniel saw a "man-like figure" approaching the Ancient of Days; and (2) by this "man-like figure" the vision contrasts the first four kingdoms, which are symbolized by *beasts,* and the last one, which is symbolized by the *"man-like* figure," the point being that as different in nature as a man is from beasts, so different in nature is the fifth kingdom ("the Kingdom of God") from the four kingdoms ("kingdoms of evil men") that preceded it.

Beyond these two matters of general accord, Old Testament scholars have divided over whether the "man-like figure" is symbolic of a corporate entity or of an individual. Critical scholars widely agree, on the basis of 7:18, 22, 27, that the "man-like figure" symbolizes the "saints of the Most High" alone—*with no reference whatsoever to an individual.* Evangelical scholars have noted, however, that if this is so—that the saints alone are symbolized—it would herald an unheard-of, the first-of-its-kind kingdom-without-a-king in human history, and would suggest that Daniel was not simply non-Messianic but positively anti-Messianic in his eschatology, which we know from Dan. 9:25-26 he was not. Furthermore, they dispute the critical conclusion that there is no basis in the passage for interpreting the "man-like figure" as an individual, for Dan. 7:17 ("these great beasts, which are four, are four *kings* [not kingdoms!]" provides just this basis. Just as the four beasts symbolized "four kings," the "man-like figure," as Vos notes, "in like manner approximates the King of the fifth kingdom, although this does not, of course, exclude the possibility of the thus described King symbolizing the nature of the Kingdom over which He is to rule" (*Self-Disclosure of Jesus,* p. 45). A concrete, individual figure, who can hardly be anyone other than the Messiah, is surely present in the passage, and, in fact, our Lord individualized it when He applied this title to Himself. This is conclusive proof that the title should be individualized.

40. Vincent Taylor writes, for example, "Jesus's use of the title was independently derived from reflection upon the basic Old Testament passage, Dan. vii. 13" (*The Names of Jesus* [London: Macmillan, 1953], p. 27). Many others would strongly support this position; for example, Benjamin B. Warfield, *The Person and Work of Christ* (Philadelphia: Presbyterian and Reformed, 1950), p. 64; *The Lord of Glory* (reprint, Grand Rapids: Baker, 1974), pp. 24, 30; Vos, *Self-Disclosure of Jesus,*

A common objection raised against Daniel's "man-like figure" as the source of Jesus' "Son of Man" sayings is the alleged absence of the suffering motif in the Daniel 7 description, while, when Jesus uses the title, the idea of suffering is often attached. But to deny that the Danielic "man-like figure" is the background figure for Jesus' *suffering* Son of Man for this reason is unconvincing and has not gone unchallenged. Some scholars, such as Moule and Longenecker, urge that Daniel 7:21, 25 suggests that, while the Son of Man is a transcendent and glorified figure, His glorification and vindication come through suffering.[41] It is true that Vos and Marshall are not persuaded by this proposal.[42] Vos, for example, suggests as an alternative that suffering is joined to the Son of Man title not by analysis but by the principle of contrast. "It is not that He must undergo humiliation, suffering and death *because* He is the Son of man, but that, *although* He is the Son of man, such a destiny is, paradoxically, in store for Him."[43] The problem with this, of course, is how a true "joining" is derived from a "contrast"? The apocalyptic figure does not in itself imply the suffering figure. The principle of contrast is drawn simply from the two kinds of statements themselves, but says nothing about *how* suffering properly belongs to the figure. Another possibility is Carson's suggestion that Jesus reflected not only on Daniel 7, but also on the other occurrences of the phrase in Psalm 8:4 and Ezekiel 2:1 passim, where "the chasm between frail, mortal man and God Himself" is underscored. This reflection led Jesus to combine within the one title "these multiform backgrounds."[44] But it is also just possible that Dodd, Bruce, and others are correct when they propose that the combining of both suffering and glory within the framework of the one title simply goes back to the creative insight of Jesus Himself, who drew upon both Daniel's Son of Man and Isaiah's Suffering Servant and combined them, as the Old Testament intended them to be, under the one title to describe the ministry of the

p. 232; T. W. Manson, *The Teaching of Jesus* (Cambridge: University Press, 1951), p. 227; C. H. Dodd, *According to the Scriptures* (London: Nisbet and Co., 1952), p. 117; C. K. Barrett, *Jesus and the Gospel Tradition* (London, SPCK, 1967), pp. 41ff.; M. D. Hooker, *The Son of Man in Mark* (London: SPCK, 1967), pp. 11-74; Longenecker, *Christology of Early Jewish Christianity*, pp. 86-87; George Eldon Ladd, *A Theology of the New Testament* (Grand Rapids: Eerdmans, 1974), pp. 145-58, esp. p. 147; C. F. D. Moule, *The Origin of Christology* (Cambridge: University Press, 1977), pp. 11-22; F. F. Bruce, in *Christ the Lord*, pp. 53-54; D. A. Carson, *Matthew*, pp. 209-13; R. G. Gruenler, in *Evangelical Dictionary of Theology*, p. 1034; R. H. Stein, ibid., p. 584. Moule in the work cited even makes the novel suggestion that the article uniformly attached to "Son of Man" in the Greek New Testament has virtual demonstrative force: "[That] Son of Man [in Daniel 7]."

41. Longenecker, *Christology of Early Jewish Christianity*, pp. 87-88.
42. Vos, *Self-Disclosure of Jesus*, pp. 235-36; Marshall, *Origins of New Testament Christology*, pp. 75-76.
43. Vos, *Self-Disclosure of Jesus*, p. 236.
44. Carson, *Matthew*, pp. 212-13.

Messiah.[45] I prefer this suggestion over Carson's because there is some question whether Psalm 8:4 intends to underscore man's frailty and mortality; it seems more likely that David intended to highlight man's elevated station over the work of God's creation. And God's addressing Ezekiel as "Son of man," while it means "O Man," does not necessarily intend that the prophet's frailty and mortality are being set off over against God Himself. But whatever the correct solution, this review of proposed options points up how Jesus could have conceived the Son of Man figure as bearing not only the apocalyptic features but the weight of suffering as well. There is no ground, then, for saying that any one of the groups of sayings is not authentic because it does not fit the parameters of the Danielic "man-like figure."

I conclude, then, that when Jesus employed the title, He was self-consciously claiming to be the Danielic "man-like figure," and hence the Messiah, uniting within the one Old Testament figure two motifs: Isaiah's Suffering Servant and Daniel's Son of Man coming apocalyptically to judge the earth and complete the Kingdom of God.

"Son of David"

One further title should receive some comment in connection with Jesus' perception of His messiahship—the title "Son of David."

That the Old Testament had declared that the Messiah would be of Davidic lineage is clear from Isaiah 9:7; 11:1, 10; 55:3; Psalm 89:3-4, 20-29, 35-37; Hosea 3:5; Amos 9:11-12; Micah 5:2 et al. And that the early church believed in Jesus' lineal descent from David "according to the flesh" is equally evident from (1) the genealogies in Matthew 1:6-16, 17 and Luke 3:23-31 (cf. also Matt. 1:20 and Luke 1:27; 2:4); (2) the Lukan report of Gabriel's message to Mary (1:32; cf. 2:11), Zechariah's *Benedictus* (1:69), and Peter's first sermon (Acts 2:30); (3) Paul's letters (Rom. 1:3; 2 Tim. 2:8); and (4) John's Revelation (5:5; 22:6). This in itself, of course, does not prove Jesus' messiahship, inasmuch as there were doubtless other families in Jesus' time that could have claimed Davidic descent. But clearly it was a settled conviction of both the Old Testament Scriptures and Israel's understanding of those Scriptures that without such a lineal descent no one could have legitimately claimed to be the Messiah and thus the rightful heir to the Davidic throne (cf. Matt 12:23; 21:42; Mark 12:35; Luke 20:41; John 7:42). In other words, lineal descent from David did not in itself mean messiahship, but the absence of such descent disqualified as a false Christ anyone who

---

45. Dodd, *According to the Scriptures*, pp. 108-10; F. F. Bruce, in *Christ the Lord*, pp. 60-61.

made the claim of messiahship. The early church clearly held the conviction that Jesus met this qualification, and there is no reason whatever to question the validity of this conviction.

Because the conviction that the Messiah would be of Davidic descent was a "commonplace" in Israel's hope, it should come as no surprise that the title "Son of David" came to be regarded in some branches of popular Judaism as a Messianic title.[46] The question now is this: Did Jesus claim to be the "Son of David" in the Messianic sense? If we base our response solely on explicit claims, we have to answer this question in the negative. But there is indisputable testimony from the Gospels that Jesus tacitly claimed to be the Messianic "Son of David." When addressed as such by the two blind men in Matthew 9:27 and later by blind Bartimaeus and his fellow beggar in 20:30-31 (Mark 10:47-48; Luke 18:38-39), Jesus did not disclaim it. To the contrary, He healed all of them in response to their appeal to Him, although in the former case He performed the healing within the privacy of a house to dampen Messianic expectations.[47] When He rode into Jerusalem on a donkey as Zechariah 9:9 had foretold, the crowds addressed Him along the way and in the temple as the promised Messianic "Son of David" by their cries of "Hosanna! . . .Blessed is the Kingdom of our Father David that is coming" (Mark 11:9-10; Matt. 21:9: "Hosanna to the Son of David" [cf. 21:15]; Luke 19:38: "Blessed is the King who comes in the name of the Lord"; John 12:13: "Blessed is He who comes in the name of the Lord, even the King of Israel"). Jesus tacitly accepted their address, for when the Pharisees said, "Teacher, rebuke your disciples," He answered, "I tell you, if these were silent, the very stones would cry out" (Luke 19:39-40). Then later, when the temple leadership became indignant over the children's ascribing the title to Him, Jesus defended the children and expressed His approval of their acclamation by referring to Psalm 8:2 (Matt. 21:15-16).

I am not suggesting that those who took recourse to Him under the aegis of the Son of David title properly comprehended all that the role entailed. There can be no doubt, however, that the blind men and the crowds intended by their cries to ascribe Messianic stature to Jesus, and that, responding as He did, He accepted their ascription as proper and true. But

---

46. Carson, *Matthew*, p. 62; Carson, "Christological Ambiguities in the Gospel of Matthew," in *Christ the Lord*, p. 104.

47. Carson, *Matthew*, p. 233. That the title should have often been on the lips of the blind should not be surprising, as Carson notes, inasmuch as "the Messianic Age was to be characterized as a time when 'the eyes of the blind [would be] opened and the ears of the deaf unstopped,' when 'the lame [would] leap like a deer, and the tongue of the dumb shout for joy.' If Jesus was really the Messiah, the blind reasoned, then he would have mercy on them; and they would have their sight" (ibid.). Cf. in this connection Jesus' response to John's question from prison in Matt. 11:4-5.

as with the title "Christ," He had a certain reticence before His triumphal entry to relate Himself to the Son of David title, this reticence doubtless due to the same concern we noted in our discussions of "Christ" and "Son of Man," namely, to avoid raising erroneous Messianic expectations.

And as with the title "Christ," this again could be the end of the discussion were it not for the fact that liberal and traditio-historical form-critical scholars have, in one way or another, denied all of the foregoing data and the conclusions that the church has traditionally based upon that data.

For example, some have construed Jesus' famous question and comment concerning the Messiah's relationship to David in Matthew 22:41-46 (Mark 12:35-37; Luke 20:41-44), "if genuine," to be no more than "an academic discussion on Messianic doctrine." Most likely, they urge, the pericope is "a reflection of the debate of the early church."[48] Others, following W. Wrede, understand the point of the pericope to be Jesus' outright denial of the Messiah's identity with the Son of David. But if this were His point, it is incomprehensible why the Evangelists would incorporate the pericope into their Gospels when it is apparent that this identity is precisely what they wished to uphold (cf. Matt. 1:1; Luke 18:38-39; 19:38-40). Far from this being a mere "academic discussion on Messianic doctrine" or "a reflection of the debate of the early church," or far from denying the identification of the Messiah with the Son of David, it was rather Jesus' purpose, not only to affirm the connection (the Jewish response was correct as far as it went), but also to challenge the religious leaders to rethink their narrow Messianic expectations, to integrate the idea that the Messiah's sonship cannot be explained merely in terms of human descent. It must embrace as well an unprecedented supernatural origin on the scale of divine sonship.

R. H. Fuller's thorough reworking of the accounts of the triumphal entry (an event found in all four Gospels, which fact itself strongly supports the event's authenticity and historicity) along non-Messianic lines, suggesting rather that Jesus' only "intention was to go to the temple to lay down the final challenge of his eschatological message at the heart of Judaism,"[49] is highly speculative and has only the presuppositions of traditio-historical criticism to commend it.

"Son of David" is certainly not a dominant title in the Gospels; yet when it does occur, it clearly ascribes messiahship to Jesus; and all the evidence supports, and none weighs against, His approving acceptance of it.

From our cursory study of the three titles "Christ," "Son of Man," and "Son of David," we have found more than ample reason to conclude that

48. R. H. Fuller, *Foundations of New Testament Christology*, p. 111.
49. Ibid., p. 114.

Jesus claimed, in fact, to be the Messiah the Old Testament had foretold. We noted that Jesus did not Himself directly appeal with any frequency to the titles "Christ" or "Son of David" to describe His role of Messiah (though He accepted these titles in direct address from others upon occasion). He preferred the Danielic (7:13) Messianic title "Son of Man" because, we have suggested, it allowed Him, due to its ambiguity in the public mind, to make His Messianic claims with a minimum of interference from the recalcitrant religious leadership and from others among the populace who expected the Messiah to deliver the nation from Gentile oppression and extend the nation's political influence throughout the world, and hence who would have attempted to declare Him Israel's king in opposition to Rome (cf. John 6:15). But Jesus' preferred self-designation possessed a certain "openness" about it as well, which permitted Him to shape its significance as a Messianic designation by His own teaching and work.[50] This concern to avoid terminology that would raise inappropriate and misleading Messianic expectations is doubtless what lay behind Jesus' command that demons (Mark 1:25, 34; 3:12; Luke 4:35, 41), those whom He healed (Matt. 8:4; 9:30; 12:16; Mark 1:44; 5:43; 7:24, 36; 9:30; Luke 5:14; 8:56), and His own disciples (Matt. 16:20; 17:9; Mark 8:30; 9:9; Luke 9:21) remain silent and tell no one that He was the Messiah before He was ready to reveal Himself publicly. (We may properly speak in this sense of the "Messianic secret" over against the contrived [and erroneous] view of Wrede that Mark created this theme in order to explain why [so Wrede thought] Jesus was never recognized as the Messiah during His lifetime.) This is doubtless also the reason behind His practice of teaching the crowds about the Kingdom of God in parables (Matt. 13:10-17, 34-35; Mark 4:10-12, 33-34; Luke 8:9-10). But as for His claim as such to be the Messiah, we have seen enough to conclude that this He most assuredly did! And claiming that role, as we shall now see, He laid claim to its requisite corollary—that is, to deity—as well!

Jesus' Claim to Deity

The Old Testament prophets, with increasing clarity, had spoken of a

---

50. Cf. Vos's comment:

> There must have existed in our Lord's mind a potent reason why He preferred this way of designating Himself to all others. Other names He might acknowledge, or at least not repudiate, but this name stands alone as the name that was His favorite, and as a result became in His use almost eliminative of other names, the name Son of God only excepted, though even the latter did not attain to the same frequency as Son of man upon His lips. If we see correctly, this potent reason lay in the fact that the title Son of man stood farthest removed from every possible Jewish prostitution of the Messianic office. . . . It moves in an altogether different sphere from the kingdom which the spirit of Judaism favored and expected (*Self-Disclosure of Jesus*, pp. 253-54).

Messiah who would possess divine titles (Isa. 9:6; cf. 7:14) and whose coming to His people would be in some sense the coming of God Himself to them (Pss. 45:6; 96:13; 98:9; Zech. 12:10; Mal. 3:1) in the person of His Son the King (Ps. 2:7; Isa. 9:6).

When we turn to our Lord's self-estimation of His person and work in those teachings authenticated as His own, even by the form critic's own criteria, we discover that everything Old Testament revelation anticipated the Messiah to be, Jesus believed Himself to be. Consider again His self-designation as "the Son of Man" and His teaching concerning Himself as the Son of Man.

The Implications of Deity in Jesus' "Son of Man" Sayings

Commenting upon the significance of the "Son of Man" title, Vos writes:

> In close adherence to the spirit of the scene in Daniel from which it was taken, it suggested a Messianic career in which, all of a sudden, without human interference or military conflict, through an immediate act of God, the highest dignity and power are conferred. The kingship here portrayed is not only supernatural; it is "transcendental."[51]

Even a cursory examination of the Daniel 7 passage and Jesus' Son of Man sayings will bear out all that Vos asserts here and more. The "man-like figure" in the Daniel 7 passage (cf. n. 39 for my reasons for understanding the "man-like figure" individualistically as well as corporately)—said to be "man-like" only in order to highlight the contrast between Himself and the beast-empires and their kings—is assuredly more if not other than man in nature. He is depicted there as a *superhuman*—let us say it frankly—even a *divine* figure. This is evident from the following: There is an "unearthly," heavenly cast about the scene that lifts the entire vision out of the *natural* order of things. And His "coming with clouds," that is, in connection with or "surrounded by" clouds, as He does, is a phrase descriptive of both divine presence and divine activity in the execution of judgment against His enemies (cf. Pss. 18:9-11; 97:2; 104:3; Isa. 19:1; Jer. 4:13; Nah. 1:3) and in the deliverance and protection of His saints (Exod. 13:21; 19:9; 1 Kings 8:10-12; Ezek. 10:4). The free access He enjoys as He is escorted into the presence of the Ancient of Days suggests the supernatural character of His person. Finally, the universal and everlasting dominion He receives from God and the universal and everlasting worship He receives from men imply that He is

51. Ibid., p. 254.

in possession of divine qualities (cf. Pss. 2; 45; 110; Isa. 9:6-7; Mic. 5:4, 5a).

On Jesus' lips this title, as Vos remarks, "connotes the heavenly, super-human side of Jesus' mysterious existence,"[52] expressing what is commonly called His preexistence. To Nicodemus Jesus declared, "No one has ever gone into heaven except the One who came from heaven—the Son of Man" (John 3:13). And to His own disciples He exclaimed, "What if you see the Son of Man ascend to *where He was before* [ὅπου ἦν τὸ πρότερον]" (6:62). Jesus also claimed as the Son of Man to have the authority to forgive sins (Matt. 9:6; Mark 2:10; Luke 5:24)[53] and to regulate *even* the observance of the divine ordinance of the Sabbath (Matt. 12:8; Mark 2:28; Luke 6:5),[54] clearly prerogatives of deity alone. To speak against the Son of Man, He said, although forgivable, is blasphemy (Matt. 12:32; cf. Mark 3:28). The angels are His (Matt. 13:41), He said, clearly implying thereby His own superangelic status

52. Ibid., 239.

53. To those scholars who insist that "Son of Man" in these verses means simply "man as such," because of the presence of the word "man" in Matt. 9:3 and Mark 2:7, and because of Matthew's statement in 9:8, Vos's comment is a sufficient response:

> These reasons can avail little in the face of the indisputable fact that, according to the common Christian and Jewish faith, the forgiveness of sins was exclusively a divine prerogative. How can we impute to Jesus the monstrous idea that every man has the authority to forgive sin? A modern Jesus, assimilating man to God, without principial difference, might perhaps have thought so, but scarcely the historical Jesus. If he actually proceeded to forgive sin on the basis of the "rights of men," then all we can say is that the scribes were right in their insinuation, and Jesus was wrong in His religious usurpation. Surely, what our Lord laid claim to cannot have been this, but only that the Son of Man possessed this right (ibid., p. 51).

His entire discussion (pp. 51-53) may still be read with profit.

54. The καί in Mark 2:28, translated "even" (or "also"), suggests that *in addition to* other things "of relatively lesser importance, to which the authority of the Son of Man extended, it covers also such an important matter as the Sabbath" (ibid., p. 53; cf. Warfield, *Lord of Glory*, p. 99).

To those who would urge that "Son of Man" here means simply "man as such," because the phrase must have the same sense in the "therefore" (ὥστε) clause as ἄνθρωπος has in the premise clause, it is again sufficient to point out, with Vos, that

> the argument is just as conclusive when Son of Man is understood of the Messiah. This Messianic name suggested to Jesus . . . that all things affecting the interests of man lay particularly within His jurisdiction. Inasmuch as the Sabbath partook of this character to a high degree ("made for man"), He possessed the right to regulate its observance (*Self-Disclosure of Jesus*, p. 53).

It is heinous exegesis that imputes to Jesus here the monstrous intention to relegate such a venerable religious sanctity as the Old Testament Sabbath to the area of "things" indifferent by insisting that He meant by His statement that the observance of the Sabbath should be left to the free choice of men. To the contrary, as Vos asserts:

> The general law underlying Jesus' reasoning seems to be that in the service of the Theocracy the lower must give way to the higher, and provisions for the special servants of God and the performance of their functions must take precedence over the ordinary routine of religious duty; the ceremonial must give way to the ethical. But the decision about such things is not left to the free choice of men; the Son of Man is sovereign over it (ibid.).

and lordship over them. He said, it is true, that He would know, as the Son of Man, a period of humiliation, having no place to lay His head (Matt. 8:20; Luke 9:58) and finally even dying the cruel death of crucifixion; but He would suffer and die, He declared, only to the end that He might ransom many (Matt. 20:28; Mark 10:45). A man's eternal destiny would turn on his relationship to the Son of Man, He taught, for unless the Son of Man gives a man life, there is no life in him (John 6:53). As the Son of Man, He would rise from the dead and "sit at the right hand of power," and "come in clouds with great power and glory" (Matt. 24:30; Mark 13:25; Luke 21:27)—coming with all His holy angels in the glory of *His Father*, true enough (Matt. 16:27; Mark 8:38), but coming in *His own glory* as well (Matt. 25:31). And when He comes, He declared, He would come with the authority to execute judgment upon all men precisely *because* (ὅτι) He is the Son of Man (John 5:27). Clearly, for Jesus the Son of Man sayings, above all others, embodied His conception of messiahship; and beyond question its associations were supernatural, even divine, in character. Warfield can hardly be accused of overstating the matter when he writes:

> In the picture which Jesus Himself draws for us of the "Son of Man" . . . we see His superhuman nature portrayed. For the figure thus brought before us is distinctly a superhuman one; one which is not only in the future to be sitting at the right hand of power and coming with the clouds of heaven . . . , but which in the present world itself exercises functions which are truly divine,—for who is Lord of the Sabbath but the God who instituted it in commemoration of His own rest (2:28), and who can forgive sins but God only (2:10, cf. verse 7)? The assignment to the Son of Man of the function of Judge of the world and the ascription to Him of the right to forgive sins are, in each case, but another way of saying that He is a divine person; for these are divine acts.[55]

The Implications of Deity in Jesus' "Son [of God]" Sayings

A great deal more can be said in favor of Jesus' claim, as the Messiah, to deity. On two of the five occasions when He openly acknowledged Himself to be the "Christ," explaining the significance of that title in terms of the Danielic Son of Man (Peter's confession—Matt. 16:16-21; Mark 8:29-31; Luke

---

55. Warfield, *Lord of Glory*, p. 41. We must conclude from this entire discussion of the significance of the Son of Man sayings that such early Fathers as Ignatius (*Ephesians*, 20:2), the anonymous author of *The Epistle of Barnabus* (12:10), Irenaeus (*Against Heresies*, 3:16; 7; 17:1), and Justin Martyr (*Dialogues*, 76:1; 100) were in error when they assumed that "Son of God" referred to Jesus as God and "Son of Man" designated Him simply as man.

9:20-22; and His trial before the high priest—Matt. 26:64; Mark 14:62; Luke 22:67-70), He claimed as well to be the Son of God, not in an ethico-religious, official, or nativistic sense of the title,[56] but in what the church would later come to describe as the sonship of the intratrinitarian relation, denoting essential oneness and sameness with the Father. This was clearly the case at His trial, for when He acknowledged that He was the "Son of God" (or "Son of the Blessed"), His judges accused Him of blasphemy worthy of death (Matt. 26:65-68; Mark 14:63-64; Luke 22:71), the basis of which judgment Jesus made no attempt to repudiate.

His claim to divine sonship opens for us an entirely new area of investigation—that of the significance of the titles, "Son of God," and, more simply, "the Son." In the next two sections of this chapter (pp. 68-92), as we develop this point, I shall contend that by those titles He was registering a claim tantamount to possessing essential divine oneness with God.

Jesus claimed by His "Son [of God]" sayings essential divine oneness with God in the Synoptic Gospels in Matthew 11:27 (Luke 10:22); 21:37-38 (Mark 12:6; Luke 20:13); 24:36 (Mark 13:32); and 28:19; and in the Gospel of John in (at least) 5:17-29; 6:40; 10:36; 11:4; 14:13; 17:1. To these must be added those instances in the Fourth Gospel when He claimed that God was His Father in such a unique sense that the Jewish religious leadership correctly perceived that He was claiming a sonship with God of such a nature that it constituted essential divine oneness and equality with God and thus, from their perspective, was committing blasphemy deserving of death (John 5:17-18; 10:24-39, especially verses 25, 29, 30, 32-33, 37, 38; cf. also 19:7). To an exposition of the more significant occurrences of this title we will now turn.

The "Son" Sayings in the Synoptic Gospels
Matthew 11:25-27 (Luke 10:21-22): The Three Great Parallels

This passage, judged by Vos as "by far the most important seat of the testimony which Jesus bears to His sonship" and "the culminating point of our Lord's self-disclosure in the Synoptics,"[57] brings us face to face with some of the most wonderful words Jesus ever spoke. Because of their clear, unmistakable, and forthright testimony to Jesus' self-advocacy of His own

56. By "ethico-religious," I refer to the sense in which the term may designate the Christian (or, for that matter, anyone else) simply as a "child of God"; by "official," I mean the sense in which it describes "office," not essential nature; and by "nativistic," I refer to the sense in which (some scholars argue) the Messiah is the Son of God as the direct supernatural work of God in the virginal conception. Cf. Vos, *Self-Disclosure of Jesus*, pp. 141-42.

57. Ibid., p. 143.

divine nature and sonship, it is not surprising that liberal critics have rigorously assailed their authenticity even though, since both Matthew and Luke report Jesus' words, they are in "the supposedly most ancient source of the sayings of Jesus,"[58] that is, in "Q," which on source-critical grounds assures its existence to within a score or less of years from the time our Lord presumably uttered them, hardly sufficient time for a radical reshaping of a more original saying to have gained acceptance with disciples who had actually been with Jesus. But, because that theological quarter has rejected, *a priori*, the ontological deity of Jesus Christ, it must ask whether the passage is authentic.

Consequently, these scholars cite three difficulties with the passage: (1) It has a "Johannine ring" to it. (K. A. von Hase describes the passage as a "thunderbolt [meteor] from the Johannine heaven.") (2) Both its form and content suggest that it is a "product of late Christian Hellenization." (3) "The greatest barrier to the acceptance of the genuineness of [Matt. 11:27] is the supposition that Jesus could not have made such an absolute claim for himself"[59] because, these critics say, the simple title "the Son" was not a common title for the Messiah until after Easter.

These problems, more created and imagined than real, have been ably answered by John Chapman, A. M. Hunter, I. Howard Marshall, and D. A. Carson, to name a few.[60] But before I consider the passage itself, a review of the responses to these so-called difficulties is in order.

Its "Johannine" Ring. There is no question that our Lord's words in this context have a "pronounced Johannine sound" to them (cf. John 3:35; 5:20-21; 6:46; 8:19; 10:15, 30; 14:6, 9). But this in no way invalidates its authenticity, "unless" as A. M. Hunter writes, "we make it a canon of criticism that any saying in the Synoptics with a parallel in John must *ipso facto* be spurious."[61] The fact is that, regardless of its "tone," on grounds

58. Ibid., p. 144.

59. David Hill, *The Gospel of Matthew* (London: Oliphants, 1972), p. 206.

60. John Chapman, "Dr. Harnack on Luke X 22: No Man Knoweth the Son," *The Journal of Theological Studies* 10 (1909): 552-66; A. M. Hunter, "Crux Criticorum—Matt. XI. 25-30—A Re-Appraisal," *New Testament Studies* 8 (1962): 241-49; I. Howard Marshall, "The Divine Sonship of Jesus," *Interpretation* 21 (1967): 91-94; D. A. Carson, *Matthew*, pp. 276-77.

61. Hunter, "Matt. XI. 25-30," p. 245; cf. also Cullmann, (*Christology of the New Testament*, p. 287) for a similar conclusion. Hunter in the same context points out that instead of the pericope being spurious, "the precise opposite might indeed be argued: that if we find in John a logion with parallels in the Synoptics, John either depends on the Synoptics or else draws upon an independent tradition." G. B. Caird says virtually the same thing:

Many scholars have doubted whether Jesus could really have made the claims attributed to him in this passage [Luke 10:21-22]. Hase described it as "an aerolite from the Johannine

recognized by the critical scholar, the pericope is still an integral part of so-called "Q," and, as Jeremias points out, is not a precise parallel to anything that John wrote.[62]

Its Late Christian Hellenization. As for the second difficulty—that its form and content reflect a late Hellenistic rather than a Jewish milieu—Hunter's judgment again is worthy of note:

> Still less is it permissible to dismiss the saying blandly as a Hellenistic "revelation word". The Hellenistic parallels to it . . . were never impressive and . . . the discovery of the Dead Sea Scrolls has altered the whole picture. So large a role does "knowledge" play in the Scrolls that it is quite "unnecessary to go outside a Jewish milieu to account for our passage".[63]

G. B. Caird concurs:

> The whole passage abounds in Semitic turns of phrase and follows the rhythms of Hebrew verse, so that it cannot be regarded as a theological product of the Greek-speaking Church.[64]

Increasingly today, the scholarly consensus is that the provenance of the passage is Palestinian.

The Presence of the So-called Late Title "the Son." Radical form critics who

heaven," the implication being that such a theological affirmation has no place in the more terrestrial narrative of the Synoptic Gospels, that the historical Jesus could not have used the terms Father and Son in this absolute fashion (cf. Mark 13:32). Modern scholars would be a little more hesitant about the assumption that sayings found in John's Gospel are necessarily unhistorical. If we find a "Johannine" saying in Q, the oldest strand of the Synoptic tradition, the natural inference is, not that Q is untrustworthy, but that John had access to a reliable sayings source (*The Gospel of Luke* [London: Adam and Charles Black, 1968], p. 146).

Leon Morris, in fact, has cogently argued that John did not allow his theological interests to warp his view of the facts he reported ("The Fourth Gospel and History," in *Jesus of Nazareth: Saviour and Lord*, ed. Carl F. H. Henry [London: Tyndale, 1966], pp. 123-32), a conclusion that I infinitely prefer to James D. G. Dunn's regrettable declaration that "despite the renewal of interest in the Fourth Gospel as a historical source for the ministry of Jesus, *it would be verging on the irresponsible to use the Johannine testimony on Jesus' divine sonship in our attempt to uncover the self-consciousness of Jesus himself*" (*Christology in the Making: A New Testament Inquiry into the Origins of the Doctrine of the Incarnation* [London: SCM Press, 1980], p. 31, emphasis original).

62. Joachim Jeremias, *The Prayers of Jesus*, trans. John Bowden and Christoph Buchard (London: SCM Press, 1967), p. 48.

63. Hunter, "Matt. XI. 25-30," p. 245. Cf. also Alan Richardson, *An Introduction to the Theology of The New Testament* (London: SCM Press, 1961), p. 43.

64. Caird, *Gospel of Luke*, p. 146.

affirm this objection must assume that this title is spurious everywhere else it occurs in the Synoptic tradition (Matt. 24:36 and the Marcan parallel in 13:32, and Matt. 28:19)—and they, in fact, do. But in light of Jesus' frequent reference to God as Αββα ("[the] Father"), there is no reason to doubt that He referred to Himself as "the Son," particularly in light of the Old Testament references (in Messianic contexts) to the "Son" (1 Chron. 17:13; Ps. 2:7; Isa. 9:6) and the "great acknowledgment" from heaven in Matthew 3:17 (Mark 1:11; Luke 3:22): "This is My Son, whom I love; with Him I am well pleased."

Hunter's final estimate of the matter, in light of this data, certainly seems justified.

> If men reject this logion, they reject it not because they have proved it a Hellenistic revelation word, or because its Johannine ring condemns it, but because they have made up their minds, *a priori*, that the Jesus of history could not have made such a claim.[65]

But such a basis for rejecting the saying only underscores the bias with which the radical form critic approaches the biblical text—especially since the arguments for its authenticity are exceedingly strong. I am not convinced that any evidence or argument advanced to date compels one to doubt its authenticity; therefore, I will proceed with its exposition, assuming that Matthew 11:25-27 (also Luke 10:21-22) confronts us with one of Jesus' authentic sayings.

The Three Great Parallels. In this saying, Jesus asserts the unique and intimate nature of the Father-Son relationship, drawing three parallels between God as "the Father" and Himself as "the Son" (cf. Matt. 3:17; Mark 1:11; Luke 3:22). Only perhaps in certain of the utterances of the Fourth Gospel did Jesus make any higher claims, and because Jesus expresses His intimacy with the Father precisely in terms of these parallels, my exposition of this saying will focus on them.

The *first* parallel has to do with the *exclusive, mutual knowledge each has of the other.* Jesus declares in 11:27, "No one knows [ἐπιγινώσκει] the Son except the Father, and no one knows [ἐπιγινώσκει] the Father except the Son." Note here Jesus' emphasis upon the exclusiveness of this mutual knowledge ("no one knows except").[66] Even more striking, as a moment's reflection

---

65. Hunter, "Matt. XI. 25-30," p. 245.

66. The exclusiveness of Jesus' knowledge is not invalidated by His following remark, "and to whomever the Son wills to reveal Him," since the very point of His statement is that men must acquire their saving knowledge of the Father *from Him.* They can acquire it *in no other way* (John

shows, is the inference that the nature of this knowledge lifts Jesus above the sphere of the ordinary mortal and places Him "in a position, not of equality merely, but of absolute reciprocity and interpenetration of knowledge with the Father."[67] Vos observes:

> That essential rather than acquired knowledge is meant follows . . . from the correlation of the two clauses: the knowledge God has of Jesus cannot be acquired knowledge [it must, from the fact that it is God's knowledge, be direct, intuitive, and immediate—in a word, divine—knowledge, grounded in the fact that the Knower is divine[68]]; consequently the knowledge Jesus has of God cannot be acquired knowledge either [it too must be direct, intuitive, and immediate—in a word, divine—knowledge, grounded in the fact that Jesus as God's Son is divine], for these two are placed entirely on a line. In other words, if the one is different from human knowledge, then the other must be so likewise.[69]

The only conclusion that this correlation of the two clauses warrants is that God has this exclusive and penetrating knowledge of the Son because He is the Father of the Son, and that Jesus has this exclusive and penetrating knowledge of God because He is the Son of the Father. The knowledge Jesus here claims for Himself could not possibly have resulted from the investiture of the Messianic task but must have originated in a sonship that, of necessity, would have been *antecedent* to His Messianic investiture. It is plain, then, that Jesus' sonship and the Messianic task with which He had been invested do not describe identical relationships to the Father—the former must have preceded the latter and provided the ground for it.

14:6), whereas His knowledge of the Father is intrinsic to the filial relationship He sustains to the Father.

67. Warfield, *Person and Work of Christ*, p. 65.
68. Cf. Ladd, *Theology of the New Testament*, p. 166.
69. Vos, *Self-Disclosure of Jesus*, p. 149. As with the case regarding the exclusiveness of His knowledge (n. 66), so with the nature of Jesus' knowledge: its direct, intuitive, and immediate character is in no way jeopardized by the clause that relates men to His knowledge inasmuch as, again, their knowledge, from the very fact that it is derived from the revelatory transaction, is clearly not intuited and direct but acquired. Ladd correctly observes:

> As the Father exercises an absolute sovereignty in revealing the Son, so the Son exercises an equally absolute sovereignty in revealing the Father; he reveals him to whom he chooses. This derived knowledge of God, which may be imparted to men by revelation, is similar but not identical with the knowledge that Jesus has of the Father. The Son's knowledge of the Father is the same direct, intuitive knowledge that the Father possesses of the Son. It is therefore on the level of divine knowledge. The knowledge that men may gain of the Father is a mediated knowledge imparted by revelation through the Son. The knowledge of the Father that Jesus possesses is thus quite unique; and his sonship, standing on the same level is equally unique. It is a derived knowledge of God that is imparted to men, even as the sonship that men experience through Jesus the Son is a relationship mediated through the Son (*Theology of the New Testament*, pp. 166-67).

The *second* parallel, which rests upon the first, comes to focus in Jesus' assertion of the *mutual necessity of the Father and the Son each to reveal the other* if men are ever to have an acquired saving knowledge of them. This parallel may be seen in Jesus' thanksgiving to the Father, Lord of heaven and earth, that He—the Father—had hidden (ἐκρύψας) the mysteries of the Kingdom, which are *centered in the Son* (cf.11:19-24), from the "wise" (that is, spiritual "know-it-alls") and had *revealed* (ἀπεκάλυψας) them to "babies" (that is, to men like Peter; cf. Matt. 16:17) (11:25), and His later statement that "no one knows the Father except the Son and to whomever the Son wills to *reveal* [ἀποκαλύψαι] Him" (11:27).

The reason that the Messianic task was invested in the Son becomes even plainer, if that is possible, from this parallel: Not only does the Son alone know the Father with the depth of understanding (that is, to infinity) necessary to a true revelation of Him, but also, precisely because He alone has such knowledge, the Son alone can be the revelatory channel of salvific blessing to the Father (John 14:46). Therefore, the Messianic investiture had to repose in Him.

The *third* parallel is that of the *mutual absolute sovereignty each exercises in dispensing His revelation of the other*. The Father's sovereignty is displayed in Jesus' words: "for this was Your *good pleasure*" (εὐδοκία) (11:26); the Son's in His words: "to whomever the Son *wills to reveal*" (βούληται ἀποκαλύψαι) (11:27).

A higher expression of parity between the Father and the Son in possessing divine knowledge and sovereignty and dispensing saving knowledge is inconceivable. Warfield is surely justified when he writes that this is "in some respects the most remarkable [utterance] in the whole compass of the four Gospels."

> In it our Lord asserts for Himself a relation of practical equality with the Father, here described in most elevated terms as the "Lord of heaven and earth" (v. 25). As the Father only can know the Son, so the Son only can know the Father: and others may know the Father only as He is revealed by the Son. That is, not merely is the Son the exclusive revealer of God, but the mutual knowledge of Father and Son is put on what seems very much a par. The Son can be known only by the Father in all that He is, as if His being were infinite and as such inscrutable to the finite intelligence; and His knowledge alone—again as if he were infinite in His attributes—is competent to compass the depths of the Father's infinite being. He who holds this relation to the Father cannot conceivably be a creature.[70]

70. Warfield, *Lord of Glory*, pp. 82-83; cf. also pp. 118-19. Ned B. Stonehouse similarly declares:

Such a parity is surely the basis upon which our Lord grounds His following invitation to the weary—an invitation to come not to the Father but *to Himself* as the Revealer of the Father—surely an unholy usurpation of divine place and privilege if He were not Himself deity. And it is not without significance, I urge, that His invitation, in its all-encompassing scope (*"all* you who are weary and burdened") and its absolute certainty and unqualified promise of blessing ("I will give you rest"), parallels in form the divine invitation in Isaiah 45:22.

> Isaiah 45:22: "Turn to Me, all the ends of the earth, and be saved [that is, I will save you]."
>
> Matthew 11:28: "Come to Me, all you who are weary and burdened, and I will give you rest."

Clearly, by His promise to succor *all* who come to Him, Jesus claimed for Himself a place of power and privilege as the Son of the Father altogether on the level of deity.

Matthew 21:37-38 (Mark 12:6; Luke 20:13): The Parable of the Wicked Farmers

In this parable Jesus tells the story of a landowner who leased his vineyard to some farmers and then went into another country. When the time arrived for him to receive his rental fee in the form of vineyard fruit, he sent servant after servant to his tenants, only to have each one of them beaten, stoned, or killed. Finally, he sent his son (Luke: his "beloved son"; Mark: "yet one [other], a beloved son," which evokes the earlier words of the Father from

Here [in Matt. 11:25-27] Jesus claims such an exclusive knowledge of the Father, and a consequent exclusive right to reveal the Father (both corresponding with the Father's exclusive knowledge and revelation of the Son), that nothing less than an absolutely unique self-consciousness, on an equality with that of the Father, is involved. To summarize Zahn's comment on this passage, the Son is not only the organ of revelation but is himself a mystery to be revealed; the knowledge of the Father and the knowledge of the Son are two sides of the same mystery, which is now revealed, and so the Father and the Son in fellowship with one another are both subject and object of revelation (*The Witness of Matthew and Mark to Christ* [Philadelphia: Presbyterian Guardian, 1944], p. 212).

Stonehouse also writes in another place:

Most clearly of all, perhaps, the claim to divine Sonship in a form excluding subordination altogether is found in Luke x. 22, which closely parallels Mt. xi. 27. The Son's knowledge of the Father and the Father's knowledge of the Son are set forth with such exact correspondence and reciprocity, and are moreover made the foundations of their respective sovereign revelational activity, that all subordination is excluded, and the passage constitutes an unambiguous claim of deity on the part of the Son (*The Witness of Luke to Christ* [London: Tyndale, 1951], p. 167).

heaven [Mark 1:11; 9:7]), saying, "They will respect my son." But when the tenants saw the landowner's son, they said, "This is the heir; come, let's kill him and take his inheritance." This they did, throwing his body out of the vineyard. When the landowner came, he destroyed the tenants and leased his vineyard to others.

The metaphorical equivalents of the parable, as Carson notes,[71] are obvious: the landowner is God; the vineyard the nation of Israel (Isa. 5:7); the farmers the nation's leaders; the servants the prophets of the theocracy (Matt. 23:37a); and the son is Jesus Himself, the Son of God.

As with all the other passages we have considered, in which a high Christology is evident, this passage has also suffered at the hands of the form critic. W. G. Kümmel in particular argued that the parable in its present form is a creation of the first-century church.[72] Since I. Howard Marshall, however, has adequately demonstrated its essential authenticity in the form in which it appears in the canonical Gospels, concluding that "we may . . . add this saying to the texts . . . which throw light on the mind of Jesus,"[73] I will proceed to the elucidation of its Christology.

The central teaching of the parable was obvious to its original audience (Matt. 21:45): after having sent His prophets repeatedly to the nation and its leaders to call the nation back to Him from its sin and unbelief, only to have them rebuffed and often killed, God, the true owner of Israel, had in Jesus moved beyond sending mere (human) servants. In Jesus God had *finally* sent His beloved (that is, His "one and only") Son who would be similarly rejected. But *His* rejection, unlike the rejections of those before Him, would entail, not a mere change of politico-religious administration, but "the complete overthrow of the theocracy and the rearing from the foundation up of a new structure in which the Son [the elevated Cornerstone] would receive full vindication and supreme honor."[74]

The parable's high Christology—reflecting Jesus' self-understanding, I suggest—finds expression in the finely arranged details of the story. Vos

---

71. Carson, *Matthew*, p. 451.

72. W. G. Kümmel, *Promise and Fulfilment* (London: SCM Press, 1957), pp. 82f.

73. I. Howard Marshall, "Divine Sonship of Jesus," *Interpretation* 21 (1967), pp. 97-98. Cullmann (*Christology of the New Testament*, p. 289), also supports the authenticity of Jesus' reference to Himself as "the Son" in this parable. A. B. Bruce represents the prevailing interpretive understanding of the "one beloved Son" of the parable: "It is natural to suppose that as that son represents the Speaker, He claims for Himself all that He ascribes to the former. In that case this text must be associated with the remarkable one in the eleventh chapter [v. 27] of Matthew as vindicating for Jesus a unique position in relation to God" (*The Parabolic Teaching of Jesus*, 5th ed. rev. [New York: George H. Doran, 1886], p. 457).

74. Vos, *Self-Disclosure of Jesus*, p. 162.

brilliantly elucidates the following aspects of that Christology:[75]

1. By virtue of His sonship, Jesus possesses "a higher dignity and a closer relation to God than the highest and closest official status known in the Old Testament theocracy."[76] This is apparent from the highly suggestive "beloved" attached to the title "Son," not to mention the title "Son" itself over against the word "servant."

2. The Son's exalted status in the salvific economy of God is apparent from the *finality* of the Messianic investiture, which He owns. From the word ὕστερον ("finally") (cf. Mark: "He had yet *one* other," and ἔσχατον—"finally"; also Luke: "What shall I do?"), it is clear that Jesus represents Himself as the *last*, the *final* ambassador, after whose sending none higher can come and nothing more can be done. "The Lord of the vineyard has no further resources; the Son is the highest messenger of God conceivable" (cf. Heb.1:1-2).

3. The former two points cannot be made to answer merely to an official "Messianic" sonship, as some theologians would like to believe. This is apparent because Jesus represents Himself as the Son *before His mission*—and He is the "beloved Son" *whether He be sent or not!* "His being sent describes . . . His Messiahship, but this Messiahship was brought about precisely by the necessity for sending one who was the highest and dearest that the lord of the vineyard could delegate. . . . The sonship, therefore, existed antecedently to the Messianic mission." And because He was, as the Son, the "heir" (in all three Synoptics; cf. also Ps. 2:8; Heb. 1:2, where the Son is the heir of all things prior to His creating the world), His sonship is the underlying ground of His messiahship.[77]

It is impossible to avoid Jesus' strong suggestion here of His preexistence with the Father as the latter's "beloved Son," James D. G. Dunn's opinion to the contrary.[78] Here His divine station in association with His Father prior to His Messianic commitment in space-time history is confirmed. The "Son" in this parable, Jesus' *self*-portrait, is clearly divine.

---

75. Ibid., pp. 161-63.
76. Cf. Jesus' "greater than" teaching in this connection. He is "greater than" Abraham (John 8:56; cf. 8:53), Jacob (John 4:12-14), David (Matt. 22:41-45), Solomon (Matt. 12:42), Jonah (Matt. 12:41), and the temple (Matt. 12:6). For the demonstration that Jesus rather than worship, the love command, or the Kingdom is the subject-referent of the neuter "one greater than" in Matt. 12:6, that Jesus rather than His deliverance from death is the subject-referent of the neuter "one greater than" in Matt. 12:41, and that Jesus is the subject-referent of the neuter "one greater than" in Matt. 12:42, cf. Carson, *Matthew*, pp. 281-82, 296-97.
77. Vos, *Self-Disclosure of Jesus*, pp. 162-63.
78. Dunn, *Christology in the Making*, pp. 28, 280 n. 106.

Mark 13:32 (Matt. 24:36): The Ignorant Son

In his 1901 article, "Gospels," appearing in *Encyclopaedia Biblica*, Paul Wilhelm Schmiedel included Mark 13:32 among his nine "foundation-pillars for a truly scientific life of Jesus." These pillars "prove that in the person of Jesus we have to do with a completely human being," that "he really did exist, and that the gospels contain at least some absolutely trustworthy facts concerning him," and that "the divine is to be sought in him only in the form in which it is capable of being found in a man."[79] For Schmiedel, these nine passages (Mark 3:21; 6:5; 8:12, 14-21; 10:17-18; 13:32; 15:34; Matt. 11:5; 12:31-33) could serve as a base for "a truly scientific life of Jesus" because each in its own way affirms of Him something that would be appropriate to a human Jesus but that would be *impossible* for a divine Jesus. The reason, of course, for the inclusion of Mark 13:32 among his nine "pillar passages" is Jesus' admission of His ignorance of the day and hour of His return in glory. But does this passage affirm, as clearly as Schmiedel and a host of other writers since him have believed, that Jesus was clearly a man who truly existed, and just as clearly, because of His professed ignorance, the impossibility of His being divine? I say no, and I will argue this in a moment.

But first, we must ask, Is the saying authentic? I believe we must conclude, because there is no significant textual variant at Mark 13:32, that in Mark the saying is textually secure. I affirm the same for Matthew 24:36, even though the phrase "not even the Son" is lacking in the majority of the Matthean witnesses, including the late Byzantine text. "On the other hand," Metzer declares:

> the best representatives of the Alexandrian, the Western, and the Caesarean types of text contain the phrase. The omission of the words because of the doctrinal difficulty they present is more probable than their addition by assimilation to Mk 13.32. Furthermore, the presence of μόνος ["alone"] and the cast of the sentence as a whole (οὐδὲ . . . οὐδὲ ["not even . . . not even"] belong together as a parenthesis, for εἰ μὴ ὁ πατὴρ μόνος ["except the Father alone"] goes with οὐδεὶς οἶδεν ["no one knows"]) suggest the originality of the phrase.[80]

I believe we may also conclude, against Marshall's cautious reserve,[81] that it

---

79. P. W. Schmiedel, "Gospels," *Encyclopaedia Biblica*, ed. T. K. Cheyne and J. Sutherland Black (New York: Macmillan, 1914), p. 1881. For Warfield's response, cf. his "Concerning Schmiedel's 'Pillar-Passages,' " *Christology and Criticism* (New York: Oxford University Press, 1929), pp. 181-255.

80. Metzger, *Textual Commentary on the Greek New Testament*, p. 62.

81. Marshall, *Origins of New Testament Christology*, p. 116. He seems to be not as cautious in his earlier article, "The Divine Sonship of Jesus," *Interpretation* 21 (1967): 94-95. Cullmann (*Christology*

is highly unlikely that anyone in the early church would have invented a saying in which the Son confesses His ignorance—not even to offset the influence of apocalyptic enthusiasts who claimed they knew the time of His coming. I believe that one must accept the saying in both Matthew and Mark as authentic (however much we might prefer to have it otherwise because of the doctrinal difficulty it poses for us) and treat it as a further saying that reveals something of Jesus' understanding of Himself as the Son of the Father. But what does it reveal?

It is too facile to assume, as did Schmiedel, that because of Jesus' assertion of ignorance about this specific datum[82] the Son is *entirely* and *merely* human. This fails to take into account Jesus' equally plain claim in Matthew 11:27 to an all-encompassing knowledge equal to that of the Father Himself. (The fact that this claim is found in Matt. 11:27 might explain why a scribe would have omitted "not even the Son" from Matt. 24:36 but would have allowed it to remain in Mark 13:32, since Mark does not contain the so-called "thunderbolt from the Johannine heaven.") But it is equally too facile a handling of the text simply to declare, as does the Roman Catholic decree, *Circa quasdam propositiones de scientia animae Christi* (1918), that Christ does not mean here that as man He did not know the day of judgment, that the idea of any limitation to the knowledge of Christ cannot possibly be taught in view of the hypostatic union of the two natures.[83] Clearly, dogmatic bias is governing Roman Catholic exegesis here. What then is one to say who is interested in "hearing" the text?

That Jesus speaks here as One with a divine self-consciousness is apparent, I urge, for three reasons: (1) This is the meaning of the simple "the Son" when it is associated as it is here with "the Father," as we have already observed in Matthew 11:27 and will observe in Matthew 28:19. (2) Jesus speaks in this passage (cf. Matt. 25:31) of His coming as *the Son of Man* in glory, which Danielic figure, as we have noted, is supernatural, even divine

---

of the New Testament, pp. 288-89) supports the authenticity of this saying. Fuller (*Foundations of New Testament Christology*, p. 114) thinks it was originally a "Son of Man" saying. This I reject because there is no textual evidence for his conjecture, but even if it were the case, it would make no substantial difference to my basic conclusion as to the meaning of the saying.

82. "We may wonder why the 'day and hour' of His own return should remain among the things of which our Lord's human soul continued ignorant throughout His early life. But this is a matter about which surely we need not much concern ourselves. We can never do more than vaguely guess at the law which governs the inclusions and exclusions which characterize the knowledge-contents of any human mind, limited as human minds are not only qualitatively but quantitatively; and least of all could we hope to penetrate the principle of selection in the case of the perfect human intelligence of our Lord; nor have the Evangelists hinted their view of the matter" (Warfield, *Biblical and Theological Studies*, p. 180).

83. Cf. G. C. Berkouwer (*The Person of Christ*, trans. John Vriend [Grand Rapids: Eerdmans, 1954], pp. 211-15) for his discussion of the Roman Catholic exegesis of this passage.

in character. (3) Since the phrase "not even the Son" comes *after* the reference to angels, Jesus places Himself, on an ascending scale of rank, above the angels of heaven, the highest of all created beings, who are significantly marked out here as supramundane (cf. Matthew's "of heaven," Mark's "in heaven"). Clearly, He classifies Himself with the Father rather than with the angelic class, inasmuch as elsewhere He represents Himself as Lord of the angels, whose commands they obey (Matt. 13:41, 49; 24:31; 25:31; cf. Heb. 1:4-14). And if this be so, and if for these two Synoptic Evangelists, Jesus is not merely superhuman but superangelic, "the question at once obtrudes itself whether a superangelic person is not by that very fact removed from the category of creatures."[84]

But if Jesus is speaking here out of a divine self-consciousness, as we believe we have just demonstrated, how can He say of Himself that He is ignorant of the day and hour of His coming in glory? In response, I submit that in both Jesus' statements about Himself and those of the later New Testament writers about Him a theological construction, quite common in their language, governs their speech. For the reader to grasp the precise point I have in mind, it will be necessary to provide a little theological background.

In light of all of the biblical data concerning Christ's person (which we are here reviewing), the church has seen it doctrinally appropriate to affirm that Jesus, "being the eternal Son of God, became man, and so was, and continueth to be, God and man in two distinct natures, and one person, forever" (*Westminster Shorter Catechism*, Ques. 21). This means that the eternal Son of God, without in any way divesting Himself of His divine attributes (which is to say, His deity), took human nature into union with His divine nature in the one divine person. In sum, He continued to be God when he became a man. But, of course, this means that He possessed two whole and entirely distinct complexes of attributes—the divine and the human. Now in Scripture—and this is the theological construction to which I referred a moment ago—because of the union of the two distinct natures in the one person, Christ is sometimes *designated* in terms of what He is by virtue of one of His natures when what is then *predicated* of Him, so designated, is true of Him in virtue of what He is because of His other nature. As the *Westminster Confession of Faith* says:

> Christ, in the work of mediation, acts according to both natures, by each nature doing that which is proper to itself; yet, by reason of the unity of

---

84. Warfield, *Lord of Glory*, p. 37; cf. p. 81. Cf. also David F. Wells, *The Person of Christ* (Westchester, Ill.: Crossway Books, 1984), p. 44.

the person that which is proper to one nature *is sometimes in Scripture* attributed to the person denominated by the other nature (VIII, vii; emphasis added).

This means that, regardless of the designation Scripture employs, the *person* of the Son, and not one of His natures, is always the subject of the statement. To illustrate: When what is predicated of Christ is true by virtue of *all* that belongs to His person as essentially divine and assumptively human, for example, "that He might become a . . . high priest" (Heb. 2:17), it is the *person* of Christ, as both divine and human, and not one of His natures, who is the subject. Again, when what is predicated of Christ, designated in terms of what He is as human, is true of Him by virtue of His divine nature, for example, He is "the Man from heaven" (1 Cor. 15:47-49), it is still the *person* and not His human nature who is the subject. Finally, when what is predicated of Christ, designated in terms of what He is as divine, is true of Him by virtue of His human nature, for example, "they crucified the Lord of Glory" (1 Cor. 2:8), it is still His *person* and not His divine nature who is the subject.

Now the application of all this to Mark 13:32: As in the case of the last category above, I submit that Christ designates Himself as divine ("the Son" of "the Father"), but then what He predicates of Himself, namely, ignorance as to the day and hour of His return in heavenly splendor, is true of Him as human, though it is not true of Him as divine. As the God-man, He is simultaneously omniscient as God (in company with the other persons of the Godhead) and ignorant of some things as man (in company with the other persons of the human race). Warfield has quite properly assessed the governing conditions in this present regard when he writes:

> When He speaks of "the Son" (who is God) as ignorant, we must understand that He is designating Himself as "the Son" because of His higher nature, and yet has in mind the ignorance of His lower nature; what He means is that the person properly designated "the Son" is ignorant, that is to say with respect to the human nature which is as intimate an element of his personality as is His deity.[85]

So what we have in Mark 13:32, contrary to Schmiedel's "pillar for a truly scientific life of Jesus" as a mere man, is as striking a witness by our Lord Himself as can be found anywhere in Scripture (1) to His supremacy as God over the angels, the highest of created personal entities, and at the same time (2) to His creaturely limitations as a man, as well as (3) to the unity of

---

85. Warfield, *Person and Work of Christ*, p. 63.

both complexes of attributes—the divine and the human—in the one *personal* subject of Jesus Christ. I conclude that in this saying, which brings before us "the ignorant Son," Jesus, as "the Son," places Himself outside of and above the category even of angels, that is, outside of and above *creatures* of the highest order, and associates Himself as the divine Son with the Father, while testifying at the same time to His full, unabridged humanity.[86]

Matthew 28:19: The Son of the Triune "Name"

Sometime between His resurrection and His ascension to the right hand of His Father forty days later, our Lord gathered with His eleven disciples and commissioned them to "go and make disciples of all nations."

As a prelude to the commission itself, our Lord declared that all authority in heaven and on earth had been given to Him, words reminiscent of Daniel 7:13-14, claiming thereby an all-encompassing, unrestricted *sovereignty* over

---

86. In arriving at this conclusion, in addition to employing exegesis, I employed the hermeneutical "key" that the Reformed world believes explains the way that Scripture speaks about Jesus Christ. But I am aware that the question still remains how a person can be simultaneously both omniscient and finite in knowledge. For this reason I am in entire sympathy with Vos when he writes:

> As to how this matter-of-fact ignorance is to be explained in One who elsewhere claims for Himself a knowledge of God equal to God's knowledge of Himself (Matt. 11:27), cannot . . . be indicated on the basis of this passage alone. Of course it is necessary to maintain that whatever ignorance existed in the Son must have existed only within the limits of His human nature. But this is no more than a statement—highly valuable, indeed, as such—by which we guard the vital doctrine of the two natures of Christ. It does not really elucidate the problem psychologically, if we may so speak. In reality it only leads us to the threshold of the ulterior problem as to how the interaction of the two natures possessed by one subject, and that particularly in the matter of knowledge, is to be understood (*Self-Disclosure of Jesus*, p. 168).

The "ulterior problem" to which Vos alludes is usually addressed by the systematic theologian, who proposes some solution such as the likely presence of different levels of consciousness within Jesus. But it was necessary to say this much here in order to draw the conclusion that I believe the entire tenor of Scripture would have us reach regarding "the ignorant Son" saying.

As for the second problem for Vos and others in this saying—how, that is, our Lord can issue here an avowal of unqualified ignorance as to the day and hour of His coming and yet earlier have made some rather definite prediction "to some extent . . . concerning its hour of coming" (since Vos gives no Scripture references, I can only assume that He has reference to such earlier passages in Matt. as 10:23; 24:4-8, 9-14, 15-31, and, most particularly, 32-34), I suggest that the problem is more imagined than real. If one will only recognize that Matt. 10:23 and that part of the Olivet discourse found in 24:4-35 both have to do with Jesus' "coming" in judgment at the destruction of Jerusalem in A.D. 70, which did occur before that generation passed from the scene, while 24:36–25:46 is dealing with His coming in eschatological glory at the end of the age, all becomes clear. Jesus did know about the time of His coming in judgment against Jerusalem in A.D. 70 (this He could have known being divine and the Controller of events and/or by the Spirit's prophetic enabling); He did not know as man, by prior divine decree, the day or the hour of His advent in global glory.

the entire universe. In His postlude to it, He declared He would be with His church ("I am with you"), words reminiscent of the Immanuel title of Isaiah 7:14 and Matthew 1:23 and implying that the attributes of *omnipresence* and *omniscience* were His. In His additional words, "always, even to the end of the age," He implied His possession of the attribute of *eternality*. Between the prelude and the postlude—both pregnant with the suggestion of deity— comes the commission itself (Matt. 28:19-20a). In its words, "all nations . . . teaching them to observe all that *I have commanded* you," His universal *lordship* is affirmed. Sovereignty, omnipresence, omniscience, eternality, and lordship—if we were to say no more, we have demonstrated that the risen Christ claimed to be divine. But more can and must be said.

Before we look at the "the Son" saying, which is our central concern here, we must say something respecting the widely held opinion that we have in Matthew 28:16-20 "a Matthean redaction of a [more] primitive apostolic commissioning."[87] Of course, for those radical form-critical followers of Bultmann, such as the *Myth of God Incarnate* scholars, for whom the resur- rection of Christ is only an existential (nonhistorical) experience ("myth"), this saying must necessarily be the later creation of Matthew, reflecting the developing theological attitudes and practices of the early church. But even among the less radical form critics who actually accept the historicity of the resurrection of Jesus (for example, Robert H. Gundry[88]) the saying has been regarded as a Matthean creation and not the actual words of the risen Christ. Two main reasons for rejecting its authenticity are these: (1) the resistance of the Jewish church to the Gentile mission, these critics say, is inexplicable if Jesus had actually enjoined His disciples to evangelize the world; and (2) Christian baptism throughout the New Testament (Acts 2:38; 8:16; 10:48; 19:5; cf. Gal. 3:27; Rom. 6:3) is uniformly administered not in the name of the Trinity but in the name of Jesus alone.

With respect to the first difficulty, that of the disciples' hesitancy about evangelizing and receiving Gentiles into the church if they had really been charged by Christ to embark on the evangelization of the world, Tasker writes:

> It was surely not to be expected that they would be able to grasp all at once the full implication of their commission, or that a "catholic" church would immediately emerge from what was originally a movement within Judaism. Many difficulties had to be overcome, and many adjust-

87. I have borrowed the phrase from B. J. Hubbard's study by the same name (Missoula, Mont.: Society of Biblical Literature and Scholars' Press, 1974).

88. Robert H. Gundry, *Matthew: A Commentary on His Literary and Theological Art* (Grand Rapids: Eerdmans, 1982), p. 596.

ments had to be made, before it was fully understood that "in Christ Jesus there is neither Jew nor Gentile."[89]

Surely Tasker's perception of the situation shows a greater sensitivity to the in-bred Jewishness that controlled the first disciples in much of their early reflections on the task before them. Luke records Jesus' same universal commission (Acts 1:8), and yet only a few chapters later, in spite of Christ's commission, he must report Peter's reticence to "eating anything common or unclean," that is, to Gentile evangelism (Acts 10:9-16), and God's insistence that Peter must be about the job of discipling the nations, beginning with Cornelius and his household (cf. also Gal. 2:11-12). Form critics who expect those first Jewish disciples to understand instantaneously the implications of Christ's commission to them and thus to submit to that commission with no psychological resistance, display an insensitivity to the position in which the first Jewish disciples found themselves.

Concerning the second difficulty, that Jesus' commission to baptize in the triune name must be an anachronism in light of the reported Christian baptisms in Acts and elsewhere, two things can be said. (1) There is nothing irregular, abnormal, or unexpected about our Lord mentioning all three persons of the Godhead here in what appears to be something of a summary of His teaching. He had made repeated mention of "the Father" and "the Son" previously, as we have already seen (Matt. 11:27; 24:36; cf. also His Αββα references in the Sermon on the Mount and His references to "the Father" and "the Son" in the Fourth Gospel). And He had referred to "the Spirit" in an extended fashion in John 14:25-26; 15:26; 16:7-15. Moreover, references to "the Spirit" are found in both the Lukan and Johannine versions of the commission (Luke 24:49; Acts 1:4-5, 8; John 20:22). So there is no biblical-theological reason why the mention of all three persons could not have occurred on this occasion. (2) It is just as possible that Acts gives only an abbreviated form of the words actually used in the baptismal ceremony, highlighting by using Jesus' name the fact that these persons were being admitted to the *Christian* church, as it is that Matthew reflects a later redactional form of the baptismal formula. Alfred Plummer suggests that Jesus in Matthew 28:19 might not have been giving primarily a formula to be used as much as an explanation of "what becoming a disciple really involves: it means no less than entering into communion with, into vital relationship with, the revealed Persons of the Godhead." He concludes,

89. R. V. G. Tasker, *The Gospel According to St. Matthew* (Leicester: Inter-Varsity Press, 1961), p. 275.

If, then, in this important passage our Lord was explaining the import of Christian baptism rather than enjoining a particular mode of administration, the difficulty of believing that He uttered this saying is greatly diminished, if it does not vanish altogether.[90]

I see no compelling reason, then, to conclude that this saying must be a Matthean redaction, and every reason to believe that here we are afforded further entrance into (the now risen) Jesus' own self-understanding. My exposition will proceed accordingly.

We are particularly interested in calling attention at once to the precise form of the so-called "baptismal formula." Jesus does not say, (1) "into the names [plural] of the Father and of the Son and of the Holy Spirit," or what is its virtual equivalent, (2) "into the name of the Father, and into the name of the Son, and into the name of the Holy Spirit," "as if we had to deal with three separate Beings."[91] Nor does He say, (3) "into the name of the Father, Son, and Holy Spirit," (omitting the three recurring articles), "as if 'the Father, Son, and Holy Ghost' might be taken as merely three designations of a single person."[92] What He does say is this: (4) "into the name [singular] of *the* Father, and of *the* Son, and of *the* Holy Spirit," first "[asserting] the unity of the three by combining them all within the bounds of the single Name, and then [throwing] into emphasis the distinctness of each by introducing them in turn with the repeated article."[93]

To comprehend fully the import of Jesus' statement, one must appreciate the significance of the term "the name" for the Hebrew mind. In the Old Testament, the term does more than serve as the mere external designation of the person. Rather, it refers to the essence of the person himself. "In His name the Being of God finds expression; and the Name of God—'this glorious and fearful name, Jehovah thy God' (Deut. xxviii. 58)—was accordingly a most sacred thing, being indeed virtually equivalent to God Himself"[94] (cf. Isa. 30:27; 59:19). "So pregnant was the implication of the Name, that it was possible for the term to stand absolutely . . . as the sufficient representation of the majesty of Jehovah"[95] (cf. Lev. 24:11). Warfield's conclusion is worthy of quotation in full:

When, therefore, our Lord commanded His disciples to baptize those

---

90. Alfred Plummer, *An Exegetical Commentary on the Gospel According to S. Matthew* (London: Robert Scott, 1915), pp. 433-34.

91. Warfield, *Biblical and Theological Studies*, p. 42.

92. Ibid.

93. Ibid.

94. Ibid., pp. 42-43.

95. Ibid., p. 43.

whom they brought to His obedience "into the name of . . ." He was using language charged to them with high meaning. He could not have been understood otherwise than as substituting for the Name of Jehovah this other Name "of the Father, and of the Son, and of the Holy Ghost", and this could not possibly have meant to His disciples anything else than that Jehovah was now to be known to them by the new Name, of the Father, and the Son, and the Holy Ghost. The only alternative would have been that, for the community which He was founding, Jesus was supplanting Jehovah by a new God; and this alternative is no less than monstrous. There is no alternative, therefore, to understanding Jesus here to be giving for His community a new Name to Jehovah and that new Name to be the threefold Name of "the Father, and the Son, and the Holy Ghost."[96]

What are the implications for His own deity in a saying, as Warfield declares elsewhere, that places Him as "the Son" along with the Father and the Holy Spirit and equally with them, "even in the awful precincts of the Divine Name itself"?[97] The answer is obvious: Jesus is affirming here His own unqualified, unabridged deity! And that this is unquestionably His intent may be seen, still further, from an analysis of just that portion of the saying that precedes the mention of "the Son," namely, the phrase "the name of the Father." Clearly, in this abbreviated context, the phrase "the name" must carry the highest connotation, even that of deity itself, inasmuch as it is the Father's name and thus the Father's nature that is so designated. But it is precisely this same "name" to which the Son (along with the Holy Spirit) stands related, evincing His equality with the Father as Himself deity.

Our examination of the occurrences of "the Son" in the Synoptic Gospels is now completed. The significance of the title, "the Son," for the Synoptic Evangelists is consistent and pervasive: as "the Son" of "the Father," Jesus Christ is deity incarnate!

The "Son" Sayings in the Fourth Gospel

When we press our investigation of the meaning of Jesus' "Son [of God]" sayings into the Fourth Gospel, we find no new doctrinal content in them but only a more pervasive testimony, if that is possible, to the same doctrine of Jesus' divine sonship we discovered in the Synoptic Gospels. The Synoptic Gospels only infrequently report Jesus' self-designation as "the Son" (we have just reviewed the instances), preferring to preserve for the church that

96. Ibid., pp. 43-44.
97. Warfield, *Lord of Glory*, p. 156.

Jesus publicly favored the title "Son of Man." John does not ignore this, but he, more than the Synoptic Evangelists, informs us that our Lord employed with great frequency the title "the Son" in direct association with "the Father," and used "the Father" by itself some seventy additional times and "My Father" by itself almost thirty more times.

I will consider the implications of the more significant occurrences of this title in a moment, but it is necessary to say something first about the authorship of John's Gospel in order to validate my conclusions.

My studied opinion is that John the apostle wrote the Gospel that bears his name. When I say this, I do not, of course, intend to suggest that I believe that every single word came from his pen. For example, appended to 21:24 is a non-Johannine "validation" "and we know that this witness is true."[98] But B. F. Westcott's massive argument for the over-all authorship of John bar Zebedee, I believe—with Leon Morris—"has not so much been confuted as bypassed."[99] Westcott argues first from what he terms "indirect evidence" (Carson: "in concentric circles from circumference to centre") that the author was a Jew, a Jew of Palestine, an eyewitness, an apostle, and finally John the apostle. Then from what he construes to be "direct evidence" (1:14; 19:35; 21:24) he reaches the same conclusion. Finally, he shows that this conclusion is supported by early patristic evidence.[100] This means, of course, if Westcott is correct, that the Gospel was written by one who had been an eye- and ear-witness to Christ's ministry, His Passion, the empty tomb, and His postresurrection appearances, which in turn implies that its author would have needed no assistance from the Synoptic Gospels or the so-called Synoptic literary sources of "Ur-Markus" or "Q," "M" or "L." Nor would he have needed to rely on other literary or oral sources for the content of his Gospel. The facts about Jesus, surely the major concern of John himself as he composed his Gospel (19:35), are certified to us by his own pen as one of the original Twelve. His Gospel should be viewed, then, as a supplement to the Synoptic Gospels. Aware of their existence and their content, John wrote his Gospel self-consciously as a climax to the other three. And although John's supplementary depiction of Christ differs from those of the Synoptic Gospels in that it takes on the decided character of a

---

98. I am also aware of the widely held view that John 21 in its entirety is a later supplement, but cf. Grant R. Osborne, "John 21: Test Case for History and Redaction in the Resurrection Narratives," in *Gospel Perspectives*, vol. 2, ed. R. T. France and David Wenham (Sheffield: JSOT Press, 1981), pp. 293-328.

99. Leon Morris, *Gospel According to John*, p. 9. For Morris's sustained defense of Westcott's argument for John the apostle's authorship, cf. his "The Authorship of the Fourth Gospel," *Studies in the Fourth Gospel* (Grand Rapids: Eerdmans, 1969), pp. 215-92.

100. B. F. Westcott, *The Gospel According to St. John* (London: John Murray, 1908), pp. ix-lxvii.

Christology "from above," beginning as it does with the intratrinitarian relations between the Father and the Son in eternity and tracing the "descent" of the divine Word to His enfleshment as Jesus of Nazareth, *there is no evidence that John ascribes to Jesus anywhere a self-understanding that is not already implicit in the Synoptics.* Critics argue that John allowed the later faith of the church and his own more mature theological reflections to distort Jesus' true self-understanding. But this is hardly likely since John himself often carefully distinguishes between something Jesus said and the meaning that he and the other disciples only later (after the resurrection) comprehended (cf. 2:18-22; 7:37-39; 12:16; 21:18-23; cf. also 20:9).

But precisely because John's high Christology is unacceptable to much of current New Testament critical scholarship, they have rejected his authorship and traced the Gospel that bears his name to other sources—Jewish Wisdom, Hellenistic, Gnostic, and so on. The general critical opinion today is that the Fourth Gospel is probably literarily independent of the Synoptics but, like the Synoptics, is ultimately dependent upon a hazy "layer" of oral tradition about Jesus that lies behind the "literary sources" that were used in composing John's Gospel as we have it today. Now it goes without saying that if these postulated literary sources cannot be isolated from each other, neither can they be analyzed for the historical authenticity of the events they report or for the philosophico-theological influences they bring to bear on the total make-up of the "Johannine" Christology. Consequently, a great amount of effort has been and is being expended on source-criticism of the Fourth Gospel. R. Bultmann in his commentary on John postulated that underlying the Fourth Gospel are a "signs source," a revelatory discourse source (originally in Aramaic and based on Gnostic material), a Passion and resurrection narrative (which is independent of the tradition of the Synoptics), plus contributions from the Evangelist and a later editor. While his particular view has not found general acceptance among New Testament scholars, it has spawned a number of other theories, among them being those of J. Becker, R. Schnackenburg, W. Nicol, R. Fortna, H. Teeple, and S. Temple. But these have faired no better in attracting a following. D. A. Carson has critically analyzed these attempts to discover the literary sources for John, only to conclude that "it is doubtful if [these attempts] are demonstrable, even in the limited sense of commanding sustained assent to their probability." He concludes his survey of them with an "appeal for probing agnosticism in these matters."[101]

---

101. D. A. Carson, "Current Source Criticism of the Fourth Gospel: Some Methodological Questions," *Journal of Biblical Literature* 97 (1978): 428. Morris had earlier reached the same conclusion:

In a more recent article, in which Carson critically analyzes C. H. Dodd's form-critical study of John, entitled *Historical Tradition in the Fourth Gospel*, and the responses of a number of reviewers of that work, Carson reaches a conclusion similar to his earlier one.[102] He also makes the point that the form-critical scholar's presuppositions, rather than the method he uses, all too often are the determining factors in the conclusions he reaches, and he calls upon those engaged in this method to exercise more objectivity than they have in the past.[103] I could not agree more; my own research bears out both the highly subjective nature of the form critic's application of his so-called "criteria of authenticity" and (at times) his failure to see the "forest of meaning" for the "trees of minutia" that engross him. With both Morris and Carson, therefore, I am not persuaded that any argument against the apostolic authorship of John's Gospel to date compels one to abandon the view that, until more recent times, enjoyed virtually universal acceptance in the church. I will turn, then, to the exposition of Jesus' "Son of God" sayings in John's Gospel with the studied opinion that we are considering eye- and ear-witness testimony.

I would begin by calling attention to Oscar Cullmann's insight that, beginning and ending his Gospel as John does with the description of Christ as θεός (1:1; 20:28), if there is merit in the literary device of inclusion, "there can be no doubt that for him all the other titles for Jesus which are prominent in his work . . . ultimately point toward this final expression of his Christological faith."[104] Even a cursory examination of the Johannine occurrences of the christological titles "the Son" and "the Son of God" bears out the accuracy of Cullmann's assertion.

John 5:17-29: The Divine Son

For John, the title "the Son of God" is at least Messianic, this borne out

> If John did take sources he has so re-worked them and made them his own that in the judgment of many competent scholars it is now impossible to discern which were sources and which was John's own material. What B. H. Streeter said about a particular view has a much wider application: "if the sources have undergone anything like the amount of amplification, excision, rearrangement and adaptation which the theory postulates, then the critic's pretence that he can unravel the process is grotesque. As well hope to start with a string of sausages and reconstruct the pig." It seems much safer to take the Gospel as it stands and assume it comes from the Evangelist (*Gospel According to John*, p. 58).

Cf. also C. S. Lewis ("Modern Theology and Biblical Criticism," in *Christian Reflections*, ed. Walter Hooper [London: Geoffrey Bles, 1967], pp. 152-66), who, as only Lewis can do, points up the weaknesses of the Bultmannian source-critical and form-critical methods of New Testament analysis.

102. D. A. Carson, "Historical Tradition in the Fourth Gospel: After Dodd, What?" in *Gospel Perspectives* (1981), 2:112-14, 135.

103. Ibid., pp. 121, 135.

104. Cullmann, *Christology of the New Testament*, p. 308.

from its appearance in his Gospel alongside the clearly Messianic titles of "the King of Israel," "the Christ," and "He who was to come into the world" (1:49; 11:27; 20:31). But that it connotes more than the Messianic office *per se* is clear from its occurrences in several of Jesus' discourses in the Gospel. In John 5:17-29, after healing the lame man on the Sabbath day, Jesus justified His act before the offended religious hierarchy by claiming both the ability and prerogatives of "seeing" and "doing" as "the Father" does:

"My Father is working still, and I am working" (5:17);

"The Father loves the Son, and shows Him all that He Himself is doing" (5:20);

therefore,

"The Son does . . . what He sees the Father doing" (5:19a).

Indeed,

"Whatever he does, that the Son does *likewise* [ὅμοιος]" (5:19b).

Furthermore, as "the Son," Jesus claimed to have the "Father-granted" sovereign right to give life. "The Son gives life to whom He is pleased to give it" (5:21b). There is no contextual consideration that warrants our placing any limitation on the denotation He intends here, either to spiritual or to physical life, for as *spiritually* dead men hear the voice of "the Son of God," they "live" (5:24-25: cf. 6:40a), and as *physically* dead men someday hear His voice, they will come forth from their graves (5:28-29; cf. 6:40b). And when they do the latter, He declared, they do so only to stand before *Him* in the judgment inasmuch as the Father has committed all judgment to Him (5:22-27). These are clearly activities within the province and powers of deity alone to perform; and in making these claims Jesus also claimed coordinate engagement in every work of the Father. In short, in this one brief passage, Jesus claimed, as "the Son," to be—coordinate with "the Father"—the Sovereign of life, of salvation, of the resurrection, and of the final judgment. But perhaps His most emphatic claim to equality with the Father comes in 5:23 when He makes one's honoring of "the Father" turn on the issue of whether one honors "the Son," that is, Jesus Himself. With these words Jesus claimed the right to demand, equally with the Father, the honor (that is, the devotion and worship) of men!

Is it any wonder, given that the religious leaders assumed He was only a man, that they thought Him worthy of death under Jewish law (cf. Lev.

24:16)? By declaring that this unique relationship existed between Himself and "the Father," He was making Himself "equal [ἴσον] with God" (5:18).

In view of Jesus' statements that "the Son can do nothing by Himself; He can do only what He sees His Father doing" (5:19), and "by Myself I can do nothing" (5:30), as well as His later declaration that "the Father is greater than I" (14:28), one might at first conclude that the charge that He was making Himself "equal with God" was unfounded and one He was expressly disavowing: that in declaring Himself to be "less than the Father" He was explicitly making Himself "less than God." There can be no doubt that in making these statements, our Lord was asserting in some sense a subordination to the Father. But *in what sense*—in the ontological, the covenantal, or the functional sense? That is the issue. Warfield sensitizes us to the problem and offers words of caution here:

> There is, of course, no question that in "modes of operation," as it is technically called—that is to say, in the functions ascribed to the several Persons of the Trinity in the redemptive process, and, more broadly, in the entire dealing of God with the world—the principle of subordination is clearly expressed. . . . The Son is sent by the Father and does his Father's will (Jn. vi.38). . . . In crisp decisiveness, Our Lord even declares, indeed: "My Father is greater than I" (Jn. xiv.28). . . . But it is not so clear that the principle of subordination rules also in "modes of subsistence," as it is technically phrased; that is to say, in the necessary relation of the Persons of the Trinity to one another. The very richness and variety of the expression of their subordination, the one to the other, in modes of operation, create a difficulty in attaining certainty whether they are represented as also subordinate the one to the other in modes of subsistence. Question is raised in each case of apparent intimation of subordination in modes of subsistence, whether it may not, after all, be explicable as only another expression of subordination in modes of operation. It may be natural to assume that a subordination in modes of operation rests on a subordination in modes of subsistence; that the reason why it is the Father that sends the Son . . . is that the Son is subordinate to the Father. . . . But we are bound to bear in mind that these relations of subordination in modes of operation may just as well be due to a convention, an agreement, between the Persons of the Trinity—a "Covenant" as it is technically called—by virtue of which a distinct function in the work of redemption is voluntarily assumed by each. It is eminently desirable, therefore, at the least that some definite evidence of subordination in modes of subsistence should be discoverable before it is assumed.[105]

105. Warfield, *Biblical and Theological Studies*, pp. 53-54.

Here are words of wisdom that we would do well to heed! It is not at all evident that Jesus, in "subordinating" Himself to "the Father," was denying His essential oneness with the Father. When the charge of blasphemy for making Himself "equal with God" was leveled against Him, He said nothing to allay the hardened suspicions of the religious leaders, but followed their charge with this very discourse in which He laid claim to the powers and privileges that belong to deity alone! No wonder the charge of blasphemy hounded Him to the very end of His life and finally became the basis for His death sentence (cf. 8:58-59; 10:33; 19:7; in the Synoptics, Matt. 26:65-66; Mark 14:61-62; Luke 22:70-71).

John 10:22-39: The Unity of "the Son" and "the Father"

In His "Good Shepherd" discourse, Jesus grounded the security of His sheep in their being kept by both the Father and Himself (10:28, 29). Then He explained that the *coordinated* keeping was grounded in the essential oneness of "the Father" and "the Son." "I and the Father are one [ἕν ἐσμεν]," He declared (10:30; cf. 12:45; 14:9, 23). About this declaration B. F. Westcott writes:

> It seems clear that the unity here spoken of cannot fall short of unity of essence. The thought springs from the equality of power (*my hand, the Father's hand*); but infinite power is an essential attribute of God; and it is impossible to suppose that two beings distinct in essence could be equal in power.[106]

He was thus confronted by the religious leaders who took up stones to kill Him, charging Him again with blasphemy because "you, being a man, make yourself God" (10:33). If they were hoping that some word from Him would relieve their suspicions, they were disappointed. Instead of declaring that they had misunderstood Him, He insisted that if human judges, as recipients of and administrators of the justice of the Word of God, could be called "gods" (cf. Ps. 82:6), how much greater right did He—"the One whom the Father sanctified and sent into the world" (10:36)—have to call Himself "the Son of God." Note that Jesus' claim to be "the Son of God," both here (10:36) and earlier (5:25), invoked the same response from the Jewish opposition, namely, the charge of blasphemy. How wrong the modern popular perception is that Jesus, in claiming "sonship," intended

---

106. B. F. Westcott, *The Gospel According to St. John*, (1881; reprint, Grand Rapids: Eerdmans, 1958), p. 159.

something less than the claim of deity! "He is not God; He is the *Son* of God," the saying goes; but the religious leadership of Jesus' day understood His claim as just the opposite, namely, as claiming deity, and Jesus did not correct them. That He intended to claim deity is evident also from the word order of "sanctified" and "sent" in Jesus' explanation of His right to the title "the Son of God." Vos notes, "He places the sanctifying before the sending into the world, because it preceded the latter, and a suggestion of pre-existence accompanies the statement."[107] Jesus says clearly that "the Son" is transcendent—He is not "the Son" because He was sent, but rather was "the Son" and was "sanctified" (that is, was "set apart" through the investiture of the Messianic task) *before He was sent*; and He was sent precisely because only One such as Himself, "the Son," could carry out the Messianic task.

The Eternal Preexistence of the Son

Vos's observation above catapults us into the center of this raging contro-versy: Did Jesus claim for Himself preexistence, and if so, in what sense—in the ontological (eternal) or in the ideal ("foreknown") sense?[108] For one who takes Jesus' words at face value, it is evident that Jesus affirmed Himself as not just preexistent, but *eternally* preexistent: "Glorify Me, Father," He prayed, "with Yourself, with the glory which I had with You before the world was" (17:1, 5), indeed, with "My glory which You have given Me because You loved Me before the foundation of the world" (17:24).

This claim to an eternal preexistence with His Father is not an aberration on the surface of John's Gospel, for Jesus speaks elsewhere of that same preexistence:

"No one has ascended into heaven but He who descended from heaven, even the Son of Man" (3:13);

"I have come down from heaven, not to do my own will, but the will of Him who sent me" (6:38; cf. 6:33, 50, 58);

"[No one] has seen the Father except Him who is from [παρά with genitive; that is, from the side of] the Father" (6:46);

---

107. Vos, *Self-Disclosure of Jesus*, p. 198.
108. Cf. R. G. Hamerton-Kelly, *Pre-Existence, Wisdom, and the Son of Man* (Cambridge: Uni-versity Press, 1973), and the numerous short discussions of the issue of Christ's preexistence throughout Dunn, *Christology in the Making* (cf. index), for the questions being raised and the critical answers being offered.

"What if you were to see the Son of Man ascending where He was before [τὸ πρότερον]?" (6:62).

"You are from below, I am from above; you are from this world, I am not from this world" (8:23);

"I speak of what I have seen with the Father" (8:38);

"I came out and came forth from [ἐκ with genitive] God" (8:42);

"I came out from [ἐκ παρά] the Father, and have come into the world" (16:28; cf. 9:39; 12:46; 18:37).

But perhaps the greatest assertion among all of His claims to eternal pre-existence is found in His "I am" saying of 8:58. Most of Jesus' "I am" sayings He supplied with a subjective complement of some kind, such as the following:

"I am the bread of life" (6:35, 48, 51);
"I am the light of the world" (8:12; 9:5);
"I am the door of the sheep" (10:7, 9);
"I am the good shepherd" (10:11, 14);
"I am the resurrection and the life" (11:25);
"I am the way, the truth, and the life" (14:6); and
"I am the vine" (15:1, 5).

But I agree with D. A. Carson that "two are undoubtedly absolute in both form and content . . . and constitute an explicit self-identification with Yahweh who had already revealed himself to men in similar terms (see especially Isa. 43:10-11)."[109] The two instances Carson refers to are in John 8:58 and 13:19, but there could be other instances as well, such as His "I am" usages in John 6:20; 8:24, 28; and 18:5-8. In John 8:58, standing before men

---

109. D. A. Carson, " 'I Am' Sayings," in *Evangelical Dictionary of Theology*, p. 541. Carson goes on to say in the same article that "these two occurrences of the absolute 'I am' suggest that in several other passages in John, where 'I am' is *formally* absolute but a predicate might well be supplied from the context (e.g., 4:26; 6:20; 8:24, 28; 18:5, 6, 8), an intentional double meaning may be involved" (ibid). I personally believe that, with the exception of the single occurrence in 4:26, all of the other "I am" statements Carson cites, because of some detail(s) in the context, should be regarded as absolute in form and content, reflecting Jesus' ascription of deity to Himself through using the great Old Testament "I am" language. Cf. Dodd, *Interpretation of the Fourth Gospel*, p. 345 on 6:20; p. 95 on 8:28 (cf. also Isa. 43:10 LXX). Cf. Morris, *Gospel According to John*, p. 447 on 8:24; pp. 743-44 on 10:5, 6, 8. Cf. also G. C. Berkouwer, *Person of Christ*, p. 168 on 8:24. For another general discussion of the "I am" sayings, cf. Raymond E. Brown, *Gospel According to John I-XII*, pp. 533-38.

who already regarded Him as demonic and who had told Him as much, Jesus declared, "Before Abraham was, I am." Thus, He not only invoked the phrase that Yahweh in the Old Testament had chosen as His own special term of self-identification, but He also claimed a preexistence appropriate only to one possessing the nature of Yahweh. Unbiased exegesis of these words, Henry Alford reminds us, "must recognize in them a declaration of the essential pre-existence of Christ."[110] His meaning was not lost on His audience, for "they took up stones to throw at Him" (8:59). "They understood that Jesus ascribed divine existence to himself and made himself equal with God."[111] After His "I am" in 13:19 Jesus Himself explicated His unity with the Father and in turn His own Yahwistic identity when He declared, "He who receives Me receives Him who sent Me" (v. 20). In 6:20, by His "I am, be not afraid" saying, Jesus admittedly might have been simply identifying Himself to His terrified disciples, yet, as Carson notes, "Not every 'I' could be found walking on water."[112] Then in 8:24, following immediately as it does His declaration that He was "from above" and "not from this world," Jesus' "I am" statement, "If you do not believe that I am, you will die in your sins," surely carries with it divine implications. Finally, consider John's eyewitness account of Jesus' arrest in 18:5-8: As soon as Jesus uttered, "I am," His would-be captors "drew back and fell to the ground." It is difficult *not* to conclude that John's readers were to recognize in Jesus' acknowledgment that He was the one whom they sought also His implicit self-identification with Yahweh.

In all these declarations, Warfield reminds us, "the subject of the affirmation is the actual person speaking; it is of Himself who stood before men and spoke to them that Our Lord makes these immense assertions."[113]

Jesus' Teaching, Acts, and Attributes

Returning from His conflict with "the strong man" (cf. Matt. 12:29), Jesus, "in the power of the Spirit" (Luke 4:14), began His public ministry as the Messiah. Having called Andrew, Simon, Philip, and Nathaniel to be His disciples while in Judea (John 1:35-51), He journeyed to Cana in Galilee where He performed His first "miraculous sign"—the changing of the water into wine (John 2:1-11). After a brief stay in Capernaum (John 2:12), Jesus

110. Henry Alford, *The Greek Testament*, vol. 1 (Cambridge: Deighton, Bell, and Co., 1868), p. 801.
111. Berkouwer, *Person of Christ*, p. 165.
112. Carson, " 'I Am' Sayings," p. 541.
113. Warfield, *Person and Work of Christ*, p. 60.

returned to Jerusalem and drove the money changers out of the temple (John 2:13-14), the first of two such "temple cleansings," the second occurring during the Passion Week. By this "act of zeal" (John 2:19), He provoked opposition from the religious leaders, whose antipathy would follow Him throughout His ministry and at whose instigation He would finally be crucified by the Roman procurator.

It is interesting to note that even at this first temple cleansing, at this early stage of His ministry, He refers to God as "My Father" (John 2:16), indicating His awareness of His unique sonship. In fact, He had already revealed this awareness at the age of twelve. And only weeks before this temple cleansing the heavenly voice had confirmed His special sonship at His baptismal "commissioning." And forty days after that Satan himself had had to acknowledge Jesus' sonship. On this occasion Jesus also spoke of His resurrection, though His disciples did not comprehend His meaning.

Also during this early Judean stage of His ministry He spoke with Nicodemus (John 3:1-15). Note that His "new birth" discourse features themes that would surface again and again throughout His teaching ministry—for example, references to the "Kingdom of God" (3:5, 8) and to the Spirit as a distinct person of the Godhead (3:5,8), His early use of "the Son of Man" title (3:13, 14; cf. 1:51), and even a veiled allusion to His death by crucifixion ("the Son of Man must be lifted up"). Such early references highlight the sustained continuity of the content of His teaching ministry.

After only a brief ministry in Jerusalem (John 3:23) and in the surrounding countryside (3:22), Jesus returned to Galilee (John 4:3). On His way He ministered to the woman at the well of Samaria, evidencing His supernatural awareness of her past (4:17) and expressly claiming to be the Messiah (4:25-26). Arriving in Galilee and calling James and John, He launched what New Testament scholars call His "great Galilean ministry," proclaiming that the Kingdom of God was "near" (that is, had come in its "mystery" form) (Matt. 4:17) and giving evidence of the same by "healing every disease and sickness among the people" (Matt. 4:23-25). Wherever He went the supernatural was present in both His words and deeds—and in both His divine character was manifested.

His Teaching

As illustrations of His general teaching, one may cite (1) His Sermon on the Mount (Matt. 5–7), at the end of which, we are told, "the crowds were amazed at His teaching, because He taught as One who had authority, and not as the teachers of the law" (Matt. 7:28-29); (2) His lesson on the nature of the kingdom of heaven (Matt. 13), which He sovereignly related in parable form because, so He informed His disciples, "The knowledge of the secrets of the kingdom of heaven has been given to you, but not to them," that is, to the people at large (Matt. 13:11); (3) His Bread of Life Discourse (John 6:25-59), in which He repeatedly claimed, as "the Bread of Life," that He had come down from heaven (6:33, 38, 51, 58); (4) His Good Shepherd Discourse (John 10:1-18, 25-30), in which He claimed that He and the Father were one (10:30) and that He was "the Son of God" (10:36); (5) His Olivet Discourse (Matt. 24–25), in which He foretold the destruction of Jerusalem in A.D. 70 and His own future coming in power and great glory to consummate the Kingdom of God, and (6) His Upper Room Discourse, in which He revealed the most intimate details of the relations within the Godhead itself (14:10, 16, 18, 26–15:26; 16:12-15). Three themes in His general teaching demand comment.

The Law of God. Admittedly, this is only an indirect indication that Jesus understood Himself to be divine, but never anywhere in His general deliverances to the people does He claim the Spirit's inspiration as the origin of His teaching. Never does He say, "Thus the Lord says." Always He taught as if He was Himself the divine Oracle. Take, for example, the authoritative manner in which He expounded the law of God to His contemporaries. He claimed to know the will and true intention of God that lay behind the law (cf. His "I say to you"—Matt. 5:22, 28, 32, 34, 39, 44, and His many sayings introduced by ἀμήν ["Truly"]—Matt. 6:2, 5, 16). In speaking the way He did, writes Marshall, He

> made no claim to prophetic inspiration; no "thus says the Lord" fell from his lips, but rather he spoke in terms of his own authority. He claimed the right to give the authoritative interpretation of the law, and he did so in a way that went beyond that of the prophets. He thus spoke as if he were God.[114]

The Kingdom of God. His teaching concerning the Kingdom of God, acknowledged on all sides as the central theme of His teaching ministry, also suggests that Jesus' self-understanding included the self-perception of deity. According to Jesus, while the Kingdom or rule of God will come some day in the future in power and great glory in conjunction with His own return (Matt. 25:31-46, particularly v. 34), it had already invaded history in the

114. Marshall, *Origins of New Testament Christology*, pp. 49-50. Marshall's entire chap. 3, "Did Jesus Have a Christology?" (pp. 43-62), can be read with real profit, for he defends, on grounds that pass radical criteria of authenticity, the unique authority of Jesus and Jesus' claim to messiahship.

soteric/redemptive sense (its "mystery" form) *in His own person and ministry* (cf. Matt. 11:2-6 against the background of Isa. 35:5-6; 12:28; 13:24-30, 36-43. *In Him* God's Kingdom had invaded the realm of Satan, and He had bound the "strong man" Himself (Matt. 12:29; Mark 3:27), a claim clearly carrying *Messianic* implications. But Jesus was equally explicit that the Kingdom of God is both supernatural in essence and supernaturally achieved. George Eldon Ladd explains:

> As the dynamic activity of God's rule the kingdom is supernatural. It is God's deed. Only the supernatural act of God can destroy Satan, defeat death (I Cor. 15:26), raise the dead in incorruptible bodies to inherit the blessings of the kingdom (I Cor. 15:50ff.), and transform the world order (Matt. 19:28). The same supernatural rule of God has invaded the kingdom of Satan to deliver men from bondage to satanic darkness. The parable of the seed growing by itself sets forth this truth (Mark 4:26-29). The ground brings forth fruit *of itself*. Men may sow the seed by preaching the kingdom (Matt. 10:7; Luke 10:9; Acts 8:12; 28:23, 31); they can persuade men concerning the kingdom (Acts 19:8), but they cannot build it. It is God's deed. Men can received the kingdom (Mark 10:15; Luke 18:17), but they are never said to establish it. Men can reject the kingdom and refuse to receive it or enter it (Matt. 23:13), but they cannot destroy it. They can look for it (Luke 23:51), pray for its coming (Matt. 6:10, and seek it (Matt 6:33), but they cannot bring it. The kingdom is altogether God's deed although it works in and through men. Men may do things for the sake of the kingdom (Matt. 19:12; Luke 18:29), work for it (Col. 4:11), suffer for it (II Thess. 1:5), but they are not said to act upon the kingdom itself. They can inherit it (Matt. 25:34; 1 Cor. 6:9-10; 15:50), but they cannot bestow it upon others.[115]

Jesus, so declares David F. Wells in this connection, clearly saw Himself as the Messiah and as bringing in this supernatural Kingdom. And "if Jesus saw himself as the one in whom this kind of Kingdom was being inaugurated, then such a perception is a Christological claim which would be fraudulent and deceptive if Jesus was ignorant of his Godness."[116] Warfield would surely have concurred, concluding as he did about Jesus' teaching that "in its insight and foresight it was as supernatural as the miracles themselves. . . . The theme of His teaching was the kingdom of God and Himself as its divine founder and king."[117]

---

115. George Eldon Ladd, "Kingdom of Christ, God, Heaven," in *Evangelical Dictionary of Theology*, p. 609.

116. Wells, *Person of Christ*, p. 38.

117. Warfield, *Person and Work of Christ*, p. 31.

Claims From the Passion Week. Coverage of the last week[118] of our Lord's life occupies a major portion of the four Gospels. If sheer amount of material is any indication, one may safely conclude that for the Evangelists that last week was the most significant week of Jesus' entire ministry. And, of course, it was—since its events were to bring Him directly to "the hour" for which He had come (John 12:23-27), and to the "cup" that His Father had ordained He should drink (Matt. 26:39, 42).

Much of His time that week was spent teaching in the temple courts[119] (Luke 19:47), debating with those who were plotting His death and communing with His small band of disciples, whose spirits He sought to fortify against the fears and disappointments that would overwhelm them as a result of the events of that first "Good Friday." But certain things He did and said that week make it clear that He was laying claim both to an essential divine sonship, as over against a Messianic or functional sonship, and to the Messianic investiture, which in its own way implied the former. Because of space limitations I must restrict myself to only the more significant items of evidence in this regard, grouping that evidence by the days of the Passion week for easier presentation.

Matthew 21:1-11; Mark 11:1-11; Luke 19:28-44; John 12:12-19: Palm Sunday
The one major event of the first day of that momentous week was, of course, Jesus' entry into Jerusalem riding on a young donkey, with the crowds of pilgrims on their way to the Passover festivities hailing Him as "the Son of David" and "the King of Israel." Jesus, quite clearly, intended that this act, in accordance with Zechariah 9:9, be regarded as His public announcement that He was Israel's Messianic King; and coming as He did—not on a military charger with armies behind Him but on a donkey— He came as the Prince of Peace of Isaiah 9:6 (cf. Matt. 21:5: "gentle"; John 12:15: "Do not be afraid").

There can be little doubt that the crowds did not grasp the significance and symbolism in the humble entry He had arranged. In their hailing Him as "the Son of David" (Matt. 21:9), "the King who comes in the name of the

118. T.W. Manson suggests in his "The Cleansing of the Temple" (*Bulletin of the John Rylands Library* 33 [1951]: 271-82), which suggestion receives some support in William L. Lane's *The Gospel According to Mark* ([Grand Rapids: Eerdmans, 1974], pp. 390-91, 489), that the traditional "week" commencing with Jesus' entrance into Jerusalem may, in fact, have been a period of approximately six months extending from the Feast of Tabernacles the previous fall to the Passover in the spring. This, in my opinion, is precluded by John's explicit statements that date Jesus' Jerusalem entry five days before the Passover (John 12:1, 12-15).

119. Godet says He "resided in the temple, as if in His palace, and exercised there a sort of Messianic sovereignty" (*Commentary on the Gospel of John,* vol. 2, 3rd ed. [1893; reprint, Grand Rapids: Zondervan, 1968] p. 216).

Lord" (Luke 19:38), and "the King of Israel" (John 12:13), they doubtless were thinking of Him for the most part, if not exclusively, in terms of a political Messiah. In fact, John informs us that even His disciples did not understand the real significance of this aspect of His announcement until after His resurrection (John 12:16). They too were still capable of thinking of His messiahship in nationalistic and political terms. But there can be no legitimate doubts regarding Jesus' intentions. Notwithstanding Bultmann's view that the opinion I am espousing here is "absurd," Jesus, I submit, intended His entrance into Jerusalem on the unridden young ass, in accordance with and in fulfillment of Zechariah 9:9, to be His formal proclamation to Jerusalem that He was the promised Messiah. The time for Messianic secrecy was past.[120] Nor can there be any legitimate questioning of the fact that both the crowds and the disciples perceived Jesus' act as Messianic. Finally, there are no legitimate grounds to deny the historicity of the event.

It is not my intention to argue here that Jesus (1) was exercising the attributes of divine prescience and omnipotence over the actions of men in His acquisition of the donkey, or (2) was asserting divine lordship over the ordinary laws of nature when He rode the unbroken animal, or (3) was intending by His use of "the Lord" (ὁ κύριος) (Matt. 21:3; Mark 11:3; Luke 19:31) to refer to Himself as "the (real) Owner" of the colt over against "the owners"(οἱ κύριοι) (Luke 19:33), since one may propose reasonable alternative interpretations. I will only say that I believe a reasonable case can

---

120. C. E. B. Cranfield (*The Gospel According to Saint Mark* [Cambridge: University Press, 1966], pp. 352-54) argues that certain details in the Gospel records—for example, the fact that Jesus' entry on the donkey and the accompanying demonstration are not mentioned at the Jewish trial, the crowd's designation of Jesus as (only) "the Prophet" (Matt. 21:11), John's remark in 12:16, and Mark's "incredibly quiet ending" to the demonstration (11:11)—indicate that, while Jesus was fulfilling Zech. 9:9, He intended to do so "in circumstances so paradoxical as to make the meaning of his action hidden. It was a veiled assertion of his Messiahship. . . . The messianic hiddenness is still maintained." Lane (*Gospel According to Saint Mark*, pp. 393-94) concurs. But I vigorously disagree with this interpretation of the event. Jesus was *unambiguously* claiming to be the Messiah— and the biblical evidence indicates that the crowds perceived this (cf. John 12:13)—but in terms the *full* significance of which only the spiritually illumined, such as Mary (John 12:7; cf. Matt. 26:12), would understand. After all, to present oneself publicly as the King in the terms of Zech. 9:9 is to claim *unambiguously and publicly* to be the Messiah. John does not intend by his remark in 12:16 to say that no one perceived "the fact" of His messiahship. As I have already just said, he expressly implies otherwise by his report of the crowd's exclamations in 12:13. And the disciples had realized for some time that He was the Messiah (John 1:41, 49; Matt. 16:16). John tells us by the remark in 12:16 that the disciples "did not understand the real significance of these events. They did not comprehend the nature of Jesus' kingship. . . . John is not affirming that the multitude correctly evaluated the Person of the Lord. They thought of Him as King in the wrong sense. After the glorification the disciples thought of Him as King in a right sense" (Morris, *Gospel According to John*, p. 588). But publicly and unambiguously declare Himself by His Jerusalem entry to be the Messiah—this Jesus most assuredly did, though neither the crowds nor the disciples perceived that the cross yet stood between Him and the crown.

be made in each of the above situations for a supernaturalist interpretation.

I wish to underscore here one point: In presenting Himself as the promised King of Zechariah 9:9 by consciously arranging the circumstances of His entry to conform to the Old Testament prophecy (cf. Matt. 21:4-5; John 12:14-15), Jesus was claiming, by implication, to be the fulfiller of every other Old Testament Messianic prophecy: the "Shiloh" of Genesis 49:10; the "Star" and "Scepter" of Numbers 24:17; the "King" and "Son" of Psalm 2:6-7; the "Mighty One" and the "God" of Psalm 45:3-6; David's "Lord" and the "Priest forever in the order of Melchizedek" of Psalm 110:1-4; the "Immanuel" and the "wonderful Counsellor, mighty God, enduring Father, and Prince of peace" of Isaiah 7:14 and 9:6; the "Son of Man" and the "Messiah" of Daniel 7:13-14 and 9:25-26; the suffering "Servant" of Isaiah 53 and "the One whom they pierced" of Zechariah 12:10; and the "Lord who would suddenly come to His temple" of Malachi 3:1. Simple consistency requires us to say this. And, it is specifically to fulfill this last prophecy that He would cleanse the temple the following day.

Matthew 21:18-19, 12-17; Mark 11:12-19; Luke 19:45-58:
Monday: the Day the Lord Came

The following morning, Jesus left Bethany, where He had spent the night (Mark 11:11), and, on His way into the city, He cursed the barren fig tree. He then entered the temple and drove out the merchants and the money changers,[121] healed the blind and the lame who came to Him there, and accepted the praise of the children over the protests of the chief priests and teachers of the law, citing Psalm 8 as His justification for doing so. Then He returned to Bethany for the night.

Each of His recorded acts that day was clearly Messianic, and in one way or another gave evidence of His deity. His cursing of the barren fig tree symbolically underscored His divine prerogative to judge and gave symbolic prominence to the truth He would express the following day in His parable of the wicked farmers that the Kingdom of God was to be taken from fruitless Israel and given to a people (the Gentiles) who would produce its fruit (Matt. 21:43). Which is just to say that as Israel's God He was going to reject ("curse") the nation and turn to the Gentiles for praise.

With regard to His actions at the temple that day, Malachi's words need to be recalled:

---

121. I am following Mark's arrangement of events here. Matthew gives the impression that the cleansing of the temple occurred on Sunday, immediately after Jesus entered the city, but he is doubtless following here his practice of arranging material topically rather than chronologically. Cf., for another illustration of this, Matt. 21:18-20 and Mark 11:12-14, 20-21.

Behold, I will send My messenger, who will prepare the way before Me. Then suddenly the Lord you are seeking ["the God of justice," from 2:17] will come to His temple; the Messenger of the covenant, whom you desire, will come, says the Lord of Hosts. But who can endure the day of His coming? Who can stand when He appears? For He will be like a refiner's fire or a launderer's soap. He will act as a refiner and purifier of silver; He will purify the Levites and refine them like gold and silver. Then the Lord will have men who will bring offerings in righteousness, and the offerings of Judah and Jerusalem will be acceptable to the Lord, as in days gone by, as in former years. So I will come near to you for judgment. I will be quick to testify against sorcerers, adulterers and perjurers, against those who defraud laborers of their wages, who oppress the widows and the fatherless, and deprive aliens of justice, but do not fear Me, says the Lord of Hosts (3:1-5).

There really can be little doubt that this awesome prediction saw at least the initiation of its fulfillment when Jesus—the Lord whose temple it was— walked into the temple that day and drove out those who had turned it into a house of dishonest merchandising. Note that here Jesus does not refer to the temple as "My Father's house," as He had done in John 2:16 at the time of His first temple cleansing. Citing Isaiah 56:7 and Jeremiah 7:11, He speaks of it as *"My* house." And His work did have the salutary effect not too long after, as Malachi had predicted, of "purifying the Levites," for we read in Acts 6:7, "A large number of priests became obedient to the faith."

That He was thinking of Himself as He so acted in terms of one with divine authority is brought out, not only by His reference to the temple as "My house," but also by what immediately followed His acts of healing. Some children, having just witnessed the authority by which He cleansed the temple and the power by which He healed the blind and lame, began to repeat the cries of their elders that they had heard the day before—"Hosanna to the Son of David." The chief priests and teachers of the law insisted that Jesus silence their cries of praise. But, as we have already noted, Jesus defended their praise by appealing to Psalm 8:2 (Heb., 8:3), which speaks of God ordaining that children should praise Him. The point of the psalm is that God has ordained that He would receive praise from children, and the point of Jesus' citation of Psalm 8 is clear. As Carson writes:

> The children's "Hosannas" are not being directed to God [in heaven, in this instance] but to the Son of David, the Messiah. Jesus is therefore not only acknowledging his messiahship but justifying the praise of the children by applying to himself a passage of Scripture applicable to God alone.[122]

122. Carson, *Matthew*, p. 443.

It is clear from His citation of Psalm 8:2 that Jesus not only viewed Himself as divine, but also believed He was acting throughout that day as the divine Messiah!

Matthew 21:20–25:46; Mark 11:20–14:37; Luke 20:1–21:27; John 12:20-36:
Tuesday: Jesus' Last Day of Public Ministry

Tuesday was not only Jesus' final day of public ministry but perhaps also His busiest. It was filled with conflict, but it concluded with God's confirming voice coming to Him from heaven for the third time in the recorded accounts of His public ministry, the previous two times being at Jesus' baptism and transfiguration.

On His way into Jerusalem that morning, passing the fig tree that had withered (Mark 11:20), Jesus delivered a short homily to His disciples on the need for and power of faith in prayer. Then entering the temple again, He taught the people and debated the religious opposition throughout the day. Against the chief priests and teachers of the law, who questioned His authority for acting as He had been doing, He raised the issue of their attitude toward John's baptism. Then against their stubbornness and hardness of heart, He delivered His parables of "the two sons," "the wicked farmers," and "the wedding banquet." Then He found Himself in debate with the Pharisees and the Herodians over the question of whether Jews should pay taxes to Caesar. Then the Sadducees accosted Him with their casuistic question concerning the resurrection. Finally, the Pharisees confronted Him again over the question of which is the greatest commandment.

Jesus, having either amazed them or put them to silence with His answers in each of these conflicts, then asked them His questions concerning the sonship of the Messiah: "Whose Son is He?" "If David . . . calls Him 'Lord,' how is He his son?" Turning then to the crowds and to His disciples, He issued His stinging discourse of warnings and woes against the teachers of the law and the Pharisees, just as Malachi had said He would (cf. Matt. 23 and Mal. 3:5). Following this and His commendation of the widow for her great act of love in "giving all she had," He delivered His Olivet Discourse.

Sometime, probably on that day in light of John's remark in 12:36 and perhaps just before He departed from the temple for the Mount of Olives where He delivered His Olivet Discourse, some Greeks who had come to Jerusalem for the Passover celebration expressed their desire to see Jesus.[123]

---

123. Another proposal is that this event occurred on Sunday, immediately after Jesus had entered the city and had arrived at the temple "to look around," because of the connection suggested by John's reference to the "crowd" in 12:17 and 12:19. Cf. Brown, *Gospel According to John I-XII*, p. 469. Morris does not commit himself (*Gospel According to John*, p. 596).

It was on this occasion, as He was reflecting on His imminent death, that the Father spoke from heaven, assuring Him that He would glorify His name in His Son's forthcoming death. When Jesus had delivered His Olivet Discourse, He returned to Bethany, His public ministry completed, to spend Wednesday in Bethany with His disciples, and to await the events of Thursday.

So many details in the reports of this day's events indicate Jesus' divine sonship and Messianic investiture that it is not an overstatement to say that one could write a chapter on them alone. I, of course, can only note the more obvious ones and for convenience will simply itemize them.

1. The fig tree that by Tuesday morning had withered from His previous day's imprecation indicates the power that was His and that was present, of course, in all of His mighty works, including those of the previous day. These in turn, He Himself had said, indicated both His supernatural, divine origin (cf.John 2:11; 5:36; 10:24-25, 37-38; 14:11) and His Messianic investiture (cf. Matt. 11:4-5; Luke 7:22).

2. His question about John's baptism is significant in that, if the Pharisees had said John's baptism (i.e., ministry) had been authorized by Heaven, He would have said, as they themselves rightly surmised, "Then why did you not believe him?" But why did Jesus ask them this specific question about John when obviously He could have asked them any number of questions? The answer is clear and plain: because John had publicly identified Jesus as "the One mightier than I, whose sandals I am not worthy to remove," in whose hands resided the sovereign prerogatives of salvation and judgment (heaven and hell), whose baptism of salvation John had said that he himself needed, and who was, in fact, the preexistent Son of God and the One in whom all men should place their trust (Matt. 3:11-12, 14; John 1:15, 30, 34; Acts 19:4).

3. In His parable of the wicked farmers, as we have already demonstrated, He portrayed Himself as the "only beloved Son" and the "heir" of the landowner (God) to the vineyard (Israel), and as the Son He existed *before He was sent* and was loved *whether He be sent or not*. In His application of the parable, He applied the Messianic passage in Psalm 118:22-23 to Himself and taught thereby that He was the "chief Cornerstone" of God's "true temple" (the church), which Israel was in the process of rejecting, thereby sealing its own fate (Matt. 21:42-44).

4. In His parable of the wedding banquet Jesus represented Himself as the "king's son," the title denoting, at the very least, His Messianic dignity, but more likely bearing the full significance for Him that the titular "Son" had in His previous parable.

5. In His conflict situations with the Pharisees, Herodians, and Sadducees He displayed special insight into the Scriptures, even explicating a previously unrecognized implication in one of the Old Testament titles for God, and demonstrated the divine wisdom "that comes down from above" (James 3:15). Not only did His wisdom amaze His opposition and often silence them, but in every instance in which He employed or interpreted Scripture, He acted as if He knew the very will and mind of God on the meaning of Scripture.

6. By His question concerning the Messiah's sonship (Matt. 22:41-46; Mark 12:35-37; Luke 20:41-44) He intimated that the person of the Messiah is not fully explained if one says He is only David's son, inasmuch as David by the Spirit of God called Him "Lord," thus assigning a superior status to Him (Ps. 110:1). This can properly be understood within the context of the theology of the New Testament to mean only one thing: while the Messiah traced His human side back to His father David, He, as David's "Lord," was on the divine side the Son of God as well (cf. Rom. 1:3-4).

Critical scholars have written much on this pericope and the intention behind Jesus' question, "If David then calls [the Messiah] 'Lord,' how is He his son?" Such scholars as F. Hahn contend that the pericope, and specifically the question, is not authentic but arose in the Hellenistic church because Jesus' Davidic sonship was being denied by the church's detractors. Marshall neatly summarizes the arguments against the pericope's authenticity and rebuts them.[124] For example, it is highly unlikely that the later church created a story in which Jesus questions the Messiah's Davidic sonship, first, because the Messiah's Davidic descent is too clearly taught in both the Old Testament and Judaism (cf. also Matt. 1:1, 6-17; Luke 3:23-31), and second, because there is no evidence that such a denial was being registered against Jesus' ancestry. But if in this pericope Jesus is not questioning the Messiah's Davidic descent but is in some sense affirming the Messiah's lordship over His father David, and if the church had created the pericope to apply the question to Jesus (why else would *His* church have "created" it?), it is exceedingly strange that the church did not make its application to Christ more explicit and obvious. The very fact that Jesus leaves its point "hanging" lends the ring of authenticity to Jesus' question. Marshall concludes that there is simply no convincing *Sitz im Leben* for the pericope in the later early church.

Assuming, then, for good reason, that the pericope is authentic and that Jesus was not denying the Messiah's Davidic descent, the question still remains, How is it that David would call his son his "Lord"? There can be no

124. Marshall, *Gospel of Luke*, pp. 744-47.

question that part of the answer must be found in David's knowledge that God would raise his son, the Messiah, from the dead (Ps. 16:8-11; cf. Acts 2:25-31) and exalt Him to His own right hand (Ps. 110:1 [the verse Jesus cites]; cf. Acts 2:32-36). In other words, the Messiah's "functional" lordship over David, according to Luke (the author of Acts) and Peter (the preacher in Acts 2), is found in the exaltation of the Messiah to the Lord's right hand through His resurrection and ascension. But can nothing more be said? Can a case be made for the Messiah's being *intrinsically*, that is, ontologically, David's Lord, apart from and, indeed, prior to His resurrection? I submit that, for the following reasons, David understood that the Messiah would be divine: (1) According to the writer of Hebrews (1:5), when David wrote Psalm 2:7, he was ascribing such superangelic dignity to the Messiah that the further supreme titles of "God" and "Lord" (the Yahweh of Ps. 102), with all the attributes and functions these titles connote, could also be rightly ascribed to Him. (2) According to the same writer (1:13), it was this *divine* Son of whom David was speaking when he asserted His superangelic dignity in Psalm 110:1.

The writer of Hebrews is only affirming what Jesus Himself taught. For though Jesus did not apply the citation to Himself in a direct way in this pericope, He did do so in Matthew 26:64 and the Synoptic parallels, showing clearly that He understood His lordship over David entailed more than His exaltation through resurrection. This is evident for four reasons: (1) His claim that He would shortly be sitting at the right hand of God (an allusion to Ps. 110:1) immediately followed His claim to be the Son of God, which, as we saw, denotes divine status; (2) to "sit on the right hand of the Mighty One" implies not only mere *occupancy* of the place of highest honor in the heavens but also *participation* in the very dignity and power of that Mighty One; (3) to "come on clouds of heaven," an allusion to Daniel's transcendent "man-like figure," which He also employs in the later pericope, describes not human but divine activity (Nah.1:3); and (4) all of the Synoptic Evangelists record that the Sanhedrin branded His claim to sonship in these terms as blasphemy worthy of death.

When all of this data is taken into account, it becomes obvious that Jesus was speaking of His own sonship and was thinking of that sonship as essentially divine and entailing divine attributes.

7. In general, His pronouncement of woes against the teachers of the law and the Pharisees (cf. Matt. 23) reflects His prerogative as the Messiah (Deut. 18:15). But His denunciation also transcended the prophets who preceded Him: never did He say "Thus the Lord says." Several other very significant features in the denunciation itself underscore that He knew He

was the Son of God as well. By implication He declared Himself to be the Christ, and as such the *only* legitimate "Teacher" and "Master" of men (23:8-10).[125] He declared that it was He, "the Wisdom of God" (cf. Luke 11:49),[126] who "sends prophets to you" (23:34). When one recalls that according to Old Testament teaching a man could only be a "prophet" (נביא) if there was a "god" behind him as his authority (Exod. 4:15; 7:1), and it was Yahweh who commissioned and sent the prophets to Israel, one can hardly find a more explicit claim to deity anywhere in Jesus' teaching (cf. John's exposition of Isa. 6:1-7 in 12:39-41, where we learn that it was the preincarnate Son, whose glory Isaiah saw, who commissioned Isaiah to go for the Godhead). When Jesus then cried, "O Jerusalem, Jerusalem, you who kill the prophets and stone those sent to you, how often I longed to gather your children together. . . ," the immediate context suggests that the temporal extent of His expressed longing is not to be restricted to the years of His personal ministry but embraced the Old Testament economy as well. What lay behind His judgment against *His* generation that placed the guilt of the blood of all the prophets upon it, was the fact that His generation (descendants of the "fathers who murdered the prophets") was not simply rejecting the prophets whom He had sent to them but was dismissing *the very One who had sent all of the prophets throughout past generations.*

He concluded His denunciation against them by applying the Messianic passage in Psalm 118:26 to Himself, declaring that they would not see Him after the events of the next few days until they said, "Blessed is He who comes in the name of the Lord." Throughout the warp and woof of the entire denunciation are strong intimations of His divine consciousness and Messianic dignity.

8. It is quite likely that it was at this time that the Greeks expressed a desire to see Him (John 12:20-36). From His reaction it is evident that Jesus saw the Gentiles' desire for an audience with Him as a "sign" that His death was imminent. Morris observes:

> Jesus recognizes in their coming an indication that the climax of his mission has arrived. . . . The fact that the Greeks had reached the point of wanting to meet Jesus showed that the time had come for Him to die for the world. He no longer belonged to Judaism, which in any case has rejected Him.[127]

125. Cf. Warfield, *Lord of Glory*, pp. 67-68. Vos (*Self-Disclosure of Jesus*, p. 133), writes: "The uniqueness of even the teacher-dignity of Jesus, and the admixture of religious reverence evoked by it, are recognizable in the saying of Matt. 23:8. . . . This uniqueness is no less than that [uniqueness] of the religious fatherhood, when predicated of God . . . (Matt. 23:9)."

126. "That Jesus could be and actually was identified with the Wisdom of the Old Testament is inferred from Matt. 23:34-36 (Luke 11:49-51)" (Vos, *Self-Disclosure of Jesus*, p. 146).

127. Morris, *Gospel According to John*, p. 590. Cf. the words of the Pharisees in 12:9 and John's illustration of it in 12:20.

And so Jesus began to contemplate the cross work that lay before Him in a fresh and vivid way, so much so that His contemplation created in Him "a foretaste of Gethsemane," evoking from Him the cry, "Now is My soul troubled. And what shall I say? 'Father, save Me from this hour'? But for this purpose I came to this hour! Father, glorify Your name!" (12:27-28).

At that moment, a voice, audible even to the crowds, came from heaven: "I have glorified it, and will glorify it again" (12:28). Responding directly to Jesus' prayer to His Father, the voice speaking in the first person was clearly that of God the Father. Here then is the third instance when the Father confirmed to Jesus and/or attested to others the unique filial relationship in which He stood as "the Son" to God as "the Father," and surely His claim to Messianic investiture received fresh confirmation as well.

9. In His Olivet Discourse one can find a sustained emphasis on Jesus' consciousness of both His divine sonship and Messianic prerogatives and functions. By contrasting Himself with the "false Christs" who would come in *His* name, He declared Himself to be the *true* Christ (24:5). By placing His reference to Himself as "the Son" in the particular order that He did in Matthew 24:36 (cf. Mark 13:32), He implied that His was a superangelic existence. By foretelling both the destruction of Jerusalem in A.D. 70 and His own second advent in power and great glory, He demonstrated His possession of supernatural prescience. He spoke of sitting someday on His glorious throne with all the angelic hosts behind Him and all the nations before Him (25:31). And as "the King" (who speaks of God as "My Father"—25:34, 40), He declared that He would judge the nations and decide their eternal destinies. The criterion of His division among men would be ultimately their relationship to Him (25:40,45), and the outcome of His judgment would mean either eternal life or eternal punishment (25:46). The portrait He draws of Himself in this final judgment scene is so awesome and majestic that it is simply moral perversity that prevents one from viewing Him here in terms of His full divine character as God and His Messianic investiture as One conducting the affairs of His Father.

Matthew 26:17-75; Mark 14:12-72; Luke 22:7-65; John 13:1–18:27:
Thursday: The Last Passover

Jesus spent Wednesday in Bethany with His disciples. The next day, being "the first day of Unleavened Bread, when the Passover lamb was being sacrificed" (Mark 14:12), Jesus made preparations to eat His last Passover with His disciples in Jerusalem. When it was evening (which by Jewish reckoning would have been the day of Passover), Jesus gathered with His disciples in the upper room and ate the Passover with them. At that time He instituted the Lord's Supper, washed His disciples' feet, and said His farewell to them (John 13–16), closing the meal with His great high-priestly prayer (John 17). Then He went to the Garden of Gethsemane to pray. There He was arrested and taken for trial first before Annas and then before Caiaphas.

The accounts of these events are so filled with intimations of Jesus' understanding of Himself as the divine Messiah that I can only mention the more significant ones. Again, I will itemize them according to the events in which they are found for easier presentation.

1. At the Passover meal, the arrangements for which may well have been carried out in accordance with details known to Jesus by divine prescience (Mark 14:13-16; Luke 22:8-13), Jesus gave several indications that He regarded Himself as the Messiah. He declared that what was about to befall Him was coming to pass "just as it had been written" (Matt. 26:24; Mark 14:21; Luke 22:22). He cited the following specific Old Testament verses in this regard: Psalm 41:9 (John 13:18); Psalm 69:4 (John 15:25); and Isaiah 53:12 (Luke 22:37), declaring in connection with this last citation, "This which has been written must be fulfilled in Me: 'And with the transgressors He was numbered'; yes, what concerns Me is reaching its fulfillment" (Luke 22:37). This last citation is most significant in that it is the one occurrence of record where we find Jesus Himself explicitly relating His Messianic work to the Servant of Isaiah 53, no doubt a major reason why the New Testament writers later felt at liberty to do so (cf. Matt. 8:17; John 12:38; Acts 8:32-33; Rom. 15:21; 1 Pet. 2:22).[128] And as the Servant who would "bear the sin of

---

128. Because of the connection Jesus makes here between His Messianic work and the sacrificial work of the Servant of Isaiah 53, this saying has been viewed by many modern form-critical scholars as a product of the early church's over-all efforts to give scriptural support to its representation of Jesus' death as sacrificial. If Jesus' authority could be added to everything else favoring this view, so the argument goes, this representation of His death would be greatly enhanced. But Donald Guthrie in his *New Testament Theology* ([Leicester: Inter-Varsity Press, 1981], pp. 261-62) defends the authenticity of the saying and argues that Jesus' citation of Isa. 53:12 raises the "strong probability that he saw himself as fulfilling the whole role [of the Servant] including the vicarious suffering." Many students of the Gospels have detected other references to Isa. 53 in single words in the sayings of Jesus, for example, "rejected" in Mark 9:12 (cf. 53:3) and "taken away" in Mark 2:20 (cf. 53:8). Furthermore, Isa. 53:7 appears to be reflected in Jesus' deliberate silence before His judges (Mark 14:61; 15:5; Luke 23:9; John 19:9), 53:12 in His intercession for His executioners (Luke 23:34), and 53:10 in His "laying down His life" for others (John 10:11, 15, 17). Martin Hengel, in fact (*The Atonement: The Origin of the Doctrine in the New Testament*, trans. John Bowden [London: SCM Press, 1981], pp. 33-75), argues that Isa. 53 and Jesus' understanding of it lies behind His "ransom sayings" (Matt. 20:28; Mark 10:45) and His "supper sayings" (Matt. 26:26-28; Mark 14:22-24). The later New Testament uses of Isa. 53 (53:1 in John 12:38; 53:4 in Matt. 8:17; 53:5, 6, 9, 11 in 1 Pet. 2:22-25; 53:7-8 in Acts 8:30-35; 53:12 in Phil. 2:7) surely go back to the mind of Jesus Himself.

many," Jesus saw Himself as the Mediator of the New Covenant of Jeremiah 31:31-34, His own life being offered in sacrifice for the sins of many (Luke 22:20). And with Messianic authority, Jesus declared, "I confer on you a kingdom, just as my Father conferred one on me, so that you may eat and drink at my table in my kingdom . . ." (Luke 22:29-30). Then in His high priestly prayer (John 17:3), He actually referred to Himself in the third person as "Jesus *Christ,* whom You have sent."[129]

His perception of Himself as divine was brought out plainly when He revealed Judas' forthcoming betrayal. Citing Psalm 41:9 as the Old Testament prediction of it, He asserted, "I am telling you now before it happens, so that when it does happen you will believe that *I am*" (John 13:19; emphasis added). "The ["I am"] expression almost certainly has overtones of deity as in 8:28," declares Morris.[130] Divine prescience is evident also in Jesus' prediction, down to minute detail, of Peter's denial—"before the cock crows *twice,* you will deny me *three* times."

In His words of farewell in John 14–16 and His prayer of John 17 His essential divine sonship is acutely evident. So sustained is Jesus' emphasis on His sonship here that I can do little more than mention the recurring themes. He speaks, for instance, of His pretemporal eternal preexistence with His Father (14:24; 15:21; 16:27, 28; 17:5, 24), of His coming out from His Father into the world to do His Father's will (14:10, 31; 15:10, 15; 16:5, 28; 17:3, 8, 18, 21, 23, 25) and of His return to His Father (14:2, 12, 28; 16:5, 10, 28; 17:13). He speaks of the fellowship that was His with the Father and of the love He continued to know by His union with the Father throughout His earthly sojourn (14:10, 11, 20; 15:10; 17:11, 21, 22, 23). Clearly, here is the "stuff" of which the church's incarnational Christology is made!

With the celebration of the Passover completed, after singing a concluding psalm, Jesus left the upper room and went to the Garden of Gethsemane.

2. In the garden, Jesus agonized before His Father in prayer over "the cup" His Father had placed before Him to drink. On the way there He cited Zechariah 13:7 as foretelling what was about to happen to "the Shepherd" and His "sheep" (Matt. 26:31; Mark 14:27), further evidence that Jesus perceived that the way He was going was the way that had been foretold for

---

129. Cf. Warfield, (*Lord of Glory,* pp. 183-86) for his extended defense of the phrase "Jesus Christ" in John 17:3 as an authentic self-designation on Jesus' part.

130. Morris, *Gospel According to John,* p. 623. T.W. Manson proposed that the formula ἐγώ εἰμι ("I am") really means, "The Messiah is here" (cited by B. Daube, "The 'I Am' of the Messianic Presence," *The New Testament and Rabbinic Judaism* [London: Athlone, 1956], p. 325). But Brown writes, "There is not much in the context of the Johannine passages that would incline us to think that Jesus is speaking of messiahship. A more common explanation . . . is to associate the Johannine use with ἐγώ εἰμι employed as a divine name in OT and rabbinic Judaism" (*Gospel According to John I-XII,* p. 533).

the Messiah. And during His stay in Gethsemane, if the text is original, an angel from heaven came to strengthen Him (Luke 22:43), further evidence that He was walking in the way the Father had willed for Him.

Then His arresters came, led by Judas. Stepping forward, in reply to their declaration that they were seeking Jesus of Nazareth, He declared, "I am!" (John 18:5).[131] At this, they retreated and fell to the ground. Surely both in His words and their reaction to them is further evidence of His deity. Then after Peter, impulsively trying to protect Jesus, had cut off Malchus' ear, Jesus healed him, saying, "Do you think I cannot call on My Father and He will at once put at My disposal more than twelve legions of angels? But how then would the Scriptures be fulfilled that say it must happen this way?" (Matt. 26:53-54). This remark clearly suggests His consciousness of His unique sonship and His Messianic investiture. Then He submitted to His captors, saying again, "This has all taken place that the writings of the prophets might be fulfilled" (Matt. 26:56; Mark 14:49).

3. At His trial before Caiaphas, in response to the high priest's question, He affirmed that He was both "the Christ" and "the Son of God," both Daniel's "Son of Man" who would come on clouds of heaven and David's "Lord," the One who would sit at the right hand of God. Here are unmistakable claims both to messiahship and to deity, for which they judged Him a blasphemer and worthy of death.

Throughout the recorded events of this day, our Lord testified to His deity in so many ways that to deny this testimony and explain it away as the later "mythical" creation of the church, appears to be, to say the least, a mere expediency. More likely, something deeper than mere scholarly reserve or the "assured results of scholarly research" underlies this denial by much of modern scholarship.

Matthew 27:1-61; Mark 15:1-47; Luke 22:66–23:56; John 18:28–19:42:
Friday: The Hour When Darkness Reigned

At daybreak, the council of elders decided to put Jesus to death for blasphemy (Luke 22:66-71). But because the Jewish authorities did not have the authority to execute criminals (John 18:31), they determined to hand Jesus over to Pilate, the Roman procurator, on the trumped-up charge that He opposed paying taxes to Caesar and that He, by claiming to be the Messiah, posed a political threat to Rome (Luke 23:2). After Herod and Pilate

---

131. "The answer is in the style of deity" (Morris, *Gospel According to John*, p. 743). "The fact that those who hear it fall to the ground when he answers suggests a form of theophany which leaves men prostrate in fear before God" (Brown, *Gospel According to John I-XII*, p. 534).

had examined Him, however, they both concluded that there was no substance to these charges. So Pilate sought to have Him released. But he finally
capitulated to their protests and turned Him over to the soldiers to be
crucified. After six hours on the cross, Jesus died, making the practice of
crurifragium unnecessary in His case, thus fulfilling the Scriptures once
again (John 19:33, 36). His body was then taken down from the cross by
friends and placed in the tomb of Joseph of Arimathea.

While the intimations of Jesus' deity are not as many, they were still
present on this day up to the very end. At His final early morning trial before
the Sanhedrin, Jesus again affirmed that He was both the Danielic "Son of
Man" who would sit at the right hand of the Mighty God and the Son of God
(Luke 22:69-70), further attestation by Jesus that He was the divine Messiah.

Before Pilate, Jesus affirmed that He was the "King of the Jews," but not in
the sense that His accusers had represented Him (Matt. 27:11; Mark 15:22;
Luke 23:3; John 18:33-37). Concluding that His claim was no apparent threat
to Caesar, Pilate attempted to have Him released. It was then that the Jews
admitted their real reason for hostility toward Him: "We have a law [a
reference probably to Lev. 24:16] and according to that law he must die,
because he claimed to be the Son of God" (John 19:7). From His enemies'
acknowledgment, we learn again that Jesus had claimed to be the Son of
God, a claim tantamount to claiming deity.

Denying responsibility for His death, Pilate released Jesus to the soldiers,
who took Him away and crucified Him.

Even on the cross, Jesus expressed His consciousness of (1) His sonship
("*Father*, forgive them"; "*Father*, into Your hands . . . "),[132] (2) His assur-
ance that He was going to His Father ("Today, you will be *with Me* in
paradise"; "*Father, into Your hands* I commit My spirit"); (3) His need as the
Messiah to fulfill all Scripture ("I thirst"; cf. John 19:28 and Ps. 69:21), and
(4) His having completed the objective requirements of the Messianic task
that the Father had assigned to Him ("It is finished").

His Mighty Acts

"The purport of His miracles was that the kingdom of God was already

132. There is ground for legitimate doubt whether the "first saying from the cross" ("Father,
forgive them") is a part of the original Gospel of Luke. Found as it is only in Luke 23:34, it is absent
even there in such early and diverse witnesses as P75, B, the original hand of D, W, Θ, and several
significant versions, a "most impressive" group of witnesses (Metzger, *Textual Commentary on the
Greek New Testament*, p. 180). But the textual support for its retention is not weak either, being
found in the original hand of ℵ, A, C, L, N, and several other versions. Harnack, Schlatter, Zahn,
and a host of fine commentators support the authenticity of this prayer, as does the editorial
committee of the UBS Greek New Testament who consider the logion as dominical in origin even
though, writes Metzger, it is "probably not a part of the original Gospel of Luke" (ibid., p. 180).

present in its King."[133] Specific healing miracles are mentioned in the Gospels: (1) the royal official's son (John 4:46-54), (2) Peter's mother-in-law (Matt. 8:14-17; Mark 1:29-31; Luke 4:38-40), (3) the woman with the hemorrhage of blood (Matt. 9:20-22; Mark 5:25-34; Luke 8:43-48), (4) the centurion's servant (Matt. 8:5-13; Luke 7:1-10), (5) the man suffering from dropsy (Luke 14:1-6), (6) the blind (Matt. 9:27-31; John 9:1-7; Matt. 20:29-34; Mark 10:46-52; Luke 18:35-43), (7) the deaf (Mark 7:31-37), (8) the paralyzed and lame (Matt. 9:1-8; Mark 2:1-12; Luke 5:17-26; John 5:1-15; Matt. 12:9-13; Mark 3:1-5; Luke 6:6-10; 13:10-17), (9) lepers (Matt. 8:1-4; Mark 1:40-45; Luke 5:12-16; 17:11-19), and (10) Malchus' ear (Luke 22:49-51). One must also mention both His exorcisms of demons, which, in demonstrating His mastery over the forces of Satan, signalized in a unique way His divine authority over and Messianic assault against the cosmic kingdom of evil and sin (Matt. 8:28-34; Mark 5:1-20; Luke 8:26-39; Mark 1:23-27; Luke 4:33-37; Matt. 15:21-28; Mark 7:24-30; Matt. 17:14-21; Mark 9:14-29; Luke 9:37-43) and the raising again to life of Jairus' daughter (Matt. 9:18-19, 23-26; Mark 5:22-24, 35-43; Luke 8:41-42, 49-56), the widow's son (Luke 7:11-16), and Lazarus (John 11:1-54).

In addition to these specific examples of healing—against which much effort has been expended to explain them away—we have those general narrative statements found in all of the Synoptic Gospels that are not so easily explained away:

> Jesus went throughout Galilee . . . healing every disease and sickness among the people. News about Him spread all over Syria, and people brought to Him all who were ill with various diseases, those suffering severe pain, the demon-possessed, the epileptics and the paralytics, and He healed them (Matt. 4:23-24).

> When evening came, many who were demon-possessed were brought to Him, and He drove out the spirits with a word and healed all the sick (Matt. 8:16).

> Jesus went through all the towns and villages . . . healing every disease and sickness (Matt. 9:35).

> When Jesus landed and saw a large crowd, He had compassion on them and healed their sick (Matt. 14:14).

> People brought all their sick to Him and begged Him to let the sick just

---

133. Warfield, *Person and Work of Christ*, p. 31; cf. also Wells, *Person of Christ*, p. 40.

touch the edge of His cloak, and all who touched Him were healed (Matt. 14:35-36).

Great crowds came to Him, bringing the lame, the blind, the crippled, the dumb and many others, and laid them at His feet; and He healed them. The people were amazed when they saw the dumb speaking, the crippled made well, the lame walking and the blind seeing (Matt. 15:30-31).

The people brought to Jesus all the sick and demon-possessed. The whole town gathered at the door, and Jesus healed many who had various diseases. He also drove out many demons (Mark 1:32-34).

So He traveled throughout Galileee . . . driving out demons (Mark 1:39).

He had healed many, so that those with diseases were pushing forward to touch Him (Mark 3:10).

And everywhere He went—into villages, towns or countryside—they placed the sick in the marketplaces. They begged Him to let them touch even the edge of His cloak, and all who touched Him were healed (Mark 6:56).

When the sun was setting, the people brought to Jesus all who had various kinds of sickness, and laying His hands on each one, He healed them (Luke 4:40).

A large crowd of His disciples was there and a great number of people from all over Judea, from Jerusalem, and from the seacoast of Tyre and Sidon, who had come to hear Him and to be healed of their diseases. Those troubled by evil spirits were cured, and the people all tried to touch Him, because power was coming from Him and healing them all (Luke 6:17-19).

The crowds . . . followed Him. He welcomed them and spoke to them about the kingdom of God, and healed those who needed healing (Luke 9:11).

ıtthew and Luke also report Jesus' own general description of His minis-
in His response to John the Baptist's query:

The blind receive sight, the lame walk, those who have leprosy are cured, the deaf hear, and the dead are raised (Matt. 11:4-5; Luke 7:22).

He furthermore declared that if His "powers"—which had been done in Chorazin, Bethsaida, and Capernaum—had been done in Tyre, Sidon, and even Sodom, those ancient cities would have repented (Matt. 11:20-24; Luke 10:12-13). Even His enemies acknowledged His authority over demons (Matt. 12:22-32; Mark 3:20-30; Luke 11:14-23).

In addition to His own miraculous works, Jesus gave His twelve disciples the authority to "drive out evil spirits and to cure every kind of disease and sickness" (Matt. 10:1), including even the authority to raise the dead (Matt. 10:8); and Mark informs us that "they went out and . . . drove out many demons and anointed many sick people with oil and healed them" (Mark 6:13). Then later, He commissioned seventy (-two) other disciples to go and do the same thing (Luke 10:1, 9, 17, 19). With pardonable overstatement, Warfield writes, "For a time disease and death must have been almost banished from the land."[134]

To these "signs and wonders" of alleviating human suffering, one can add the so-called "nature miracles," such as (1) the changing of water into wine (John 2:1-11), (2) the two miraculous catches of fish (Luke 5:1-11; John 21:1-14), (3) the stilling of the storm (Matt. 8:23-27; Mark 4:35-41; Luke 8:22-25), (4) the feeding of the five thousand (Matt. 14:15-21; Mark 6:34-44; Luke 9:12-17; John 6:5-14), (5) the walking on the sea (Matt. 14:22-27; Mark 6:45-52; John 6:16-21), (6) the feeding of the four thousand (Matt. 15:32-39; Mark 8:1-10), (7) the four-drachma coin in the fish's mouth (Matt. 17:24-27), and (8) the cursing of the fig tree (Matt. 21:18-22; Mark 11:12-14, 20-21).

If the New Testament record is reliable here, never had any other age of the world witnessed such a dazzling display of "wonders," "signs," "powers," and "works" of God. Of course, much effort has been expended through the centuries, as I have already said, to explain away Jesus' works of power, some explanations more speculative, some more crassly rationalistic than others, but all having as their chief aim the reduction of Jesus to manageable "human" dimensions. Baruch Spinoza (1632–77), the Dutch rationalist philospher of Jewish parentage, for example, argued in his *Tractatus Theologico-politicus* (1670) that God was a God of such unchangeable order that were He to work a miracle, since that miracle would then be as much God's law as the law of nature it violated, He would violate the unchangeable order He had decreed for the laws of nature and thus contradict Himself. David Hume (1711–76), the Scottish skeptic and empiricist philos-

---

134. Warfield, *Person and Work of Christ*, p. 31.

opher of the Enlightenment, argued in his "Essay on Miracles," a section of his *Philosophical Essays Concerning Human Understanding* (1748), that the only case in which the evidence for a miracle could prevail over the evidence against it would be that situation in which the falseness or error of the affirming witnesses would be a greater miracle than the miracle they attest. Friedrich Schleiermacher (1768–1834), often called the father of liberal Protestant theology, contended in his *The Christian Faith* (1821) that Christ's "miracles" were such only for those in respect to whom they were first done but not miracles in themselves, being but the anticipation of the discoveries of the laws that govern in the kingdom of nature. Christ, it seems, by the providence of God, simply possessed a deeper acquaintance with the laws of nature than any other man before or after Him and was able to evoke from the hidden recesses of nature those laws already at work therein and to employ them for others' benefits. Another German theologian of the same period, Heinrich Paulus (1761–1851), in his *Exegetical Handbook Concerning the First Three Gospels* (3 vols., 1830–33) argued that the Evangelists did not intend their reports to be understood as miracles but only as ordinary facts of everyday experience. Thus Christ

> did not heal an impotent man at Bethesda, but only detected an imposter; He did not change water into wine at Cana, but brought in a new supply of wine when that of the house was exhausted; He did not multiply the loaves, but, distributing His own and His disciples' little store, set an example of liberality, which was quickly followed by others who had like stores, and thus there was sufficient for all; He did not cure blindness otherwise than any skilful oculist might do it;—which indeed, they observe, is clear; for with His own lips He declared that He needed light for so delicate an operation—"I must work the works of Him that sent Me, while it is day; the night cometh, when no man can work" (John 9:4); He did not walk on the sea, but on the shore; He did not tell Peter to find a stater in the fish's mouth but to catch as many fish as would sell for that money; He did not cleanse a leper, but pronounced him cleansed; He did not raise Lazarus from the dead, but guessed from the description of his disease that he was only in a swoon, and happily found it as He had guessed.[135]

Then there was David Strauss (1808–74), another German theologian, who under the influence of Hegelian thought, in his famous *Life of Jesus, Critically Examined* (2 vols., 1835–36), argued that the supernatural elements in the Gospels, including the miracles of Jesus, were simply Hellenistic "myth," created between the death of Christ and the writing of the Gospels in (so he

135. Cited by Richard C. Trench, *Notes on the Miracles of our Lord* (London: SPCK, 1904), pp. 82-83.

thought) the second century. R. Bultmann also espoused a position similar in its final conclusion to that of Strauss. And Joachim Jeremias, in his *New Testament Theology* (I) (Eng. trans. 1971), after critical literary and linguistic analyses, comparisons with Rabbinic and Hellenistic miracle stories, and form-critical analyses of the individual miracle stories, contends that one is left with only a "historical nucleus" of "psychogenous" healings (exorcisms) and healings through "overpowering therapy"—in short, healings produced by psychic powers. G. Vermes in his *Jesus the Jew* (1973) takes a different approach, categorizing Jesus as a "charismatic" similar to other "Galilean charismatics" such as Honi the Circle-Drawer and Hanina ben Dosa. Another view is that of Morton Smith, the title of whose book, *Jesus the Magician* (1978), leaves little to guesswork respecting his estimate of Jesus. A. E. Harvey's *Jesus and the Constraints of History* (1982) is not as radical in its denials as the former two books, but he reduces the authentic miracles of Jesus to eight in number—those dealing with healings of the deaf, dumb, blind, and lame.

A detailed response in support of the historicity and authenticity of Jesus' mighty works would require far more space than is possible here. Suffice it to say that this has been done, ably and often when the need arose, by such men as R. C. Trench in his *Notes on the Miracles of Our Lord* (cf. chap. V, "The Assaults on the Miracles"); J. B. Mozely in his *Eight Lectures on Miracles;* J. Gresham Machen in his *Christianity and Liberalism* (cf. chap. V, "Christ"); C. S. Lewis in his *Miracles;* Bernard Ramm in his *Protestant Christian Evidences* (cf. chap. V, "Rebuttal to Those Who Deny Miracles"); H. Van der Loos in his *The Miracles of Jesus;* Norman L. Geisler in his *Miracles and Modern Thought;* the Inter-Varsity Press volume *Gospel Perspectives: The Miracles of Jesus,* edited by David Wenham and Craig Blomberg; and Craig Blomberg in his *Gospel Truth: Are the Gospels Reliable History?* (cf. chap. III, "Miracles"). These scholars have shown time and again that every assessment of Christ's miracles as spurious or rationally explicable results from the antagonist making his own *a priori* judgment about the nature of God or the world the touchstone of what is and is not possible. The Christian, of course, places the question of the historicity and authenticity of Jesus' miracles, first, within the total context of Christian theism *per se*. "Once admit," Machen writes, "the existence of a personal God, Maker and Ruler of the world, and no limits, temporal or otherwise, can be set to the creative power of such a God. Admit that God once created the world, and you cannot deny that He might engage in creation again."[136] And second, the Christian places the

136. J. Gresham Machen, *Christianity and Liberalism* (Grand Rapids: Eerdmans, 1923), p. 102.

question of the historicity and authenticity of Jesus' miracles in the more narrow context of the specific requisite occasion of the reality of sin. He realizes that man's only hope of conquest over it is in supernatural aid coming to him from outside the human condition.[137] He believes this exigency is fully met in the supernatural Savior who gave evidence of His supernatural origin and character through, among other means, the working of miracles. Grant, in other words, the fact of the infinite, personal God and the exigency of human sin and no philosophical or historical barrier stands in the way of the historicity of any of the miracles of Scripture. The distinct likelihood of the miracles of the Gospels follows as a matter of course.

Now within the context of biblical theism, the weight of Jesus' miracles, separately and collectively, point, according to Jesus' own testimony, to a twofold conclusion. They testified to the coming of the Messianic Age in the person of the Messiah (Matt. 12:28), as we have already noted, but they also testified to His own divine character as the Son of God who visited this poor planet on a mission of mercy (Matt. 20:28; Mark 10:45) to seek and to save that which was lost. Consider Jesus' own testimony regarding His miraculous works.

John 5:36. In the John 5 context, where may be found a most amazing series of claims to equality with God, in addition, He said, to John the Baptist's witness (5:33-35), the Father's witness (doubtless including but not to be restricted to the confirmation from heaven at the time of His baptismal "commissioning") (5:37), and the witness of the Old Testament Scriptures (5:39, 46), "the works that the Father has given Me to finish, the very works which I am doing, testify concerning Me, that the Father sent Me" (5:36). These unique works—unique because they were "works . . . which no one else did" (15:24), unique because they "bear upon them the hallmark of their divine origin"[138]—underscored, He says, His uniqueness as One not of human origin but as One whom "the Father sent" from heaven.

John 10:24-25, 37-38. In these verses, in direct response to the demand from the religious leaders, "If you are the Messiah, tell us plainly," Jesus replied, "I did tell you, but you do not believe. The miracles I do in My Father's name speak for Me." He then said, "Do not believe Me unless I do what My Father does. But if I do it, even though you do not believe Me,

---

137. Ibid., pp. 104-6.
138. Morris, *Gospel According to John*, p. 328.

believe the miracles, that you may learn and understand that the Father is in Me and I in the Father." By these remarks, Jesus asserts that His miracles witnessed both to His Messianic investiture and to that intimate union between the Father and Himself which He describes in terms that some theologians have urged come nothing short of a mutual indwelling or interpenetration of the persons of the Father and the Son.

John 14:11. In His Upper Room Discourse, after making the marvelous claims that "anyone who sees Me has seen the Father" (14:9) and that He and the Father were in personal union one with the other (14:10-11), Jesus urged His disciples to believe Him for His own words' sake, but if they had any hesitancy concerning His words, then "at least," He said, "because of the works themselves believe." Again, His works, He declared, testified to His divine nature.

Matthew 11:4-5; Luke 7:22. As confirmation to John the Baptist that He was indeed the "One who was to come," that is, the divine Messiah, Jesus said to John's disciples, "Go back and report to John what you hear and see: the blind receive sight, the lame walk, those who have leprosy are cured, the deaf hear, the dead are raised, and the good news is preached to the poor." Clearly, Jesus implies, His miracles validated and authenticated the fact that the Messianic Age had come in His own person as the divine Messiah.

Matthew 9:1-8; Mark 2:1-12; Luke 5:17-26. As we noted earlier in our discussion of the Son of Man title, on this occasion Jesus vindicated His right to forgive sin—a prerogative of God alone—by healing the paralytic.[139]

We can only conclude that Jesus' miraculous works, when viewed as Jesus intended they should be viewed, both authenticated His teachings and were themselves direct and immediate indications of the presence of the Messianic Age and His own divine character as the Messianic King.

But in addition to His mighty miracles ("powers"), which were designed

---

139. We are considering Jesus' self-witness here, but the reader might note the testimony of John and Peter in this connection. By His first miracle, John informs us in 2:11, Jesus "revealed His glory." And what glory was that? Just "the glory of the one and only [Son] who came from the side of His Father" (John 1:14). What is it, then, that John says this miracle, as a "sign," signified but just Jesus' glory as the divine Son of God! Then Peter's opening remark (Acts 2:22) in his sermon on the Day of Pentecost is also quite revealing: "Jesus of Nazareth, a man attested to you by God with miracles and wonders and signs which God performed through Him in your midst" (cf. Acts 10:38-39). Here Peter attests to the authenticating value of Jesus' miracles—they testified to God's approval of the "man" Jesus. But then this means that God approved of His teaching as well. And in that teaching He claimed to be the Son of God, one with the Father, and in possession of the rights and privileges of deity.

to authenticate His Messianic claim (Matt. 11:2-6; John 5:36; 10:25, 38; 14:11; Acts 2:22) and to reveal His glory (John 2:11), instances of Jesus' exercise of other divine prerogatives (like His public claims to deity itself, as we have seen) occur with sufficient frequency to warrant our notice of them as further aspects of His self-witness.

The Forgiving of Sins

We have already noted that Jesus claimed, as the Son of Man, to have the authority to forgive sins (Matt. 9:6; Mark 2:10; Luke 5:24) and, in fact, did forgive men of their sins against God both by the spoken word (Matt. 9:2; Mark 2:5; Luke 5:20; 7:48) and by His attitude in eating meals with sinners (Luke 15:1-2). This authority, as the teachers of the law who were present when Jesus healed the paralytic rightly judged, is the prerogative of God alone. The one fact they did not recognize, but which would have explained His act to them, is His deity. Of course, a man may forgive the transgressions of another man against himself, but Jesus forgave men of their sins against God! Only One who is Himself divine has that right.

The Hearing and Answering of Prayer

In a remarkable passage in John's Gospel, Jesus declared that He would answer the prayers of His disciples (14:13), but equally significant for our purpose, He represented Himself as One to whom prayers may properly be addressed. Morris writes on 14:14: "The true text appears to be 'if ye shall ask me anything in my name.' Prayer may be addressed to the Son as well as to the Father."[140] In verse 14, Jesus stated again that He Himself would answer His disciples' prayers, surely an implicit claim to deity. While many other examples might be cited, the instances of prayer addressed to Jesus in Acts 1:24; 7:59; 9:10-17; and 2 Corinthians 12:8 bear out the literalness with which the disciples understood Jesus' promise and show also their immediate recognition of His divinity.

The Receiving of Men's Adoration and Praise

Immediately after His triumphal entry into Jerusalem, when asked by the indignant chief priests to silence the children who were praising Him (Matt. 21:16), Jesus defended their praise by appealing to Psalm 8:2 (Heb., 8:3), which speaks of children praising *God*. On this appeal to Psalm 8:2, Carson writes:

140. Morris, *Gospel According to John*, p. 647.

God *has* ordained praise for himself from "children and infants" . . . Jesus' answer is a masterstroke . . . 1. It provides some kind of biblical basis for letting the children go on with their exuberant praise. . . . 2. At the same time thoughtful persons, reflecting on the incident later (especially after the Resurrection), perceive that Jesus was saying much more. The children's "Hosannas" are not being directed to God but to the Son of David, the Messiah. Jesus is therefore not only acknowledging his messiahship but justifying the praise of the children by applying to himself a passage of Scripture applicable only to God.[141]

Later, on the occasion of His second appearance to the disciples a week after His resurrection, He accepted Thomas's adoring ascription of Him as his "Lord and God." There can be no doubt, in light of these clear instances when Jesus accepted and approved the adoration and praise of men, that He was endorsing the notion of His own deity. R. T. France believes that New Testament Christology "was first perceived functionally" and was expressed in the worship of Jesus. This functional Christology "was then necessarily worked out in ontological terms" by the later church, this later ontological Christology, of course, describing what was already true about Jesus from the beginning.[142] I applaud France's forthright defense of the doctrine of Christ's full deity on the ground that He was regarded by the Christian community as a proper object of worship, but I feel quite strongly that we must insist that virtually from the beginning, even prior to His resurrection, in concert with the "functional" aspects of its Christology, the disciples also held an ontological Christology taught by Jesus Himself, which was the basis for Thomas's belated confession only a week after Jesus' resurrection and which is the only ground upon which the worshiping community could have *worshiped* Jesus as early as Acts 1.

The Proper Object of Men's Faith

In the familiar saying of John 14:1, whether the two occurrences of πιστεύετε εἰς (" believe in [with unreserved trust]") are both to be rendered indicatively ("You believe in") or imperatively ("Believe in"), or whether the former is to be translated indicatively with only the latter to be rendered imperatively (or vice versa), makes no difference to our present purpose. The outcome is exactly the same: Jesus places Himself on a par with the

---

141. Carson, *Matthew*, p. 443.

142. R. T. France, "The Worship of Jesus: A Neglected Factor in Christological Debate," in *Christ the Lord*, pp. 17-36.

Father as *equally* with Him the proper object of men's trust. If Jesus was not in fact divine, such a saying would constitute blasphemy of the first order. The only ground upon which His goodness may be retained in the light of such teaching is to affirm His Godness. He cannot be a mere man and at the same time good while teaching men to trust Him as they would trust the Father.

His Attributes

Jesus, in addition to exercising divine powers and claiming divine prerogatives, claimed to possess divine attributes as well. Before we consider them individually, I should explain what I mean by "attribute." I mean a "characteristic" of the nature of a person or thing. A person's nature is the sum total of the attributes or characteristics that are necessary to his being what he is. Put another way, one may say that precisely in the sum total of his attributes the nature of a person subsists. This is what we mean by "attribute." Now we say that God has a nature. We speak accordingly of the "divine nature" and by the phrase ascribe to God that complex of attributes, whatever and however many they might be, that are essential to His being God. When I say, then, that Jesus claimed to possess divine attributes, I mean that Jesus, of necessity, would have had to think of Himself as divine in order to do so. I do not mean that a claim to every divine attribute may be found in so many words in Jesus' discourses. But a sufficient number may be found in His statements to conclude that He believed Himself to be divine and thus in possession of them all.

We have had occasion already to note certain of Jesus' claims to divine attributes. I list them as a group for the benefit of the reader with brief comments on each.

Eternal Preexistence. I refer the reader to the discussions of Matthew 28:20; John 8:58; and 17:5 for our reasons for ascribing this attribute to Jesus.

Sovereignty and Omnipotence. In claiming the authority to reveal the Father to whomever He chose (Matt. 11:27) and to give life to whomever He chose (John 5:21), in claiming both the prerogative and the power to call all men someday from their graves (5:28-29) and the authority to judge all men (John 5:22, 27), in claiming the authority to lay down His life and the authority to take it up again (John 10:18), in declaring he would return someday "in power and great glory" (Matt. 24:30), and in claiming that all authority in heaven and on earth had been given to Him by the Father (Matt. 28:18),[143] Jesus was claiming, implicitly and explicitly, an absolute sovereignty and power over the universe. If any other man made such claims, we would rightly regard him as insane; but Jesus, because He is the divine Son, deserves men's adoration and praise.

Omnipresence. When Jesus promised that "where two or three gather together in my name, there am I with them [ἐκεῖ εἰμι ἐν μέσῳ αὐτῶν]" (Matt. 18:20), and when He promised "I am with you always [ἐγὼ μεθ' ὑμῶν εἰμι πάσας τὰς ἡμέρας]" (Matt. 28:20), not only was He invoking the language of the Immanuel title but He was also claiming that He is Himself personally always with His own, not just in the power and presence of His Holy Spirit but present with them Himself as the omnipresent Savior.

Omniscience. When Jesus surprised Nathaniel with His comment, "I saw you while you were still under the fig tree before Philip called you" (John 1:48), "it is difficult," as Morris observes:

> to explain Jesus' knowledge of the incident on the level of merely human knowledge. Nathaniel had never met Him before this moment. We are required to understand that Jesus had some knowledge not generally available to the sons of men.[144]

When Jesus claimed for Himself the prerogative to hear and to answer the prayers of His disciples, He was claiming omniscience. One who can hear the innumerable prayers of His disciples—offered to Him night and day, day in and day out throughout the centuries—keep each request infallibly related to its petitioner, and answer each one in accordance with the divine mind and will would need Himself to be omniscient.[145]

And when Jesus claimed to have not only an *exclusive* knowledge of the

---

143. It would be a major mistake theologically to infer from the ἐδόθη in Matt. 28:18 (or for that matter the ἔδωκεν in John 5:26) that Jesus was given authority to exercise universal dominion for the first time *as God's Son* only at His resurrection. As we shall argue later (cf. pp. 220-22), when Jesus declared here that authority "was given" to Him, we must understand Him as saying this about Himself in His mediatorial role *as the divine-human Messiah*. But as the *divine* Messiah and being as such the eternal Son of God, Jesus continued as He always had done to exercise over his creation the powers and lordly rights that were intrinsically His as God the Son (cf. Calvin, *Institutes*, II, 13, 4).

144. Morris, *Gospel According to John*, p. 167.

145. This is one of the insuperable difficulties inherent within the Roman Catholic dogma of the veneration of Mary (*hyperdulia*) because of her supposed mediation for the earthly petitioner. In allowing her to hear the prayers of Christians on earth, that church regrettably ascribes to her a knowledge and an ability found only in God, and in so doing virtually ascribes divinity to her.

Father, but also a knowledge whose object is God the Father Himself in all the infinite depths of His divine being (Matt. 11:27), He was again claiming to possess, as "the Son," a degree of knowledge falling nothing short of omniscience itself.

We conclude then that, not only in the specific titles He employed but also in the explicit claims He made and the works He did, Jesus *believed* Himself to be and claimed to be in possession of attributes normally the property of God alone; in making this claim He was claiming to be God incarnate.

Before I draw this section of our study to a close, lest I be accused of ignoring a piece of Jesus' self-witness that flies in the face of this conclusion, I feel it imperative to say something about one of Jesus' statements that Arians in the fourth century and liberals in our own day allege to be His disclaimer of being in any sense of the word divine. I refer to Jesus' response to the rich young ruler's strange[146] address to Him ("Good Teacher," διδάσκαλε ἀγαθέ—Mark 10:17; Luke 18:18; cf. Matt. 19:16): "Why do you call Me good? No one is good except one, even God" (τί με λέγεις ἀγαθόν; οὐδεὶς ἀγαθὸς εἰ μὴ εἷς ὁ θεός—Mark 10:18; Luke 18:19; cf. Matt. 19:17). These theologians infer that Jesus drew a contrast between Himself (cf. the enclitic με) on the one hand and God on the other, and they argue that Jesus not only disclaimed being divine but that He even confessed creaturely moral imperfection.

But does Jesus' response imply the contrast between Himself and God that is the core of this interpretation? The enclitic (unemphatic) με Jesus employs to refer to Himself simply will not bear the weight of this inferred contrast. Nor will its position in the sentence support the weight of this inferred contrast either, since, as Blass and Debrunner observe, "the old rule, observable in Greek and cognate languages, that unemphatic (enclitic) pronouns and the like are placed as near the beginning of the sentence as possible . . . applies also to the NT."[147] Moreover, such an inferred contrast "throws into chief prominence a matter which lies quite apart from the main subject under discussion,"[148] that is, the contrast not between God and Jesus, but (as Matthew's account brings out clearly by reporting Jesus' question, "Why do you ask Me about what is good?") between God as the

---

146. Warfield, citing Edersheim, Plummer, and Dalman, says of the young man's address that it is "apparently unexampled in extant Jewish literature," throwing into relief "the levity with which the young man approached Jesus of whom he knew so little, with so remarkable a demand" (*Person and Work of Christ*, pp. 156-57). Marshall also describes it as a "strange" address, citing only one other example of it, but that one is from the fourth century A.D. (*Gospel of Luke*, p. 684).

147. F. Blass and A. Debrunner, *A Greek Grammar of the New Testament and Other Early Christian Literature*, translation of 9th-10th German edition (Chicago: University of Chicago Press, 1961), p. 249, sec. 473 (1).

148. Warfield, *Person and Work of Christ*, p. 161.

only true standard of goodness and any and all others who prescribe other standards for acquiring eternal life. Jesus' implied point is that, as a Jew, the man already had God's revelation on the matter. Warfield explains:

> The whole emphasis is absorbed in the stress laid upon God's sole right to announce the standard of goodness. The question of the relation of Jesus to this God does not emerge: there is equally no denial that He is God, and no affirmation that He is God. The young man is merely pointed to the rule which had been given by the good God as a witness to what it is requisite to do that we may be well-pleasing to Him. He is merely bidden not to look elsewhere for prescriptions as to life save in God's revealed will. The search for a master good enough to lead men to life finds its end in God and His commandments.[149]

This is the contrast Jesus intended, not a contrast between Himself and God. Immediately after His opening response He declared, "You know the commandments" (Mark 10:19); "If you would enter life, keep the commandments" (Matt. 19:17).

I. Howard Marshall agrees with Warfield that Jesus intended no contrast between or comparison of Himself and God in the passage. The point He wished to make was altogether another matter:

> Jesus' answer is meant to do away with any cheapening of the idea of goodness. True goodness belongs to God, as the OT testifies. . . . There is no reason to regard Jesus' statement as a confession of sinfulness, since this would be at variance with the rest of the Synoptic tradition. . . . The Christian reader may go to the other extreme and see here a tacit identification of Jesus with God, but this lies beyond what the passage actually says.[150]

So this saying, by which critics allege that Jesus rejected any thought of being divine, actually does not address the issue one way or the other.[151] Neither should it be construed as a confession of sin on Jesus' part.

As we draw this first phase of our study to a close, I remind the reader that we set for ourselves at the beginning of this chapter the task of answering two questions:

1. Did Jesus believe Himself to be—and teach others—that He was the promised Messiah?

---

149. Ibid., pp. 158-59. So also Alexander, Swete, Lagrange, Plummer et al.
150. Marshall, *Gospel of Luke*, p. 684.
151. Warfield's article ("Jesus' Alleged Confession of Sin,"*Person and Work of Christ*) should be read in its entirety by any who remain unconvinced that this is the proper construction to place on Jesus' remarks.

2. Did Jesus believe Himself to be—and teach others—that He was more than a man, that He was, in fact, divine?

To answer these two questions, we restricted ourselves in this chapter to considering only Jesus' teaching and the things He did. At this stage we ignored the testimonies of God Himself, angel, disciple (unless expressed in His presence), Evangelist, or apostle (the task addressed in the next four chapters), being concerned as we were to discern Jesus' *self*-understanding.

From our examination of the occurrences of the Messianic titles "Christ," "Son of Man," and "Son of David," we found more than ample reason to conclude that Jesus did, in fact, claim to be the promised Messiah of the Old Testament. We noted too the significant fact that Jesus preferred "Son of Man" over the other Messianic titles as His favorite public self-designation because it stood at the farthest remove from the purely political associations by which the Messianic concept and hope had been debased in and by the popular imagination.

This brought us to our second concern. From our examination of Jesus' "Son of Man" and "Son [of God]" sayings, we concluded that He believed Himself to be divine and taught men so. As the "Son of Man," Jesus claimed to possess both attributes and prerogatives of deity (John 3:13; 6:62; Matt. 9:6; 12:8). As "the Son" of "the Father," He claimed to possess an exclusive, direct, intuitive, and absolute knowledge of "the Father," and the exclusive, sovereign right to reveal "the Father" to whomever He chose (Matt. 11:27). He further claimed as "the Son" to be the highest and final messenger from God (Matt. 21:37-38), placing Himself outside of and above the angelic order (Mark 13:32), indeed, within the "awful precincts of the Divine Name itself" (Matt. 28:19), that is, within the venue of deity. Jesus claimed as the Son of God the right to exercise, in conjunction with "His own Father," sovereign lordship over life, determine the eternal destinies of men, effect the eschatological resurrection, and act as arbiter at the final judgment (John 5:17-29), claims that His enemies understood, quite correctly, as claims to equality with God Himself (John 5:18; 10:33). As the Son of God, He claimed, furthermore, to be in essential union with the Father (John 10:30). Indeed, He claimed to be the eternal "I am" of the Old Testament (John 8:58 et al.), insisting upon His own eternal preexistence, omnipotence, omnipresence, and omniscience and representing Himself as the One who forgives men of their sins, who hears and answers their prayers, and who deserves their adoration and praise, their honor and worship, as well as their trust.

Jesus indicated that His sonship is *ontologically anterior* to the (covenantally grounded) functional, or economical, messiahship with which He was invested. That is to say, He received from His Father the Messianic investiture because He is the Son of God; He is not the Son of God because He received the Messianic investiture.

Many critical scholars, of course, do not like the verbal portrait Jesus drew of Himself. Yet they wish, quite possibly in order to meet their own religious needs, to cleave to Him still as in some sense the Man for all men, universally significant but not universally perceived yet as such. So while they explain away His high claims to deity by applying their form-critical analyses and the "criteria of authenticity" to His teachings in a highly subjective way, they solicitously leave themselves with some form of functional Christology. But the issue every purely functional christologist must squarely face, as I have suggested earlier, is that a functional Christology alone cannot sustain the uniqueness and universal significance for Christ that its advocate desires.

Much more consistent are those who, offended at His claims, simply dismiss them as the claims of one suffering delusions of grandeur, to put it as mildly as possible. They seem to have grasped much better the point C. S. Lewis made in the third of his famous BBC radio broadcasts on "What Christians Believe":

> There suddenly turns up a man who goes about talking as if He was God. He claims to forgive sins. He says He has always existed. He says He is coming to judge the world at the end of time. Now let us get this clear . . . I'm trying here to prevent anyone from saying the really silly thing that people often say about Him: "I'm ready to accept Jesus as a great moral teacher, but I don't accept His claim to be God." That's the one thing we mustn't say. A man who was merely a man and said the sort of things Jesus said wouldn't be a great moral teacher. He'd either be a lunatic—on the level with the man who says he's a poached egg—or else he'd be the Devil of Hell.
>
> You must make your choice. Either this man was, and is the Son of God; or else a madman or something worse. You can shut Him up for a fool, you can spit at Him and kill Him as a demon; or you can fall at His feet and call Him Lord and God. But don't let us come with any patronising nonsense about His being a great human teacher. He hasn't left that open to us. He didn't intend to.

THE PRERESURRECTION
WITNESS TO JESUS

In the previous chapter we investigated whether Jesus understood Himself to be and in fact claimed to be the Messiah the Old Testament had promised. We found a great deal of evidence supporting the classic Christian insistence that He did, and that, in the process of doing so, He claimed to be divine as well.

Now we turn to the larger New Testament witness and will consider in this and the following chapters other major lines of testimony on the basis of which the Christian church confessed, with Jesus, from the beginning that He is the Messiah, and both God and man (*vere Deus vere homo*) and thus God incarnate. In this chapter, we will consider preresurrection testimony (assuming for the present the fact of Jesus' resurrection), presenting it under five heads: the nativity accounts, the baptism accounts, the temptation accounts, the transfiguration accounts, and the disciples' understanding of Jesus.

Testimony From the Nativity Accounts
Luke 1:17, 76: "before Him," "before the Lord"
The word-revelation aspect of the Old Testament epoch had come to a close with the prophetic word of Malachi holding forth the promise of the two (related) comings (1) of the Lord's "forerunner" (whom Yahweh describes both as "My messenger who will prepare the way *before Me*" [3:1a] and "the prophet Elijah" [4:5]) and (2) of the Lord of Hosts Himself (who describes Himself as "the Lord [אדון] you are seeking" and "the Messenger of the covenant" [3:1]). Four hundred years of revelatory silence then ensued, finally broken by the angel Gabriel announcing to Zechariah, according to Luke 1:11-17,[1] that he and his barren wife Elizabeth would have a son in their old age.

---

1. Cf. J. Gresham Machen (*The Virgin Birth of Christ*, 2nd ed. [London: James Clarke and Co.,

What is remarkable about this first revelatory disclosure of the New Testament age is that embedded in Gabriel's description of the child's future ministry are the words, "And he will go *before Him* in the spirit and power of Elijah" (1:17), clearly a compressed allusion to both Malachi 3:1a and 4:5, words with which the revelatory aspect of the Old Testament epoch had concluded, marking out John the Baptist as the promised forerunner of the Lord. The word-revelation aspect of the New Testament epoch, in other words, begins precisely where the Old Testament word-revelation aspect had terminated. From the New Testament perspective, all of history now stood on the brink of its most stupendous moment—the Lord of Hosts Himself was about to make His long-promised coming a space-time reality.

To whom do the words "before Him" (ἐνώπιον αὐτοῦ) in 1:17 refer? Possibly their referent is "the Lord their God" in Luke 1:16, referring then simply to God in the unspecified totality of His majestic being and not necessarily to the Messiah directly. Inasmuch as the phrase "the Lord their God" is the closest possible antecedent, a case can be made for this interpretation. But the "Elijah-forerunner," who we are now informed was John the Baptist, was to be the forerunner of the Lord of Hosts (אָדוֹן and יהוה צבאות) who was Himself to "come to His temple" (Mal. 3:1, and Zechariah later says of his son John that he was to be the "prophet of the Most High . . . [who] shall go before the Lord [ἐνώπιον κυρίου] to prepare His way" (Luke 1:76; again an allusion to Mal. 3:1a). It is much more likely, then, that by his words "before Him" Gabriel referred to the One before whom John actually went in the temporal sense, whose coming he actually announced, namely, the Messiah.

If this is so, and it certainly is the most natural implication of the words of 1:76,[2] then inasmuch as the reference to "the Lord" in the Lukan passages alludes to the God of the Malachi prophecy who is just Yahweh Himself

---

1932], pp. 44-61) for his valuable demonstration that Luke 1:5–2:52, which he describes as "probably the most markedly Semitic section of the whole New Testament" (p. 46) and "a strikingly Jewish and indeed Palestinian narrative" (p. 62), is an original part of Luke's Gospel. His defense of the textual integrity of the Lucan birth narratives (pp. 119-68), particularly 1:34-35, is still unparalleled though naturally dated somewhat by the passage of time. I. Howard Marshall's defense of 1:5-25 (*The Gospel of Luke* [Exeter: Paternoster Press, 1978], pp. 50-51), although it moves in the same direction, is, in my opinion, too cautious and not to be preferred over Machen's defense. The latter's book is still one of the best on the subject anywhere in print. I would also highly recommend Robert G. Gromacki's *The Virgin Birth: Doctrine of Deity* (Grand Rapids: Baker, 1974).

2. F. Godet's comment on 1:76 (*A Commentary on the Gospel of St. Luke*, vol. 1, 5th ed. [Edinburgh: T. & T. Clark, 1870], p. 114) is pertinent: "In saying *the Lord* Zacharias can only be thinking of the Messiah . . . but he could not designate Him by this name, unless, with Malachi, he recognized in His coming the appearing of Jehovah."

who, as "the Lord you are seeking" speaks of His own coming that will follow the coming of "my messenger who will prepare the way before me" (Mal. 3:1a), it follows that we are given here in the very first revelatory disclosure of the New Testament era a clear intimation of Jesus' identity as Yahweh incarnate. This conclusion receives additional support from (1) Gabriel's announcement to Mary, which follows immediately (1:30-37), (2) Elizabeth's greeting (1:43), and (3) the angel's announcement to the shepherds (2:11).

Luke 1:30-37: Gabriel's Announcement to Mary

In connection with the first of these, the support to which I refer comes in a threefold form: *first*, in the name Mary is instructed to give her Son (1:31; Matt. 1:21); *second*, in the fact of Jesus' virginal conception itself (1:34-35); and *third*, in the two titles Mary's Son would bear (1:32, 35).

Luke 1:31; Matthew 1:21: The Name "Jesus." Mary was instructed to name her Son "Jesus." Although Luke does not draw attention to its significance, Matthew does (1:21). (It can hardly be the case, however, that Luke was unaware of its significance since he alone of the Synoptic Evangelists employs σωτήρ ["Savior"] as a christological title [2:11].) Matthew records that Joseph was instructed to name Mary's Son "Jesus, for He will save His people from their sin." According to W. Foerster, the name "Jesus" in its full form is a "sentence name, in which the subject comes first and represents a form of the divine name יהוה, and in which the verb is a subsidiary form of the verb ישע which . . . means 'to help.'"[3] "Jesus" means then "Yahweh saves" and its essence is captured by Luke's "Savior." This in itself does not need to mean that the one who bears this name is identical with Yahweh; others bore the name under the Old Testament economy to symbolize the fact that Yahweh was at work in the salvation of His people. But I suggest that in Jesus' case we should understand that it connotes more than a mere symbol, inasmuch as

> some intimation of the identity between Jehovah and the Messiah seems to be contained in the words of the angel (Matt. 1:21). Here the name Jesus, to be given to the child, is understood in its etymological sense: "Jehovah is Salvation." . . . Jesus bears the name . . . because He (Jesus) saves His (Jesus') people from their sins. We have, therefore,

3. W. Foerster, "Ἰησοῦς," *Theological Dictionary of the New Testament*, ed. G. Kittel, vol. 3 (Grand Rapids: Eerdmans, 1965), p. 289.

in close succession the statements, that Jehovah is salvation, and that Jesus saves, that Israel (Jehovah's people) are Jesus' people.[4]

The suggestion is quite strong, then, because of this close succession of ideas and particularly because of the pronoun "His" in the expression "*His* people," that this "Jesus" who saves *His* people is just Yahweh Himself. Agreeing with this interpretation, Warfield writes:

> Here [in Matt. 1:21] [the simple name "Jesus"] is represented as itself a gift from heaven, designed to indicate that in this person is fulfilled the promise that Jehovah shall visit His people,—for it is He [Jesus] who, in accordance with the prediction of the Psalmist (130:8), shall save His people—*His* people, although, in accordance with that prediction, they are Jehovah's people—from their sins.[5]

When one adds to this compelling data first the fact that Yahweh again and again in the Old Testament declares that He alone is Israel's "Savior" (Isa. 43:3, 11; 45:21; 49:26; 60:16; Hos. 13:4; cf. 1 Sam. 10:19; 14:39; 2 Sam. 22:3; Pss. 7:10; 17:7; 106:21; Isa. 45:15; 63:8; Jer. 14:8) and then the fact that Jesus is often declared (along with God the Father) to be "the Savior" in the New Testament (Luke 2:11; John 4:42; Acts 5:31; 13:23; Eph. 5:23; Phil. 3:20; 1 Tim. 4:10; 2 Tim. 1:10; Titus 1:4; 2:13; 3:6; 2 Pet. 1:1, 11; 2:20; 3:2, 18; 1 John 4:14), it is difficult to avoid the conclusion that when Jesus was named "Yahweh saves," the name connoted more than merely that He stood as one more in the long line of "saviors" (cf. Judg. 3:9, 15; 6:36; 2 Kings 13:5; Neh. 9:27). Rather His name meant that in Him, as Himself Yahweh incarnate, the line of "saviors" had now been consummated in a transcendent manner. If

---

4. Geerhardus Vos, *Biblical Theology* (Grand Rapids: Eerdmans, 1948), pp. 331-32. He also writes:

> The very words of the annunciation in 1:21 suggest the Deity of the child, in the form of equivalence to Jehovah. Of course the appointment of the name Jesus—"Jehovah is salvation"—does not of itself affirm this, for as before under the Old Covenant, so now also the name might have been borne by the child as a standing witness to the fact that Jehovah is salvation, without thereby meaning that the child is Jehovah. In reality, however, the context here makes the situation far more concrete than would be the case under general circumstances. When after the appointment of a name meaning "Jehovah is salvation" there is immediately added the explanatory statement, "For it is he that shall save his people from their sins," no other interpretation remains possible than that Jesus will function as Jehovah, and that this truth is conveyed by His name. Still even this does not go to the extent of putting the close identification with God in the form of Jesus' being the Son of God. It is not rash to infer, however, that this latter lay actually in the mind of the Evangelist, since it is hard to tell how he could have conceived the identification in "saving" with Jehovah on any other principle than that of sonship (*The Self-Disclosure of Jesus* [1926; reprint, Phillipsburg, N.J.: Presbyterian and Reformed, 1978], p. 182).

5. Benjamin B. Warfield, *The Lord of Glory* (reprint, Grand Rapids: Baker, 1974), p. 91.

there is some lingering doubt that this is an appropriate deduction to draw, it should be dispelled as we consider the next aspect of the angel's announcement to Mary—namely, the momentous fact that this One, so named, was to be *virginally* conceived. What are the implications of this for our present purpose?

Luke 1:34-35; Matthew 1:18-25: The Virginal Conception of Jesus. In the words of Machen, "It is perfectly clear that the New Testament teaches the virgin birth of Christ; about that there can be no manner of doubt. There is no serious question as to the *interpretation* of the Bible at this point."[6] Clear indications that the Bible teaches the doctrine of Jesus' virginal conception are found in Isaiah 7:14 ("the virgin will be with child"), Matthew 1:16 ("out of *whom* [fem.] was born Jesus"), 1:18 ("before they came together, she was found to be with child through the Holy Spirit), 1:20 ("that which has been begotten in her is through the Holy Spirit"), 1:22-23 ("All this happened in order that [ἵνα] the utterance [τὸ ῥηθὲν] of the Lord through the prophet might be fulfilled: 'Behold, the virgin will be with child, and shall bear a son, and they shall call His name "Immanuel" '—which means, 'God is with us' "), 1:25 ("He knew her not until she gave birth to a son"), Luke 1:27 ("to a virgin . . . and the virgin's name was Mary"), 1:34 ("How shall this be, since I know not a man?"), 1:35 ("The Holy Spirit will come upon you, even the Power of the Most High will overshadow you. Wherefore, the One to be born will be called holy—[after all, He is] the Son of God"), and 3:23 ("being the son, so it was supposed, of Joseph"). The reader is also referred to (1) Mary's musings in Luke 2:19 and 2:51b; (2) the snide intimations that something (illegitimacy?) was unusual about His birth in Mark 6:3, when compared with its parallels in Matthew 13:55 and Luke 4:22, as well as in the suggestions of John 8:41 and 9:29; and (3) Paul's "made of a woman" reference in Galatians 4:4. In light of this biblical data, the most indisputable fact about the tradition respecting Jesus' conception is that it occurred out of wedlock—we have, in other words, either a virginal conception or an illegitimate conception. And the Bible clearly endorses the former as the ground of the rumors of the latter.

We must acknowledge that only two New Testament writers—Matthew and Luke—directly mention the virginal conception of Jesus, but then they are the only two to record His birth at all. As to whether other New Testament writers knew of His virginal conception, it certainly seems likely that Paul, working as closely as he did with Luke and being familiar with

6. Machen, *Virgin Birth of Christ*, p. 382.

Luke's Gospel as he was (cf. 1 Tim. 5:18 and Luke 10:7), would have known about it. And it is also most likely that John, writing his Gospel after Matthew and Luke, would have known about it as well. He certainly understood that "the Word became flesh" (1:14) by human birth (19:37) and that He had a human mother (2:1; 19:25). And in the light of his recurring statements that Jesus "came from above," "came down from heaven," "came into the world," and "was sent by the Father," John would have had to believe that some form of supernatural intervention intruded itself at the point of Jesus' human conception if all of the features he reports about Jesus are to be harmonized. This much is clear: *No New Testament writer says anything to contradict the Matthean and Lukan testimony.*

Furthermore, on how the church has understood the Matthean and Lukan birth narratives, there is no doubt that Jesus' literal virginal conception has been uniformly seen in them, as evidenced by the united testimonies of Irenaeus (Asia Minor and Gaul), Ignatius (Antioch of Syria), Tertullian (North Africa), Justin Martyr (Ephesus and Rome), and the Old Roman Baptismal Symbol in the second century[7] right down through the great creeds of the church to the present day (cf. the Apostles' Creed; the present "Nicene Creed"; the Definition of Chalcedon; the so-called "Athanasian Creed" [*homo est ex substantia matris,* that is, "He is man from the substance (nature) of His mother"]; the *Augsburg Confession,* Article III; the *Belgic Confession,* Article XVIII; the *Westminster Confession of Faith,* Chapter VIII; and the *Thirty-Nine Articles,* Article II). The suggestion of some modern scholars that Matthew (in particular) was writing "midrash" (the expansion and embellishment of actual history with the "nonhistorical") is simply unproven. There is, in fact, a real question whether midrash was a common literary genre at the time when Matthew wrote. At any rate, the early church fathers did not understand Matthew's birth narrative as a midrash. So when men like E. Brunner and W. Pannenberg, whatever their reasons and however well-intentioned they be, deny the fact of the virginal conception of Jesus, it is not only the New Testament witness but also the consistent, universal testimony of the church that they reject—no small departure from Christian doctrine on the part of any man. For myself, I accept the fact of the virginal conception of Jesus[8] and am simply concerned here to draw out its

7. For specific references in the writings of these early Fathers, cf. ibid., pp. 2-43 (chap. 1, "The Virgin Birth in the Second Century"). There were, of course, some sects that dismissed the story of Christ's virginal conception (the Jewish Ebionites, the heretic Marcion), but they clearly understood what the birth narratives intended to report, namely, history and not myth.

8. My reasons for believing in Christ's virginal conception in the womb of Mary through the power of the Holy Spirit are as follows: In addition to the *biblical* teaching, which, of course, is

implications for the nature of Jesus' person. Given His virginal conception, what was its purpose relative to Jesus Himself?

We begin our answer to this question by underscoring two things that we must not say its purpose was.

1. We must not understand the birth narratives as teaching that Mary's virginal conception of Jesus through the power of the Holy Spirit was the efficient cause or source of His deity. Vos quite properly declares that while "there is truth in the close connection established between the virgin birth of our Lord and His Deity," it would be "a mistake to suspend the Deity on the virgin birth as its ultimate source or reason." To do so "would lead to a lowering of the idea of Deity itself."[9] What we mean to highlight here is the obvious fact that "neither sinful nor holy human parents could produce an offspring *who is God*. That is beyond their humanity. And neither could a virgin human mother do this!"[10] If our understanding of New Testament

paramount, and the weight of the church's *historical* testimony, which I reviewed in a cursory way above, there is the *Christian theistic* reason: Jesus' virginal conception is simply one aspect of the total supernaturalism of Scripture and of Christian theism in general; if one can believe, for example, Gen. 1:1, or that God speaks to men in Scripture, or in Jesus' miracles, or that He rose from the dead and ascended to His Father, it is asking very little more to believe that Jesus was virginally conceived. There is also the *psychological* reason: only the virginal conception can explain Mary's willingness to be included in the company of those who *worshiped* Jesus as the Son *of God* (Acts 1:14); it taxes one's credulity to accept that Mary could have believed that her Son died for her sins and was her *divine* Savior deserving of her worship if she knew in her heart that His origin was like that of every other man. There are the *theological* reasons: (1) the virginal conception of Jesus is the Bible's explanation for the Incarnation, and (2) while the virginal conception is not necessarily the total explanation for Jesus' sinlessness, it is a fact that if Jesus had been the offspring of the union of a human father and mother, such a natural generation would have entailed depravity (John 3:6) and implicated Jesus in Adam's first sin (Rom. 5:12, 19). Finally, there are the *apologetic* or *polemical* reasons: (1) if Jesus was not virginally conceived, then the Bible is in error and ceases to be a trustworthy guide in matters of faith (cf. ibid., pp. 382-87); (2) if Jesus was not virginally conceived, serious gaps are left in any effort to understand the person of Christ and the Incarnation (ibid., 387-95); and (3) if Jesus was conceived like all other men, then He stood under the Adamic curse like the rest of those who descend from Adam by natural generation, as we have already noted, and this in turn means that He would not have been an acceptable Savior of men before God. But this would mean in turn the end of Christianity as the religion of redemption of men from their sins since there would then be no one who could offer himself up to God as an acceptable, unblemished sacrifice to satisfy divine justice and to reconcile God to man. I fully realize that this last point assumes a particular doctrine of sin ("original and race sin") and a particular view of the atonement ("satisfaction"); but then the Bible teaches this doctrine of sin (Rom. 5:12-19), and Jesus accomplished that kind of atonement by His sinless life and substitutionary death on the cross. The reader is referred to Warfield's brief but magnificent article, "The Supernatural Birth of Jesus" (*Biblical and Theological Studies* [Philadelphia: Presbyterian and Reformed, 1952], pp. 157-68), for further argument in behalf of the salvific necessity of the virgin birth of Christ.

9. Vos, *Self-Disclosure of Jesus*, p. 191 n. 15.

10. Kenneth S. Kantzer, "The Miracle of Christmas," *Christianity Today* 28, no. 18 (December 14, 1984): 15.

Christology is correct, another ground exists for believing that Jesus Christ is God, namely, that as God the Son, He was God prior to and apart from His virginal conception. So we say again, His virginal conception in Mary's womb must not be viewed as the ultimate cause or source of His deity. Nor did the virginal conception, we must say in this same connection, produce a hybrid or a sort of demi-god, an offspring of the union between God (the Holy Spirit) and a human woman, who was neither fully God nor fully man but only half-God and half-man. This is simply mythology for which there is *no* scriptural warrant. Another purpose, as we hope to show, underlay the virginal conception of Jesus.

2. The virginal conception of Jesus by Mary through the power of the Holy Spirit was probably not the efficient cause of Jesus' sinlessness (cf. 2 Cor. 5:21; Heb. 4:15). At least, it is most unlikely as some have espoused, that Jesus' virginal conception was essential to His sinlessness because "original [or race] sin" is transmitted through the *male* line. Women, as well as men, share in the sinfulness of the human race and are corrupted by it, and this pervasive sinfulness encompassed Mary as well, who possessed a sinful nature, committed sins, and confessed her need of a Savior (Luke 1:47). All the biblical, not to mention the biological, evidence suggests that the woman contributes equally to the total physical, spiritual, and psychic make-up of the human offspring that comes from natural generation. It is striking, for example, that in his great penitential psalm, David specifically mentions his mother when he traces his sinful deed back to his sinful nature: "With sin," he declares, "did my *mother* conceive me" (51:5). There is reason to assume, therefore, that except for a special divine work of preservation beyond the virginal conception itself, Mary would have transmitted the human bent to sin to her firstborn. John Calvin was even willing to assert as much:

> We make Christ free of all stain not just because he was begotten of his mother without copulation with man, but because he was sanctified by the Spirit that the generation might be pure and undefiled as would have been true before Adam's fall.[11]

Luke 1:35, to be discussed in a moment, also suggests as much, if we construe ἅγιον ("holy") as a predicate and understand it in the moral/ethical sense. John Murray also entertains the same possibility, although with a certain degree of discretionary reserve:

11. John Calvin, *Institutes of the Christian Religion,* trans. Ford Lewis Battles (Philadelphia: Westminster Press, 1960), II. 13. 4; p. 481.

[Jesus' preservation from defilement] may reside entirely in the supernatural begetting, for it may be that depravity is conveyed in natural generation. [Note that he does not place the transmission of racial sin in the male line *per se* here but rather in the "natural generation" that involves the union of male *and* female.] In any case, natural generation would have entailed depravity (John 3:6). Yet it may not be correct to find the whole explanation of Jesus' sinlessness in the absence of natural begetting. So it may well be that preservation from the stain of sin (cf. Psalm 51:5) required another, supernatural factor, namely, the preservation from conception to birth of the infant Jesus from the contamination that would otherwise have proceeded from his human mother.[12]

Obviously, great care should be expended in any explanation of the ground of Jesus' sinlessness. But until we know a great deal more than we do about natural generation and human reproduction, we would be wise to refrain from suspending Jesus' sinlessness simply and solely on the obvious fact that in the virginal conception the male factor had been eliminated in His human generation. In any event, it seems quite safe to say, even if Jesus' sinlessness is an indirect effect of the virginal conception, that His sinlessness was not the effect that His virginal conception was primarily intended to bring about.

What then was the primary purpose of Jesus' virginal conception? Before I respond directly, I would note that Jesus' conception in a *human* mother's womb, although virginal in nature, was followed by His normal development in that human mother's womb and His altogether normal passage from that human womb into the world, as recorded in both Matthew and Luke. These features of His human origination insure and guarantee to us that Jesus was and is truly and fully human. The Bible is quite adamant that Jesus' full and true humanity was in no way threatened or impaired by the miracle of His virginal conception, but just to the contrary, by being conceived by a human mother He "shared" our humanity (Heb.2:14) and was "like" us in every way (Heb. 2:17). To the objection of some, that a virginal conception precludes at the outset the possibility of our Lord being truly and fully man, I say that such an objection is hypothetical and indemonstrable.

When we then penetrate to the mysterious and marvelous primary purpose of the Christmas miracle, we must conclude that both Evangelists intend that we understand *before everything else* that, by means of the virginal

12. John Murray, *Collected Writings*, vol. 2 (Edinburgh: Banner of Truth Trust, 1977), p. 135; cf. also James Oliver Buswell, *A Systematic Theology of the Christian Religion* (Grand Rapids: Zondervan, 1962), 1:251; 2:57.

conception, "the [preexistent] Word *became flesh*" (John 1:14)! Mary's virginal conception, in other words, was the means whereby *God became man,* the means whereby He who "was rich for our sakes became poor, that through His poverty, we might become rich" (2 Cor. 8:9). It is the Bible's answer to the question that naturally arises in men's minds as soon as they learn that Jesus Christ is the God-man: "How did this occur?" The virginal conception is the effecting means of the "Immanuel event" (Isa. 7:14; Matt. 1:22-23), which made God man with us, without uniting the Son of God to a second (human) person, which would have surely been the effect of a *natural* generation. But by means of Mary's virginal conception, God the Son, without ceasing to be what He is—the eternal Son and Word of God—took into union with His divine nature in the one divine person of the Son our *human nature* (not a *human person*) and so came to be "with us" as "Immanuel." Any other suggested purpose for the virginal conception of Jesus as reported in the Matthean and Lukan birth stories, whatever truth it may contain, pales into insignificance in the glorious light of this clear reason. And when this is clearly perceived, we acknowledge that the Matthean and Lukan birth narratives take their rightful place along with the other lines of evidence in the New Testament—grander no doubt than some—for the deity of Jesus Christ and thus for the classical doctrine of an incarnational Christology.

Luke 1:32, 35: The Two Titles Jesus Is to Bear. Many scholars today argue that the pericope in which the first of these two titles is found (1:26-33) and the one in which the second is found (1:34-37) represent two oral traditions, the second being an interpolation, either by Luke or by an earlier hand, introducing the virginal conception motif into an earlier story. This is highly unlikely. As we noted in our first footnote to this chapter, Machen defended, first, the birth narrative as an original part of Luke's Gospel; second, its genuinely primitive and Palestinian character; and third, the textual integrity of the Lukan birth narrative as a whole. I. Howard Marshall has more recently demonstrated, from an analysis of the two purported traditions, the high probability of the narrative's unity against the views of such scholars as G. Schneider and J. Geweiss.[13] I will proceed to the exposition accordingly, with the assumption that Gabriel's announcement is an original and single unit, reflecting accurate, authentic information Luke acquired, probably from Mary herself, in the course of investigating the evidence to compose his Gospel (cf. 1:1-4).

13. Marshall, *Gospel of Luke,* p. 63.

The two titles Gabriel employs descriptively of Mary's offspring are "the Son of the Highest" (1:32) and "the Son of God" (1:35), titles obviously intended as virtual equivalents. Scholars of all theological persuasions commonly hold that both should be understood in this context in the nativistic sense, that is to say, that Jesus "will be called" (that is, "will be") "the Son of the Highest" and "the Son of God" *because* the origin of His human nature is directly traceable to a *paternal* act on the part of God. In other words, with respect to Jesus' humanity, while Mary was to be His mother, God was to be His "Father," and accordingly Jesus was to be "the Son of God." Luke 1:35, in fact, is cited more than any other New Testament verse as biblical support for this nativistic sense of the title in Scripture. (It is virtually the only verse that *can* be cited in support of Jesus' "nativistic" sonship.[14]).

But it seems altogether inadequate to suggest that the significance of the title in 1:32 is exhausted by a nativistic sonship, if it is even present at all, given that (1) the birth is not connected with the title as the causal explanation of the title,[15] and (2) the virginal conception had as its primary purpose the marvelous design of enfleshing the eternal Son of God. There is simply no evidence in the context of 1:32 to warrant the conclusion that the title is to be construed in the so-called nativistic sense.

The διὸ καὶ (literally, "because of which also") in 1:35 might appear to bring the Child's supernatural conception into causal connection with His "Son of God" title. But does it? Did Gabriel mean at least here, if not in 1:32, insofar as this specific announcement is concerned, that Mary's offspring "would be called" (that is, "would be") "the Son of God" because of God's "fatherly" act in effecting His virginal conception—that the significance of the title, in other words, at least in this context, is exhausted by His nativistic

---

14. Cf., for example, Vos, *Self-Disclosure of Jesus*, pp. 142, 209; and L. Berkhof, *Systematic Theology* (Grand Rapids: Eerdmans, 1941), p. 92. A number of modern scholars, including Zahn, Blass, Loisy, R. Seeberg, and Burney, in addition to Vos and Berkhof, also cite John 1:13 in support of the nativistic sense of Jesus' sonship, but this interpretation of John 1:13 seems forced. The singular ("he who was born") is a very poorly attested reading, while the plural ("who were born") is attested by all the Greek manuscripts as well as the versions and most patristic witnesses.

15. Vos explains the absence of a connection between Mary's bearing a son and Jesus' being called "the Son of the Highest" on the ground that "in the first greeting the mode of birth is not yet defined as supernatural, it simply being stated that she has found grace with God, and will conceive and bear a son" (*Self-Disclosure of Jesus*, pp. 182-83). But this suggestion is not very convincing. The motif of a supernatural birth is clearly present in the allusions in 1:31 to the virginal conception of Isa. 7:14 and in 1:32 to the divine Son of Isa. 9:6-7. It is precisely the implicit suggestion of an irregularity about the birth in 1:31 that provokes the question that Mary, as a virgin (1:27, 34), asks. Besides, there was nothing to prevent Gabriel, who certainly was aware that the birth was to be supernatural, from making the causal connection between the birth and the title in this context if such a connection existed.

sonship? I suggest not; indeed the title is not directly related to the διὸ καὶ at all, for two reasons.

First, the christological title, "the Son of God," most uniformly designates Jesus in His essential relationship to the Father, and His claim to be "the Son of God" in this sense became, in fact, the ground of His enemies' charge of blasphemy against Him in all four Gospels (Matt. 26:63-66; Mark 14:61-64; Luke 22:69-71; John 10:33-39; 19:7). But mention of the *Father* is conspicuously absent in both the Matthean and Lukan birth accounts as the divine person effecting the miraculous conception. Rather, both Evangelists uniformly trace the virginal conception to the activity or agency of the Holy Spirit (cf. Matt. 1:18, 20; Luke 1:35;[16] *N.B.:* the words in 1:35, "the Power of the Highest," placed as they are in synonymous parallelism with "the Holy Spirit," denote a *title* of the Holy Spirit and not a reference to the creative power of the Father). In other words, Scripture uniformly represents Jesus' virginal conception as a miracle wrought by the Holy Spirit. If one person of the Godhead rather than another is to be regarded as the "father" of Jesus in the nativistic sense, it would seem that it should be the Holy Spirit, with Jesus in turn to be regarded, again in the nativistic sense, as the Son of the Holy Spirit. But such a representation of the matter is out of accord with the uniform representation of Jesus as "the Son of God," that is, as the Son of the Father.[17] Therefore, precisely because the Father's activity is absent in the birth accounts, I urge this as the first reason for understanding "the Son of God" in 1:35 in a sense other than the so-called nativistic one.

Second, there is a syntactical reason to question whether "the Son of God" phrase is the predicate of "will be called." Κληθήσεται ("will be called"), the future passive of καλέω, when introducing a title or description (but not a proper name), regularly *follows* in word order the predicate (cf. Matt. 2:23; 5:19 [twice]; 21:13; Mark 11:12; Luke 1:32, 76; 2:23; cf. Matt. 5:9; Rom. 9:7; Heb. 11:18). But in 1:35 it *precedes* the title of "the Son of God" (cf. the punctuation in *The Greek New Testament* [UBS], RV, RSV, NEBmg, NIVmg). This strongly suggests that the anarthrous ἅγιον ("holy"), which κληθήσεται does follow in word order, is alone the predicate, underscoring what we suggested earlier—namely, that through the Holy Spirit's sanctify-

16. It is true that the words "Holy Spirit" appear anarthrously each time they occur in these verses, but this fact means nothing. C. F. D. Moule writes, "It seems to me rather forced to interpret the anarthrous uses [of πνεῦμα ἅγιον] (e.g., in the Gospels) as uniformly meaning something less than *God's Holy Spirit"* (*An Idiom Book of New Testament Greek* [Cambridge: University Press, 1970], pp. 112-13).

17. Cf. Kantzer: "Jesus Christ is not the son of the Holy Spirit as to his humanity. Rather, Jesus Christ, with respect to his humanity, *had no father.* We have here no mythological mating of a divine being with a human mother" ("Miracle of Christmas," p. 15; emphasis added).

ing influence the Child would be preserved from all defilement from sin while in the womb—and intimating that the title following the verb is the ultimate reason for His being preserved "holy"—"[After all, He is] the Son of God!"[18] By this construction, the title "the Son of God" would not describe what He would become (or be) as the result of the virginal conception but rather would specify the ultimate reason for His humanity being preserved from sin's defilement from the moment of His conception to the time of His birth—because it was the eternal Son of God who was taking otherwise sinful flesh into union with Himself. Accordingly, I urge that the title in 1:35, as in 1:32, does not refer to what He would be by virtue of His virginal conception; rather, it speaks of His personal and eternal relationship to the Father in the trinitarian sense. In my opinion, this accords more nearly with the central message of the angel: his announcement of the staggering, *ultimate* aim of the virginal conception, namely, the effecting of the incarnation itself, not the creating of a man-child through supernatural agency. Consequently, I maintain that these two titles, properly interpreted, are designations of Jesus' divine sonship, and as such, should be allowed to add their testimony to the New Testament's incarnational teaching.

Luke 1:43: Elizabeth's Greeting

Having been informed by Gabriel, as a confirmation that God can do the impossible (1:36-37), that her relative Elizabeth would bear a child in her old age, Mary hurried to Elizabeth's home in the hill country of Judea and greeted her older relative. At her greeting, the unborn John leaped in his mother's womb for joy—"the beginning of John's witness to Jesus" (1:41, 44).[19] Elizabeth, responding under prophetic inspiration from the Holy Spirit (1:41), exclaimed, "Blessed are you above all other women, and blessed is the Child you bear! Why has this high favor been granted to me, that the mother of my Lord should come to me?" (1:42, 43).

The high evaluation Elizabeth places on Mary she makes entirely dependent upon the nature of the One Mary carries in her womb, as indicated by her description of Mary as the mother of "my Lord." That Elizabeth is speaking by divine illumination (1:41) when she addresses Mary follows from the fact that nothing had been said to her previously respecting the momentous thing that had happened to her young relative. In fact, apart

18. Cf. Buswell (*Systematic Theology*, vol. 1, p. 106) for the suggestion that the proper translation of Luke 1:35 is "that which is born will be called holy. [He is] the Son of God."
19. Marshall, *Gospel of Luke*, p. 77.

from divine illumination, she had no way of knowing Mary was even pregnant, if indeed at that moment she was.

Elizabeth calls Jesus here "my Lord" (τοῦ κυρίου μου). Speaking most likely in Aramaic or Hebrew, she probably actually described Him as מָארִי, or as אֲדֹנִי. But assuming that Luke's κύριος captures the dynamic essence of her word, it is hardly likely that she intended to ascribe to Mary's unborn infant simply Messianic status and sovereignty (this, even so, would carry divine implications, as we have seen). Rather, it is virtually certain that she intended more: Zechariah had doubtless instructed her (through writing) what name would be given her own son (cf. 1:13, 60); he most likely also informed her that John was to be the Elijah-forerunner of the אֲדוֹן of Malachi 3:1, of Yahweh Himself, as Zechariah expressly states later (1:76). So under the Holy Spirit's illumination, she immediately perceived through the sign of John's leaping in her womb for joy that Mary's Son was "the Lord" before whom her own son would go to prepare His way. Furthermore, it is doubtful, to say the least, from Luke's repeated employment of κύριος to denote the Deity throughout his account of Jesus' birth (cf. 1:6, 9, 11, 15, 16, 17, 25, 28, 32, 38, 45, 46, 58, 66, 68, 76; 2:9 [twice], 11, 15, 22, 23 [twice], 24, 26, 39) that he could have failed to realize that this is the meaning his readers would most naturally attach to the word he put in Elizabeth's mouth.

When all these features of Luke's narrative are taken into account, it appears that Elizabeth intended, certainly not the veneration of Mary (which is where modern Roman Catholicism inappropriately places the emphasis), but the ascription of deity to Mary's Son with special emphasis on the lordship intrinsic to that deity.

Luke 2:11: The Angel's Announcement to the Shepherds[20]

Addressing the shepherds in the Judean fields on the night of our Lord's birth, the angel of the Lord (Gabriel perhaps; cf. 2:9 with 1:11, 19, 26) declared, "Today in the town of David a Savior has been born to you, who is Christ the Lord" (2:11). There are some textual variants to the *hapax* "Christ [the] Lord" (Χριστὸς κύριος), but Metzger explains, "It was to be expected that copyists, struck by the unusual collocation [instead of the more frequent Χριστὸς κυρίου—"the Lord's Messiah" (cf., for example, Luke 2:26)],

---

20. For a defense of the integrity of Luke 2:1-20 as an original *Christian* story and not an adaptation of a pre-Christian legend, cf. Machen, *Virgin Birth of Christ*, pp. 317-79, particularly pp. 348-63, and Marshall, *Gospel of Luke*, p. 97.

should have introduced various modifications, none of which has significant external attestation."[21] The phrase does, in fact, then, intend to describe the newborn Savior as "the Messiah [and] the Lord" or as "the Messiah [who is] the Lord."

What is the meaning of κύριος ("[the] Lord")? Some scholars suggest that κύριος is merely a Lukan elucidation of "Messiah" to aid non-Jewish readers, but two contextual features make it more likely that κύριος, as the climactic term in the angel's description of Jesus, was used to *add* significantly to the meaning of the person designated Χριστός. If this is so, since "Christ" already entails kingly sovereignty and overtones of deity, what remains to be added can hardly be anything other than the direct ascription of deity to the Messiah. What are these two considerations?

First, the angel, it should be carefully noted, describes the newborn Savior, not as "Christ *your* Lord," but as "Christ, [the] Lord"—the Sovereign, in other words, not just of men but of angels as well, "for it is an angel who speaks these words."[22] This feature of the angel's declaration— that this One is the Lord in the unqualified sense of Sovereign over both men *and* angels—ascribes a dignity superseding even the dignity of the angels to the Savior-Messiah, which is just to say that "the adjunction of 'Lord' is intended to convey the intelligence that the 'Christ' now born is a divine Christ."[23]

Second, we must not overlook the fact that Luke employs κύριος three times in this very context, referring to Yahweh (2:9: ἄγγελος κυρίου—"an angel of the Lord," and δόξα κυρίου—"the glory of the Lord"; 2:15: ὅ ὁ κύριος ἐγνώρισεν "which the Lord made known"). As we said earlier, it is difficult, if not impossible, to believe that Luke would not have realized, if he or the angel had actually intended something less than deity by this term, that his readers would nonetheless make a connection between his references to the angel of *the Lord* and the glory of *the Lord*, on the one hand, and Christ *the Lord*, on the other, and would ascribe such superangelic majesty and glory to Christ by this connection as to justify an assessment of Him rising to the level of just deity itself as His essential character. Not only would his readers make this connection and draw this conclusion, but I submit that the angel (and/or Luke) intended they should. This view alone comports with the *aim* and *end* of the virginal conception itself, which in this very context is brought to its consummation—namely, the bringing of the

21. Bruce M. Metzger, *A Textual Commentary on the Greek New Testament* (New York: United Bible Societies, 1971), p. 132.

22. Warfield, *Lord of Glory*, p. 108.

23. Ibid., p. 144.

God-man into the world. Can any lesser meaning be attached to this word κύριος and still do justice to the miraculous and unique character of the birth event itself? I think not.

In the preceding pages we have discussed the pertinent passages in the nativity stories that affirm the deity of Christ and the fact of the incarnation. We have demonstrated that Matthew and Luke intended their readers to learn that Jesus was Yahweh incarnate, the One before whom John, His "Elijah-forerunner," was to go temporally as the "preparer of His way." This same block of material also highlights that the two Evangelists also intended their readers to learn that Jesus, as God incarnate, is also the promised Messiah. This is clear from the following passages:

1. Luke 1:32-33, in which Gabriel declared that "the Lord God will give Him the throne of His father David, and He will reign over the house of Jacob forever; His kingdom will never end";

2. Mary's song (Luke 1:46-55), in which Mary affirmed that God "has helped His servant Israel, remembering to be merciful to Abraham and his descendants forever, even as He said to our fathers";

3. Zechariah's song (Luke 1:68-76; cf. 1:69-70, and the references to "salvation from our enemies" and the "forgiveness of sins");

4. The angel's explicit identification of Jesus as "the Messiah" (Luke 2:11);

5. Simeon's song (Luke 2:29-32, cf. 2:26) and his prophetic oracle (2:33-35);

6. Anna's proclamation (Luke 2:38; cf. Isa. 52:9);

7. Matthew 1:16 (cf. 1:18) wherein Jesus is described as the One "who is called Christ" (ὁ λεγόμενος Χριστός);

8. The Magi's description of Jesus as the "king of the Jews" (Matt. 2:2), and their presentation of gifts to Him (2:11);

9. Herod's question concerning the place of "the Messiah's birth" (Matt. 2:4);

10. The reference to Jesus in the Micah prophecy as "[the] ruler who shall shepherd my people Israel" (Matt. 2:6); and

11. Matthew's application to Him of Old Testament passages (2:15, 23).

Just as we saw when we examined His self-understanding that Jesus claimed to be both the divine Son and the Messiah, the former the ultimate antecedent ground of the latter, so also here in the Matthean and Lukan birth narratives we see these same two themes: that Jesus is God incarnate and that He, as such, is the promised Messiah of the Old Testament.

Testimony From the Accounts of Jesus' Baptism

All four Gospels record something of the ministry of John the Baptist leading up to Jesus' baptism. In all four he is either represented by the Evangelists as "a voice crying in the wilderness to prepare the way for the Lord" (Matt. 3:3; Mark 1:2-3; Luke 3:4) or he represents himself in that role (John 1:23). All four Gospels record his warning that coming after him was One more powerful than he whose sandals "I am not fit to carry" (Matt. 3:11) or "stooping down, to untie" (Mark 1:7; Luke 3:16; John 1:26). All four Gospels record John's description of Jesus as the "Spirit-Baptizer" (Matt. 3:11; Mark 1:8; Luke 3:16; John 1:33). And all four Evangelists (John by allusion) know of Jesus' baptism at the hand of John (Matt. 3:13-17; Mark 1:9-11; Luke 3:21-22; John 1:32-34). These corroborating literary facts put beyond reasonable doubt the historicity of the baptismal event *per se*.

Those (for example, Bultmann) who insist that early Hellenistic Jewish Christians added the miraculous features in the accounts (the Spirit's descent and the Father's voice from heaven) to an earlier non-Messianic tradition in order to interpret the event Messianically offer as support for their view mainly the form-critical conclusion that the *Sitz im Leben* of the pericope is Hellenistic. But there is nothing particularly Hellenistic about the account—indeed, I suggest that the accounts report quite accurately what occurred. As Edwin Hoskyns and Noel Davey declare, "At no point is the literary or historical critic able to detect in any stratum of the synoptic material evidence that a Christological interpretation has been imposed upon an un-Christological history."[24] And Marshall, more recently, has asserted, "When the narrative can be fully understood on its own terms, it is doubtful whether we are entitled to press back to a conjectural earlier form and function by which we may hope to explain it more amply."[25]

The view of some that the baptism narratives only record God's "adoption" of Jesus as His "Son" has nothing ultimately to commend it either. The birth narratives of both Matthew and Luke (cf. again Luke 1:32, 35) set forth the clear purpose of the virginal conception as the means by which the Son of God became flesh, and in Matthew 2:15 ("Out of Egypt I have called My Son")

---

24. Edwin Hoskyns and Noel Davey, *The Riddle of the New Testament*, 2nd ed. (1931; reprint, London: Faber and Faber Limited, 1958), p. 145.

25. Marshall, *Gospel of Luke*, p. 151.

Matthew represents Jesus *before* His baptism as *already* God's Son. Against this background, it simply makes no sense to view the baptism story as an "adoption" story marking the point when Jesus was "adopted" as "the Son of God." It should be apparent that, at least for Matthew and Luke, the baptism story cannot be an "adoption" story, but rather is the Father's "commissioning" Jesus to public ministry by personal confirmation (cf. Luke 3:22; Mark 1:11) and public attestation (Matt. 3:17) of His messiahship and divine sonship.

Because Mark says nothing about Jesus' supernatural entrance into the world, unlike Matthew and Luke, Wellhausen, Bultmann, and others have urged that at least in Mark the baptism narrative suggests an adoptionist Christology; as Wellhausen writes, "[Jesus] descended into the water a simple man and comes out of it as Son of God." Responding to that claim Stonehouse correctly declares:

> The conception that Jesus, according to Mark, became the Son of God at the moment of his baptism, that is, that he then received appointment as Messiah and underwent a certain transformation, presupposes that the reference to the fact of God's choice in the second clause, "on thee my choice has fallen," explains the appellation "Son" in the first clause, "Thou art my beloved Son." The divine voice declares then that Jesus becomes the Son of God because he has been chosen as Messiah. The chief difficulty of such an interpretation is, however, that the utterance then becomes tautological. It understands the first clause in the sense: "thou hast now become my Son," or "thy name has now become Son." But this presumes a past tense where the present is employed, and substitutes the idea of *becoming* for the expressed thought of *being*. As the text stands, however, there is a contrast between the two clauses, the former describing an essential relationship, a relationship conceived without reference to its origin, and the latter a past choice for the performance of a particular function. That the present tense cannot envisage an historical act receives powerful confirmation from the use of similar language in the transfiguration scene in Mark 9:7. Jesus did not any more become the Son of God at the baptism through the pronouncement of the words, "Thou art my beloved Son," than he became Son again at the transfiguration when the divine voice declared, "This is my beloved Son." He is seen to be the divine Son quite apart from the word spoken to him. The essential relationship . . . is clearly a completely distinctive relationship. The relationship of the second clause to the first in 1:11, while not expressed, is therefore by implication more properly viewed as resultative: *because* of the unique filial relationship of Jesus he has been chosen to the task upon which he is about to enter.[26]

26. Stonehouse, *The Witness of Matthew and Mark to Christ*, pp. 18-19.

If Jesus' earthly ministry was, in fact, Messianic, and we have already itemized the evidence given in the accounts prior to His baptism for such an understanding of His life's purpose, then there is nothing incredible about an event, similar in character to a "prophetic commission," that "set Him apart" and authenticated Him as divine and His work as Messianic. This, I suggest, is the main purpose of His baptism and the intent behind the heavenly manifestations.

The Baptist's Christology

Before we consider the significance of the two heavenly manifestations that accompanied Jesus' baptism, something should be said about the Baptist's Christology. John's testimony concerning Jesus is found in four contexts in particular. We will look at each in turn.

Matthew 3:10-12; Mark 1:7-8; Luke 3:16-17. Prior to his baptizing Jesus, John had announced to the people coming to him at the Jordan River:

> I am baptizing you with water unto repentance. But He who comes after me is mightier than I, whose sandals I am not worthy to carry. He shall baptize you with the Holy Spirit and [judge you] with fire.

In this declaration John states that the Coming One was more powerful than he, whose sandals he was not worthy to carry. These features of his pronouncement imply at least that for John the Messiah possessed a lofty, exalted, kingly office. But John intends more, for he goes on to say that the Coming One, by prerogative, administrates both eternal salvation ("He will baptize you with the Holy Spirit") and eternal judgment ("and [judge you] with fire"—cf. the parallelism in the three occurrences of "fire" at the end of Matt. 3:10, 11, and 12; the occurrences of "fire" in Luke 3:16-17; and the fact that where Mark does not mention the "[judging] with fire," neither does he mention any other reference to "fire"). The prerogatives in the Messiah's possession explain why John insisted in his intercourse with Jesus later that he (John) had need of being baptized (with salvation) by Jesus (Matt. 3:13). Such prerogatives belong only to One with divine stature (cf. the parallelism between the two "this is . . ." statements in John 1:33 and 34); only One who is God can exercise such authority!

John 1:15, 30. When John was asked about his relation to the One coming after him, twice he expressed himself in the following words:

> He who comes after me [or, "A Man is coming after me who"] was

before me [ἔμπροσθέν μου γέγονεν], because He was before me [πρῶτός μου ἦν].

Here is an enigmatic statement on John's part. Arndt and Gingrich suggest that the middle assertion has to do with status, and they translate the phrase, "ranks higher than I."[27] But there are sound reasons for moving in a different direction, from evidence that suggests that John is thinking *temporally*, that is, in terms of time, throughout the verse. This is certainly his intent in the first clause ("He who comes *after* me"), and almost as certainly his intent in the third clause ("He *was* [ἦν] *before* me", the ἦν here doubtless having as its background the three occurrences of ἦν in John 1:1. These features strongly suggest that the middle clause should also be construed as bearing some reference to time. But what then is John saying? Clearly, he does not mean by the last two clauses the same thing, inasmuch as different words underlie the surface similarity in the English translation above. Furthermore, the ὅτι ("because") suggests that the third clause provides the explanation for how the thought of the middle clause can be so. I suggest, therefore, following Vos,[28] that John is saying this: "He who comes *after* me was *before* me [in His active involvement as the Angel of the Lord, indeed as Yahweh Himself, in Old Testament times], because [that is, the reason I can say this of Him is] He was *eternally before* me [as the eternal God]."[29]

It is simply farcical, in light of the biblical data reviewed thus far, for Raymond E. Brown, following J. A. T. Robinson,[30] to suggest that John did not perceive his role to be that of Malachi's "Elijah" but rather saw himself as the forerunner of the promised Elijah, and thus he was speaking of Elijah when he made these statements in John 1:15, 30. That is, John was saying something on the order of the following: "Elijah, who comes after me, ranks higher than I, because he was before me." Brown has cleared the way by this construction to suggest the further conclusion that John regarded Jesus as

27. William F. Arndt and F. Wilbur Gingrich, *A Greek-English Lexicon of the New Testament* (Chicago: University of Chicago Press, 1957), p. 256f.

28. Vos, *Biblical Theology*, p. 347.

29. Oscar Cullmann also argues that the last phrase alludes to the "absolute time of the prologue:

> The proposition introduced by the ὅτι, looking at the matter from the standpoint of absolute chronology, which is that of the prologue, explains this general statement: He is before me because, being at the beginning of all things, ἐν ἀρχῇ, the ὁ ὀπίσω μου ἐρχόμενος is πρῶτος in an absolute way ("'Ὁ ὀπίσω μου ἐρχόμενος," *The Early Church* [London: SCM Press, 1956], p. 181).

Cf. also his *The Christology of the New Testament*, trans. Shirley C. Guthrie and Charles A. M. Hall (London: SCM Press, 1959), p. 28.

30. John A. T. Robinson, "Elijah, John and Jesus," *Twelve New Testament Studies* (London: SCM Press, 1962), pp. 28-52.

the Elijah who was to come, who in turn was to be the forerunner of Yahweh.[31] This view is easily dispelled by noting that nowhere does John even remotely intimate such, but to the contrary, expressly states that he was sent ahead of the Messiah Himself (John 3:28).

John 1:34. After he had baptized Jesus, having seen on that occasion the Spirit descend upon Jesus and having heard the voice from heaven declare, "This is My beloved Son, in whom I am well pleased," John testified of Jesus, "This is the Son of God."[32] The significance of the Baptist's epithet at this time is insightfully elucidated by Vos:

> That [the title "Son of God"] can not be lower in its import than the same title throughout the Gospel follows from the position it has as the culminating piece of this first stage of witnessing, when compared with the statement of the author of the Gospel (20:31). According to this statement the things recorded of Jesus were written to create belief in the divine sonship of the Saviour. With this in view a series of episodes and discourses have been put in order. Obviously the John-the-Baptist section forms the first in this series, and therein lies the reason, why it issues into the testimony about the Sonship under discussion. That it carried high meaning also appears from [John 1:15, 30], in which nothing less than the preexistence of the Messiah has already been affirmed.[33]

In sum, John intended by his epithet to ascribe nothing short of deity to Jesus, and here accordingly at the very dawn of the New Age in the forerunner's testimony is the highest conceivable declaration about Him.

John 3:27-36. This passage falls into two sections (vv. 27-30 and vv. 31-36), the first of which is clearly the Baptist's testimony, the second possibly his. In the first, John the Baptist applies the epithets of "Bridegroom" to Jesus and "the friend of the Bridegroom" to himself, adding, "It is necessary that He [His light (cf. John 1:7-8; 3:19-21)] increase and I [my light] decrease." It is

---

31. Raymond E. Brown, "Three Quotations from John the Baptist in the Gospel of John," *The Catholic Biblical Quarterly* 22 (1960): 297-98; cf. also his *The Gospel According to John I-XII*, Anchor Bible Series (Garden City, N.Y.: Doubleday, 1966), p. 64.

32. The variant readings at this point in the Greek text—mainly Western, "the Chosen One," "the Chosen Son," and "the only Son"—do not either singly or collectively have sufficient textual support to overthrow the reading "the Son," supported as it is by P66, P75, A, B, C, K, L, P, and corrected ℵ. Metzger (*Textual Commentary on the Greek New Testament*, p. 200) declares that both the "age and diversity" of the textual witnesses support "the Son."

33. Vos, *Biblical Theology*, p. 351.

only barely conceivable that John's disciples could have heard this reference to the "Bridegroom" and not have been reminded of the Old Testament references to Yahweh as the Bridegroom of Israel (cf. Isa. 62:5; Hos. 2:2-23; 3:1; Jer. 2:2). It is also just barely possible that John did not intend this comparison to be drawn.

The second section, Vos suggests, may be "needed to round off the argument of the Baptist on the absurdity of endeavoring to rival Jesus."[34] The NASB and the NIV apparently concur, as evidenced by their handling of the quotation marks. Jesus is described as "the One who comes from above," "the One who comes from Heaven," the One who is "above all," "the One whom God sent," "the One to whom God gave the Spirit without measure," "the Son whom the Father loves, into whose hands all things have been placed," and the One who brings eternal life to those who believe in Him. In light of the Baptist's other testimony respecting Jesus (cf. again John 1:15, 30; the details surrounding Jesus' baptism itself; and Acts 19:4), there is not one single description in this second section that the Baptist could not have expressed concerning Jesus, although it may be the apostle John's testimony after all. But if it is the Baptist's testimony, we must conclude that for John Jesus was the Christ, the Lord who was to come to His temple, the Messenger of the Covenant who was to come, indeed, Yahweh Himself who was speaking in Malachi 3:1, and thus the divine Son of God. It is difficult to imagine a higher Christology anywhere in Scripture unless it be the Christology of Jesus Himself.

Having reviewed the Baptist's perception of Jesus, we are now in a position to consider the implications for the nature and office of Jesus in the two heavenly manifestations that accompanied His baptism.

Matthew 3:16; Mark 1:10; Luke 3:22; John 1:33: The Spirit's Descent

All four Gospels refer to the fact that at Jesus' baptism the Holy Spirit descended upon Him in the form of a dove. John describes this as an indication that the Spirit had been given to Him without limit (1:34), and Jesus would say later, referring to the whole event, "On [the Son of Man] God the Father has placed His seal of approval" (John 6:27). Luke, describing Jesus immediately thereafter as "full of the Holy Spirit" (4:1), tells his readers (as do Matthew in 4:1 and Mark in 1:12) that Jesus was "led by the Spirit" into the wilderness (4:1) and then "returned to Galilee in the power of the Spirit" (4:14). In Nazareth on the Sabbath day, Luke reports, Jesus

34. Ibid., p. 352.

went to the synagogue and read in the hearing of the assembly the words of
Isaiah 61:1-2: "The Spirit of the Lord is on Me, because He *has anointed Me*
[ἔχρισέν με: (note the allusion in the verb to the lexical meaning of "Messiah"] to preach good news to the poor. He *has sent Me* to proclaim freedom
for the prisoners and recovery of sight for the blind, to release the op-
pressed, to proclaim the year of the Lord's favor" (emphasis added). "Today," Jesus declared, "this Scripture is fulfilled in your hearing" (4:21).
Many healing and nature miracles then issued from His hand (Matt. 4:23-24;
9:35; cf. Acts 10:37-38), which, at least in regard to demonic exorcisms, He
performed "by the Spirit of God" (Matt. 12:28; cf. Luke 11:20). What is the
meaning of the Spirit's descent upon Jesus and His empowering Him to
perform these mighty works? To every enlightened Jew the meaning was
obvious: the Messianic age had dawned! David F. Wells aptly remarks:

> Jews knew that the coming of the Messianic age would be signaled by
> the Spirit's outpouring. . . . That Jesus realized that he was bringing
> with him the age of Messiah was, from the time of the baptism at least,
> beyond question. It was visibly signaled [the Spirit's descent] and
> audibly declared [the voice from heaven]. And the Synoptic authors
> plainly wanted their readers to understand this.[35]

What, then, is the meaning of the Spirit's descent or anointing? Let Jesus
Himself answer: "If I drive out demons by the Spirit of God, then the
Kingdom of God has come upon you" (Matt. 12:28). In other words, the
Spirit's descent upon Jesus visibly designated Him as the Messiah and
indicated the inauguration of the Messianic age![36]

Matthew 3:17; Mark 1:11; Luke 3:22: The Voice From Heaven

Accompanying the Spirit's descent upon Jesus was the Father's (inferred
from the words, "My Son") personal confirmation, "You are My Son, the
Beloved, in whom I am well pleased" (Mark and Luke). Matthew represents
the heavenly Witness as *publicly* attesting Jesus' sonship by rendering the
divine statement in the third person: *"This is My Son. . . ."*[37] It is doubtful

35. David F. Wells, *The Person of Christ* (Westchester, Ill.: Crossway Books, 1984), pp. 38-39.
36. Cf. Vos (*Biblical Theology*, pp. 344-46) for his insightful discussion of the significance of the
Spirit's descent upon Jesus. In the main, he agrees that it represented God's designation of Jesus
as the Messiah and His equipping "for the execution of His Messianic task."
37. The additional words, "Today I have begotten You," following the phrase, "You are my
Son," at Luke 3:22 are found in one fifth- to sixth-century Greek manuscript (D) and a few Western
readings. It is clearly an assimilation to Ps. 2:7 and thus secondary, but the fact that it was "widely
current during the first three centuries" (Metzger, *Textual Commentary on the Greek New Testament*,

that both renderings were actually spoken. It is more likely the case that Matthew, interested as he is in "interpreting" Jesus for his readers as God's Son and Messiah (cf. 1:23), while certainly retaining the substance of the divine oracle, took the next step beyond the *confirmation* in the "You are" of Mark and Luke and represented the oracle as an *attestation* to or *proclamation* of Jesus as Son and Messiah.

The oracle itself consists of two parts. The first is "You are My Son," universally acknowledged as a reminiscence of the divine oracle in Psalm 2:7, with this one difference—that the word order has been altered by the Evangelists away from the Septuagint (which reflects the Hebrew word order) "to stress the fact that it is Jesus who is God's Son rather than that the dignity of sonship has been conferred on the person addressed."[38] There are those who insist that "Son" here is the Messianic title given to Jesus on the occasion of His "institution into the office of the eschatological king,"[39] and that no ontological overtones should be read into it. But there are six compelling reasons to understand the title otherwise—as entailing, beyond its Messianic implication, a preexistent *personal* relationship to God that preceded His messiahship and that served as the basis of both it and that self-understanding of His as "the Son" found in such passages as Matthew 11:27; Mark 14:61-62; and Luke 20:13.

1. If in other situations the idea of personal sonship is present and represented as antecedently behind the Messianic sonship, it seems totally unlikely, on the only two occasions in the Gospel accounts (the transfiguration is the second) when Heaven itself bore witness to Jesus' sonship, that the sense of "Son" therein was solely official and nonpersonal.[40]

2. "Beloved" (ὁ ἀγαπητός) should probably be construed as an adjective rather than as a second title, leaving us with the full phrase, "You are My *beloved* Son." But whether it is construed this way or as a second title, it points to a unique and personal sonship. Consider Genesis 22:2, 12, 16 in the

---

p. 136), and found in such Fathers as Justin, Origen, Hilary, and Augustine, illustrates how apparent the words "You are My Son" are as an allusion to Ps. 2:7.

38. Marshall, *Gospel of Luke*, p. 155.

39. E. Schweizer, "υἱός" (in the New Testament), *Theological Dictionary of the New Testament*, vol. 8 (Grand Rapids: Eerdmans, 1972), p. 368. James D. G. Dunn writes, "Mark thought of Jesus' sonship as from his anointing with the Spirit at Jordan and in terms particularly of his suffering and death" (*Christology in the Making: A New Testament Inquiry into the Origins of the Doctrine of the Incarnation* [London: SCM Press, 1980], p. 50; cf. also p. 47). So too must be mentioned here R. W. Lyon who states in his article, "Baptism of Jesus," "The significance here of the sonship is service to the Father rather than any particular reference to Jesus' divine nature. The expression [the Father's confirmation] is teleological rather than ontological" (in *Evangelical Dictionary of Theology*, ed. Walter A. Elwell [Grand Rapids: Baker, 1984], p. 120).

40. Vos, *Self-Disclosure of Jesus*, p. 186.

Septuagint: here, Isaac is described in precisely the same terms, as Abraham's "beloved son" (ὁ υἱός σου ὁ ἀγαπητός), and ἀγαπητός translates the Hebrew יְחִיד, which means "one and only." Obviously, Isaac's sonship must be understood in an *intensely* personal way; it is virtually certain that the phrase means the same thing in the heavenly allocution. Vos declares, "A sonship so unique [that is, a sonship grounded in the Father's love for His *only* Son] does not permit us to restrict its meaning to that of a bare figure for Messiahship."[41]

3. The phrase "My beloved Son" (τὸν υἱόν μου τὸν ἀγαπητόν) is found in Jesus' parable of the wicked farmers (Luke 20:13) that we considered in the previous chapter. There we saw that Jesus portrays Himself as "the beloved Son" *before His mission* and as enjoying a preexistent relationship with the Father *whether He be sent or not*. Jesus' representation of Himself in Luke 20:13 strongly suggests that the similar phrase in Luke 3:22 means the same thing—preexistent, personal sonship.

4. It more accords with the backgrounds of the birth narratives in Matthew and Luke and the titles in Matthew 2:15 and Luke 1:32, 35 (not to mention Jesus' youthful reference to God as "My Father" in Luke 2:49), in which the referent in every case is to His antecedent personal sonship, to understand the heavenly utterance in the ontological, divine sense rather than simply in a Messianic sense.

5. John the Baptist testified that his vision of the divinely appointed sign of the Spirit's descent had brought him to two conclusions: (1) that the One coming after him, who would baptize with the Spirit, was Jesus, and (2) that Jesus was "the Son of God" (John 1:34). If John *saw* the Spirit descending as a dove (John 1:33-34), then, likely, his testimony about Jesus as "the Son of God" reflects the fact that he *heard* the divine oracle as well. And, as we have already noted, his witness to Jesus as "the Son of God" cannot be lower in its import than the same title intends throughout the Gospel, that is, identity with God in nature and distinct from the Father in person. If John the Baptist meant by "Son" *divine* sonship (and all that John the Evangelist says suggests he did), and if he was correct in this assessment of Jesus (and John implies that he was), and if he deduced this in this historical context on the basis of what he had heard from heaven, then it follows that the prior heavenly oracle had in view *divine* sonship.

6. According to the writer of Hebrews, the title "Son" in Psalm 2:7, to which the heavenly utterance at the baptism alludes, ascribes to Jesus a sonship to God that entails such superangelic dignity that the supreme titles of "God" (1:8) and "Lord" (1:10), with all the dignity, attributes, and

41. Ibid., p. 187.

functions that these two titles connote, may also rightly be ascribed to Him—not, however, as titles additional to "Son" but rather as explications of the content of that *one* "more superior name [than "angel"]" of "Son." From the writer of Hebrews, as a legitimate commentator on the meaning of the title of "Son" in Psalm 2:7 and by extension on the heavenly oracle under consideration, it is evident that "the Son, the Beloved" in the heavenly oracle goes beyond Messianic sonship and embraces the super-official, personal, divine sonship lying behind it.

For these six reasons—compelling, in my opinion—I conclude that by His statement "You are My Son," the Father attested to Jesus' antecedent, personal, and eternal sonship that lay behind His Messianic investiture and that provided the ground and precondition of it.[42]

This is not to suggest that no allusion whatever to Jesus' Messianic role can be found in the heavenly utterance, for indeed there is. The second part of the heavenly witness is "in whom I delight [εὐδόκησα]." This appears to refer to a phrase in Isaiah 42:1: "My chosen One, in whom My soul delights." While it reflects a Greek translation unknown to us in the Septuagint tradition, it does accord with the translation of Isaiah 42:1-4 in Matthew 12:18-21, which reflects the influence of the Septuagint but with various alterations for the sake of closer conformity to the Hebrew or to bring out more clearly the Messianic application. Vos even argues, because εὐδόκησα in the traditional rendering is both tautological and anticlimactic relative to the preceding "Beloved," that it means in the aorist something akin to "upon whom My good pleasure has *settled*" or "whom I have *chosen* in My good pleasure." (He cites the statement in 1 Maccabees 10:47, "Having the choice between Alexander and Demetrius, they chose [εὐδόκησαν ἐν] Alexander," to support his contention.[43]) If this is so, this points even more strongly to Isaiah 42:1 as the Old Testament background to the divine statement, for it becomes the dynamic equivalent to the fuller statement in the Hebrew: "My *chosen* one, in whom My soul *delights*."

Since Isaiah 42:1 is the introduction to the first of the Servant Songs in

---

42. Cf. Vos's entire discussion of the divine testimony at the baptism in *Self-Disclosure of Jesus*, pp. 186-87. Cf. also Warfield, *Lord of Glory*, p. 80 (also p. 80 n. 29).

It is by the term "My Son" above all that God Himself bore witness to Him on the two occasions when He spoke from heaven to give Him His testimony . . . adding to it moreover epithets ["the Beloved, in whom I am well-pleased" and "the Chosen One" (in the case of Luke 9:35 at the transfiguration)] which emphasized *the uniqueness of the Sonship* thus solemnly announced. It would seem quite clear, therefore, that the title "Son of God" stands in the pages of the Synoptics as the supernatural Messianic designation by way of eminence, and represents the Messiah *in contradistinction from children of men as of a supernatural origin and nature* (Warfield, *Lord of Glory*, p. 139, emphasis added).

43. Vos, *Self-Disclosure of Jesus*, p. 186, 186 n. 12.

Isaiah, I infer that the second half of the divine utterance *does* allude to Jesus' Messianic investiture, and, if so, it suggests that when Jesus later ascribed to Himself both intra-divine sonship and the Servant task spoken of in the four Servant Songs of Isaiah (cf. Matt. 11:27a, 29b; 20:28; Mark 10:45; Luke 22:37), He was only following the pattern established by the heavenly oracle at the time of His Messianic commissioning. In sum, there is sound justification for seeing in this divine utterance the attestation to and confirmation of both Jesus' divine sonship and His messiahship.

Testimony From the Accounts of Jesus' Temptation

All three Synoptic Gospels report that immediately following His "baptismal commissioning," Jesus, upon whom the Spirit was now "remaining" (John 1:33), was led by the Spirit into the desert to be tempted by the devil (Matt. 4:1-11; Mark 1:12; Luke 4:1-13). The primary accounts are those of Matthew and Luke. These two reports are quite uniform, except that Luke reverses the order of Matthew's second and third temptations. (But even in doing so, Luke retains the substance of the temptations. The Evangelists obviously reserved the right to arrange their material to suit their own plans and purposes for their respective Gospels [a legitimate observation of "redaction criticism"], but this in no way suggests that they took liberties with history and created events out of thin air.)

As with so many other events in the Gospel accounts, radical form critics see in the temptation narratives evidence of later Hellenistic influence, which, they argue, indicates that the story was created by the Hellenistic Christian community. But Marshall observes that

> the narrative displays such a strong combination of Jewish features that it is impossible to assume that it went through a preliminary Hellenistic stage before receiving its present Jewish form. In particular, the objection that the use of the LXX here (and elsewhere in the Gospels) betrays a Hellenistic origin should be forgotten once and for all; the evidence implies nothing more than that when the story was told in Greek the narrator made use of the current Greek translation of the OT. Finally, it must be insisted that it is one thing to show how a narrative was used in the early church [an exercise which the radical form critic claims that he is very good at doing but whose conclusions have been shown all too often to be erroneous], and quite another thing to claim that because it was used for a particular purpose in the church, it must have been created by the church without any historical basis.[44]

44. Marshall, *Gospel of Luke*, pp. 167-68.

It has often been noted that there must have been a single historical explanatory event lying behind Jesus' statement in Matthew 12:29 concerning His "binding the strong man" (cf. also Mark 3:27; Luke 11:21-22). Such a necessary antecedent is most admirably met by the temptation event.[45] The Evangelists represent Jesus' demonic exorcisms as occurring in the objective world of space and time, and "there can be no doubt that Jesus regarded the demons as actually existing supernatural beings, who could be spoken to and give answer, and [who] exercised a wide sphere of baneful power."[46] And the reason He was able to exercise the authority and power He did over them was to be traced, He said, to the fact that He had "first tied up the strong man" of the "house" He was now plundering, thereby enabling Him to plunder that "strong man's house" at will. That "binding" would of necessity have had to happen also in and through an objective, historical event, and this occurred, most naturally, at the temptation.

Those who take exception to the spiritual phenomenon of a personal Satan as being distasteful to the modern mind must, of course, find all the references in the New Testament, indeed, in the whole Bible, to Satan and his demons as unhistorical reflections of ancient and/or pagan mythology. But these references are too deeply embedded in the very warp and woof of Scripture and particularly in the Gospel accounts of Jesus' healing miracles, both in number and significance, to be cavalierly dismissed on the *a priori* assumption that they are mythological.

We are not told in what form—whether tangible and visible or not—Satan came to Jesus after His fast of forty days, but "an encounter between persons, especially in the supersensual world, can be perfectly objective without necessarily entering into the sphere of the corporeally perceptive."[47] To decide such a question is not pertinent to our present purpose. The point that we want to underscore is that when Satan employed the title "[the] Son of God" in his conversation with Jesus (Matt. 4:3, 6; Luke 4:3, 9),[48] he acknowledged Jesus' divine sonship.

Now it is true that the title occurs on each occasion in the temptation accounts in the protasis of a conditional sentence (the "if" clause), but in each case the protasis according to Greek syntax is a "first-class condition," which means that the condition expressed is regarded, from the speaker's

45. Cf. Vos, *Biblical Theology*, pp. 355-56.
46. Ibid., p. 357.
47. Ibid., p. 356.
48. The anarthrous υἱός, coming before the copula, should be regarded as definite in accordance with E. C. Colwell's observations ("A Definite Rule for the Use of the Article in the Greek New Testament," *Journal of Biblical Literature* 52 [1933]: 20). Cf. also Moule, *Idiom Book of New Testament Greek*, pp. 115-16.

perspective, as real and factual. An English translation on the order of *"Since You are the Son of God"* will make clear what I mean here, although I am not suggesting that the εἰ ("if") should necessarily be so rendered by the English versions of the Bible. However, three textual features support this interpretation.

1. The near juxtaposition of Satan's employment of the title to the preceding occurrence of the title in the heavenly oracle during Jesus' baptism, highlighted by the Matthean "then" (4:1) and the Marcan "at once" (1:12), can hardly be accidental. By this juxtaposition the Evangelists surely intended that the fact of Jesus' sonship and the meaning of the title in the immediately preceding event extend themselves to govern the fact and meaning of the latter event. And since the Father had just attested in Jesus' hearing that He *was* the Son of God, it is hardly likely that Satan only days later believed it to be contrary to fact and was seeking proof of Jesus' sonship by suggesting ways that Jesus might demonstrate His divine sonship both to Himself and to Satan. But then, if Jesus' sonship is not to be understood in the "if" clauses as a condition contrary to fact, we must assume that Satan was not questioning the status of Jesus but, to the contrary, was assuming that Jesus was the Son of God and devising the forms of the several temptations accordingly. This suggests that we should view the force and intent of the temptations as Satan's recognition that Jesus was the Son of God. A paraphrase of them will bring out my meaning here. It is as if he were saying, "One who enjoys such inherent station and rank as resides in Your status as God's Son should not have to endure such deprivation as hunger or have to walk the Servant's road in order to win the right to govern the kingdoms of the world; therefore, repudiate the Messianic investiture, which entails such humiliation, and exercise the powers and functions native to the sonship God Himself has confirmed is Yours and achieve the same end." Satan's assumption that Jesus' sonship is fact and *not* contrary to fact more clearly meets the demands the temptations call for.

2. All three Synoptic Evangelists inform us that "whenever the unclean spirits [demons] saw Him, they fell down before Him and cried out, 'You are the Son of God' " (Mark 3:11; cf. Luke 4:41[49]), or that they addressed Him as

---

49. Regarding Luke's comment following the demons' cries—"You are the Son of God"—to the effect that Christ would not allow them to say more "because they knew He was the Christ" (4:41), Marshall writes in *The Gospel of Luke:*

Luke's elucidation of the title in terms of the Messiah does not mean that he has downgraded "Son of God" to become merely an attribute of the Messiah; this is impossible in the light of 1:32-35 [Marshall's view of the earlier passage accords with my own that the titles in the Lucan birth narrative refer to Jesus' personal rather than to a nativistic or a Messianic Sonship; cf. pp. 67, 68, 71]. Rather the term "Messiah" is seen to be applicable to a

"Son of God" (Matt. 8:29) or "Son of the Most High God" (Mark 5:7; Luke 8:28). From other things they say in these contexts, there is no uncertainty in *their* understanding of who He was: He was deity incarnate. Whence the source of *their* understanding?

It is *theoretically* possible that Satan had informed his demonic cohorts, but it is *theologically* highly unlikely that such was the source of his demons' knowledge of Jesus' sonship. Such a representation of the origin of their understanding is probably too crassly literalistic to truly reflect the supernaturally charged intercourse among spirits. Rather, while theirs was not in any sense an omniscient apprehension of things, their understanding would have been an intuitive, supernatural kind of awareness. Because they were themselves supernatural spirit beings, they would have "scented," to use Wrede's picturesque characterization, the supernatural in Jesus. As Vos aptly comments, "It was a case of spirit recognizing spirit."[50] And if this is what lay behind the demons' awareness of Jesus' station, it would follow that it would be equally true for Satan himself. Therefore, to Satan's likely awareness of the heavenly oracle's witness to Jesus' sonship we must add the likelihood that lying behind Satan's "Since You are the Son of God" was his "scented" recognition of the reality of Jesus' sonship. Of course, it is also possible that Satan (and his demons) simply recognized his Creator on the basis of a knowledge of the fact of the incarnation.

3. By the form of the temptations themselves Satan implicitly recognized that Jesus possessed the *power* to work miracles (turning stones to bread), a *special right* to divine care, and the *entitlement to the kingdoms of this world*. Why, otherwise, in the last case, for example, does he offer the kingdoms of the world then and there *to Him* rather than to someone else if He would only worship the Tempter? Clearly, here is an acknowledgment that Jesus possessed Messianic powers, privileges, and prerogatives, "a type of Messiahship lifting Him far above the level of the natural."[51] But this is just to say that the prior sonship, which in this context governs these Messianic privileges, is supra-mundane as well and thus divine. I submit, therefore, that here we find the arch-demon of all dark spirits himself affirming the divine sonship of the Son of God.

more-than-earthly figure, able to exorcise demons, and on a different level from political saviours. At the same time, Luke's purpose may be to indicate that "Son of God"must not be understood in purely Hellenistic categories as a reference to a charismatic, semi-divine figure, but must be seen in the light of Jewish messianic expectations (p. 197).

50. Vos, *Self-Disclosure of Jesus*, p. 171.
51. Ibid., pp. 172-73.

Testimony From the Accounts of Jesus' Transfiguration

Peter's great confession at Caesarea Philippi that Jesus was "the Christ, the Son of the living God" (Matt. 16:16; cf. Mark 8:29; Luke 9:20) marked the beginning of a new emphasis in Jesus' instruction of His disciples. Now that they were fully convinced that He was the Messiah, Jesus began (ἤρξατο) to emphasize the necessity of His death and resurrection[52] (which latter event, as the instrumental means to His enthronement at the Father's right hand, He apparently thought of in "shorthand" fashion for His resurrection *and* ascension, since He says nothing about the latter event, but rather assumes it when He later speaks about His parousia) (Matt. 16:21; Mark 8:31; Luke 9:22). Assured by Peter's confession, Jesus found it now both possible and needful to infuse the Messianic concept with the content of the Servant Song of Isaiah 52:13–53:12 and to correct the purely nationalistic associations that still lingered in the disciples' minds (cf. Matt. 16:22-23; Mark 9:32-33; 10:35-37; Luke 9:46). So from that moment on to the end of His ministry, even though His disciples did not understand Him (Mark 9:32; Luke 18:34), He kept constantly and prominently before them the "departure which He was about to accomplish at Jerusalem" (Matt. 17:22-23; 20:17-19, 22, 28; 21:39; 26:2, 11-12, 24, 28; Mark 9:31; 10:32-34, 38, 45; 12:8; 14:8, 21, 24; Luke 9:51, 53; 13:33; 17:11; 18:31-33; 22:20).

But He not only began to speak more often than He had before about *His* suffering and death; in this context He also informed them that His disciple must be prepared to die as well and must never be ashamed of Him, else "the Son of Man will be ashamed of him when He comes in His glory and in the glory of His Father and of the holy angels" (Luke 9:23-26; cf. Matt. 16:24-27; Mark 8:34-37). Solemn words these—concerning both His own

---

52. This incident at Caesarea Philippi should not be regarded as the point of emergence of a totally new *doctrine* in Jesus' teaching. Rather, it pinpoints only the beginning of a new *emphasis* upon a doctrine found in His earliest teaching. For example, He had spoken earlier of His death (John 3:14; by implication also in Matt. 9:15; Mark 2:20; Luke 5:35) and resurrection (John 2:19-22). And His earlier warnings that His disciples would be persecuted (Matt. 5:11, 44; 10:16-39) because of Him assumes that He will be persecuted as well. Vos writes:

> Our Lord simply takes for granted that there will be a breach between His followers and the world. And, since the cause of the breach is placed in their identification with Him, the underlying supposition doubtless is that the same conflict is in store for the Master Himself, only after a more principial fashion. And there is no point in Jesus' life where this mental attitude can be said to have first begun. The "sunny" and untroubled days of "fair Galilee" are, when exploited in such a sense, a pure fiction. There never was in the life of Jesus an original optimistic period followed later by a pessimistic period. As the approaching of the dread crisis did not render Him despondent towards the end, so neither did its comparative remoteness render Him sanguine at the beginning. The intrusion of such a terrifying thought as the thought of His death, in the specific form belonging to it, must have been, could not have failed to leave behind it the evidence of a sudden shock. But there is no evidence of any such sudden shock in the Gospels (*Self-Disclosure of Jesus*, pp. 278-79).

Passion and His demand for His disciples' unflagging loyalty. All of the
Synoptic Evangelists report that, immediately following this reference to
His return in glory (which is in itself an implicit claim to the Messianic
investiture), our Lord then cryptically declared, "Some who are standing
here shall not taste death before they see the Son of Man coming in His
kingdom" (Matt. 16:28),[53] words that I think were intended to counter-
balance the apprehension His previous words about martyrdom must have
invoked in their minds. The cryptic saying implicitly enjoined them to view
His Passion and their own persecution against the background of His and
(by extension) their own ultimate and eternal glory.

C. E. B. Cranfield neatly summarizes seven suggestions for the fulfilling
referent of this saying,[54] any one of which, I submit, is infinitely preferable
to the widely held view that Jesus mistakenly expected His parousia to take
place within the lifetime of that generation of disciples. For myself, with
Cranfield,[55] W. L. Lane,[56] and (I suspect) most evangelicals, I believe that
Jesus was referring to His transfiguration, which took place a week later and
which all three Synoptic Gospels place immediately after the saying. Such a
fulfillment meets all the requirements of the saying:

1. The phrase, *"some* who are standing here," would refer to His "inner
circle" of disciples—Peter, James, and John—who alone were present at the
transfiguration.

2. The phrase, "shall not taste of death," that is, "shall not die," finds the
explanation for its presence in the reference Jesus had just made to the need
for the disciple to "take up his cross" and "lose his life for Me." The

53. The other Synoptists report this "Son of Man" saying in essentially the same way. Luke's
account reads simply, "until they see the kingdom of God" (9:27), which I take to mean, because in
all the Gospels the Kingdom of God and the person of Jesus as the Messiah are integrally and
inseparably bound together, "until they see the kingdom of the divine Messiah"; Mark's account
reads, "until they see the kingdom of God having come in power" (9:1), which adds the idea that
the Messiah's kingdom will have come with accompanying manifestations indicating the presence
of divine omnipotence. Cf. Royce G. Gruenler, "Son of Man," in *Evangelical Dictionary of Theology*,
p. 1036, for the view that Jesus employs the title in a *corporate* sense both here and in Matt. 10:23.
54. C. E. B. Cranfield, *The Gospel According to Saint Mark* (Cambridge: University Press, 1966),
pp. 285-88. The seven, briefly, are as follows: (1) Dodd's use of it in support of his view of "realized
eschatology"; (2) the view that "shall not taste of death" refers to spiritual death, from which
faithful disciples will be exempted; (3) Michaelis's view that the meaning is that there will be some
at least who will have the privilege of not dying before the parousia, but that it is not said when
these will live and not implied that they must belong to Jesus' contemporaries; (4) the destruction
of Jerusalem in A.D. 70; (5) Pentecost; (6) Vincent Taylor's view that Jesus was referring to a visible
manifestation of the rule of God displayed for men to see in the life of the elect community; and
(7) the transfiguration.
55. Ibid., pp. 287-88.
56. William L. Lane, *The Gospel of Mark* (Grand Rapids: Eerdmans, 1974), pp. 313-14.

argument of some that if Jesus' transfiguration is made the fulfilling referent of Jesus' remark, then the "some" in the first phrase would imply that at least some if not all of the others there present *would* die in the next few days, is surely a *non sequitur*. For while Jesus' remark implies that the majority of those present would not see this thing themselves in their lifetime, it does not mean that they must necessarily die before *some* did see it.

3. The phrase, "before they *see*," fits well with the sustained emphasis in the transfiguration narrative on this inner circle of disciples *seeing* Him in His "unearthly" radiance (cf. the phrases "transfigured *before* them" and "what you have *seen*" in Matt. 17:2, 9; the phrases "transfigured *before* them," "there *appeared* before them," and "what they had *seen*" in Mark 9:2, 4, 9; and the phrases "they *saw* His glory" and "what they had *seen*" in Luke 9:32, 36).

4. The phrase, "the Son of Man coming in His kingdom" (Mark: "with power"), as Cranfield notes, "is a not unfair description of what the three saw on the mount of Transfiguration,"[57] for Jesus' transfiguration was, although momentary, nonetheless a real and witnessed manifestation of His sovereign power and glory that pointed forward, as an anticipatory foretaste, to His parousia when His kingdom would come "with [permanent] power and glory" (Mark 13:26).

Before we comment on the event of the transfiguration itself, I need to say something about its historicity in view of three assaults upon it. Regarding the view of Bultmann, which continues to find steady support to this day, that "it is an Easter-story projected backward into Jesus' life-time,"[58] that is, a legendary resurrection appearance mistakenly displaced and put in the preresurrection material, it need only be said that G. H. Boobyer[59] and C. H. Dodd[60] have convincingly demonstrated that nothing about it resembles the later resurrection appearances. For example: (1) All of the accounts of the resurrection appearances in the Gospels begin with Jesus being absent, but here He is present from the beginning. (2) In all of the accounts of Jesus' resurrection appearances, Jesus' spoken word is prominent, but here He gives no encouragement or instruction to His disciples. He speaks, but to Moses and Elijah about His *future* death (Luke 9:31). (3) The presence of

57. Cranfield, *Gospel According to Saint Mark*, p. 288.

58. R. Bultmann, *Theology of the New Testament*, vol. 1, trans. Kendrick Grobel (London: SCM Press, 1952), pp. 26, 27, 30, 45, 50.

59. G. H. Boobyer, *St. Mark and the Transfiguration Story* (Edinburgh: T. & T. Clark, 1942), pp. 11-16.

60. C. H. Dodd, "The Appearances of the Risen Christ: An Essay in Form Criticism of the Gospels," in *Studies in the Gospels*, ed. D. E. Nineham (Oxford: Basil Blackwell, 1955), pp. 9-35. Cf. also J. Schniewind, *Das Evangelium Nach Markus* (Göttingen: Vandenhoeck and Ruprecht, 1949), p. 123.

Moses and Elijah here is strange, if this is a resurrection appearance, since no figure from the beyond ever appears at the same time with Him in the postresurrection appearances. (4) This account contains none of the features one might expect if it is an appearance in the context of which Peter is present as a guilt-ridden disciple (cf. John 21). Consequently, Dodd declares:

> To set over against these points of difference I cannot find a single point of resemblance. If the theory of a displaced post-resurrection appearance is to be evoked for the understanding of this difficult *pericope*, it must be without any support from form-criticism, and indeed in the teeth of the presumption which formal analysis establishes.[61]

Against the view of Lohmeyer[62] and others that it is a nonhistorical, symbolical expression of a "theological conviction" concerning Jesus, derived from imagery drawn from the Old Testament Feast of Tabernacles (cf. Peter's reference to "booths"), Cranfield marshalls details in the account that are very strange if the pericope was only a theological statement created by the early church, for example, Mark's "after six days" and Peter's use of "Rabbi" and his absurd statement about the "booths." This title for Jesus and Peter's thoughtless statement are hardly likely to have been put in the mouth of a chief apostle, if the post-Easter church was creating a symbolic narrative to make a theological statement about Jesus.[63] The fairer analysis concludes that Mark was relating something that really happened.

Finally, Matthew's τὸ ὅραμα ("the vision") (17:9), which I translated earlier by "what you have seen," need not mean that what is reported here occurred merely in a vision the disciples had. Three facts register tellingly against the view that Jesus' transfiguration was simply a visionary experience shared by the three disciples. First, a single vision is not shared, at least normally, by several persons at the same time. Second, ὅραμα may be used of what is seen in the ordinary way (cf. Deut. 28:34). And third, Luke expressly declares that the disciples "had been very sleepy," but it was when "they became fully awake" that "they saw His glory and the two men standing with Him" (9:32).

Everything about the Gospel accounts suggest that the Evangelists reported an event that actually happened and could have been seen by others had they been present; furthermore, no argument has been advanced by

---

61. Dodd, in *Studies in the Gospels*, p. 25.

62. E. Lohmeyer, *Das Evangelium des Markus* (Göttingen: Vandenhoeck and Ruprecht, 1937), pp. 173-81.

63. Cranfield, *Gospel According to Saint Mark*, pp. 293-94.

solid scholarship to date that overthrows the traditional view of the church that the transfiguration was an actual occurrence. Therefore, I will presume the historicity of the event and proceed to its exposition.

The "Metamorphosis" Itself

The accounts all begin by informing the reader that a week after Jesus' cryptic prophecy,[64] Jesus took Peter, James, and John up into a mountain.[65] Luke alone adds, "to pray." And while He was praying, we are told, Jesus was "transfigured" (μετεμορφώθη) before them. We are not left to wonder about the nature of this "metamorphosis." Two aspects of His physical appearance are singled out for comment: His face (but this probably included His entire body as well because of the reference to His garments) and His clothing. While Luke simply states that "the appearance of His face was changed" (9:29), Matthew writes, "His face shone like the sun" (17:2). And while Matthew simply states that "His clothes became as brilliant as the light" (17:2), Mark adds that they became "dazzling white, whiter than any cleaner on earth could bleach them" (9:3), and Luke writes that they were "gleaming as lightning" (9:29). If this transformation took place at night, as some details in the Lukan account suggest (cf. 9:32, 37), the scene unfolding before the disciples must have been all the more fearsomely awesome (Mark 9:6), beyond the capacity of words fully to describe.

This "transfiguration" in Jesus' appearance Luke characterizes in two words: it was a revelation of "His glory" (9:32), a momentary substantiation of the essence of His prophecy in Luke 9:26 where He makes mention of "His glory." Because Luke declares that Moses and Elijah, whose appearances are mentioned by all three Synoptics, also appeared in "glorious splendor" (9:31), one might at first be disinclined to make too much of Jesus' transfiguration, so far as indicating anything unique about Him is concerned, and conclude that the combined glory of all three is simply indicative of the "supernaturalism" of the occasion. But Peter declares later that, in

---

64. Matthew's and Mark's "after six days" could place the event on the seventh day, especially if it occurred at night after the close of the sixth day, whereas Luke's "some eight days after," by inclusive reckoning, as in John 20:26, also means "on the seventh day." In any event, Luke's ὡσεί ("about") suggests that he was conscious that his number of days was an approximation to the figure in the other Gospels.

65. Cf. Walter L. Liefeld ("Theological Motifs in the Transfiguration Narratives," in *New Dimensions in New Testament Study*, ed. R. N. Longenecker and M. C. Tenney [Grand Rapids: Zondervan, 1974], p. 167 n. 27) for an interesting defense of Mt. Meron, rather than the more traditional Mt. Tabor or Mt. Hermon, as the most likely site of the transfiguration. I mention this fact to underscore the space-time historical character of the transfiguration.

seeing this, the disciples were made "eyewitnesses of [Jesus'] μεγαλειότης" (2 Pet. 1:16), that is, His "grandeur," "sublimity," or "majesty." He says nothing about Moses and Elijah. This word is used on only two other occasions in the New Testament—as an attribute of God in Luke 9:43 and of the goddess Diana of Ephesus in Acts 19:27—a word that can and does clearly designate the glory of deity. For Peter the word took on the idea also of divine power (cf. δύναμις, 2 Pet. 1:16). So Jesus' "metamorphosis" was a visible manifestation, we conclude, of His divine "glory" (Luke 9:32) and "majesty" (2 Pet. 1:16), revealed in "power" (2 Pet. 1:16).

The Voice From the Cloud

Peter, awestruck, said thoughtlessly, "Rabbi, it is good for us to be here. Let us put up three shelters—one for You, one for Moses, and one for Elijah" (Mark 9:5). In response and in order to remove even the remotest notion that these three "glorious" figures should be regarded in any sense "equal in power and glory," God appeared theophanically in the form of a bright cloud that enveloped them, and a terrifying voice from the cloud said: "This is My beloved Son, in whom I am well pleased. Listen to Him" (Matt. 17:5-6). Whereas the Father's voice from heaven at His baptism *confirmed to Jesus* His rightful claim to sonship, here it *attests to His disciples* His unique station as the Son of God. Here, as there, these words signalized Jesus' personal and essential divine sonship as the antecedent ground and precondition of His Messianic investiture, which is alluded to in the final words, "Listen to Him," words reminiscent of Deuteronomy 18:15, "The Lord your God will raise up for you a Prophet like me [that is, Moses; recall his presence here on this occasion] from among your brothers. *You must listen to Him.*" Peter later confirmed that the voice was that of God the Father and that the Father's attestation "honored" and "glorified" the Lord Jesus Christ (2 Pet. 1:17). Here, then, in the Father's attestation to His Son, in addition to the feature of the transfiguration itself, we find the second indication in the transfiguration accounts of Jesus' essential deity.

The Disciples' Question

Coming down from the mountain the next day (Luke 9:27), the disciples asked Jesus, "Why, therefore, do the teachers of the law say that Elijah must come first?" (Matt. 17:10; Mark 9:11). Their mention of Elijah, of course, was prompted by the fact that they had just seen him. But what lay behind their question about him? There can be no doubt that something in Malachi's prophecy was perplexing them. Malachi had said that "Elijah" would come *before* the Lord came (3:1), *before* the great and terrible day of the Lord (4:5), which they had just seen "in miniature." The implications of their question for Jesus' identity must not be lost on the reader. The only conclusion that one can fairly draw is that for them Jesus—just attested as such by the glory of His deity shining through His humanity and by the heavenly voice—was Malachi's "Lord who was to come," the Yahweh of the Old Testament, but the order of their historical appearances—Jesus had first appeared, then Elijah—seemed to them to be the reverse of what Malachi had predicted. This seeming inversion of the prophet's order was creating the quandary that provoked their question. Jesus solved their problem by informing them that "Elijah" (in the person of John the Baptist) had indeed come first and Jesus had then followed as that "Elijah's" Lord. By His exposition of Malachi's prophecy here, Jesus unmistakably claimed to be the Lord of Hosts, the Messenger of the Covenant, who had promised He would come *after* "Elijah," His messenger, had come.

The entire account of the transfiguration is replete—resplendent might be the more appropriate word—with indications of Jesus' essential divine sonship. It is not surprising that those who deny His deity seek so solicitously to reduce this event to legend or myth. But the accounts stand, unfazed by the attempts of critical scholarship to make them into something they are not, and thus these accounts lend their combined voice to the larger witness of Scripture to Jesus' essential divine sonship in the Godhead.

Testimony From the Disciples' Understanding of Jesus

As our last area of investigation in this chapter, we shall examine the disciples' precrucifixion understanding of Jesus for the light that their understanding sheds on Jesus' person and work. It is, of course, theoretically possible that they could have been mistaken in their understanding of Him, and the Scriptures indicate that they often were mistaken. But when they express their understanding of Him in His presence and are not corrected or rebuked by Him but, to the contrary, are actually encouraged to continue in their expressed perception of Him, we may safely conclude that their understanding received His endorsement and coincided with His own. It is this kind of testimony that I intend now to consider.

We have already called attention to Jesus' many mighty works. But what we did not mention earlier is the impact His "glorious deeds" (ἐνδόξοις) (Luke 13:17) made on the crowds that swarmed around Him almost daily. Not only do the Evangelists report that the crowds, as a result of His miracles, "marveled" (Mark 1:27), "wondered at" (Mark 5:20; Luke 9:43), were "amazed" (Mark 2:12; Luke 8:56), were "utterly astonished" (Mark 7:37), were "overcome with fear" (Luke 8:37; cf. 5:26; 7:16), and "rejoiced" (Luke 13:17); but they also report some of the crowd's direct comments:

> What is this? A new teaching with authority! He commands even the unclean spirits, and they obey Him! (Mark 1:27).

> What is this word, that with authority and power He commands the unclean spirits, and they obey! (Luke 4:36).

> We have never seen anything like this! (Mark 2:12).

> Nothing like this was ever seen in Israel! (Matt. 9:33).

> He has done all things well! He makes even the deaf to hear and the dumb to speak! (Mark 7:37).

> We have seen marvelous things today! (Luke 5:26).

> A great prophet has appeared among us! (Luke 7:16).

> God has visited His people! (Luke 7:16).

Now if His miracles affected the crowds in this fashion, we should not wonder that the disciples who were with Him almost constantly throughout His earthly ministry and who saw virtually all of His "powers" (δυνάμεις) (Matt. 11:20-23; Luke 10:13) were also deeply affected by what they beheld and formed certain definite opinons about Him, several of which they openly expressed in His hearing. We shall consider eight of these expressions of belief.

John 1:49: Nathaniel's Testimony

We will pass over Andrew's designation of Jesus as "the Messiah" (1:41) and Philip's description of Him as the object of Old Testament prophecy ("the One about whom Moses wrote in the Law, and about whom the prophets spoke") (1:45) simply because they were not spoken in Jesus' presence. But I would like to make this observation about them: these early testimonies should not be entirely discounted as "reflections of a later theological development" merely because the Synoptic Gospels suggest that it took some time for the disciples to come to a deeply held conviction about the nature of *His person*. It is one thing to call Jesus "Messiah" and to do so in a "dawning" way, and it is quite another to have a fully adequate understanding of the Messianic concept and how Christ's person relates to it. But both are legitimate stages in the growth process, and both stages represent degrees of *true* awareness—the latter stages, of course, entailing greater degrees of knowledge. True, the evidence indicates that there were many "false starts" in the disciples' understanding and a good many "ebbs and flows" as well before they finally came to a settled conviction about Him (cf. Mark 4:41; 6:51-52; 8:32; 10:31-32). But Andrew's and Philip's testimonies, even though they appear in the early days of Christ's public ministry, should be allowed nonetheless to stand as authentic statements as two "true starts," and to add their weight, however minor, to the overall New Testament witness to Jesus' messiahship.

Now to the matter before us. At Philip's invitation, Nathaniel came to Jesus to investigate for himself the question of Jesus' messiahship (1:45-47). We know nothing about Nathaniel, outside of this single incident, beyond the fact that he was from Cana in Galilee and was with six other disciples when Jesus appeared to the seven of them by the Sea of Galilee in one of His postresurrection appearances (21:2). This latter fact surely indicates that he was a disciple of Jesus, but whether he was one of the original Twelve is another question. It has been suggested that Nathaniel is the Bartholomew of the Synoptics (for the reasons, cf. the commentaries), but it is entirely possible that he was not one of the original Twelve. Jesus, after all, had many disciples besides the twelve apostles. But whatever the actual case in this regard, "there is no evidence that Nathaniel is a purely symbolic figure."[66]

Before we actually consider the titles Nathaniel employed to describe Jesus, we should note Nathaniel's response to Philip's invitation to come to Jesus, for in it we can detect a glimpse of his attitude toward the Messianic hope *per se*. Even though his question, "Can anything good come out of Nazareth?" (1:46), may be a local proverb reflecting the rivalry often existing between small towns in close proximity to one another, it still describes his estimation of the Messianic hope as something "good." Then when we find Jesus addressing Nathaniel later as a "true Israelite [literally, "truly an Israelite," but the adverb has the equivalent force here of an adjective] in whom there is no guile" (1:47; cf. Gen. 27:35), we may conclude, since Jesus was not one to pander to men's egos with empty flattery, that Nathaniel, like Simeon and Anna, was waiting for the "consolation of Israel" (cf. Luke

---

66. Brown, *Gospel According to John I-XII*, p. 82. Cf. Leon Morris, *The Gospel According to John* (Grand Rapids: Eerdmans, 1971), p. 164.

2:25-38). And because he later applies both "Son" and "King" to Jesus, it is a virtual certainty that he knew the prophetic Scriptures and had the words of Psalm 2:6-7 in mind in his titular descriptions of Jesus. Furthermore, the entire report clearly suggests that, in his thinking, the Messiah would do just such works as Jesus did here, that is, would display *supernatural* abilities, for as a result of only the briefest exchange between them, in which he was confronted with Jesus' supernatural knowledge of his heart (1:45-48),[67] he concluded that Jesus, far from being clairvoyant, was his "Rabbi" (literally, "my Teacher"), and exclaimed, *"You* [emphatic] are the Son of God; *You* [emphatic] are the King of Israel" (1:49).

Now in reaching a correct interpretation of these two latter titles, we must keep constantly in mind that *both* titles reflect conclusions Nathaniel derived from Jesus' supernatural insight into the very thoughts of his heart. Consequently, although the latter title is tantamount to a confession of Jesus' messiahship,[68] it must be seen, because it was provoked spontaneously by Jesus' supernatural insight into his inmost thoughts, to be a confession "on a higher plane than that of the Messiah in vs. 41."[69] It is thus entirely possible that even with the title "King of Israel" Nathaniel attributed deity to Jesus, for here was someone who could read his heart, "here was someone who could not be described in ordinary human terms."[70] (That the title "the King of Israel" could describe deity is clear from Isaiah 44:6, where it serves as a title of Yahweh.) But whatever the real case may be, by this second title Nathaniel clearly confessed faith (1:50) in Jesus as "the King of Israel" and thus as *his* Messiah, inasmuch as *he* was a "true Israelite."

With regard to his first title for Jesus—"the Son of God"—for two reasons I suggest that by it Nathaniel was confessing that he stood in the presence of deity. *First,* whatever experience in Nathaniel's past to which Jesus alluded when He said, "I saw you while you were still under the fig tree before Philip called you," it was clearly an experience so *intimate* and *private* that only *God* could have known about it, for Nathaniel's reaction to Jesus' comment suggests that it was an experience known to no *man* other than himself. And the fact that Jesus alluded to it implies that He knew this to be the case—this was His reason for alluding to it. But for *Jesus* to know about it (and recall that

67. Cf. Morris: "It is difficult to explain Jesus' knowledge of the incident on the level of merely human knowledge. Nathaniel had never met Him before this moment. We are required to understand that Jesus had some knowledge not generally available to the sons of men (cf. 2:24f.)" (*Gospel According to John,* p. 167).

68. C. H. Dodd, *The Interpretation of the Fourth Gospel* (Cambridge: University Press, 1953), p. 88; C. K. Barrett, *The Gospel According to St. John* (London: SPCK, 1955), p. 155.

69. Brown, *Gospel According to John I-XII,* p. 87.

70. Morris, *Gospel According to John,* p. 168.

Nathaniel was so amazed by Jesus' knowledge that he *immediately* confessed faith in Jesus' messiahship) could only mean for Nathaniel that Jesus stood in the closest possible relationship to God—that filial relationship ascribed to the Messiah in Psalm 2:7 (cf. Heb. 1:5) and elsewhere, a sonship of essential oneness with God. In other words, as the dove descending on Jesus, by divine appointment, was the sign to John the Baptist that Jesus was the Son of God, so Jesus' knowledge of his very private past became, under the Spirit's illumination, the sign to Nathaniel that Jesus was not only the Messiah but also the Son of God in a supra-natural sense.

Second, just as earlier with John the Baptist's attestation of Jesus as the Son of God, the title here cannot be lower in its import than the same title in John's statement of purpose for writing his Gospel (20:31), which, because of its proximity to Thomas's confession in 20:28, indicates both identity with God as to His nature and distinction from the Father as to His person. To suggest that John *knowingly* incorporated a pericope in which the title occurs but where its user (Nathaniel) meant less by it than its import in his overall purpose raises a serious question about John's integrity and vitiates to some degree the validity of his entire argument for Christ's divine sonship. But this possibility is most unlikely in light of both his stated concern for truth in reporting (19:35) and the validation the Gospel receives from those who knew him and the facts he reports (21:24). To suggest he did it *unknowingly* questions his competence as a writer and as a witness to Christ. This possibility is excluded by both the literary skill and the rich theological insights that even the most radical critics acknowledge are present in every sentence he wrote.

Against this title meaning essential sonship with God, two objections have been raised. First, placing the title *before* "the King of Israel" suggests that it too carries Messianic import rather than denoting essential oneness with God. However, this juxtaposition is one of the strongest arguments against it simply meaning a Messianic "sonship." We have already seen that the latter title—"the King of Israel"—does signify messiahship. To make the former also signify messiahship results in the following harsh tautology: "You are the Son of God [that is, the Messiah]; You are the King of Israel [that is, the Messiah]." If the two are synonymous for "Messiah," the second could have been connected as a simple apposition. As it is, the occurrence of σὺ εἶ ("You are") with both titles precludes their synonymy.

Second, if the former title denotes essential rather than Messianic sonship, since the former title would then be the more significant of the two titles, the order would be anticlimactic. But this does not follow if the former title is being treated as the ground of the latter and the latter as the covenantal consequence of the former (cf. the same order in Ps. 2:7; Matt. 3:17; 17:5).

Now it is exceedingly important that we note Jesus' reaction to Nathaniel's attestations. Jesus did not register any objections to either of Nathaniel's descriptions of Him. To the contrary, Jesus assured Nathaniel that he would see even greater things than Jesus' disclosure of the thoughts of his heart. Adding solemn certainty to His next words by introducing them with His authoritative "Truly, truly I say to you," Jesus declared that Nathaniel would (someday) see heaven opened, and the angels ascending and descending on the Son of Man (1:51; very likely an allusion to the words in Gen. 28:12-13). Employing the Danielic "Son of Man" figure, Jesus here confirmed Nathaniel's estimation of Him as the Messiah; and by the *apocalyptic* imagery He employed (the heavens opened and the Son of Man surrounded by the angels of God), He spoke prophetically of His future glorious return,[71] underscoring thereby both His supernatural character as the divine Son of God and His role as Israel's Messiah.

Consequently, I conclude that Nathaniel confessed faith in both Jesus' divine sonship and His Messianic investiture and that Jesus confirmed his confession. I also submit that Nathaniel's confession resulted from his awareness of Jesus' supernatural ability to know what only God could have known. And because Jesus did nothing to correct either his confession or the ground upon which he based it, we have another instance where the New Testament affirms the deity of Jesus.

Luke 5:8: Peter's Confession of Jesus as "Lord"

Jesus addressed the crowds from the haven of Peter's boat (Luke 5:1-11), and after He had finished speaking, Jesus invited Peter to put out into deep water and let down his nets for a catch. Although Peter mildly protested that it would do no good inasmuch as he had been fishing all night and had caught nothing, nevertheless, addressing Jesus as his "Master" (Έπιστάτα), he agreed to do as he was instructed. Immediately, he caught so many fish that his nets began to break, and when the second boat came alongside to assist, the catch was so plentiful that both boats began to sink!

Before we consider the implications of Peter's response in words and actions, something should be said about the historicity of the incident. Because certain details in the story resemble the miracle in John 21:1-14, Bultmann and his school have urged that Luke has ante-dated a post-Easter

---

71. Cf. J. H. Bernard, *A Critical and Exegetical Commentary on the Gospel According to St. John,* International Critical Commentary (Edinburgh: T. & T. Clark, 1928), 1:68.

story,[72] but again, C. H. Dodd has shown that the account lacks the essential "form" of a resurrection story and must be placed in the preresurrection period.[73] The mere fact that the accounts of the two incidents resemble one another in some details does not necessarily mean that they both reflect one original story in the "tradition." There are numerous examples in the Gospels of pairs of similar but distinct incidents (cf. Matt. 9:27-31 and 20:29-34; Luke 7:37-39 and John 12:1-3). There is no reason to deny either the historicity or the authenticity of the Lukan account.

At the display of not only Jesus' supernatural knowledge of but also His supernatural power over the creatures of nature, and overcome with the numinous[74] awareness of his own sinfulness in the presence of Jesus' majestic holiness,[75] Peter fell at Jesus' knees, crying, "Depart from me, because I am a sinful man, O Lord!" Although Marshall states that "no precise connotation (e.g., of divinity) can necessarily be attached to [Peter's use of κύριος ("Lord")],[76] Peter's act of prostrating himself at Jesus' knees, accompanied with his acknowledgment of his sinfulness, is an act of religious worship. Whereas godly men and angels always condemned such prostration before them as an act of misplaced devotion, indeed, as an act of idolatry (cf. Acts 10:25-26; 14:11-15; Rev. 19:9-10; 22:8-9), Jesus issued no such prohibition to Peter. To the contrary, He endorsed Peter's adoration by calling him to follow Him as a "fisher of men." (The parallel between Peter's action here and Isaiah's action in Isa. 6:1-7 is quite remarkable.) Concerning Peter's address of Jesus as "Lord" (κύριε), Warfield remarks that it

> seems to be an ascription to Jesus of a majesty which is distinctly recognized as supernatural: not only is the contrast of "Lord" with "Master" here expressed (cf. v. 5), but the phrase "Depart from me; for I am a sinful man" (v. 8) is the natural utterance of that sense of unworthiness which overwhelms men in the presence of the divine [cf. Job 42:5-6; Isa. 6:5; Dan. 10:16; Luke 18:13; Rev. 1:12-17], and which is

72. R. Bultmann, *Theology of the New Testament*, p. 45.

73. Dodd, *Studies in the Gospels*, pp. 9-35.

74. By "numinous" here I refer to that sense of religious awe that is aroused in the soul when one is suddenly confronted by the presence of the Holy. Cf. Rudolf Otto's *The Idea of the Holy* and J. D. Spiceland, "The Numinous," in *Evangelical Dictionary of Theology*, p. 783.

75. Vos writes: "The disciples came into awesome contact with [Jesus' holiness] through the miracle of the great draft of fishes and the perspective it opened to them of the supernatural Messianic potencies stored up in the Person of Jesus (Luke 5:1-11). The experience made Peter exclaim: 'Depart from me, for I am a sinful man, O Lord.' [His holiness] also explains, to some extent, the atmosphere of mystery enveloping Jesus as He walks through the Gospels. And it is one of the channels through which the apperception of *that which was even higher than Messiahship* broke in upon His followers" (*Self-Disclosure of Jesus*, p. 110; emphasis added).

76. Marshall, *Gospel of Luke*, p. 204.

signalized in Scripture as the mark of recognition of the divine presence.[77]

There can be no legitimate doubt that Peter here regards Jesus as divine and addresses Him accordingly as "Lord."

Matthew 14:33: The Disciples' Confession of Jesus as "the Son of God"

It had been an awe-inspiring day for the disciples—they had just witnessed Jesus' miraculous feeding of "about five thousand men, not counting women and children" with only five loaves and two fish (Matt. 14:13-21). But now, only hours later, they were on the Sea of Galilee some three and a half miles from shore (John 6:19); and with a strong wind against them, they found themselves in "rough sea." And it was night. Suddenly they saw Jesus walking toward them on the sea's surface, unhindered by the strong winds that were causing them such difficulty. And until Jesus reassured them that it was He, the disciples, terrified, imagined they were seeing a ghost (a sea-demon of some kind?). Peter requested that he might be allowed to go to Jesus, and with Jesus' permission and by His power, Peter walked, not without a lapse of faith, on the sea's surface as well. As soon as they both were received into the boat, the wind died (another demonstration of Jesus' sovereignty over nature?). All of this could not but make a great impression on the disciples—so much so, as Matthew informs us, that "those who were in the boat worshiped Him, and said; 'You are truly the Son of God' " (14:33).[78]

Before we consider the meaning of this exclamation, it is again necessary to deal with the historicity of the incident. We must insist at the outset that

77. Warfield, *Lord of Glory*, p. 142. Cf. also F. Godet: "Peter here employs the more religious expression *Lord*, which answers to his actual feeling" (*Commentary on the Gospel of St. Luke*, vol. 1, p. 257); Alfred Plummer: "The change from Ἐπιστάτα ["Master" to "Lord"] is remarkable, and quite in harmony with the change of circumstances. It is the 'Master' whose orders must be obeyed, the 'Lord' whose holiness causes moral agony to the sinner" (*A Critical and Exegetical Commentary on the Gospel According to St. Luke*, International Critical Commentary [Edinburgh: T. & T. Clark, 1896], p. 145); William Hendriksen: "Peter stands in awe of his Master and confesses him to be his 'Lord.' Astonishment and fear had seized him, and not only him but also his men . . . and his partners, James and John. They have become aware of the fact that Jesus is superhuman; in fact, that he is God! Again and again in the Septuagint . . . the title *Lord* is used as an equivalent of God. Instantaneously, under the impression of the astounding miracle, Simon Peter knew in his heart that his 'Master' was at the same time his 'Lord,' truly worthy of worship and adoration. Over against this 'Lord' Peter was nothing but a 'sinful man' " (*The Gospel of Luke* [Grand Rapids: Baker, 1978], p. 284); Marshall: "What Simon expressed was the sense of unworthiness . . . and fear . . . which men should feel in the presence of the divine. . . . The revelation of Jesus' divine power in this epiphany sufficed to demonstrate to Simon that he was in the presence of the Holy One . . . and to make him aware of his own inadequacy" (*Gospel of Luke*, pp. 204-5).

78. According to T. Zahn, the "truly" should be construed not as the indicator that the statement is an asseveration, that is: "Truly, you are . . ." but should rather be taken adverbially

there is no real ground for seeing this pericope as another displaced story or a resurrection appearance. Cranfield writes:

> The close connection between this section and the preceding makes [this] most unlikely. The character of the detail with which the section abounds makes it also unlikely that the narrative is a pious legend or a symbolical story; it suggests rather the memory of an actual incident. When the third person is changed to the first person plural, the section reads like the vivid reminiscence of one of the Twelve. . . . It seems very likely that we have here Petrine reminiscence.[79]

As for the disciples' confession itself, because neither Mark (6:45-51) nor John (6:16-21) mentions it, critical scholars commonly hold that Matthew has taken redactional liberties, in line with his purpose, and has created this feature of the story. This is all the more likely, they argue, since Mark declares that the reaction of the disciples was not what Matthew suggests—one of faith—but one of amazement (6:51), a statement critics interpret as incomprehension because of the words that follow: "for they had not understood about the [miracle of the] loaves, but their hearts were hardened" (6:52). But Mark's words do not need to be interpreted in such a manner. Vos's suggestion is very plausible that the disciples' amazement should not be interpreted in terms of utter lack of comprehension but rather in terms of "dawning apprehension [which makes room for Matthew's account of their confession], a sign that the hardening of their hearts was now to some extent passing away."[80] Mark's point would then be that if they had grasped earlier the significance of the miracle of the loaves (which had occurred the previous day), they would have realized *then* the mystery of Jesus' person and not later, after the frightening experience they had just gone through.

We are left, then, with Cullmann's two difficulties with the pericope: first, he judges that "within Matthew itself it has no special significance whatsoever," and second, "it seems inconsistent that this recognition should come in Matt. 14.33, when, according to the structure of the Gospel of Matthew, the disciples first recognized Jesus in Matt. 16.16."[81] As for his first problem, I suggest that it is reckless on Cullmann's part to say that the pericope "has no special significance whatsoever." That is not for Cullmann

with εἰ, that is, "You are truly . . ." underscoring the nature of this One in whose presence they were. This accords, says Zahn, with the fact that Matthew does not use Ἀληθῶς (as Luke does in 12:44; 21:3) like ἀμήν (*Das Evangelium des Matthäus* [Leipzig: A. Deichertsche, 1922], p. 514). Cf. Arndt and Gingrich, *Greek-English Lexicon of the New Testament*, p. 36, no. 1.

79. Cranfield, *Gospel According to Saint Mark*, p. 224; cf. also Lane, *Gospel of Mark*, p. 234.

80. Vos, *Self-Disclosure of Jesus*, p. 178, citing Weiss.

81. Cullmann, *Christology of the New Testament*, p. 277, 277 n. 3.

to say; Matthew apparently thought otherwise. If he reports a miracle that actually occurred, that is a significant fact in itself. And if it is also true that, as a result of the miracle, the disciples were brought to a fresh and deeper appreciation of Jesus' superhuman character and were led to affirm that fact, that too is significant—both for themselves and for the guidance and instruction of the church throughout all subsequent generations.

Cullmann's second problem is based upon a false assumption. Nowhere in the pericope itself or in "the structure of the Gospel" is there the remotest suggestion that it was at Caesarea Philippi that the disciples "first recognized Jesus." The actual case is quite different. The earliest of the disciples, including Peter himself, from the beginning concluded that Jesus was the Messiah (John 1:41, 49). But because He proceeded to act differently from what they had anticipated in their preconceptions of the Messianic hope, they were often perplexed about His messiahship. But again and again, some new miracle or some new discourse would persuade them afresh of His Messianic investiture and give them clearer insight into His nature. This is what we have here in Matthew 14:33 and will see occurring later in John 6:69 and, in a most significant way, in Matthew 16:16.[82] But even after Caesarea Philippi, the disciples had difficulty taking in His teaching about

---

82. Stonehouse writes in this regard:

> It is necessary to insist . . . that the situation [in Matt. 16:16-17] is not [to be construed as a totally new disclosure of the Messiahship of Jesus], in spite of the conspicuous reference to the divine revelation. If Mt. 16:17 is viewed in the perspective which Mt. 11:27 provides, as well as in the light of the entire previous record of the activity of Christ, it will appear that no new objective revelation of the moment can be in mind. Rather, the entire history of Christ has been in the nature of a divine revelation which the disciples, with greater or lesser clarity, and with admixture of doubt and bewilderment, have come to comprehend. In Peter's confession we are invited to observe then, not a new objective revelation, but genuine subjective apprehension. And even this apprehension is not clearly intimated to be a completely new apprehension. The fundamental contrast of the narrative is not between the disciples' previous lack of apprehension and their suddenly bestowed understanding, but between the inadequate and erroneous estimates of men, who held that he was at best one of the prophets, and the evaluation of his disciples who belonged to the inner circle and who had eyes to see and ears to hear.
>
> From this perspective no difficulty is presented by the acknowledgment of Jesus as God's Son which appears in Mt. 14:33. If the confession of Peter in Mt. 16:16 represented a turningpoint in the attitude of the disciples, grounded in a completely new revelation of the person of Jesus to them, the acknowledgment of Jesus' sonship which Matthew records in the narrative of the walking upon the sea might appear to introduce confusion and inconsistency into Matthew's delineation of the historical developments. Since, however, the whole of the ministry of Jesus is viewed as constituting a divine revelation, the apprehension of the revelation expressed in the words, "Of a truth thou art God's Son," does not imply that Matthew is reading back into an earlier stage of the disciples' experience an estimate of Christ's person which actually emerged at a later juncture. In fact, the confession of 14:33 is fully as intelligible as that in 16:16 since in the context the response is called forth by the miraculous action of Jesus in walking upon the water, rescuing Peter from the deep, and apparently also quieting the wind, besides Jesus' words of challenge to faith and of rebuke for doubt (Mt. 14:24-32) (*Witness of Matthew and Mark*, pp. 126-28).

His impending cross work (cf., e.g., John 12:16). It was not until after Jesus' resurrection that all He said to them came together in a comprehensive, coherent fashion. But even the later "false starts" after Matthew 16 in no way invalidate the legitimacy and significance of their earlier expressions of faith. Cullmann's difficulties, I conclude, are more "created" than real and are not really substantive problems.

Taking the Matthean account as an authentic report of the event, then, it is apparent from their act of worship and their confession that the disciples realized afresh the supernatural character of the One who was capable of such works. Their act of worship we may deduce from the Matthean word προσεκύνησαν, which means "they [fell down and] worshiped, did obeisance to, prostrated themselves before, did reverence to." At the very least the word connotes an attitude of reverence, but because of the character of the miracle itself (cf. Pss. 89:9; 106:9; 107:23-30, which Jewish sailors and fishermen must surely have known by heart), the word must certainly be given its maximum allowable sense of worship. And is it not plain that their earlier question, "What kind of [Ποταπός] man is this? Even the winds and the waves obey Him!" (Matt. 8:27), receives here its answer: "You are truly the Son of God!" This can only mean that they believed that they were in the presence of One who was supernatural and divine. Vos can even remark that in its momentary dissociation from the idea of messiahship, the confession of Matthew 14:33 stands even higher than Peter's famous confession at Caesarea Philippi "for through it, the disciples for a moment caught a vision of this [superhuman] character of Jesus as such, apart from its reflection in the Messiahship."[83] Again, Jesus does nothing to disabuse His disciples of their perception of Him as the Messiah or to correct their apprehension of Him as a proper object of worship. And so this confession adds the weight of its testimony to the larger New Testament witness to Jesus' divine nature and thus to the church's doctrine of an incarnational Christology.

John 6:69: Peter's Confession of Jesus as "the Holy One of God"

If the last few days had been a period of acute significance for the disciples regarding the question of Jesus' person, all the more so had it been for Peter since it had been he who had actually walked with Jesus on the Sea of Galilee. Certainly Peter must be included in that small group of seamen who had on that occasion acknowledged Him by deed and word to be the divine Son of God. Now on this occasion, presumably only some hours or days

83. Vos, *Self-Disclosure of Jesus*, pp. 178-79.

later, certainly not weeks (cf. John 6:22), Peter had just listened to his Lord's discourse on the Bread of Life, in which Jesus claimed that He had come down from heaven (6:33, 38, 51, 62), was the Giver of eternal life to the world (6:33, 40, 50, 51, 53, 54, 57, 58), and was the Lord of resurrection (6:39, 40, 44, 54). Because of these exalted, exclusive, and universal claims and His insistence on man's inherent inability to believe on Him (6:44-45, 65), many of His followers departed and no longer followed Him. At this defection, Jesus turned to the Twelve and asked, "You do not want to leave too, do you?" Although the question was put to all of them, not surprisingly (in view of the events of the last few days), Peter answered for the group: "Lord, to whom shall we go? You have words of eternal life. And we have believed and we know that You are the Holy One of God" (6:68-69).[84]

Since there is no miracle to get in their way in this pericope, most critical scholars concede the general authenticity of Peter's remarks. But some critical scholars insist that this is the Fourth Gospel's variant account of Peter's confession at Caesarea Philippi, taken out of its historical setting and placed here against the betrayal that was growing in Judas's heart (cf. 6:70-71). Against such an identification, however, we may array the differences of place, Jesus' approach, the circumstances, and the wording of the confession itself.[85] There is no reason whatsoever for taking this confession as anything other than a separate, distinct, and earlier confession on Peter's part, and that is the way I intend to approach it.

In light of the several indications in the Gospels of Peter's growing apprehension of the deity of Christ, though it is true that his term of address here ("Lord") "could mean much or little" in itself, in this context, Morris writes, "There can be no doubt that the word has the maximum, not the minimum meaning" of the ascription of deity to Jesus.[86]

Peter's statement, "You are the Holy One of God," is, at the very least, a Messianic title,[87] but several things can be said with cumulative force in favor of viewing it as implying Jesus' divine origin and character. *First* is just the fact itself of Peter's growing appreciation of who Jesus was: We noted earlier his confession of Jesus as his "Lord" (and that in the divine sense) on the occasion of his call to become a "fisher of men" in Luke 5 when, awed by

---

84. With the manuscript support in its favor (P75, ℵ, B, the original hand of C, D, L, W, and others), "the Holy One of God" is surely the original reading. The variants can all be explained as assimilations to John 1:49; 11:27; and Matt. 16:16. The editors of *The Greek New Testament* (UBS) give it an "A" rating. Cf. also Metzger, *Textual Commentary on the Greek New Testament,* p. 215.

85. Cf. Morris, *Gospel According to John,* p. 388 n. 155.

86. Ibid., p. 389.

87. So Bernard, *Commentary on the Gospel According to St. John,* p. 223; Vincent Taylor, *Names of Jesus* (London: Macmillan, 1953), p. 80; Barrett, *Gospel According to St. John,* p. 253.

Jesus' supernatural knowledge and power over nature, he acknowledged his own sinfulness over against the majestic and ethical holiness of Jesus. We also noted his confession (along with the other disciples) of Jesus, in view of the miracle of the loaves and his walking with Jesus on the sea, as "truly the Son of God." And we have just noted that his title of address here ("Lord") suggests deity. I submit that once a man has begun to apprehend that Jesus is divine, no title he ever employs in referring to Him (with the exception of those that clearly mark Him out as a true man) can be totally void of ascribing deity to Him.

Second, while this title ("the Holy One of God") is applied to Jesus on only one other occasion, leaving little room for extensive comparative study of the title, that one other occasion does cast some light on its meaning here. The title comes from the mouth of the demoniac in the synagogue at Capernaum, clearly revealing the demon's intuited awareness of who Jesus was (Mark 1:24; Luke 4:34). The demon feared Jesus and implied that He had the power to cast it into hell, suggesting thereby that Jesus possessed divine authority and power; but it was as "the Holy One of God" that the demon attributed to Him this authority.

Third, the stress on holiness in the title is significant. It reminds us of the frequently occurring title for God, "the Holy One of Israel," in the Old Testament. In this connection, Morris writes, "There can be not the slightest doubt that the title is meant to assign to Jesus the highest possible place. It stresses His consecration and His purity. It sets Him with God and not man."[88]

Fourth, C. H. Dodd calls attention to the similarity between Peter's words here, "we have *believed* and we have come to *know*" and Yahweh's words, "that you may *know* and *believe* that I am He" (LXX, Isa. 43:10). Dodd writes:

> The combination [in Peter's confession] πιστεύειν καὶ γινώσκειν follows Isaiah closely; but for ὅτι ἐγώ εἰμι ["that I am"] is substituted ὅτι σὺ εἶ ὁ ἅγιος τοῦ θεοῦ ["that You are the Holy One of God"]. The content of knowledge is the unique status of Christ Himself, which is an equivalent for knowledge of God.[89]

For these reasons it appears likely that Peter's confession, stressing as it does Jesus' inward character of holiness, marks Him out not only as the Messiah, but also, by virtue of His possessing a majestic and ethical holiness identical to that of God Himself (cf. Luke 5:8), as being Himself divine. And it is

88. Morris, *Gospel According to John*, p. 390.
89. Dodd, *Interpretation of the Fourth Gospel*, p. 168.

hardly necessary to point out again that Jesus accepted Peter's assessment of Him as the Messiah and his implied identification of Him as divine.

Matthew 16:16: Peter's Confession of Jesus as "the Christ, the Son of the Living God"

Following the disciples' united confession of Jesus as "truly the Son of God," and (1) a brief trip into the region of Tyre and Sidon where He healed a Canaanite woman's daughter of demon possession (Matt. 15:21-28), (2) a brief time around the region of the Sea of Galilee where He continued His healing ministry (Matt. 15:29-31) and fed about four thousand men, not counting women and children, with seven loaves and a few fish (Matt. 15:32-37), and (3) a brief journey to the region of Magadan, probably an area on the western side of the Sea of Galilee (Matt. 15:39–16:4), Jesus journeyed with His disciples northeast to Caesarea Philippi, healing a blind man at Bethsaida (Mark 8:22-26) on the way. While at Caesarea Philippi, Jesus questioned the disciples and drew from Peter, the self-appointed spokesman for the group, his great confession: "You are the Christ, the Son of the living God" (Matt. 16:16; cf. Mark 8:29; Luke 9:20).

In the previous chapter, in connection with our discussion of Jesus' self-understanding, we addressed Bultmann's view that the whole episode is a legend of the early church to undergird its "Easter faith" in Jesus' messiahship and Fuller's view that Matthew 16:17-19 is a "Matthean expansion" and thus "clearly secondary" and that Mark 8:30-32 is both Marcan redaction and later tradition. He concludes that Jesus positively rejected all claims to messiahship as a "diabolical temptation." I will not repeat here the arguments we registered there against their revision of this significant pericope but refer the reader to that section and to Marshall's refutation in his commentary on the Greek text of Luke's Gospel.[90] Suffice it to say that there is no legitimate ground to question either the historicity of the event or the authenticity of Jesus' recorded response.

Given, then, that all three Synoptic Evangelists report that Peter confessed faith in Christ's messiahship (Matthew and Mark: "You are the Christ"; Luke: "You are the Christ of God"), and that in Matthew Jesus gives express approval and in Mark and Luke tacit approval to this confession, I conclude that here is a clear and incontrovertible instance when Jesus claimed to be the Messiah.

But as we have seen, Matthew reports Peter's confession as containing a

---

90. Marshall, *Gospel of Luke*, pp. 364-65.

second part: "the Son of the living God." We have no way of knowing why Mark and Luke do not report this second part; we can only assume that it did not serve their respective purposes. It has been suggested that the second part is only a further elucidation or synonym for Peter's "the Christ" and that the two Evangelists saw no need for the elucidation. But there are four cogent reasons for insisting that Peter did not intend the second part as merely a synonym of the first part but that he intended to confess Him as the "super-Messianic Son" both as to nature and origin. Those reasons are as follows:[91]

1. We argued earlier from the disciples' act of worship in Matthew 14:33 that their united confession of Jesus as "truly the Son of God" ascribed divine sonship to Him. The title, "the Son of the living God" in 16:16 can hardly carry lower import on this occasion than the same phrase did on the former occasion. In fact, the additional word "living" in this latter expression, if anything, adds weight to the import of Peter's confession, in that it particularizes the God whose Son Jesus is and by extension particularizes Him as well.

2. If the second part does not intend *more* than the ascription of messiahship to Jesus, then it follows that all that Peter was confessing here is just Jesus' messiahship. But such a confession, expressed both by Peter and others on other occasions (cf. John 1:41, 49; 6:69), hardly explains Jesus' unusual response to Peter's confession here. Why would Peter's confession of the lone fact of Jesus' messiahship elicit Jesus' declaration on *this* occasion that Peter's confession was the effect of a special, supernatural revelation when "the ordinary means of self-disclosure during our Lord's long association with Peter would have sufficed for the basis of a mere confession of Jesus' Messiahship"?[92] The question cannot be intelligently answered on the assumption that Peter's confession entailed simply the recognition of Jesus' messiahship.

3. The two facts—(1) that the two Evangelists who do not report the second part of Peter's confession do not report Jesus' response to Peter either, whereas Matthew reports both, and (2) that Peter refers to Jesus as "the Son" in his second part and Jesus refers to God in His response to Peter not as "God," which would have been appropriate in the light of Peter's reference to "the living God," but as "My Father"—strongly suggest that

91. I am indebted for some of the thoughts in the following paragraphs to Vos (*Self-Disclosure of Jesus*, pp. 179-81) where he himself is following Zahn's exposition for the most part. But his second and third points of argument, which the interested reader may assess for himself, appear too abstruse to me and decidedly weak.

92. Ibid., p. 180.

Jesus' benediction was not a response to the first part (although the first part cannot be divorced from the context in which Jesus' response is interpreted) but was rather His response primarily to the second part. Now if it is true that *any* correct assessment of Jesus must be finally traced to the Father's "teaching" (John 6:45), especially is it true that the Father's "teaching" is necessary to perceive the essential sonship of Jesus. Jesus expressly declared this in Matthew 11:25-27: "No one knows *the Son* except *the Father*," He said, and if one is to know "the Son," it will be through the Father's act of revelation according to His good pleasure. Here Jesus declares Peter's confession to be the result of a supernatural revelation (16:17); and by His reference to "My Father" in 16:17, it is apparent (1) that Jesus regarded Peter's confession of His sonship as just such an instance of the revealing activity by the Father that He had spoken of in 11:25-26, and (2) that the disclosure made to Peter referred to the paternal ("Father") and filial ("Son") relationship between God and Jesus alluded to in Matthew 11:25-26 and not simply to the Messianic investiture *per se*.

4. The juxtaposition of the two occurrences of σὺ εἶ ("You are") in this context should not be overlooked: Peter's *"You are* the Christ, the Son of the living God" (v. 16), and Jesus' *"You are* Peter" (v. 18). They are very significant in determining the intent of Peter's confession, the pointed correspondence between them being highlighted very strongly by Jesus' words: "And I, on My part, say also to you" (v. 18). Jesus' "You are" lifts Simon bar Jonah by his new title "Peter" to an altogether *new* and *higher* category, that of being, as the representative of all of the apostles, the very foundation of the church Jesus was erecting (Eph. 2:20; cf. Gal. 2:9). The correspondence between Peter's "You are" and Jesus' "You are" strongly suggests that Peter's prior confession be construed similarly: Peter moves beyond describing Jesus merely by His office as Messiah, in which Jesus' supernatural nature and origin, although not absent, remain somewhat in the background, to a supra-Messianic ascription in which Jesus' anterior supernatural nature and origin receive special stress. And it is a matter of historical record that the church Jesus erected on the foundation of (the doctrine of) the apostles and prophets has never confessed Jesus simply as the Messiah but has also declared Him the divine Son of God in both nature and origin.

For these reasons, I urge that by his confession Peter self-consciously affirmed, as the result of the Father's revelatory activity, full, unabridged deity to Jesus as "the Son" of "the Father" and that Jesus, by declaring him in making such a confession to have been directly blessed by His Father, tacitly claimed to be God incarnate.

Matthew 17:10; Mark 9:11: The Inner Circle's "Elijah"Question

We have already discussed, in connection with the transfiguration accounts, the significance of the disciples' question—"Why then do the teachers of the Law say that Elijah must come first?"—for Jesus' identity as Yahweh. I do not intend to repeat the points I made there; I mention it again here to give a complete list of the most significant instances when something the disciples say in Jesus' presence implies that Jesus is divine. By their question, the disciples suggest that Jesus was the Yahweh who had promised to come, but they could not understand why He had come *before* rather than *after* Elijah whom they had just seen conversing with Jesus. This inversion of the prophet Malachi's order of appearances for them was the disciples' problem; Jesus proceeded to resolve it for them by making it clear that the "Elijah" who was to come was John the Baptist, His forerunner. The obvious conclusion of His interpretation of Malachi's "Elijah" prophecy is that Jesus believed Himself to be the Yahweh of Malachi 3:1.

John 11:27: Martha's Great Confession

After Lazarus died, Jesus consoled Martha, saying: "I am the resurrection and the life. He who believes in Me will live, even though he dies; and whoever lives and believes in Me will never die." Jesus then asked her: "Do you believe this?" With no hesitancy whatsoever, Martha replied, "Yes, Lord, I believe that You are the Christ, the Son of God, who was to come into the world" (John 11:27)—surely her finest reported hour.

Because of the complexity of the problems raised by critical scholars regarding the historicity of the entire incident recorded in John 11:1-54, it would take us far afield were we to enter deeply into a defense of its historicity (see pp. 48-49). Some critical scholars say that the fact that the miracle of raising Lazarus from the dead is not mentioned in the Synoptic Gospels is inexplicable if it had really had the effect that John ascribes to it, of setting in motion the chain of events that led to Jesus' crucifixion (cf. John 11:46-53). The Synoptic Evangelists, the same critics argue, suggest that it was the "triumphal entry" and the cleansing of the temple that initiated the events that were to issue in the crucifixion. However, these two grounds for the hostility of the religious leadership need not be viewed as contradictory but should be seen rather as complementing one another. After all, the conflict between Jesus and the Sanhedrin had been seething for some time, and many things Jesus had said and done—not just these things—had provoked them to the point of plotting His execution. Full defenses of the historicity of this miracle—competent and comprehensive—have been made and are available, such as those of Raymond E. Brown[93] and Leon Morris.[94] I refer the reader to these defenses and merely state here that I am convinced we have in John 11:1-54 real history and in 11:27 an authentic response by Martha to Jesus' query.

And so we turn to Martha's confession. "Lord," "the Christ," "the Son of God, who was to come into the world." What did Martha intend by this rich titular description of Jesus?

As for her title of address—"Lord," since theoretically it could have been nothing more than a title of respect with the equivalent meaning of our "Sir," the sense in which she intended it will in large measure turn on the meanings of the titles that immediately follow it. But I assert, in light of what I hope to show she meant by her following titles, that by it she was attributing to Jesus' unabridged *lordship* over her life—lordship properly belonging only to God Himself. I say this, not only because of the following titles but because of her unhesitating "Yes" and her "I have believed," the significance of which might be lost on the reader of John's Gospel as his attention is drawn to the following titles themselves. These two features in her answer indicate that she had placed her confidence—"once given and permanently remaining"[95] (for this is the force of πεπίστευκα—"I have and still do believe")—explicitly in Jesus. He was her "Lord" in the full, unqualified sense of the word.

By "the Christ," of course, she was acknowledging Jesus to be the Messiah of Old Testament promise and Jewish hope. And it is important to note, even if by the following words she intended nothing more than this, that here she at least ascribes to Jesus Messianic stature, which ascription Jesus did nothing to correct. Clearly, here is an instance, as I have argued in chapter 2, where, by the absence of any word of correction, Jesus tacitly claimed to be the Messiah.

But I believe that she intended more by the next title. For four reasons I urge that Martha, by her title, "the Son of God," intended the attribution of deity to Jesus. My first two reasons have engaged the reader's attention before in earlier contexts. *First*, if the title here is simply an additional ascription of Messianic stature to Jesus, as Barrett and a good many other scholars insist, it reduces the "Son of God" title to a tautology. Barrett, in fact, suggests that even the words, "He who is to come into the world,"

93. Brown, *Gospel According to John I-XII*, pp. 427-30.

94. Morris, *Gospel According to John*, pp. 532-36. I prefer Morris's remarks over Brown's inasmuch as the latter scholar is willing to question the historicity, if not of the basic story itself, at least of some of its details.

95. Ibid., p. 555.

should be construed this way as well, so that we have "three parallel titles" intending messiahship.[96] But this is to heap idle tautology on top of what is already tautology, if the first words, "the Son of God," are construed only as a title denoting messiahship.

Second, Martha's words, "the Christ, the Son of God," are precisely parallel to John's words in his stated purpose in 20:31. Because of its proximity to Thomas's full, unqualified ascription of deity to Jesus in his confession in 20:28, John's term, "the Son of God," while it distinguishes Jesus as the Son from the Father, does not distinguish Him from God. If then "the Son of God" in 20:31 includes the ascription of deity to Jesus, it is highly unlikely that the same title means less than that anywhere in his Gospel (cf. 1:34, 49; 5:25; 10:36; 11:4, 27; 19:7; 20:31). We have already argued in this section that this is precisely its import in 1:34; 1:49; and 20:31; and even those who would not agree with everything I have said in these earlier expositions must admit that its occurrence in 5:25; 10:36; and 19:7 must convey this meaning. In these three contexts Christ's enemies accuse Jesus of blasphemy for employing the term the way He did, for, they argue, He was "making Himself God." And certainly the occurrences of the unqualified title, "the Son," and the fuller title, "the one and only Son," throughout John's Gospel connote essential equality with the Father. All this being so, it seems highly unlikely that the title in Martha's confession could properly have intended less. In fact, I urge that this is precisely the reason behind John's decision to report her confession—he knew what she intended and he knew that it accorded with the purpose of his Gospel.

Third, Martha must have heard Jesus speaking about Himself as the Son of God. Where else would she have gained such an assessment of Him if not from His teaching? But, and here I am indebted to Hendriksen for the thought,

> if *others* [that is, His enemies] understood this to mean that he claimed full equality with the Father . . . *why not Martha?* She had heard the claims of Jesus, and *she* had believed them. . . . *Others* had heard the same claims, but had rejected them, calling Jesus a blasphemer.[97]

She doubtless knew, as did His enemies, what Jesus intended by the title when He used it of Himself. And since she believed Him, her use of the title must be allowed to carry the same import of deity as His own use of it.

Fourth, whether her last words, ὁ εἰς τὸν κόσμον ἐρχόμενος, are to be

---

96. Barrett, *Gospel According to St. John*, p. 330.
97. William Hendriksen, *A Commentary on the Gospel of John* (London: Banner of Truth Trust, 1959), pp. 151-52.

construed as a third title or appositionally, [98] her words εἰς τὸν κόσμον ("into the world"), coming between the article and the participle, clearly affirm of "the Son of God" a heavenly origin. These words are equivalent to the ἄνωθεν ("from above") coming in precisely the same place in ὁ ἄνωθεν ἐρχόμενος in John 3:31 (cf. 9:39; 12:46). Furthermore, Jesus Himself declares in John 16:28 that for Him to have "come into the world" involved *first* His coming "from [the side of] the Father," clearly claiming thereby the attribute of preexistence.

For all these reasons, I agree with Morris, who writes of Martha's affirmations, "[They] give us as high a view of the person of Christ as one well may have."[99] And Warfield declares,

> There is no reason to doubt that here, too . . . "Son of God" carries with it the implication of supernatural origin and thus designates the Messiah from a point of view which recognized that He was more than man.[100]

This text, then, joins the many others we have considered that attest to the deity of Christ.

John 16:30: The Disciples' Upper Room Confession

On the last evening before His crucifixion Jesus met in the upper room with the Twelve, and there He delivered what has come to be known as His Upper Room or Farewell Discourse(s) (John 14–16). At the end of His discourse, the disciples declared: "Now we know that You know all things, and You have no need that anyone should ask You anything. By this we believe that You came from God" (16:30).

Here is a remarkable "confession of faith."[101] Each clause deserves some comment. By their first statement—"Now [that You speak plainly and no longer in "dark sayings"] we know that You know all things"—they plainly ascribe to Jesus the attribute of omniscience. Barrett concedes that this

---

98. Some regard it as a third title because of its "fixed form" appearance, as in Matt. 11:3; Luke 7:19-20; 19:38. But in these contexts there is no preceding noun either, to which the articular participle could point as an antecedent. But where there is an immediately preceding noun that can serve as an antecedent as in John 11:27, and because the article and the participle are broken apart by the intervening words "into the world" (literally, "the one into the world coming"), thereby disrupting the fixed form, it is quite possible that the words should be construed appositionally, that is, "[He] who was to come into the world."

99. Morris, *Gospel According to John*, p. 552.

100. Warfield, *Lord of Glory*, p. 195.

101. Dodd, *Interpretation of the Fourth Gospel*, pp. 410, 416.

clause may be taken in this way ("You have all knowledge"), but he suggests that the universe of intent here should more likely be restricted to the immediate subject in 16:19-28.[102] But this interpretation the next clause expressly precludes: "and You have no need that anyone should ask You [anything]." What do they mean? On first reflection, one might think that they should have said, "and [as a result of Your knowing all things] You have no need to ask anyone anything." But they say the reverse: "You have no need that anyone ask You anything." Again, what do they mean? One possibility is that they were saying, "Because of Your knowledge, You have no need that anyone should ply You with questions in order to stimulate You to new and deeper levels of understanding." But it could mean also that they were ascribing such knowledge to Him as the reader of the thoughts and intents of men's hearts that He did not need men even to ask Him questions in order for Him to discern what was troubling them. This latter meaning receives the endorsement of the passage itself, for we are told in 16:17-18 that some of His disciples were asking one another, "What does He mean by saying: 'In a little while you will see Me no more, and then after a while you will see Me,' and 'Because I am going to the Father'?" They kept asking one another, "What does He mean by 'a little while'? We don't understand what He is saying." But they were not asking *Jesus* these questions! Then what do we read in 16:19? "Jesus knew that they were wanting to ask" these very questions! And so He answered their questions even before they asked Him. So the disciples by this second clause were saying that He had read their very thoughts. The *Jerusalem Bible* captures their meaning in this second clause quite nicely with its "you do not have to wait for questions to be put into words." And a man who can do this must "know all things."

Their third statement gives us their final deduction from their realization of His omniscience: "By this [that is, because we know You are omniscient], we believe that You came out from God." And by this statement they affirm His divine origin. But why do they declare that His knowledge had convinced them of His divine origin? Possibly they reasoned thus: Only God is omniscient. Jesus is omniscient. Therefore, He came out from God. But this is not what they should strictly have concluded by such a process of deduction. Rather, they should have concluded: Therefore, Jesus is God. So we still lack the missing piece that led them to draw this specific conclusion. So we ask again, why did they single out this feature of His person and declare that His knowledge had convinced them of His divine origin? He Himself provides the answer: Only a few moments before (16:28), in responding to

102. Barrett, *Gospel According to St. John*, pp. 414-15.

their unasked questions, Jesus had given them a "simple and precise reca-pitulation of all the mysteries of His past, present, and future existence"[103]—"I came out from the Father and have come into the world; again, I am leaving the world and going to the Father." And in saying this, He affirmed His own divine origin. Here is the missing piece. He had affirmed that He was "from the Father," and His omniscience gave them evidence of that. Their process of thinking then was as follows: Jesus says He is from God. How do we know He is? Jesus is Himself omniscient; this we know from the fact that He has read our very hearts. Therefore if He knows all things, He must have come from God, because He said so.

It escapes me why some commentators say the faith they now confessed lacked depth (Lightfoot), or "had not advanced as far as the Baptist" (West-cott), or was "inadequate" (Morris), because it was grounded in what Barrett calls the "slight foundation" of Jesus' display of divine knowledge.[104] What better foundation for his faith can anyone find than Jesus' omniscient word about Himself? Does not His omniscience guarantee that He knows all truth, and is truth not the ground of all healthy faith? And even if Jesus' following words be construed as a question—"Do you now believe? Behold, the hour is coming and has come that you will be scattered. . . ."—His intention could have been to dampen their new enthusiasm, for they had not yet comprehended the cross work that still lay ahead of Him. But He does not deny that they have faith; indeed, He had expressly stated earlier, "You have believed that I came out [of the being and] from [the side of] God" (16:27). Nor does He deny the content of their faith but, in fact, had Himself affirmed *that very content* only moments before (16:28). And it is entirely possible grammatically to construe His words as a statement: "Now you believe!" If this was the import of His words, then even with sharper lines does Jesus emphasize their faith in His divine origin. But in either case, it is clear from the entire episode that in this last confession of the Eleven before the crucifixion of their Lord, they confessed *in His presence* their belief in His divine origin and, by implication, also in His preexistence; and He did nothing to correct their statement of faith but had, in fact, declared the same thing about Himself only moments before.

Here, then, is an eighth occasion when, through our examination of the disciples' understanding of Jesus, we find them asserting His deity, and on

103. F. Godet, *Commentary on the Gospel of John*, vol. 2, 3rd ed. (1893; reprint, Grand Rapids: Zondervan, 1969), p. 321.

104. R. H. Lightfoot, *St. John's Gospel* (Oxford: Clarendon Press, 1956), p. 290; B. F. Westcott, *The Gospel According to St. John* (London: John Murray, 1890), pp. 235-36; Morris, *Gospel According to John*, p. 712; Barrett, *Gospel According to St. John*, p. 415.

each occasion we discover that He either expressly or tacitly acknowledged that what they were saying about Him was so.

Matthew 27:54; Mark 15:39: The Centurion's Confession

During His crucifixion, God attested that Jesus was His Son by causing darkness to come upon the land for three hours—the length and extension of the darkness and the time of the month precluding this being merely an eclipse of the sun. And at the moment of His death, God ripped the curtain in the temple in two from top to bottom, and caused the earth to shake. Jesus' utterances from the cross and the darkness and the earthquake evoked from the centurion (and the watching crowd) the one exclamation the Jewish leaders did not want to hear: *"This was truly the Son of God"* (Matt. 27:54; Mark 15:39).

What did the Roman centurion mean, and on what ground should we consider his confession—hardly the confession of one who was a disciple in the same sense that the others we have been considering were disciples—a credible witness to the identity of Jesus? I suggest that we may presume from the very fact that Mark reported his confession that what the centurion had witnessed had brought him to an understanding of Jesus' sonship. In accordance with Colwell's studied observation that "definite predicate nouns which precede the verb usually lack the article" while "a definite predicate nominative has the article when it follows the verb,"[105] the word order in the centurion's exclamation—specifically that the predicate nominative ("Son of God") precedes the copula ("was")—suggests that he affirmed Christ as *"the* Son of God." There is no justifiable reason to reduce his confession simply to an affirmation of Christ as one of many Hellenistic "divine men." He had just heard the jeers and taunts of the crowd: "He said, 'I am the Son of God' " (Matt. 27:43) and "Come down from the cross, if you are the Son of God" (Matt. 27:40). He had just heard Jesus address God from the cross as "Father" (Luke 23:34, 46). And even if he had been in Judea only a matter of days—much more if he had spent some years there—we cannot imagine that he was wholly ignorant of Christ's own claims and His authenticating deeds. He had just witnessed the serene, courageous manner in which Jesus endured His execution and the frightening natural phenomena of the three hours of darkness and the earthquake that occurred at the moment of Jesus' death. It is difficult to believe, therefore, that the centurion

---

105. Colwell, "Use of the Article in the Greek New Testament," pp. 13, 22.

attached no more meaning to his words than that suggested by the mythology of his pagan background.

It is true that Luke reports the centurion as saying, "Surely, this man was righteous" (23:47), a comment intended as a judgment against the whole sordid treatment Jesus had received at their hands. But it need not be taken to mean that the other Synoptic Evangelists' "Son of God" expression intended nothing more than that Jesus was a good man. If his confession amounted to no more than that, one might well wonder why Mark and Matthew were inspired to record for all time his confession in the manner they did. To interpret the centurion's statement to mean less in its import than we have suggested is to impute literary ineptitude to Mark and Matthew, for it suggests that they permitted the driving thrust of their respective Gospels' testimony to Jesus as "the Son of God" in the high, supernatural, divine sense to culminate in a climactic testimony that used the same title but, in actuality, meant less than they themselves intended by earlier occurrences of this title in their Gospels (cf. Mark 1:1 [?], 11; 3:11; 5:7; 9:7; 12:6; 13:32; 14:61-62; Matt. 2:15; 3:17; 8:29; 11:27; 14:33; 16:16; 17:5; 21:7; 28:19). It seems appropriate, therefore, to understand Luke's statement as supplementary to, not explanatory of, the other Synoptic Evangelists' report. And it seems equally appropriate to suggest that the centurion was confessing that Jesus was "the Son of God" in the same sense that the Evangelists' earlier uses of that title intended.

As I bring this third chapter to a close, let me remind the reader what I set out to do. I attempted to set forth major lines of preresurrection evidence that corroborate the church's confession—in concert with Jesus Himself— that He is both God and man and thus God incarnate. We considered five broad areas of testimony: the nativity accounts, the baptism accounts, the temptation accounts, the transfiguration accounts, and the disciples' preresurrection understanding of Jesus. I have not knowingly avoided a passage that would require a different confession. The over-all witness of the combined testimony of these areas in the Gospel accounts—each area arguably and demonstrably historically reliable and trustworthy—overwhelmingly supports the historic view of the church that the Christ of the Gospels is supernatural—both divine and human, God manifest in the flesh. The virginal conception was the means whereby God the Son became man. God the Father testified both at Jesus' baptism and at His transfiguration that He is the Son of God. The devil gave similar testimony at His temptation. And while His disciples were sometimes slow to come to a full appreciation of all

that their confessions implied, the evidence indicates that from the beginning of His public ministry, they confessed Him to be divine, their Lord and
their Messiah.

It is true that He was crucified as a criminal under Roman law. But His
death must not be viewed as the one event that puts the lie to the church's
confession. For, as we shall see in the next chapter, three days later the
Arimathean's tomb was empty, and the world had a resurrection on its
hands.

THE POSTRESURRECTION WITNESS TO JESUS

Jesus was crucified by Roman authorities at the instigation of the Jewish religious leaders. But in Paul's words, He "was raised on the third day according to the Scriptures" (1 Cor. 15:4). This quotation highlights not only a major theme of both the New Testament and church proclamation; more immediately, it also states the presupposition behind the title of this chapter. So before I continue my investigation of the New Testament data regarding Jesus' identity, I feel I must say something to justify this presupposition.

Christians should admit, given the first-century Jewish milieu in which Christ's resurrection occurred, that it was not at all what the nation expected. I do not mean to suggest by this comment that Jews of the first century did not believe in the resurrection of the dead, for it is well known that many Jews did indeed believe in the resurrection (cf. Acts 23:6-8). But they believed that the resurrection of the dead would occur in the future at the end of time. But suddenly, here was a small group of men proclaiming, not in some out-of-the-way place like Azotus but in Jerusalem itself—the politico-religious center of the nation—that God had raised Jesus from the dead. This was not only very strange teaching to the Jewish ear, it was also exceedingly offensive teaching to the majority of them, including Saul of Tarsus, because Jesus had been executed as a blasphemer with the sanction of the nation's highest court, the Sanhedrin.

The disciples of Jesus believed, however, that there were compelling reasons for such a proclamation, for they continued to preach that He had risen from the dead in the face of threats, bodily persecution, and martyrdom. What were these reasons? I submit that two great interlocking strands of evidence convinced them beyond all reasonable doubt that Jesus had risen from the dead just as He said He would.[1] These strands of evidence are

---

1. Jesus Himself spoke of His resurrection in John 2:19-21; Matt. 12:40; 16:21 (Mark 8:31; Luke 9:22); 17:9 (Mark 9:9); 17:23 (Mark 9:31); 20:19 (Mark 10:34; Luke 18:33); cf. also Matt. 27:63; Mark

the empty tomb and His numerous postcrucifixion physical appearances. Each of these calls for some comment.

Evidence for Jesus' Resurrection
The First Great Strand of Evidence: the Empty Tomb

All four Gospels report that on the third day after Jesus had been crucified and entombed His disciples discovered that His body had disappeared from the tomb in which it had been placed and His tomb was empty (Matt. 28:6; Mark 16:5-6; Luke 24:3, 6, 22-24; John 20:5-8). Almost immediately, as we have said, the disciples began to proclaim their conviction that Jesus had risen from the dead. Now if the tomb, in fact, had still contained His body—the women and later Peter and John all having gone to the wrong tomb (most unlikely in light of Matt. 27:61; Mark 15:47; Luke 23:55)—we may be sure that the authorities, both Jewish and Roman, would have corrected the disciples' error by directing them to the right tomb and to the fact that the tomb still contained Jesus' physical remains.

Many critical scholars over the years who have not accepted the historicity of Jesus' resurrection have felt it necessary to concede that the tomb was undoubtedly empty, but then have blunted the edge of their concession at the same time by advancing such theories as the stolen body theory and the swoon theory to explain why it was empty.

The "Stolen Body" Theory. With regard to the former theory, we may safely conclude that if Jesus' body had been removed by human hands, they were the hands of either His disciples, His enemies, or professional grave robbers. Now if His disciples had stolen His body, which was the explanation first concocted to explain His body's disappearance (Matt. 28:12-15), one must still face the questions: How could His disciples have gotten past the Roman guards (who, according to Matt. 27:62-66, had been posted there for the express purpose of preventing His disciples from stealing His body)? And how could they have rolled the stone away without being detected? The only possible explanation is that the entire Roman watch must have fallen asleep, which was part of the first concocted explanation.

It is most unlikely that disorganized, fearful disciples would have even

14:58; Luke 24:6-7. Certainly, the veracity of everything that Jesus taught is called into question if He did not rise as He said He would. Indeed, it is not saying too much to insist that if Christ rose from the dead as He said He would, the gospel is true; if He did not rise, it is false. And the faith that would believe He has risen, if in fact He did not rise from the dead, would be vain and futile (1 Cor. 15:17).

attempted such an exploit. And it is even more unlikely that the Roman guards would have fallen asleep on duty since to do so would have meant certain and severe punishment. Nevertheless, both of these "unlikelihoods" would have to have occurred simultaneously if this explanation for the empty tomb is to be sustained. Furthermore, it should be patently clear that any tough-minded interrogator would have immediately rejected the guards' explanation, for if in fact they all had fallen asleep, they would not have known who had stolen the body (cf. Matt. 28:13). There is one more problem that this proffered solution must face: If Jesus' disciples had been responsible for His body's disappearance—a most unlikely prospect in light of their reaction to everything that had just happened to Jesus (cf. John 20:19)—we must then believe that they went forth and proclaimed as historical fact a mere fiction they knew they had contrived, and, when faced by persecution and threats of execution as many of them were, not one of them, even when facing martyrdom, revealed that it was all a hoax. I submit that this scenario is highly improbable; liars and hypocrites are not the stuff from which martyrs are made.

Now if His enemies (the religious leaders) arranged for His body's removal, why would they do the one thing that contributed more than anything else to the very idea they were trying to suppress (cf. Matt. 27:62-66)? And if they, in fact, had His body or knew of its whereabouts, why did they not produce either it or reliable witnesses who could explain the body's disappearance and prove the disciples wrong when they began to proclaim that Jesus had risen from the dead?

To attribute the fact of the empty tomb, finally, to grave robbers is the least likely possibility of all. For it is to intrude on the story an explanation for which there is not a grain of evidence. Moreover, not only would thieves have been prevented from doing so by the Roman guards, but also, even if they could have somehow avoided detection and plundered the tomb, they would have hardly, having first unwrapped it, taken the *nude* body of Jesus with them, leaving His grave wrappings behind and essentially intact (John 20:6-7).

The "Swoon" Theory. If we may accept Albert Schweitzer's judgment (cf. his *Vom Reimarus zu Wrede* [1906], entitled *The Quest of the Historical Jesus* in the English translation), David Strauss dealt the "death-blow" to the swoon theory over one hundred and fifty years ago. And yet one occasionally hears it advanced as a possibility in popular discussions today. This discredited theory maintains that Jesus had not actually died on the cross but had only slipped into a coma-like state, and that in the tomb He revived and somehow made His way past the guards to His disciples, who then concluded that He had risen from the dead. He died shortly thereafter.

But to believe this pushes the limits of credibility beyond all legitimate boundaries. It requires one to believe that those responsible for His execution by crucifixion were woefully incompetent as executioners and then as judges of the state of the crucified victims when they performed the crurifragium (the breaking of the legs of the victim) (cf. John 19:31-33). It also requires one to believe that Jesus, though suffering from the excruciating pain of wounded hands and feet; the loss of blood, shock trauma, and physical weakness naturally ensuing from the horrible ordeal of the crucifixion itself; and the lack of human care and physical nourishment, somehow survived the mortal wound in His side and the cold of the tomb without human aid or succor and then pushed the huge stone away from the entrance of the tomb with wounded hands and made His way on wounded feet past Roman guards into the city and to the place where His disciples were hiding, and there He convinced His followers that He—the emaciated shell of a man—was the Lord of Life! Such a scenario is surely beyond all possibility and does not deserve any thinking man's assent. Such recent books as Hugh Schonfield's *The Passover Plot* and Donovan Joyce's *The Jesus Scroll* are only variations on this same theme and are not taken seriously by the scholarly community.

But if some critical scholars have acknowledged the fact of the empty tomb and attempted (unsuccessfully) to offer explanations for it, others have simply declared that the empty tomb was not an essential part of the original resurrection story, that the church only later created the "fact" in order to fortify its stories of the resurrection appearances. This is not true. The empty tomb was part of the church's proclamation from the outset (cf. Acts 2:31; 1 Cor. 15:4). It is simply erroneous teaching to assert that the first disciples believed that one can have a real resurrection without an empty tomb. G. C. Berkouwer has correctly observed:

> Not the empty grave but the resurrection of Christ is the great soteriological fact, but as such the resurrection is inseparably connected with the empty tomb and unthinkable without it. It is absolutely contrary to Scripture to eliminate the message of the empty tomb and still speak of the living Lord. The Gospels picture his resurrection in connection with historical data, moments, and places of his appearance. Scripture nowhere supports the idea of his living on independently of a corporeal resurrection and an empty tomb. [2]

2. G. C. Berkouwer, *The Work of Christ*, trans. Cornelius Lambregste (Grand Rapids: Eerdmans, 1965), p. 184.

The conclusion is self-evident: the theologian who dismisses the empty tomb as irrelevant to the Christian message but who still speaks of "the resurrection of Jesus" does not mean by His "resurrection" what the New Testament means or what the church has traditionally meant by it. It has become more a saving "idea" than a saving event. But such a resurrection would have been rejected out of hand by the early church as no resurrection at all (cf. 2 Tim. 2:17-18).

We have defended to this point the fact of the "empty" tomb. But now we must point out that such a description is not entirely accurate, since the tomb was not completely empty. For not only did angels appear to the women in the tomb and announce to them that Jesus had risen (Mark 16:5-7; Luke 24:3-7), but also both Luke (24:12) and John (20:5-7) mention the presence of His empty grave clothes. The strips of linen in which Jesus' body had been wrapped were still there, with the cloth that had been around His head folded and lying by itself, separate from the linen (which single fact in itself invalidates the authenticity of the Shroud of Turin). The empty grave linens suggest not only that Jesus' body had not been disturbed by human hands (for it is extremely unlikely that friends or foes would have first unwrapped the body before taking it away), but also that the body that had been bound within the wrappings had simply disappeared, leaving the wrappings behind like an empty chrysalis. It is highly significant, according to John's own testimony (John 20:3-9), that at the moment he saw the empty grave wrappings within the empty tomb he himself came to understand that Jesus had risen from the dead.

The Second Great Strand of Evidence: Jesus' Numerous Postcrucifixion Appearances

The second great strand of evidence, after the empty tomb, is the many postcrucifixion appearances our Lord made, under varying circumstances and in numerous places, to His disciples. The New Testament records at least ten such appearances, five of them occurring on that first "Easter," and the remaining five occurring during the following forty days leading up to and including the day of His ascension.

He appeared first to the women who had left the tomb (Matt. 28:8-10),[3] and then to Mary Magdalene who had returned to the tomb after telling

3. It is true that Mark 16:9 states that Jesus "appeared first to Mary Magdalene," and this may well be the case. But appearing as it does in the long ending of Mark 16, there is some question as to the authenticity of the statement. The appearance accounts, in my opinion, are more easily harmonized if one has Jesus appearing first to the women as they hurried away from the tomb (Matt. 28:8-9), and then to Mary who followed Peter and John back to the tomb after informing them that the tomb was empty (cf. John 20:1-18). But a harmonization is still possible, even if Jesus did appear first to Mary Magdalene.

Peter and John what she and the other women had seen (John 20:10-18). Then He appeared to Cleopas and the other (unnamed) disciple on the road to Emmaus (Luke 24:13-35), and then to Peter, no doubt sometime that same afternoon (Luke 24:34; 1 Cor. 15:5). His last appearance on that historic day was to the "Twelve" (actually ten in number since Judas and Thomas were not present) in the upper room (Luke 24:36-43; John 20:20-28; 1 Cor. 15:5). Of great significance on this last occasion is the fact that Jesus invited the disciples to touch Him in order to satisfy themselves that it was really He who stood among them, and He ate a piece of broiled fish in their presence as proof that His body was materially real and not merely a fantasy.

A week later He appeared again to His disciples, Thomas this time being present with the other ten disciples (John 20:26-29). Again Jesus encouraged confidence in the reality and factuality of His resurrection by inviting Thomas to do precisely what the doubting disciple had said earlier would be necessary if he was ever to believe that Jesus had risen, namely, to put his fingers into the wounds in Jesus' hands and side. Then Jesus appeared to seven disciples by the Sea of Galilee—"the third time Jesus appeared to His disciples"—and He prepared and ate breakfast with them (John 21:1-22). Then He appeared to the Eleven on a mountain of Galilee (Matt. 28:16-20), this occasion quite possibly being the same occasion when He appeared to more than five hundred disciples at one time, many of whom were still alive at the time Paul wrote 1 Corinthians (1 Cor. 15:6). Then He appeared to James, His half-brother (1 Cor. 15:7), and finally to the Eleven again when He ascended into heaven (Luke 24:44-52; Acts 1:4-9; 1 Cor. 15:7). (We will speak about His appearance to Saul of Tarsus later.)

Viewed as "evidence," it is true, of course, that the fact of the empty tomb alone does not prove that Jesus rose from the dead, but it does indicate that something had happened to His body. Jesus' numerous postcrucifixion appearances best explain what happened to His body: *He had risen from the dead.* And the fact that the appearances occurred (1) to individuals (Mary, Peter, James), to a pair of disciples, to small groups, and to large assemblies, (2) to women and to men, (3) in public and in private, (4) at all hours of the day—in the morning, during the day, and at night—and (5) both in Jerusalem and in Galilee, removes any and all likelihood that these appearances were simply hallucinations. An individual may have a hallucination, but it is highly unlikely that entire groups and large companies of people would have the same hallucination at the same time!

One more highly significant feature about the Gospel accounts of the appearances of Jesus must be noted—they lack the smooth "artificiality" that always results when men of guile have conspired to make a contrived story plausible: one immediately encounters numerous difficulties in harmonizing the four accounts of the several postresurrection appearances. Furthermore, according to the Gospel record women first discovered the empty tomb and to women Jesus first appeared after His resurrection. Given that the testimony of women was virtually worthless in that day and time, it is highly unlikely, if the disciples had conspired together to concoct the stories of the empty tomb and Jesus' several "postresurrection" appearances, that they would have begun their account with a significant detail that almost certainly would have discredited it at the outset. It was more desirable from the disciples' point of view—in order to make their proclamation more plausible—to be able to say that men had discovered the empty tomb first and that Jesus had first appeared to men. Thus, the prominence of the women's testimony in the Gospel accounts gives the disciples' reports the ring of truth.

These two great strands of New Testament data—the empty tomb and Jesus' numerous postcrucifixion appearances—put beyond all legitimate doubt the factuality and historicity of Jesus' resurrection from the dead.

In addition to these two lines of argument, one may also mention, for their inferential value, (1) the disciples' transformation from paralyzing discouragement to faith and certainty a few days after His death, (2) the later conversion of Saul of Tarsus, and (3) the change of the day of worship for Christians from the seventh to the first day of the week, each of these facts requiring for its explanation just such an event behind it as the resurrection of Christ.

Now for many critical scholars today, as we have noted more than once, the appearance stories recorded in the Gospels are legends. But it is intriguing that, while these same scholars are not prepared to admit that Jesus actually rose bodily from the dead, most, if not all of them, will acknowledge the historicity of Jesus' death by crucifixion under Pontius Pilate; the subsequent despair of His disciples; their "Easter" experiences, which they understood to be appearances to them by the risen Jesus; their resultant transformation; and the later conversion of Saul. In short, for many scholars today, while the resurrection of Jesus was not a *historical event*, they admit the disciples had some *subjective experiences* on the basis of which they proclaimed that Jesus had risen from the dead and appeared to them. What should we say to this?

Regarding the contention that the appearance stories are later legendary creations of the early church, 1 Corinthians 15:3-5 is significant. 1 Corinthians was written prior to the canonical Gospels, probably in the spring of A.D. 56, making 15:3-6 the first written account of the resurrection appearances. New Testament scholars in increasing numbers are advocating that Paul's statement reflects a quasi-official, much-earlier Christian creed that circulated within the *Palestinian* community of believers.[4] This assertion is based upon (1) Paul's references to his "delivering" to the Corinthians what he had first "received," terms suggesting that we are dealing with "tradition," (2) the stylized parallelism of the "delivered" material itself (cf. the four ὅτι clauses and the repeated κατὰ τὰς γραφάς phrases in the first and third clauses), (3) the Aramaic "Cephas" for Peter, suggesting a Palestinian milieu, (4) the traditional description of the disciples as "the Twelve," and (5) the omission of the appearances to the women from the list. It is quite likely that Paul, in fact, had "received" some of this "tradition," for example, that concerning Jesus' appearances to Peter and to James (referred to in 15:5, 7; cf. also Acts 13:30-31), directly from Peter and James during his first visit to Jerusalem three years after his conversion (cf. Acts 9:26-28; Gal. 1:18-19). This pericope then reflects what the earliest eyewitnesses to the events in Jerusalem were teaching on *Palestinian* soil within *five to eight years* after the crucifixion. This clearly implies that the material in 1 Corinthians 15:3b-5 is based on *early, Palestinian* eyewitness testimony and is hardly the reflection of legendary reports arising much later within the so-called Jewish Hellenistic or Gentile Hellenistic communities of faith. There simply was not enough time, with the original disciples still present in Jerusalem to correct false stories that might arise about Jesus, for legendary accretions of this nature to rise and become an honored feature of the "tradition." The presence of this "early confession" raises serious problems then for those who say the appearance stories in the canonical Gospels are "legendary" stories based upon non-Palestinian sources, as many Bultmannian scholars have insisted, for the facts strongly suggest otherwise.

Now it is significant that virtually all critical scholars today, as we have already noted, admit that the disciples very shortly after Jesus' death—for some reason—underwent a remarkable transformation in attitude, with confidence and certainty suddenly and abruptly displacing their earlier discouragement and despair. Even Bultmann admits the historicity of their "Easter experience"[5] and concedes that this newborn confidence created the

4. Günther Bornkamm, for example, refers to Paul's enumeration of the appearances of the risen Christ in 1 Cor. 15:3-7 as "the oldest and most reliable Easter text . . . formulated long before Paul." He says of this "old form" that it "reads almost like an official record" (*Jesus of Nazareth* [New York: Harper and Brothers, 1960], p. 182). Cf. also Wolfhart Pannenberg, *Jesus—God and Man* (Philadelphia: Westminster Press, 1968), pp. 90-91. Excellent treatments of this generally accepted view may be found in George E. Ladd, "Revelation and Tradition in Paul," in *Apostolic History and the Gospel*, ed. W. Ward Gasque and Ralph P. Martin (Exeter: Paternoster Press, 1970), pp. 223-30, particularly pp. 224-25; Grant R. Osborne, *The Resurrection Narratives: A Redactional Study* (Grand Rapids: Baker, 1984), pp. 221-25; and Gary R. Habermas, *Ancient Evidence for the Life of Jesus* (Nashville: Thomas Nelson, 1984), pp. 124-27.

5. Rudolf Bultmann writes: "The resurrection itself is not an event of past history. All that historical criticism can establish is the fact that the first disciples came to believe in the resurrec-

church as a missionary movement. What effected this transformation? If one replies, as some scholars do, that their belief that they had seen Jesus alive effected this transformation from fear to confidence, I must point out that this is tautological: in the final analysis one is simply saying that their *belief* that they had seen Jesus alive gave rise to their *faith* in Jesus' resurrection. We are still left with the question: What gave rise to their belief that they had seen Jesus alive and in person? Some prior event had to effect their belief that they had seen the risen Lord. If one replies that a visionary experience, that is, a hallucination, gave rise to their Easter faith, I must ask, What caused this visionary experience? Opinions vary, of course. Some scholars (Lampe, Schweizer, and Bornkamm, for example) have held that the resurrection appearances were mental images that the spiritual ego of the disembodied Jesus actually communicated back to His disciples from heaven, that the resurrection appearances, in other words, were real activities on the part of a "spiritualized" Jesus by which He entered into genuine personal intercourse with His disciples. Others have held that the experience of seeing Jesus after His crucifixion was a purely natural phenomenon— simply the work of auto-suggestion. Bultmann, for example, suggests that Jesus' "personal intimacy" with them during the days of His ministry among them began to nourish such fond memories that they began to experience "subjective visions" of Him and to imagine that they saw Him alive again.[6] Michael Goulder, in the first of his two contributions to *The Myth of God Incarnate,* traces belief in Jesus' resurrection back to Peter who, belonging to that psychological type, he says, whose beliefs are rather strengthened than weakened the more apparently refuted they are, underwent a "conversion experience in the form of a vision" and imagined that he saw Jesus on that first Easter morning. That night he told the other disciples of his experience, and

so great is the power of hysteria within a small community that in the

---

tion" ("New Testament and Mythology," in *Kerygma and Myth,* vol. 1, ed. Hans-Werner Bartsch [London: SPCK, 1972], p. 42). Donald Guthrie, however, is quite right to insist at this point upon an explanation of their "Easter faith": "The more pressing need at once arises for an explanation of the 'event of the rise of the Easter faith.' The fact is that the skepticism of Bultmann over the relevance of historical enquiry into the basis of the Christian faith excludes the possibility of a satisfactory explanation of any event, whether it be the actual resurrection or the rise of Easter faith. The one is in no different position from the other. The rise of faith demands a supernatural activity as much as the resurrection itself, especially since it arose in the most adverse conditions" (*New Testament Theology* [Leicester: Inter-Varsity Press, 1981], p. 183).

6. Bultmann's actual words are as follows: "The historian can perhaps to some extent account for that faith from the personal intimacy which the disciples had enjoyed with Jesus during his earthly life, and so reduce the resurrection appearances to a series of subjective appearances" (in *Kerygma and Myth,* p. 42).

evening in [the hypnotic spell (?) of] the candlelight, with [the highly charged emotional situation of] fear of arrest still a force, and hope of resolution budding in them too [on what ground?], it seemed as if the Lord came through the locked door to them, and away again. So [now note how effortlessly Goulder moves to his conclusion] . . . the experience of Easter fused a faith that was to carry Jesus to divinity, and his teachings to every corner of the globe.[7]

Now in addition to the fact that all such views (1) leave the empty tomb unexplained (it is not too much to say that they are scuttled on the "rock" of the empty tomb), and (2) fail to come to terms with the variety of objective details in the several accounts of the appearances themselves, George E. Ladd has quite correctly pointed out that

visions do not occur arbitrarily. To experience them requires certain preconditions on the part of the subjects concerned, preconditions that were totally lacking in the disciples of Jesus. To picture the disciples nourishing fond memories of Jesus after His death, longing to see Him again, not expecting Him really to die, is contrary to all the evidence we possess. To portray the disciples as so infused with hope because of Jesus' impact on them that their faith easily surmounted the barrier of death and posited Jesus as their living, risen Lord would require a radical rewriting of the Gospel tradition. While it may not be flattering to the disciples to say that their faith could result only from some objectively real experience, this is actually what the Gospels record.[8]

Even Bornkamm, one of Bultmann's most influential students, has to admit that "the miracle of the resurrection does not have a satisfactory explanation in the inner nature of the disciples," for as he himself acknowledges:

The men and women who encounter the risen Christ [in the Gospels] have come to an end of their wisdom. Alarmed and disturbed by his death, mourners, they wander about the grave of their Lord in their helpless love, trying with pitiable means—like the women at the grave—to stay the process and odor of corruption, disciples huddled fearfully together like animals in a thunderstorm (Jn. xx. 19 ff.). So it is, too, with the two disciples on the way to Emmaus on the evening of Easter day; their last hopes, too, are destroyed. One would have to turn all the Easter stories upside down if one wanted to present these people in the words of Faust: "They are celebrating the resurrection of the Lord, for

7. Michael Goulder, "Jesus, The Man of Universal Destiny," in *The Myth of God Incarnate*, ed. John Hick (Philadelphia: Westminster Press, 1977). p. 59.
8. George E. Ladd, "The Resurrection of Jesus Christ," in *Christian Faith and Modern Theology*, ed. Carl F. H. Henry (Grand Rapids: Baker, 1964), pp. 270-71.

they themselves are resurrected." No, they are not themselves resurrected. What they experience is fear and doubt, and what only gradually awakens joy and jubilation in their hearts is just this: They, the disciples, on this Easter day, are the ones marked out by death, but the crucified and buried one is alive.[9]

He goes on to say that by no means was "the message of Jesus' resurrection . . . only a product of the believing community," and concludes that "it is just as certain that the appearances of the risen Christ and the word of his witness have in the first place given rise to this faith."[10] I concur, and would insist that the "objectively real experience" of the disciples, of which Ladd spoke earlier, came to them as the result of the "many convincing proofs" (Acts 1:3) afforded them by Jesus' numerous material postresurrection appearances to them. Nothing less than His actual resurrection can explain both the empty tomb and the disciples' transformation from doubt and gloom to faith and the martyr's joy. And neither should we nor need we look for another explanation as the ground of their Easter faith.

Having set forth our reasons for affirming the historicity of Jesus' resurrection,[11] we will now continue with our investigation of the New Testament witness to Jesus' identity. In this chapter we will consider the evidence that four major historical events yield up: Christ's resurrection itself, His preascension ministry, His ascension, and the Pentecost event. Our investigation of the New Testament letters will follow in the next two chapters.

Testimonial Significance of Christ's Resurrection

At His resurrection, Jesus' ministry entered a new and momentous phase. By it His state of *humiliation*, consisting in His being "born, and that in a low condition, made under the law, undergoing the miseries of this life, the wrath of God, and the cursed death of the cross; in being buried, and continuing under the power of death for a time" (*Westminster Shorter Catechism*, Q. 27), came to an end. Also by it He entered into His state of *exaltation*, consisting in His "rising again from the dead on the third day, in

---

9. Bornkamm, *Jesus of Nazareth*, pp. 184-85.

10. Ibid., p. 183. The reader should recall, however, that Bornkamm espouses the view that Jesus' resurrection appearances were visions sent from heaven and not physical in nature.

11. I would refer those who care for more argumentation for the historicity of Jesus' resurrection as a central validating event of the Christian faith to Bernard Ramm, *Protestant Christian Evidences* (Chicago: Moody Press, 1953), pp. 184-207; Daniel P. Fuller, *Easter Faith and History* (Grand Rapids: Eerdmans, 1965); George E. Ladd, *I Believe in the Resurrection of Jesus* (London: Hodder and Stoughton, 1975); Donald Guthrie, *New Testament Theology*, pp. 375-91; G. R. Habermas, "Resurrection of Christ," in *Evangelical Dictionary of Theology*, ed. Walter A. Elwell (Grand Rapids: Baker, 1984), pp. 938-41; John Wenham, *Easter Enigma* (Exeter: Paternoster Press, 1984).

ascending up into heaven, in sitting at the right hand of God the Father, and in coming to judge the world at the last day" (*Shorter Catechism*, Q. 28). I speak intentionally of Jesus' *ministry* entering a new and momentous phase at His resurrection, for nothing could be farther from the truth than the view that suggests that at His ascension to the Father's right hand Jesus'ministry came to an end and that it is now the Holy Spirit who is at work. It is true that the Holy Spirit is at work today, but there was never a time when the Holy Spirit was not at work. It is also true that the Son of God is as active now as He always was both in providentially upholding all things and in the salvation of men. But this awaits our discussion of the meaning of His ascension and Pentecost.

As we shall see in connection with our discussion of Jesus' ascension, both His resurrection and ascension (and the glory attendant particularly upon the latter) are central in early apostolic preaching (cf. Acts 1:21-22; 2:24-36; 3:15, 21; 4:2, 10-11, 33; 5:30; 7:56; 10:40-41; 13:30-37; 17:3, 31; cf. also the ascended Jesus' glorious appearance to Paul in Acts 9:3-9, and Paul's later accounts of that incident in Acts 22:6-15 and 26:12-23). Indeed, it was not the preaching to unbelievers about the cross and its significance as much as it was the proclamation of Christ's resurrection from the dead and the implications implicit in and attendant upon His subsequent exaltation to the Father's right hand that "turned the [first-century Roman] world upside down" (Acts 17:6; AV, RSV)! Those implications we will consider in due course. It is also true that virtually all of the New Testament writers expound upon and apply in some fashion the significance of Jesus' resurrection for the edification of believers.[12] But one passage in particular highlights with singular clarity the significance of Christ's resurrection for His divine sonship. I refer to Romans 1:3-4.

In the early verses of Paul's letter to the church at Rome, he informs us of certain characteristics of the gospel. He tells us that it is *God's* gospel, that it had been *promised in the Old Testament Scriptures*, and that it "concerned His Son." But I wish to explicate what he then says concerning Jesus as "God's Son." A literal rendering of verses 3 and 4 is as follows:

> concerning His Son,
> who *became* [γενομένου—"came to be," that is, "was born"] of the seed of David according to the flesh,

---

12. Cf. Gal. 1:1; 1 Thess. 1:10; 4:14; 5:10; Rom. 4:24-25; 5:10; 6:3-11; 7:4; 8:11; 1 Cor. 9:1; 15:3-8, 12-23, 56; 2 Cor. 4:14; 5:15; Eph. 1:19-22; 4:7-12; Phil. 2:5-11; 3:10, 21; Col. 2:11-12; 3:1; 1 Tim. 3:16; 2 Tim. 1:10; 2:8, 11. Note that the writer of Hebrews sustains emphasis on Christ's present session at the Father's right hand, which presupposes His resurrection; cf. Heb. 4:14; 7:24; 13:20. Cf. 1 Pet. 1:3, 11, 21; 3:18, 21-22; Rev. 1:5, 17-18, and the signal demonstration throughout the book of Revelation on Jesus' glory and final triumph over death and Hades (20:14).

who *was marked out* [ὁρισθέντος] the Son of God in power,
  according to the Spirit of holiness, by the resurrection from the
  dead,
Jesus Christ, our Lord.

Before we say anything about the passage itself, note that these verses are not only found in the salutation of one of the four critically undisputed letters in the Pauline corpus, written around A.D. 56, but also that they comprise what many scholars regard as a *pre-Pauline* church confession.[13] This suggestion was first made by J. Weiss in his *Das Urchristentum* (1917), and the diction and the careful parallelism of the phrases admittedly do give a creedal ring to the passage. If this is so, and it well may be, it only underscores the primitive character of the doctrine we find set forth therein. This is the reason behind my decision to introduce at this time a "Pauline" statement, written some twenty-five years after the resurrection, in order to assess the significance of the event itself for Jesus' sonship. It may not have been originally "Pauline" at all but rather a confessional reflection of the faith of the original apostles and the earliest Christians in Jerusalem. At any rate, we may be sure that it accurately reflects what early Christians believed on the basis of the apostles' testimony.

The "Bracketing" Phrases

Coming now to the passage itself, I wish first to call the reader's attention to the fact that the two participial clauses, which I have indented in the translation above for easy identification (the translations of the participles are italicized), are "bracketed" between two phrases: "His Son" and "Jesus Christ, our Lord." Were it the case that Paul had omitted the intervening participial clauses entirely, we would still have here the highest kind of incarnational Christology. The former phrase ("His Son") indicates both the

---

13. Oscar Cullmann, *The Earliest Christian Confessions*, trans. J. K. S. Reid (London: Lutterworth Press, 1949), p. 55. Cf. also V. H. Neufeld, *The Earliest Christian Confessions* (Grand Rapids: Eerdmans, 1963), p. 50; O. Betz, *What Do We Know About Jesus?* (London: SCM Press, 1968), p. 95; and the bibliography in F. Hahn, *The Titles of Jesus in Christology* (1963, Ger. ed.; reprint, New York: World Publishing, 1969), pp. 268-69. R. Bultmann (*Theology of the New Testament*, vol. 1 [London: SCM Press, 1952], p. 49) views the passage as a "handed-down formula" that probably read, before Pauline syntax and additions, as follows:

(Jesus Christ) the Son of God,
Come from the seed of David,
Designated Son of God in power by his resurrection from the dead.

C. E. B. Cranfield (*A Critical and Exegetical Commentary on the Epistle to the Romans*, International Critical Commentary, 6th ed. rev. [Edinburgh: T. & T. Clark, 1975], 1:57) also regards this view as "highly probable." Cf. Habermas, *Ancient Evidence for the Life of Jesus*, p. 123.

relationship in which Jesus, as God's Son, stands with God the Father and
what He is in Himself, while the latter phrase ("Jesus Christ, our Lord")
designates what He is, as "Christ" and "Lord," to us. In view of several
contexts where Paul employs the title "Son" and specifically those in which
he speaks of God "sending [πέμψας] His own Son" (Rom. 8:3), "sparing not
His own Son" (Rom. 8:32), and "sending forth [ἐξαπέστειλεν] His Son"
(Gal. 4:4), the implication is clear that for Paul the Son enjoyed an existence
with God the Father prior to His being sent, and in this preexistent state He
stood in a relation to the Father as the Father's *unique* Son (cf. also Col. 1:13,
16-17 where the Son is said to be "before all things").[14] The reflexive
pronoun and possessive adjective respectively in Romans 8:3 and 8:32
(ἑαυτοῦ and ἰδίου), in the words of John Murray, also highlight

> the uniqueness of the sonship belonging to Christ and the uniqueness
> of the fatherhood belonging to the Father in relation to the Son. . . . In
> the language of Paul this corresponds to the title *monogenes* ["only one
> of a kind"] as it appears in John (John 1:14, 18; 3:16, 18; 1 John 4:9). It is
> the eternal sonship that is in view and to this sonship there is no
> approximation in the adoptive sonship that belongs to redeemed men.
> The same applies to the fatherhood of the first person. In the sense in
> which he is the eternal Father in relation to the Son he is not the Father
> of his adopted children.[15]

This being so, Murray is justified when he then writes concerning the
phrase, "His Son," in Romans 1:3:

> There are good reasons for thinking that in this instance the title refers

14. Paul uses the title "Son" seventeen times of Jesus: Rom. 1:3, 4, 9; 5:10; 8:3, 29, 32; 1 Cor. 1:9;
15:28; 2 Cor. 1:19; Gal. 1:16; 2:20; 4:4, 6; Eph. 4:13; Col. 1:13; 1 Thess. 1:10. Concerning Christ's
preexistence, which Paul presupposes in Gal. 4:4 and Rom. 8:3, H. N. Ridderbos writes:

> This pre-existence of Christ with the Father so emphatically declared by Paul *underlies his
> whole Christology* and makes it impossible to conceive of all the divine attributes and power
> that he ascribes to Christ exclusively as the consequence of his exaltation. It is true that he
> often speaks in this sense of the *Kyrios* exalted by God. . . . But this "exaltation Christol-
> ogy" is at the same time not for a moment to be divorced from the significance of Christ's
> person as such (*Paul: An Outline of His Theology*, trans. John R. DeWitt [Grand Rapids:
> Eerdmans, 1975], p. 68).

Hengel (*The Son of God* [Philadelphia: Fortress Press, 1976], pp. 7-15), following E. Schweizer
(*Theological Dictionary of the New Testament*, vol. 8 [Grand Rapids: Eerdmans, 1948], pp. 382ff.),
urges the interesting thesis that Paul reserves the "Son [of God]" title "for exceptional usage, at
the climax of certain theological statements" about Jesus (Hengel, *Son of God*, p. 14). One cannot
dogmatize here, but it would explain the rarity (and the location of certainly some) of the
occurrences of "Son" in Paul's letters.

15. John Murray, *The Epistle to the Romans*, vol. 1 (Grand Rapids: Eerdmans, 1960), p. 279. Cf.
also Benjamin B. Warfield, *The Lord of Glory* (reprint, Grand Rapids: Baker, 1974), p. 251.

to a relation which the Son sustains to the Father antecedently to and independently of his manifestation in the flesh. (1) Paul entertained the highest conception of Christ in his divine identity and eternal preexistence (cf. 9:5; Phil. 2:6; Col. 1:19; 2:9). The title "Son" he regarded as applicable to Christ in his eternal preexistence and as defining his eternal relation to the Father (8:3, 32; Gal. 4:4). (2) Since this is the first occasion in which the title is used in this epistle, we should expect the highest connotation to be attached to it. Furthermore, the connection in which the title is used is one that would demand no lower connotation than that which is apparent in 8:3, 32; the apostle is stating that with which the gospel as the theme of the epistle is concerned. (3) The most natural interpretation of verse 3 is that the title "Son" is not to be construed as one predicated of him in virtue of the process defined in the succeeding clauses but rather identifies him as the person who became the subject of this process and is therefore identified as the Son in the historical event of the incarnation. For these reasons we conclude that Jesus is here identified by that title which expresses his eternal relation to the Father and that when the subject matter of the gospel is defined as that which pertains to the eternal Son of God the apostle at the threshold of the epistle is commending the gospel by showing that it is concerned with him who has no lower station than that of equality with the Father.[16]

C. E. B. Cranfield concurs:

It is clear that, as used by Paul with reference to Christ, the designation, "Son of God" expresses nothing less than a relationship to God which is "personal, ethical and inherent", involving a real community of nature between Christ and God. The position of the words τοῦ υἱοῦ αὐτοῦ ["His Son"]—being placed, so to speak, outside the bracket, they are naturally taken to control both participial clauses—would seem to imply that the One who was born of the seed of David was already Son of God before, and independently of, the action denoted by the second participle.[17]

The latter phrase ("Jesus Christ, our Lord") Paul obviously intends as an explanatory extension of the former phrase. That is to say, He who stands in relation to God the Father as His own unique Son and who is in Himself the preexistent Son of God is also in His historical identity "Jesus" of Nazareth who because of His antecedent sonship received the Messianic investiture ("Christ") and as such is not only "Lord," the One who has been exalted to

---

16. Murray, *Epistle to the Romans*, 1:5. Cf. also Benjamin B. Warfield, *The Person and Work of Christ* (Philadelphia: Presbyterian and Reformed, 1950), p. 77.

17. Cranfield, *Commentary on the Epistle to the Romans*, p. 58.

the Father's right hand (Ps. 110:1; Phil. 2:9-11) and who exercises there all authority in heaven and on earth (Matt. 28:18), but also *"our* Lord," the One to whom *we* owe absolute obedience and who properly exercises such lordship over the creature as is the prerogative only of the divine Creator.

We have then in the two "bracket" phrases a pregnant summary statement of Paul's Christology: for Paul, the Son in His preexistent state is both equal with the Father as God and distinguishable from the Father as His Son. This One, in keeping with the requirements of His Messianic investiture, became man, and by virtue of His earthly work the incarnate Son was exalted to the highest place of honor in the heavens and given a name above every name (the title "Lord") "that at the name of Jesus, every knee should bow, in heaven and on earth and under the earth, and every tongue confess that Jesus Christ is Lord, to the glory of God the Father" (Phil. 2:10-11).

The "Bracketed" Clauses

It is imperative, as we turn now to the participial clauses between the "bracket" phrases, that we keep constantly in mind that what the apostle now tells us about Christ is "thrown up against the background of His deity"[18] implicit in the "bracket" phrases. This backdrop serves as a governing control over all of our subsequent exegesis. For example, something is amiss in our exegesis if, in determining the meaning of the second participle, we conclude that Paul teaches that at His resurrection Jesus was "constituted" or "appointed" as "Son of God." Such an adoptionistic Christology is precluded at the outset by Paul's representation of his subject as *being* the Son of God prior to and independently of either His "being born" of the seed of David or His being "marked out" as the Son of God. Whatever one makes of Paul's second clause, the "bracket" phrases preclude any form of adoptionism. With this caveat, we turn to the clauses in question.

With regard to the first clause, "who became [that is, "came to be" or "was born"] of the seed of David, according to the flesh," there is little dispute among recognized commentators on Romans regarding its meaning. Paul intended that his reader understand that in one sense, that is, "according to the flesh," the Son of God had a *historical beginning* as the Son of David. He says essentially the same thing in Galatians 4:4 when he writes, "When the time had fully come, God sent forth His Son, born [the same word he employs in Rom. 1:3] of a woman," only in Romans 1:3 he specifies the

18. Warfield, *Person and Work of Christ,* p. 78.

lineage out of which He came, namely, the Davidic line. Of course, by making specific mention of Jesus' Davidic lineage, Paul intended more than simply to offer his reader a brief account of Jesus' human genealogy. He wanted it clearly understood that Jesus, standing as He does in the Davidic line on His human side, was the promised Messiah, and, even more, "in declaring the Messiahship of Jesus, Paul adduces His royal dignity."[19]

But, as we have already noted, Paul does not simply say that Jesus was born of the seed of David, and then end his description of Jesus' historical beginning with that announcement; he adds the qualifying phrase, "according to the flesh." What does he intend by attaching this thought to the clause? I suggest that the phrase, as in Romans 9:5, specifies and limits the sense in which it may be said that Jesus had a historical beginning as the seed of David. There can be no question, of course, that the word "flesh" denotes Christ's human nature in its entirety. According to New Testament usage, σάρξ ("flesh"), when applied to Christ (cf. John 1:14; 6:51; Rom. 8:3; 9:5; Eph. 2:14; Col. 1:22; 1 Tim. 3:16; Heb. 5:7; 10:20; 1 Pet. 3:18; 4:1; 1 John 4:1; 2 John 7), denotes not simply the material or physical aspect of His human nature over against the nonmaterial aspect, that is, over against His human spirit. Rather, it uniformly refers to Him in the totality of His humanness as a man. Accordingly, when Paul says that Jesus had a historical beginning "according to the flesh," he concludes, as Cranfield well states,

> that the fact of Christ's human nature, in respect of which what has just been said is true, is not the whole truth about Him. "Son of David" is a valid description of Him so far as it is applicable, but the reach of its applicability is not coterminous with the fullness of His person.[20]

The sense in which the lineal description of Him as the Son of David ceases to be applicable as a full description of Jesus Paul had already implicitly stated in the first of the "bracket" phrases—He is not only David's son but He is also "His ["God's"] Son." As we shall now see, Paul makes this

---

19. Ibid., p. 79.

20. Cranfield, *Commentary on the Epistle to the Romans,* p. 60. Charles Hodge also well says: "The limitation . . . obviously implies the superhuman character of Jesus Christ. Were he a mere man, it had been enough to say that he was of the seed of David; but as he is more than man, it was necessary to limit his descent from David to his human nature" (*Commentary on the Epistle to the Romans* [1835; 9th reprint, Grand Rapids: Eerdmans, 1968], p. 18.). I find extremely interesting but do not agree with Richard B. Gaffin, Jr. (*Resurrection and Redemption* [Philadelphia: Westminster Student Services, 1978], pp. 113-21) that σάρξ ("flesh") refers to the "aeon" or "world order" from which Jesus was delivered by the resurrection. In my opinion, this construction fails to do justice to the New Testament usage of σάρξ when applied to Christ, and in particular to Rom. 9:5, where it denotes Christ's human nature. Ridderbos, *Paul,* pp. 66-67, also maintains that the "flesh-Spirit" contrast in Rom. 1:3-4 refers to "aeons," but I must withhold my endorsement of his view for the same reason.

explicit in the second participial clause.

The second clause reads, "who was marked out the Son of God in power according to the Spirit of holiness by the resurrection from the dead." This clause has proved to be more difficult than the former for exegetes, but it seems to me that, whereas the former clause speaks of the *historical beginning* for Jesus as "the Son of David" on His human side, this latter clause speaks of the *historical establishment*, by His resurrection from the dead, of Jesus as the Son of God on His divine side.[21] My reasons follow, beginning with the exegetical undergirding for my view.

The participle, ὁρισθέντος, the aorist passive of ὁρίζω, I suggest, should be translated "was marked out," "was delineated," or "was designated." The verb is used in the Septuagint in the sense of fixing or "marking out" or "delineating" boundaries (cf. Num. 34:6; Josh. 13:27; 15:12; 18:20; 23:4), and the noun ὅρια is used in both the Septuagint and the New Testament for "boundaries" or "borders" (cf. Matt. 2:16; 4:13; 8:34; 15:22, 39; 19:1; Mark 5:17; 7:24, 31; 10:1; Acts 13:50).

In accordance with its uniform usage as a periphrasis for the adverb "powerfully" (cf. Mark 9:1; Col. 1:29; 1 Thess. 1:5; 2 Thess. 1:11),[22] I construe the phrase ἐν δυνάμει ("in power")—in concert with Meyer, Hodge, Sanday and Headlam, Alford, Godet, and Warfield—with the participle rather than with "the Son of God" and translate the participle and the prepositional phrase accordingly as "was powerfully marked out" or "was powerfully delineated."

The preposition ἐκ introducing the phrase "the resurrection from [ablative use of the genitive] the dead," I submit, has a nuance different from the ἐκ in the former clause. The preposition ἐκ in the former clause, after the participle of "begetting," clearly denotes "origin," that is, "came to be [or "was born"] *out of* [or "from"] the seed of David"; in the second clause, after the passive participle "was marked out," ἐκ, I urge, denotes "instrumentality" or even "result" (on the analogy of its use in Heb. 11:35). Accordingly, I render the last phrase of the clause by "through the instrumentality of [or "as the result of"] the resurrection from the dead." This can, of course, and probably should, be reduced to the simpler "*by* the resurrection from the dead."

The final phrase to be discussed is "according to the Spirit of holiness." It is universally agreed that the phrase stands in contrast to "according to the flesh" in the first clause. I would urge, since "flesh" in the former clause, as

---

21. The italicized terms are from Warfield, *Lord of Glory*, p. 259.
22. W. F. Arndt and F. W. Gingrich, *A Greek-English Lexicon of the New Testament* (Chicago: University of Chicago Press, 1957), p. 260.

we have already argued, denotes Christ's humanity in its totality, including both corporeal and noncorporeal aspects of His human nature, that "spirit" in the latter clause cannot refer to the human spirit of Jesus. That aspect of His human nature is already included within the Davidic "flesh" He assumed at His birth. Its referent must be sought outside His humanity. Many, if not most, modern commentators assume that the phrase refers to the Holy Spirit, but I would argue that it does not refer to Him. On every other occasion in the New Testament where the word "holy" is attached to the noun "spirit" to refer to the Holy Spirit, the adjective ἅγιον is employed. But here, precisely to avoid reference to the Holy Spirit, Paul employs the genitive form of the noun ἁγιωσύνη: "the spirit *of holiness.*" If "spirit" does not refer to Christ's human spirit or to the Holy Spirit, then to what does it refer? I suggest that it refers to Christ's divine nature, to what He is, as the Son of God, on His divine side, and for the following two reasons: First, because it stands in contrast to "flesh" in the former clause, which refers to what Christ, as the Son of David, is on His human side, the implication is that "spirit" in the latter clause must also refer to something intrinsically inherent in Christ. But standing as it does in such close correlation to the title "the Son of God" in the same phrase that denotes Christ in terms of His Godness, it follows that its referent here is to what He is, as the Son of God, on His divine side, that is, to His deity. Second, in the same letter, some chapters later (9:5), Paul refers again to Christ as "from the fathers according to the flesh," intimating that something more can and must be said about Him. In this later context, Paul himself provided us this "something more" in the following phrase: "who is over all, God blessed forever." (We shall say more about Rom. 9:5 in the next chapter in connection with Paul's witness to Jesus.) In other words, in Romans 9:5 Paul declares that Christ is "of the fathers according to the flesh," but in the sense that He is not "of the fathers" and not "flesh" He was and is "over all, God blessed forever." Similarly, I would argue, in Romans 1:3-4 Paul informs us that Christ is "of David, according to the flesh," but in the sense that He is not "of David" and not "flesh," He was and is, as the Son of God, "the Spirit of holiness" (cf. 1 Cor. 15:45), that is, divine Spirit. Paul intends by this phrase in Romans 1:4 what he explicitly spells out in the later Romans 9:5 context. Warfield explains:

> [Paul] is not speaking of an endowment of Christ either from or with the Holy Spirit. . . . He is speaking of that divine Spirit which is the complement in the constitution of Christ's person of the human nature according to which He was the Messiah, and by virtue of which He was not merely the Messiah, but also the very Son of God. This Spirit he calls distinguishingly the Spirit of holiness, the Spirit the very charac-

teristic of which is holiness. He is speaking not of an acquired holiness but of an intrinsic holiness; not, then, of a holiness which had been conferred at the time of or attained by means of the resurrection from the dead; but of a holiness which had always been the very quality of Christ's being [cf. Luke 1:35; 5:8; John 6:69]. . . . Evidently in Paul's thought of deity holiness held a prominent place. When he wishes to distinguish Spirit from spirit, it is enough for him that he may designate Spirit as divine, to define it as that Spirit the fundamental characteristic of which is that it is holy.[23]

Putting all these features together now, I suggest that the entire clause can be paraphrased as follows: "who was powerfully marked out the Son of God in accordance with His divine nature by His resurrection from the dead."

Now while it is true that the verb ὁρίζω can also mean "appoint" or "constitute," Paul cannot mean that Jesus was "appointed" or "constituted" the Son of God at the point of or by reason of His resurrection from the dead inasmuch as he had already represented Jesus by the first "bracket" phrase as the Son of God prior to and independent of not only His resurrection but also His birth in Bethlehem of the seed of David. John Murray (Cranfield too) is persuaded that the verb, nonetheless, means "appoint" or "constitute" in this context and connotes, as does the former clause, a new "historical beginning" of some kind commencing with the resurrection. Accordingly, he regards the two clauses, in relation to one another, as depicting the "two successive stages of" *humiliatio* and *exaltatio* in the historical process of Jesus' incarnate Messianic state.[24] He carefully avoids what would otherwise be an adoptionist Christology by affirming that in the second of the two stages what was "constituted" was not Jesus as the Son of God *per se* but Jesus as the Son of God "in power." This addition, he writes, "makes all the difference."[25] The successive stages in Murray's construction, then, stand in a certain kind of antithesis, the former clause denoting what Jesus was *before* His resurrection, the latter clause denoting what He was *after* His resurrection. In other words, in the former stage, having been "born of the seed of David according to the flesh," Jesus, as the Son of David, was in a state of apparent *weakness;* but with His resurrection, Jesus entered a new stage of Messianic existence, one of powerful "pneumatic endowment" (according to Murray, this is the meaning of "according to the

---

23. Warfield, *Person and Work of Christ*, pp. 87-88. Haldane, Hodge, Liddon, Bengel, Lagrange, Alford, Vincent, Denney, and many other eminent theologians concur that "the Spirit of holiness" refers to Christ's divine nature.

24. Murray, *Epistle to the Romans*, 1:7. Murray is following here the suggestion of Geerhardus Vos, *Biblical and Theological Studies* (New York: Charles Scribner's Sons, 1912), pp. 228-30. Cf. also Vos, *The Pauline Eschatology* (Princeton: University Press, 1930,) p. 155 n. 10, for the same exegesis.

25. Murray, *Epistle to the Romans*, 1:10.

Spirit of holiness") commensurate with His Messianic lordship, a lordship "all-pervasively conditioned by pneumatic powers."[26] To assure the reader that I have not misrepresented Murray, I offer his very words: "The relative *weakness* of his pre-resurrection state, reflected on in verse 3, is *contrasted* with the *triumphant power* exhibited in his post-resurrection lordship."[27]

While I deeply appreciate Murray's reverent scholarship and his interpretive sentiment that seeks to avoid at all costs any taint of an adoptionist Christology, I am persuaded that my (the more traditional) view is correct: that Paul intended to teach in the second clause that Jesus was powerfully marked out as the Son of God in accordance with what He is on His divine side by His resurrection from the dead. My reasons are these.

Murray's view, representing the two clauses as "successive stages," injects a contrast between the clauses (what Jesus was before, and what He was after His resurrection) that I fail to find in the text. Murray implies that being "the Son of David according to the flesh" meant for Jesus a certain state of lowliness and weakness, this former clause (v. 3) needing to be read, at least to a degree, depreciatingly or concessively ("although He was born . . ."). But as I have already suggested in my discussion of the former clause:

> To say "of the seed of David" is not to say weakness; it is to say majesty. It is quite certain, indeed, that the assertion "who was made of the seed of David" cannot be read concessively, preparing the way for the celebration of Christ's glory in the succeeding clause. It stands rather in parallelism with the clause that follows it, asserting with it the supreme glory of Christ.[28]

In other words, while there is, of course, the intimation of the idea of a second successive stage *within* the second clause itself simply because of the mention of the resurrection, it is not the dominant thought in the passage. But as for succession *between* the clauses, it is absent from the context. The two clauses, as is evident from the parallelism of the two participles (τοῦ γενομένου, τοῦ ὁρισθέντος) with no connecting particle, stand in parallel to one another, together representing all that the Son of God is in His incarnate state. This is also made clear by Paul's similar statement in 2 Timothy 2:8, where he writes, as an encouragement to Timothy, "Remember Jesus Christ, having been *raised* out of the dead, is *of the seed of David,* according to my gospel." Clearly Christ's descent from David was, for Paul, a truth that

26. Ibid., p. 11.
27. Ibid., emphasis added.
28. Warfield, *Person and Work of Christ,* p. 81.

should cause the beleaguered Christian to rejoice, for it speaks of Christ's Messianic majesty. It in no way speaks of weakness and should not be set off over against His state inaugurated by His resurrection, for it is precisely Jesus Christ as the One who "has been raised" (the same theme as in Rom. 1:4) and who "is of the seed of David" (the same theme as in Rom. 1:3) who is in *both* aspects to be remembered by the Christian in distress. The relation of the second participial clause to the first in Romans 1:3-4 is not, then, one of opposition or contrast but one of climax, not one of supersession but one of superposition. This is obvious from the fact that Jesus did not cease to be either "the Son of David" or "flesh" at His resurrection; indeed, the resurrection insured that He would continue to be both (a fact Murray recognizes, of course). So Paul is saying by the first clause that the Son of God was born as the Davidic Messiah with all the glories that such an investiture entails; he is saying by the second clause that

> the Messiahship, inexpressibly glorious as it is, does not exhaust the glory of Christ. He had a glory greater than even this. This was the beginning of His glory. He came into the world as the promised Messiah, and He went out of the world as the demonstrated Son of God. In these two things is summed up the majesty of his historical manifestation.[29]

I offer this (following Warfield) as a respectful corrective to Murray, and conclude my exposition by saying that the primitive church offers us in these two verses a magnificent Christology: the eternal Son of God, who was born of the seed of David according to His manhood, was also the Son of God according to His deity; and this latter fact was powerfully displayed by His resurrection from the dead, as not only He Himself exercised that divine power He had often displayed in raising others from the dead by raising Himself from the dead (John 2:19; 10:18) but also His Father placed His stamp of approval on all that His Son had done by raising Him from the dead "in accordance with the working of the might of His strength which He exerted in Christ when He raised Him from the dead" (Eph. 1:19-20).

Our exposition of Romans 1:3-4 is completed. We have been concerned to highlight by our exposition of this early Christian confession—reflecting early apostolic teaching—the significance of Jesus' resurrection for His divine sonship. Romans 1:3-4 does this in a matchless fashion. In these verses we are informed, if we will have ears to hear it, that His resurrection from the dead was both His and His Father's powerful demonstration that Jesus was

29. Ibid., p. 80.

not only fully human—born the Seed of David—but also the incarnate God.

Testimony From Christ's Preascension Ministry

During the forty days the risen Christ spent with the apostles between His resurrection and ascension, as we have already shown, He gave "many convincing proofs" (NIV) that He was alive (Acts 1:3); He also continued to make, either tacitly or expressly, the same exalted claims He had begun to make in increasing clarity and number prior to His Passion. These, of course, were made in conjunction with His resurrection appearances.

When Jesus appeared to the women returning from the tomb on the morning of His resurrection, Matthew informs us, the women "clasped His feet and *worshiped* [προσεκύνησαν] Him" (28:9). We are not told what form this worship took. Because of Jesus' calming "Do not be afraid," it appears that their worship included that numinous awe that overwhelms the human spirit when it is suddenly made aware of the presence of the "transcendentally holy." Matthew's second verb makes it clear that the women did something beyond and in addition to their act of grasping Him by the feet, which act implies that they were already in a kneeling or prostrate position. There can be little doubt that their additional act involved the outpouring of their *religious* affections toward Him; it was a religious activity, constituting what any fair-minded person would acknowledge as the activity of worship. And the point to be made here, in conjunction with their worship of Him, is that Jesus did not reject their worship, nor did He rebuke them for their devotion; rather, He seems to have accepted it as proper and right. This means in turn that from the perspective of His own self-understanding He viewed Himself as divine and thus worthy of their worship.

In His appearance to Mary Magdalene (John 20:10-18), He informed her that He had not yet "returned to the Father," indicating that the unique filial relationship in which He stood to God had in no way been violated or affected negatively by His Passion. Then He instructed her to inform "His brothers" that He was returning "to My Father and your Father and to My God and your God" (20:17). It is significant that nowhere in the teaching of Jesus did He ever speak of God to His disciples as "our Father" or "our God." Throughout His ministry He consistently spoke of the Father as "the Father" or "My Father," but never as "our Father." (The "Our Father" of the so-called "Lord's Prayer" is not an exception to this inasmuch as there Jesus is instructing His disciples on how *they* should corporately address God in prayer.) Here, in keeping with His established pattern of speech, He avoided the obviously shorter form of expression ("our") and chose to remain with the longer form ("My" and "your"). I suggest that His concern here was to maintain the distinction between the sense in which He is God's Son by nature and by right and the sense in which His disciples are God's sons by grace and by adoption.[30]

In His appearance to the two disciples on the road to Emmaus (Luke 24:13-35), Jesus declared that "these things" (24:26; cf. for the referent of "these things," 24:20) *He* had just endured were only what "all the prophets" had said must happen to the Messiah before He entered His glory (24:26). By linking the events of the previous three days to the prophetic vision of the Old Testament respecting the Messiah's work, Jesus laid claim again to the Messianic investiture. And Luke the Evangelist adds his comment: "And beginning with Moses and all the Prophets, He explained to them what was said in all the Scriptures *concerning Himself*" (24:27).

That evening He appeared to the disciples in the upper room (Luke 24:36-49; John 20:19-23), and after greeting them and proving to them that it was really He by showing them His wounded hands, side, and feet and eating a piece of fish, He said to them, "This is what I told you while I was still with you: Everything must be fulfilled that is written *about Me* in the Law of Moses, the Prophets and the Psalms" (Luke 24:44). Then He opened their minds that they might understand the Scriptures (this act itself being divine) and said to them, "This is what is written: The Messiah will suffer and rise from the dead on the third day, and repentance and forgiveness of sins will be preached *in His name* to all nations, beginning at Jerusalem. You are witnesses of these things. I am going to send you what My Father has promised but stay in the city until you have been clothed with power from on high" (24:45-47). His claim again to messiahship is apparent and needs no comment. But note that He informs them that their witness is to be self-consciously Christocentric, that is, the blessings they promise men are to be related directly to Him ("in *My* name"). Surely, were any other to insist that a worldwide message should have his person made so integrally central to all that is proclaimed, we would conclude that it constituted the gravest form of self-worship and idolatry. But all of this seems perfectly natural, and rightly so, coming from the lips of the resurrected Jesus.

30. Donald Guthrie writes: "The uniqueness of the sonship of Jesus is supported by the clear statement of the risen Christ in John 20:17, when he made a distinction between 'my Father and your Father' and 'my God and your God.' The distinction is of great importance because it rules out the view that Jesus' sonship was of the same kind as man's but developed to a greater intensity. Others may be given power to become sons of God (1:12), but Jesus has no need for this since he is Son of a different kind, *i.e.*, he is essentially a son" (*New Testament Theology*, p. 313). Cf. also Leon Morris, who writes, "It seems as though He is of set purpose placing Himself in a different relationship to the Father from that which His followers occupy" (*The Gospel According to John* [Grand Rapids: Eerdmans, 1971], p. 842). Also cf. Morris: "The most natural way of taking the words is to see a difference between Jesus' relationship to God and that of the disciples" (ibid., p. 842 n. 42).

Then, after having commissioned them to be His witnesses, Jesus did a very significant thing. He breathed upon them and said to them, "Receive the Holy Spirit" (John 20:22). Now it is true that He had just said that He was going to send them the Holy Spirit, but it is equally true that He implied that it would be some days later before He did so. What is the significance, then, of this act at this time? In my opinion, on this occasion He did not actually impart nor did they actually receive the Holy Spirit in the "empowering" sense He had just spoken about. I say this, first, because the text does not state that they did, and second, because there is no indication of any kind that they immediately assumed their role as witnesses. To the contrary, in the words of E.C. Hoskyns, "The disciples still remain in secret, behind closed doors."[31] If Jesus did not impart the Spirit to them on this occasion, what, then, is the significance of this act? I submit that it was a symbolic act, analogous to His act of breaking the bread prior to His crucifixion, a visible depiction of the spiritual reality that was to occur only days later at Pentecost. On that occasion, when the Spirit was poured out upon them, with the image of Jesus' symbolic act of "on-breathing" a recent memory and still indelibly etched upon their minds, they would become aware in a powerful way that the ascended Lord was "breathing" upon them at Pentecost, that the life-infusing power of His "breath" was present with them in their proclamation and witness. In other words, He was preparing them, in a tangible way, for the event of Pentecost, assuring them that though He was to be absent from them in one sense (physically), He was to be present with them in the person and power of His "breath"—the Holy Spirit. And they would be conscious, even as He Himself would say during a subsequent appearance to them, that He was indeed "with [them], even to the end of the age" (Matt. 20:28). We shall say more about the significance of Pentecost later, but it is important that we understand Jesus' act on this occasion as a symbolic foreshadowing of what was to take place then. Also, this construction eliminates the so-called "discrepancy" that many critics allege exists between John and Acts over precisely when the Spirit was given.

John 20:28: The First Use of θεός ("God") as a Christological Title

A week later Jesus appeared to His disciples again; this time Thomas was also present. After Jesus showed Thomas His hands and side, Thomas exclaimed, "[You are] my Lord and my God!" (John 20:28). Not only did Jesus not correct Thomas's response as a misconception, but, just to the

---

31. E. C. Hoskyns, *The Fourth Gospel*, vol. 2 (London: Faber and Faber, 1947), p. 653.

contrary, Jesus declared of Thomas that he had finally "believed" (20:29). There can be no doubt that Jesus gives evidence here, by His express acceptance of Thomas's assessment of Him, that He was in His self-understanding their *Lord* to be served and their *God* to be worshiped.

John 20:28, in the words of Raymond E. Brown, is a critically secure text "where clearly Jesus is called God."[32] As such, Thomas's confession of Jesus as his "Lord [κύριος] and God [θεός]" is the "supreme christological pronouncement of the Fourth Gospel."[33] Here within a week of Jesus' resurrection, a disciple for the first time employs θεός as a christological title, and the other disciples would surely have learned from Thomas's words and Jesus' favorable response to them the appropriateness of doing so. This suggests that there is no basis in fact for some form critical scholars' view that the church only gradually came to an incarnational Christology. Christians virtually from the beginning believed that in Jesus they had to do with the Son of God incarnate.

No modern scholar has shown any interest in following the opinion of Theodore of Mopsuestia (c. A.D. 350–428) that Thomas's words do not refer to Christ, "but having been amazed over the wonder of the resurrection, Thomas praised God who raised the Christ."[34] This opinion was rejected by the Second Council of Constantinople in A.D. 553. The closest one comes to finding the idea expressed today is in the insistence of Jehovah's Witnesses that the first title was addressed to Jesus while the second was addressed to Jehovah. But Bruce Metzger is justified when he writes:

> It is not permissible to divide Thomas' exclamation. . . . Such a high-handed expedient overlooks the plain introductory words, "Thomas said *to him:* 'My Lord and my God!' "[35]

Moreover, the fact that both appellations are in nominative form should occasion no difficulty for the view that both terms are addressed to Jesus. The so-called articular nominative with vocative force is a well-known idiom in classical, Septuagint, and New Testament Greek.

Thomas's confession is an exceptionally wonderful exclamation, but it is all the more amazing when one reflects, first, on the incongruity of a confession

---

32. Raymond E. Brown, "Does the New Testament Call Jesus God?" *Theological Studies* 26, no. 4 (1965): 561.

33. Raymond E. Brown, *The Gospel According to John XIII-XXI,* Anchor Bible Series (Garden City, N.Y.: Doubleday, 1970), p. 1047.

34. Cf. H. Denzinger and A. Schronmetzer, *Enchiridion Symbolorum* (Freiburg: Herder, 1976), p. 150, sec. 434.

35. Bruce M. Metzger, "The Jehovah's Witnesses and Jesus Christ," *Theology Today* (April 1953): 71 n. 13.

of this magnitude coming from probably the least likely of the Twelve to utter it—one given to melancholy and gloom (John 11:16) and to theological dullness (John 14:5)—and, second, on the fact that "Thomas . . . makes clear that one may address Jesus in the same language in which Israel addressed Yahweh"[36] (cf. Pss. 35:23; 38:15, 21). John doubtless intended his report of Thomas's ascent from skepticism to full faith in Jesus as Lord and God under the impact of the reality of the resurrection to model what he thought should be the response of everyone when informed of Jesus' resurrection.

Two contextual features of Thomas's confession are noteworthy. *First*, only a week earlier Jesus in His conversation with Mary had spoken of His Father as "My God," using precisely the same words that Thomas used later of Him. He also said on that occasion that *His* God was also His disciples' God. And yet now, only a week later, He accepts Thomas's description of *Himself* as His disciple's God! Clearly, in Jesus' mind there was a personal manifoldness in the depth of the divine being that would permit His Father to be regarded as their God and also Himself to be regarded as their God. Here is certainly the stuff from which the church would later formulate its doctrine of the Trinity.

Second, Thomas's confession is followed immediately by John's stated intention for writing his Gospel, namely, that his readers "may believe that Jesus is the Christ, the Son of God" (20:31). If John here intended something other than or less than an ascription of full deity to Jesus by the title "Son of God," one can only impute unforgivable ineptitude to him for bringing this lesser title into such close proximity to Thomas's confession of Jesus' unabridged deity. Clearly, the only adequate explanation for the near juxtaposition of the two titles is that, while "Son of God" distinguishes Jesus as Son from the Father, it does not distinguish Him as God from God the Father. To be the Son of God in the sense John intended it of Jesus is just to be God the Son.

On the occasion of His early morning appearance to the seven disciples by the Sea of Galilee, Jesus demonstrated His supernatural lordship over nature by effecting the miraculous catch of fish. On that same occasion He called the church *"My* sheep," applying to Himself again the Old Testament imagery of Yahweh as the Shepherd of Israel, and then with divine foresight He predicted the kind of death Peter would die.

36. Brown, *Gospel According to John XIII–XXI*, p. 1047.

On the mountain of Galilee (Matt. 28:16-20), His next appearance, Jesus accepted His disciples' worship (28:17), and then made the stupendous claim that "all authority in heaven and on earth" had been given to Him. He followed this claim to universal sovereignty by commanding His followers to make all the nations His disciples. Beyond all legitimate debate, such universal authority and lordship is the rightful prerogative only of One who is Himself equal with God. And if the reader thinks this conclusion is premature, notice that it is fortified by Jesus' next utterance, "baptizing them into the Name of the Father and of the Son and of the Holy Spirit," for by this statement He assigned Himself a place as "the Son" within "the awful precincts of the divine name" and represented Himself as a co-sharer with the Father of the single ineffable divine "Name." He followed this by the claim to the "Immanuel" attributes of omnipresence ("I will be with you"; the "you" is plural) and eternality ("always, even to the end of the age"). Here is testimony replete with both overt claims to and implicit overtones of deity.

Finally, on the day of His ascension, He declared that His disciples were to be witnesses unto Him throughout the whole world, which commission can only be regarded as blasphemous idolatry on both His and their parts, in light of Isaiah 43:10 and 44:8, if He were not Himself the Yahweh of these Old Testament declarations. Then having blessed them, He ascended to heaven, sending them the promise immediately that He would return someday just as He had ascended. In that context, we are told, His disciples worshiped Him (Luke 24:52).[37] The significant thing about this act of worship is that He was no longer with them, their religious affections in worship being now directed to Him in heaven just as they would have worshiped the God of their fathers. Accordingly, we find them referring to Jesus as "the Lord" in Acts 1:21[38] and praying to Him as both the proper recipient of their

---

37. Supported as they are by weighty manuscript evidence, the words, "worshiping Him," are textually secure. Cf. Bruce M. Metzger (A Textual Commentary on the Greek New Testament [New York: United Bible Societies, 1971], pp. 189-90) for sound reasons for retaining the longer reading of Luke here.

38. R. T. France quite rightly observes that

the vocative kurie addressed to a living person need have no superhuman connotations, but when a man is described after his death as ho kurios, this is a different matter altogether, especially when those references are to his present rather than his past status. . . . Such uses immediately bring into view the associations which ho kurios inevitably carried for a Greek-speaking Jew, in that it was the standard LXX translation for the name of God. He could no more use ho kurios without thinking of its divine connotations than we could use "the Lord" of a human leader today. And this title springs into prominence immediately after the resurrection ("The Worship of Jesus: A Neglected Factor in Christological Debate?" in Christ the Lord, ed. Harold H. Rowdon [Leicester: Inter-Varsity Press, 1982], p. 29).

prayers and "the knower of all men's hearts."[39]

It is not an overstatement to say that Jesus' preascension ministry is replete with testimony that He is properly to be regarded as God, the Yahweh of the Old Testament, the divine Son of God, the Lord of the universe, and the promised Messiah.

Testimonial Significance of Christ's Ascension

Luke, both in his Gospel and in Acts, records that Jesus, upon completing His forty-day preascension ministry, bodily "ascended into heaven." He employs three verb roots to describe this momentous event: ἀνεφέρετο, "was led up" (Luke 24:51), ἀνελήμφθη, "was taken up" (Acts 1:2, 11; cf. ἀναλήμψεως in Luke 9:51), and ἐπήρθη, "was lifted up" (Acts 1:9). Of the four Gospel writers, Luke alone records the historical account of Jesus' ascension,[40] but he is by no means the only New Testament writer who refers to the event. Peter, Luke reports, referred to it in the upper room shortly after it occurred (Acts 1:22) and mentioned it in his sermons later (2:33-35; 3:21; 5:31); he also writes of it directly in 1 Peter 3:22. Stephen's statement in Acts 7:56 presupposes the past occurrence of it. Paul presupposes its historical actuality in his references to Christ's session at the Father's right hand in Romans 8:34 and Colossians 3:1; alludes to it in his words of Ephesians 1:20-22; 2:6; and Philippians 2:9-11; and expressly mentions it in Ephesians 4:8-10 and 1 Timothy 3:16. The writer of Hebrews presupposes it in 1:3, 13; 2:9; 8:1; 10:12; and 12:2; and expressly refers to it in 4:14; 6:20; and 9:24. John informs us that Jesus Himself often alluded to it (John 6:62; 7:33-34; 8:21; 13:33; 14:2, 28; 16:7-10; 20:17), and that He "knew that . . . He had come from God and was returning to God" (13:3). Finally, it is clear that Jesus presupposed it in His testimony before the Sanhedrin at His trial when He said, "You will see the Son of Man sitting at the right hand of the Mighty One" (Matt. 26:64; Mark 14:62; Luke 22:69).

---

39. Cf. also Acts 7:56, 59-60; 9:14; 1 Cor. 1:2; 2 Cor. 12:8-9. That it is Jesus that the church in the upper room is addressing by κύριε is evident both from its proximity to ὁ κύριος Ἰησοῦς in 1:21 and from the fact that the very thing they request—"Show us which of these two You have chosen to take over this apostolic ministry"—is what Jesus had done with reference to them earlier (1:2: "the apostles whom He chose"). In both 1:2 and 1:24-25 the same Greek words are employed. This being so, we have in their description of Him as the "Knower of the hearts of all men" a further evidence of the early church's perception of the ascended Lord Jesus as divine (cf. also John 2:24-25). Cf. Warfield, Lord of Glory, p. 208.

40. The longer ending of Mark (16:19-20) records that Jesus "was taken up [ἀνελήμφθη] into heaven and He sat at the right hand of God" (16:19). This section is textually suspect, but it does reflect a later tradition that accords with the Lukan report. It appears, in fact, to have been based mainly on the Lukan testimony.

The Bultmann school, not surprisingly, relegates Christ's ascension to the realm of legend; Bultmann himself writes,

> According to 1 Cor. 15:5-8, where Paul enumerates the appearances of the risen Lord as tradition offered them, the resurrection of Jesus meant simultaneously his exaltation; not until later was the resurrection interpreted as a temporary return to life on earth, and this idea then gave rise to the ascension story.[41]

This construction reflects his overarching aversion to the "intrusion" of the supernatural into the realm of space-time history, the ascension particularly mirroring for him the so-called "mythological" (nonscientific) "three-story universe" concept of the ancient world. But as Guthrie states, this is not the construction that is to be placed on the ascension data:

> The upward movement [of Jesus' physical figure] is almost the only possible method of pictorially representing complete removal. The OT instances of Enoch and Elijah present certain parallels. Inevitably a spatial notion is introduced, but this is not the main thrust of the Acts description. The focus falls on the screening cloud, precisely as it does in the transfiguration account. . . . The reality of the ascension is not seen in an up-there movement, so much as in the fact that it marked the cessation of the period of confirmatory appearances.[42]

B. F. Westcott, likewise, aids us by sensitively commenting on the nature of the ascension in these words:

> [Jesus] passed beyond the sphere of man's sensible existence to the open Presence of God. The physical elevation was a speaking parable, an eloquent symbol, but not the Truth to which it pointed or the reality which it foreshadowed. The change which Christ revealed by the Ascension was not a change of place, but a change of state, not local but spiritual. Still from the necessities of our human condition the spiritual change was represented sacramentally, so to speak, in an outward form.[43]

In other words, the "heavenly places" of Scripture expression, though real, are not to be conceived in spatio-temporal dimensions as "up there," but in

---

41. Bultmann, *Theology of the New Testament*, 1:45.
42. Guthrie, *New Testament Theology*, p. 395. Cf. also Gordon H. Clark, "Bultmann's Three-Storied Universe," *A Christianity Today Reader*, ed. Frank E. Gaebelein (New York: Meredith Press, 1966), pp. 173-76.
43. B. F. Westcott, *The Revelation of the Risen Lord* (London: Macmillan and Company, 1898), p. 180.

spiritual dimensions to which Jesus' *glorified* corporeal existence was capable of adapting without ceasing to be truly human, as evidenced by His activity described in Luke 24:31, 36; and John 20:19, 26. Therefore, Berkouwer quite properly declares:

> Only severe Bible criticism can lead one to a denial of the ascension and even to its complete elimination from the original apostolic *kerygma*. . . . To the Church it has always been a source of comfort to know that Christ is in heaven with the Father. And over against the denial of both the *ascensio* and *sessio* as being contrary to the "modern world conception," the Church may continue on the basis of Holy Scripture to speak of these facts in simplicity of faith.[44]

Still other critical scholars contend that the earliest ascension tradition in the church had Christ ascending to heaven directly from the cross with no intervening resurrection and preascension ministry. Traces of this are purportedly found in the early Christian hymn cited by Paul in Philippians 2:6-11, for there Christ's humiliation and exaltation are contrasted with no mention of His burial and resurrection. John's Gospel also is supposed to reflect this "ascension from the cross" teaching—with no room for the resurrection or preascension ministry—in such verses as 12:23 and 13:21 where John quotes Jesus to the effect that His hour of death would also mean His glorification. The writer of Hebrews is also said to have favored the idea that Jesus ascended to heaven from the cross because of such statements as the one in 10:12: "But when this priest had offered for all time one sacrifice for sins, He sat down at the right hand of God." Again, the point is made, there is no mention here of Christ's resurrection or preascension ministry.

Several things may be said about this effort to explain the ascension in nonliteral, nonhistorical terms. *First,* apparently the operative (but erroneous) canon of exegesis here is this: if a New Testament writer does not mention Christ's resurrection in every context where he mentions Christ's exaltation or His session at the right hand of His Father, one may conclude either that he himself was unaware of the resurrection and the subsequent preascension ministry, or that the tradition he is citing was unaware of these events. But this is a *non sequitur,* and it imposes the highly artificial requirement upon the New Testament writer, if he believed in them, always to mention the resurrection, preascension ministry, and ascension whenever he mentions Christ's session at the right hand of God. *Second,* such a contention completely ignores that all of these New Testament writers refer

---

44. Berkouwer, *Work of Christ,* pp. 206, 234.

elsewhere—indeed, in the very works where the so-called "ascension from the cross" is supposedly taught—to the postcrucifixion resurrection of Christ: by *Paul,* for instance, in Galatians 1:1; 1 Thessalonians 1:10; 4:14; Acts 17:31; 26:23; 1 Corinthians 15:4, 12-20; Romans 1:4; 4:25; 6:4, 5, 9; 7:4; 8:11, 34; Ephesians 1:20; Philippians 3:10; Colossians 1:18; 2:12; 3:1; 2 Timothy 2:8; by *John* in John 2:19-21; 20:1-29; 21:1-22; and by the *writer of Hebrews* in Hebrews 13:20. Moreover, Paul will make mention of the "many days" intervening between Christ's resurrection and ascension (Acts 13:31). *Third,* Berkouwer says in defense of the writer of Hebrews that the only way these critical scholars can interpret his work in this way is to proceed with the following formula: "The glory of Christ in Hebrews minus Hebrews 13:20 equals the ascension 'from the cross.' "[45] The same may be said in defense of all of the New Testament writers: the only way they can be used to support the idea that Christ ascended to heaven from the cross and not some weeks later is to ignore all of the references in their writings to Christ's resurrection, His postresurrection appearances, and His preascension ministry.

One can only conclude that these scholars have very little confidence in the trustworthiness of the Gospels and epistles. For myself, I am aware of no reason advanced to date that can justify the wholesale abandonment of Luke's account of the ascension. Accordingly, I turn to the significance of Christ's ascension both for men and for Himself.

The ascension of Christ meant, of course, for those first disciples and also for every other disciple since then, in a word, His *separation* from them, not "with respect to His Godhead, majesty, grace and Spirit" (*Heidelberg Catechism,* Q. 47; cf. also Q. 46), for His spiritual communion with them remains unbroken and undisturbed as a genuine and even enhanced spiritual reality, but only with respect to His physical presence among them. This separation Christ Himself spoke about in such places as Luke 5:35; John 7:33; 12:8; 13:33; 14:30; and 16:10 (cf. also 1 Pet. 1:8; 1 John 3:2).[46]

With respect to Christ Himself, the Scriptures virtually exhaust available "triumphalist" language, images, and metaphors to describe the significance of Christ's ascension for Him. At this time I can only enumerate some of these descriptions, with the expositions of these passages to follow at the appropriate places. But for now, I would note that, as His resurrection was the means to His ascension, and so a significant aspect of His total exalta-

---

45. Ibid., p. 208.

46. The trained theologian will recognize by my formulation that I am following the Reformed rather than the Lutheran tradition, which latter tradition maintains, because of its peculiar doctrine of the *communicatio idiomatum,* that Christ is, by virtue of the union of the two natures in the one person of Christ, physically ubiquitous and therefore present with us *physically* "in, with, and under" the elements of the Lord's Supper.

tion, so His ascension in turn was the means to His climactic exaltation and enthronement (*sessio*) at the Father's right hand as Holy One, Lord, Christ, Prince, and Savior of the world (Acts 2:27, 33-36; 5:31; Rom. 8:34; Col. 3:1; Phil. 2:9-11; Heb. 1:3). And what an exalted enthronement it is! If His ascension was "in [ἐν] glory" (1 Tim. 3:16), exalting Him thereby "higher than all the heavens" (Eph. 4:10; Heb. 7:26), He is also "now crowned *with* glory and honor" (δόξῃ καὶ τιμῇ ἐστεφανωμένον) (Heb. 2:9), "with angels, authorities, and powers in submission to Him" (1 Pet. 3:22), with "everything under His feet," the Father alone excepted (1 Cor. 15:26; Eph. 1:22a), sitting "far above all rule and authority, power and dominion, and every title that can be given, not only in the present age but also in the one to come" (Eph. 1:21). God has also "given" (ἔδωκεν) Him to be "head-over-everything for the church, which is His body, the fullness of Him who fills everything in every way" (Eph. 1:22-23), indeed, who fills "the whole universe" (τὰ πάντα) with His power and lordship (Eph. 4:10). In sum, He now occupies the "highest place" (Phil. 2:9) of glory and honor (Heb. 2:9) that heaven can afford, and to Him belongs *de jure* and *de facto* the title "Lord of all" (Acts 10:36; Rom. 10:12), Lord above all other lords (Acts 2:36; Phil. 2:9b; Rev. 19:16), "that at the name of Jesus, every knee should bow in heaven and on earth and under the earth, and every tongue confess that Jesus Christ is Lord" (Phil. 2:10-11a). The nature of His lordship entitles Him sovereignly to bestow gifts of every and of whatever kind upon men as He pleases (Eph. 4:7-8, 11).

There can be no question, in light of such undeniably transparent language, that upon His resurrection and ascension (these two events may be construed quite properly together, even though the former preceded the latter by forty days, as the collective two-stage means to His exaltation to lordship), as the fruit of and reward for His labors on earth, Jesus as the Messiah was granted supreme lordship and universal dominion over men. This is also suggested by the following: (1) By His own statement in Matthew 28:18—"All authority in heaven and on earth has been given to me"—Jesus speaks of that Messianic lordship He received *de jure* at His resurrection but actually began to exercise *de facto* universally from heaven upon His ascension and present session at the Father's right hand. (His references in Matt. 11:27 and John 17:2 to a possessed "delegated" dominion should be understood against the background of the covenant of redemption in the councils of eternity.) (2) Peter's statement, "God made [ἐποίησεν: "appointed," "constituted"] Him both Lord and Christ" (Acts 2:36) following His resurrection and ascension, is another declaration of His *de facto* assumption of mediatorial reign as the God-man, since Jesus was obviously both Lord and Messiah by divine appointment from the moment of His incarnation. (3) Paul, referring to Jesus' earthly work, says, "Because of which [διὸ καὶ] God exalted Him to the highest place and gave Him the name, the 'above everything' name," that is, the name of "Lord" (Phil. 2:9).

It would be a serious blunder theologically to deduce from any of this that Jesus as the Son of God, who (though in union with our flesh) continued infinitely to transcend all creaturely limitations, became "Lord" only at His exaltation and acquired *as God's Son* only then *de jure* and *de facto* universal dominion. We must never forget that, for Peter, it was "our God and Savior Jesus Christ" who "sprinkles us with His blood" (2 Pet. 1:1; 1 Pet. 1:2). For Paul, likewise, it was "the Lord of Glory" (ὁ κύριος τῆς δόξης), "the Lord to whom glory belongs as His native right," who was also both "God over all" (Rom. 9:5) and "our great God" (Titus 2:13), who was crucified for us (1 Cor. 2:8). As God the Son, then, Jesus continued as He always had done to uphold all things by the word of His power (Heb. 1:3), and to exercise the powers and lordly rights that were intrinsically His as the divine Being (cf. Calvin, *Institutes*, II, 13, 4). Consequently, when these apostles tell us that Christ Jesus was "appointed" Lord or was "exalted" and "given" authority and the title of "Lord" at His ascension, we must understand that these things were said of Him in His mediatorial role as the Messiah. It is appropriate to say these things about Him but only because He, "the Son," who is intrinsically and essentially "rich," who is "Lord" by right of nature, had *first* deigned to take into union with Himself our "flesh," becoming thereby "poor" (2 Cor. 8:9). It was as the divine-human Messiah, then, that He "acquired" or "was given" at His ascension *de facto* authority to exercise mediatorial dominion. It was not the exaltation but the prior "humiliation" that was the "strange experience"[47] to the Son *as God*. Conversely, it was not the humiliation but the "exaltation," that was the "new experience" to the Son *as the divine-human Messiah*. If we are to take history, and specifically New Testament history, seriously, we must say this. We must be willing to say that, in a certain sense, the exaltation entailed for the Son an experience that had not been His before. The "new experience" was universal dominion, not as God *per se*, of course, but as the divine-human Messiah and as the divine-human Mediator between God and man. We even learn elsewhere that this mediatorial dominion is a temporarily delegated authority. When He and His Father have subjugated finally all His and our enemies, then He will yield up not His sonship,[48] but this delegated author-

---

47. The phrase is Warfield's (cf. *Lord of Glory*, p. 225).

48. Herman Ridderbos observes that "where there is mention of the consummation of Christ's work of redemption, in the words of 1 Corinthians 15:28 ('when the Son has subjected all things to

ity as the Messiah to God, even the Father, and His special mediatorial dominion will be "re-absorbed" into the universal and eternal dominion of the triune God (1 Cor. 15:24-28). But in sum, the ascension meant for the Son, as the divine-human Messiah, the assumption of the prerogatives of the Messianic investiture on a universal scale, rights that were already His by right of nature as God the Son, but that He "won" or was "awarded" as the incarnate Son for fulfilling the obligations of the estate of humiliation intrinsic to the Messianic investiture.

This Christ, in precisely the terms of His glorious lordship, was made central to all early apostolic preaching. The apostles were solicitous to draw out the implications of Christ's exclusive lordship over the world for their audiences. None of the modern clamor for religious pluralism was present in their preaching. Because of who Christ is, the work He did, the place He presently occupies, and the title He bears, for them "salvation is in no one else, for there is no other name given among men by which we must be saved" (Acts 4:12; cf. also John 14:6; 1 Tim. 2:5). He, as Lord, will judge the living and the dead at His appearing (Acts 10:42; 17:31; Rom. 14:9; 2 Tim. 4:1). His once-for-all offering up of Himself as a sacrifice to satisfy divine justice is alone acceptable to God the Father, the "legal" representative of the Godhead in the "great transaction" of redemption and the canceling of sin (Heb. 9:24-26). His high priestly intercession alone meets with the Father's approval (Rom. 8:34; Heb. 7:24-25; 1 John 2:1). In light of their exclusive claims for Him, it is not surprising that the blessing and power of God rested upon the apostles' evangelistic efforts.

Testimonial Significance of Pentecost

E. Zeller, A. Loisy, and E. Haenchen view the Pentecost event recorded in Acts 2 as wholly the dogmatic construct of Luke's theological genius, his own redactional adaptation of an early Jewish legend about the lawgiving at Sinai in which God's voice is divided into seventy languages, which adaptation he intended as an explanation of the origin of the church. It is not my intention, as we address the meaning of that event, to weary the reader with a detailed refutation of this view; suffice it to say, there is no evidence to suggest that Luke adapted a Jewish legend to serve this purpose and every reason to believe that Luke was simply recording the occurrence of an event, the historicity of which we have no reason to doubt. As a historian, Luke

the Father, then will he himself be subjected to him, that God may be all in all'), this cannot mean the end of the Sonship. One will rather have to judge the 'post-existence' of the Son intended here in the light of what is elsewhere so clearly stated of his pre-existence" (*Paul*, p. 69).

was reporting an incident with roots deep in the earliest common Christian tradition concerning the first days of the church after Christ's resurrection and ascension.

A still-popular hypothesis associated with the name of E. von Dobschütz is that the Pentecost event is actually a variant account of the resurrection appearance to the five hundred brethren that Paul mentions in 1 Corinthians 15:6, but stripped of its appearance features by Luke himself in order to highlight the distinctive significance of Pentecost. The most that one can say about this view is that it is an interesting hypothesis that has no real supporting evidence and nothing to commend it beyond the powers of the imagination that would have it so.

Regarding the source-critical analysis of the event that urges that Luke (or his source) took an account of an experience of ecstatic glossolalia from the primitive church and, under the influence of the Babel legend or his own theological interest to portray symbolically the church's universal embrace from its very inception, transformed it into a miracle of speaking foreign languages, it must be said again that such an approach lacks evidence, is highly subjective, and smacks of being an attempt to explain on purely rationalistic grounds what Luke clearly intended as a supernatural event of deep and abiding significance.

Finally, the modern attempts to explain the Acts account psychologically on the basis of what is known about and still is being learned from the modern Pentecostal movement, in my opinion, reverse the true order of things by making the modern movement the norm for determining the nature of the Pentecost event rather than making the Acts account the norm for evaluating the validity of the current occurrences of glossolalia.

Finding nothing in these proposals that commends them as truer, more apparently real historical accountings of what actually occurred on the day of Pentecost than the Lukan account itself, I propose to take the Acts account as a straightforward narrative of what actually occurred and set forth the evidence contained in it in support of the exalted and divine character of Christ.[49]

49. Cf. James D. G. Dunn (*Jesus and the Spirit* [London: SCM Press, 1975], pp. 136-52) for a detailed form-critical defense of the likelihood of the occurrence of ecstatic speech on the day of Pentecost, in the course of which defense Dunn refutes the views mentioned above. It is regrettable that Dunn concludes that one can say no more, on the basis of Acts 2, than that a group of Jesus' disciples were suddenly caught up in a "communal experience of ecstatic worship" and others present thought they recognized the words of praise to God in other languages (ibid., p. 152), and that Luke is "only of marginal help" in providing an answer to the question of how the early Christians related the risen Christ to the Spirit as the source of their experience (ibid., p. 156). Luke provides all the help one needs in coming to a conclusion on this matter if his account is only taken at face value.

The Contextual Setting of Pentecost

The events that occurred on the Day of Pentecost are set in the context of Jesus' statement, made just prior to His ascension, that He would baptize His disciples with the Holy Spirit "in a few days" (Acts 1:5). In light of the teaching of Matthew 3:11; Mark 1:8; Luke 3:16; 24:49; and John 1:33, there can be no doubt that Jesus' statement, "you will be baptized" (Acts 1:5), means: "*I* will baptize you" (the reader should recall here also our earlier exposition of Jesus' act of breathing on His disciples [p. 212], reported in John 20:22.

This fact—that *Jesus* baptized His church on that occasion—provides the hermeneutical paradigm for understanding the event of Pentecost, as I hope to show shortly.

The Facts of Pentecost

The facts of the event that took place that day are clear enough—the disciples waiting, in accordance with Christ's instruction, in Jerusalem for the empowering gift of the Holy Spirit; the sudden "sound from heaven like the rush of a strong wind" (may we say the sudden "amplified" sound of the "expulsion of breath," in view of John 20:22?); the "tongues" of fire that came to rest upon each of the disciples; and the Spirit-wrought capacity to "declare the wonders of God" (2:11) in the "native languages" of the Jews present from the territorial regions of the then-known world (2:8-11).[50] And all these phenomena Luke himself interpreted as evidence that they had been "filled with the Holy Spirit" (2:4). This filling, it should be recalled, Christ described earlier as His "baptism" of them with the Holy Spirit.

What is not so clear, or perhaps more accurately, what is often misunderstood, is the *meaning* of the event because men have tended to concentrate their attention either on the Holy Spirit who was "poured [or "breathed"] out" and/or on the empirical phenomena accompanying His "outpouring" rather than on the "Baptizer" Himself, the One who did the "pouring." And yet its meaning is patently clear, inasmuch as Peter, with enviable clarity, explained its meaning and significance in his sermon in response to the people's query, "What does this mean?" (2:12). I propose now to "walk" the reader through Peter's sermon, that he may see for himself precisely what

---

50. Luke's list of regions in Acts 2:9-11 is supposed by some scholars to reflect "the whole world" through his mention of nations and lands purportedly assigned to the twelve signs of the zodiac. But the evidence is nil that Luke has any interest in astrological matters. Cf. Bruce M. Metzger, "Ancient Astrological Geography and Acts 2:9-11," *Apostolic History and the Gospel*, pp. 123-33.

Peter said the events of Pentecost meant for the first disciples and for the church as a whole.

The Meaning of Pentecost

The "Spirit-filling" meant, of course, for the disciples their "empowering" as witnesses—this we know from our Lord's own statements to that effect (Luke 24:49; Acts 1:8) and from Peter's sermon, which as a Christian sermon, classically illustrates the effect of this "empowering." But from the perspective of the history of redemption, it meant something else, and it is this "something else" that Peter brings out in his sermon.

Peter begins by citing Yahweh's promise in Joel 2:28-32a (he alludes later at the end of his sermon to Joel 2:32c) that in the last days He would pour out His Spirit on all kinds of "flesh"—sons and daughters, young and old men, and men and women servants (2:16-21). By his "This is that which was spoken by the prophet Joel" (2:16), Peter identifies the events of Pentecost as the (initiatory?) fulfillment of that prophecy. Then he launches into his argument. I use the word "argument" here by studied choice, for that is precisely what the remainder of his discourse comprises—one grand, sustained argument from the event of Pentecost for the lordship and Messianic investiture of Jesus Christ! There is scarcely a word of teaching about the person and work of the Holy Spirit! There is no exhortation that his audience should seek a glossolalic experience similar to that which the disciples were presently experiencing. Virtually everything he says focuses on the person and character of the work of Jesus Christ, even his appeal in 2:38-39, which includes a reference to the gift of the Holy Spirit, whom all who repent and are baptized in the name of Jesus Christ will receive.

That his remarks are a sermonic "apologetic" on behalf of the lordship and messiahship of Jesus is apparent from the outset—from his opening remark after quoting the Joel prophecy to his concluding statement in 2:36. Three times in the course of his sermon he refers to "this Jesus": (1) "Men of Israel, listen to this: *Jesus* of Nazareth, a man who was *accredited* by God to you by powers, wonders, and signs which He did through Him in your midst, as you yourselves know—*this one* . . . you killed, whom God raised, loosing the bonds of death . . ." (2:22-23a); (2) "*This Jesus* God has raised . . ." (2:32); and (3) "Therefore, let all the house of Israel know for certain that God has made Him both Lord and Christ—*this Jesus* whom you crucified" (2:36). Further indication that Peter intended his remarks as an apologetic underscoring Jesus' lordship and messiahship may be seen in his reference to God's having *accredited* Him by doing authenticating miracles through Him, in his insistence that his audience knew of Jesus' mighty works, and in his concluding "therefore" statement in 2:36. All of these features indicate that Peter's remarks prior to his "therefore" should be regarded as an argument to buttress the conclusion he himself draws in 2:36. The implication is clear that Peter believed he had said enough about Jesus prior to 2:36 to warrant such a conclusion. What specifically had he said to warrant this conclusion?

Let us follow Peter's argument, starting from his remark in 2:24 that God had raised Jesus from death. Why had God so acted? "Because [καθότι]," Peter says, "it was not possible for Him to be held by it [that is, by "death"]." And why not? Because (γὰρ), Peter declares, David had prophesied concerning Jesus' resurrection in Psalm 16:8-11. But how do we know that David was not speaking of himself when he wrote Psalm 16, since, after all, the psalm is written in the first person? First, Peter says, because David died and was buried and his tomb is "with us to this very day" (2:29). In other words, because David died and his body saw decay. (Paul will use this same argument later in Acts 13:35-37.) And second, Peter says, because David, "being a prophet, and knowing that God had sworn with an oath to seat one of his descendants on his [David's] throne—knowing this beforehand, he spoke concerning the resurrection of the Messiah that 'He was not abandoned to the grave, nor did His body see decay' " (2:30-31). In short, Peter's argument is as follows: David was obviously speaking of the Messiah's resurrection and not his own in Psalm 16 because he died and was not raised to life, and because, as an inspired prophet, he had been informed of the Messiah's resurrection and enthronement and thus, under inspiration, had written about these matters.

Before we proceed further with Peter's argument, I must call the reader's attention to the fact that, even though Psalm 132:11-12 spoke of one of his descendants sitting on *his* throne forever, when David spoke of the Messiah's glory, he was laboring under no illusion that the Messiah was to be raised from death to sit upon his (David's) earthly throne. Rather, "being a prophet," he knew that God was going to raise his descendant, God's own Messiah, from the dead to sit on God's heavenly throne. How do we know this? First, because, and here we use Peter's own argument from the history of Jesus, upon His resurrection the Messiah did not mount an earthly throne of David. Rather, He ascended to heaven and sat down on God's throne. And in the sense that any throne upon which the Messianic Son of David sat would become by that very act the Davidic throne, God's throne itself became the "Davidic throne." And second, because David, according to Peter (Acts 2:28, 33-35), made it perfectly clear that this heavenly enthronement is what he had in mind. He did so by implication in Psalm 16 itself when he has the resurrected Messiah say, "You will fill Me with joy *in your presence*, with eternal pleasures *at your right hand*" (16:11); and he did so expressly in Psalm 110:1 where he reports that Yahweh said to His Messiah, "Sit at My right hand" (cf. Matt. 26:64 and parallels).

Let us now return to our "walk" through Peter's discourse, intercepting his thought where we left it at 2:33: "Having been exalted to the right hand of God. . . ." Here Peter refers to Jesus, with David's description of His exaltation in Psalm 110 in mind. But how do we know that David was speaking of the Messiah's exaltation in Psalm 110? How do we know that he was not reflecting upon his own exaltation in the third person? Because, Peter says, "David did not ascend to heaven" (2:34)—here Peter employs the same form of argument that he had used earlier, the argument from history—"and yet he said, 'The Lord said to my Lord, sit [the same root as the one Peter had employed earlier in 2:30] at My right hand.'" The conclusion is clear: David was not speaking of himself in Psalm 110:1 but of the Messiah, not only His descendant "according to the flesh" but also his Lord, who would be exalted to the right hand of God, every detail of which prophecy had been accomplished in Jesus.

To this point, with consummate skill, Peter has demonstrated that all that had come to pass with respect to "this Jesus" David had forecast of the Messiah, and accordingly, that David had prophesied that "this Jesus" as the Messiah would be raised from the dead (Ps. 16:10) and exalted to God's right hand (Pss. 16:11; 110:1). But now we must ask, How does all of this relate to the event of Pentecost itself? Why did Peter use this occasion to argue the case for the messiahship of Jesus? There can be no doubt regarding the answer: Peter is transparently clear about the connection between the events that had just occurred and their meaning for Jesus Himself: "Having been exalted to the right hand of God, and having received the promise of the Holy Spirit from the Father [note the implication in his reference to "the Father" that the Messiah is at the right hand of "the Father" as "the Son"], He [that is, Jesus] has poured out this which you now see and hear" (2:33). What is the significance of this? When we recall the "accrediting" character of His previous miracles—the point that Peter had underscored at the outset of his discourse—it becomes clear that for Peter the event of Pentecost was to be viewed as a further tangible, concrete, miraculous self-attestation on Jesus' part that He was the Messiah. This is why Peter believed that he could conclude his remarks with his ringing "therefore": "*Therefore* [in light of (1) the attesting miracles God performed through Him during His years of earthly ministry, which miracles you, my listeners, cannot deny, (2) David's Old Testament prophecies concerning Him, and (3) now Jesus' present miraculous self-attestation from heaven that He is the Spirit-baptizer of men], let all the house of Israel know for certain that both Lord and Christ God has made Him—*this Jesus* whom you crucified."

Peter's argument is complete, and he has driven home the meaning of that event. What then is the significance of the event that occurred on the Day of Pentecost? It is not to be found primarily in the fact that the Holy Spirit had been manifested in a unique and striking fashion but rather in the fact that Jesus, the exalted Lord and Messiah, by this further display of His authority and power, had attested once again to His lordship and Messianic investiture before the nation of Israel by "breathing upon" ("baptizing") His disciples. C. H. Dodd has captured the significance of Pentecost in these simple words: "the Holy Spirit in the Church is the sign of Christ's present power and glory."[51] Also, Jesus was demonstrating to Israel by the particular character of this miracle that resident with Him, as the Baptizer, was the authority to bless and to curse, to make alive and to kill, to save and to damn, as John the Baptist had earlier said. And the present participle in John's statement in John 1:33 ("this One is *the One who baptizes* with the Holy Spirit") suggests that the Pentecostal "outpouring" illustrates that this Jesus was, is, and always will be the Lord of salvation!

But because men have tended to focus on the empirical phenomena of Pentecost rather than on the Baptizer Himself, the church's understanding of the significance of Pentecost sometimes has become warped and distorted, and the point Scripture itself emphasizes is forgotten or minimized. The emphasis today has shifted away from viewing the miracle as a self-attestation to Israel of Christ's Messianic lordship and has come to rest all too often and in too many quarters upon the person and work of the Holy Spirit. Thus the true significance of the event has been well-nigh lost. But when it is kept clearly in mind as one reads and studies Acts 2 that it was *the risen Christ* who was actively engaged that day in attesting once again in a grand, climactic way to His saving prerogatives as Israel's Lord and Messiah, two things become evident: on the one hand, how erroneous it is to represent Christ's present session at the Father's right hand as a state of relative inactivity save for His intercessory work, with the Holy Spirit now setting about the task of applying the benefits of Christ's accomplished work of redemption to men; and on the other hand, how perceptively correct the framers of the *Westminster Confession of Faith* were when, representing the work of the risen Christ, they wrote (VIII, viii):

---

51. C. H. Dodd, *The Apostolic Preaching and Its Developments* (London: Hodder and Stoughton, 1936), p. 42. Cf. also I. H. Marshall's comment: "The main theme is not so much the Spirit as the Lord" (*Luke: Historian and Theologian* [Exeter: Paternoster Press, 1970], pp. 161-62).

To all those for whom Christ hath purchased redemption, *he doth certainly and effectually apply and communicate the same*, making intercession for them, and revealing unto them, in and by the Word, the mysteries of salvation; effectually persuading them by his Spirit to believe and obey; and governing their hearts by his Word and Spirit; overcoming all their enemies by his almighty power and wisdom, in such manner and ways as are most consonant to his wonderful and unsearchable dispensation (emphasis added).

The Westminster divines are here, of course, only stating in a different fashion what they confess elsewhere when they affirm that Christ executes the offices of Prophet, Priest, and King, not only in His estate of humiliation but also in His estate of exaltation (*Shorter Catechism*, Q. 23-28).

Here then, in a sentence, is the real significance of Pentecost in the history of redemption: *It was Jesus' further self-attestation to the truth that He was Israel's Lord and Messiah*. And the nonrepeatable so-called "Samaritan Pentecost" (Acts 8:14-17) and the nonrepeatable so-called "Gentile [or, "ends of the earth"] Pentecost" (Acts 10:44-46) are to be viewed in the same light; both were Jesus' self-attestations to the church and to the people involved, at the critical junctures of the missionary endeavor He Himself had delineated in Acts 1:8, of His messiahship and saving lordship over the nations (cf. 8:14; 11:17-18).

In explaining the significance of Pentecost, Peter also said certain things that carry implications with respect to Jesus' divine character. To these features of his discourse—four in number—we now turn.

1. The very fact of His ascension and, more particularly, of His session at His Father's right hand suggests that Jesus is divine, for He who would sit as "Lord over all" the nations on the throne of God must Himself be God.[52] Certainly, His session on the throne of God attests to His superangelic nature, for "to which of the angels did God ever say, 'Sit at My right hand until I make Your enemies a footstool for Your feet'?" F. F. Bruce has well commented here:

The most exalted angels are those whose privilege it is to "stand in the presence of God" like Gabriel (Luke 1:19), but none of them has ever

52. Cf. Warfield:

In Peter's Pentecostal sermon Jesus is conceived as sitting at the right hand of God (2:34) and as having been constituted "both Lord and Christ," where the conjunction is significant (2:36): and more explicitly still He is designated in a later discourse of the same Peter, "Lord of all" (10:36), that is to say, universal sovereign, a phrase which recalls the great declaration of Rom. 9:5 to the effect that He is "God over all," *as indeed He who sits on the throne of God must be* (*Lord of Glory*, p. 211; emphasis added).

been invited to sit before Him, still less to sit in the place of unique honor at His right hand.[53]

To the divine Son alone, the writer of Hebrews affirms, this honor has been accorded (Heb. 1:4, 13).

2. The fact that it was the ascended *Jesus* who poured out the Spirit (2:33) moves in the same direction, for the connection between what Peter expressly emphasized in 2:17 by his deliberate insertion of the words "God says" into the Joel prophecy (" 'In the last days,' *God says, 'I will pour out* My Spirit' ") and his later statement in 2:33 (*"He* [the ascended Jesus] *has poured out this* which you now see and hear") cannot have been unintentional. Clearly, Peter connects the God and Yahweh of Joel 2 who promised to pour out His Spirit with the ascended Jesus of Acts 2 who poured out His Spirit.

3. The fact that the authority to apply the benefits of His redemption by His Spirit to whomever He pleases in His role as Baptizer of men by His Spirit (salvation) and by fire (judgment) means nothing less than that the prerogatives and functions of deity are His to exercise, but then this means that He Himself is God.

4. Peter, in response to his listeners' query, "Brothers, what shall we do?," urged them to "repent and be baptized *in the name of Jesus Christ*" (2:38). It is difficult to avoid the conclusion that he was urging them to avail themselves of the remedy Joel himself had prescribed in his prophecy when he said, "And everyone who calls on *the name of the Lord* will be saved" (Acts 2:21). But then this means, in turn, that for Peter Jesus was the Lord of Joel 2:32a (cf. Rom. 10:9-13), which means in turn that Jesus was the Yahweh who spoke through Joel.[54]

We discover from these features, then, that the event of Pentecost in its own striking way adds its testimony to the combined and consentient witness of Scripture to Christ's Messianic investiture and His divine nature.

In this chapter we considered four events—Jesus' resurrection, His pre-ascension ministry, His ascension, and Pentecost—for the light they throw on the nature of His sonship. Each in its own way provides data that the church has employed in confessing that Jesus the Christ is both very God and very man and thus God incarnate.

---

53. F. F. Bruce, *Commentary on the Epistle to the Hebrews* (Grand Rapids: Eerdmans, 1964), p. 24.

54. Marshall writes, "Peter spoke in Joel's words . . . of the need to call upon the name of the Lord in order to be saved. The effect of the argument is to show that Jesus is the Lord in the prophecy of Joel" (*Luke: Historian and Theologian,* p. 163).

We considered alternative interpretations to the church's historic understanding of Jesus' resurrection and found them wanting, in that they fail to explain the story itself or the church that emerged from the story. We saw that virtually from the moment of His resurrection the church confessed Jesus as Son of God in the divine sense, Thomas even employing the noun θεός itself as a christological title for Jesus. His ascension and the Pentecost event both highlighted His status as Lord of the universe and Lord of the church. We will now turn to the New Testament letters for the light they shed on Jesus' identity.

PAUL'S WITNESS TO JESUS

After the events of the Day of Pentecost, the risen Christ continued to display His divine power in the recorded events of Acts (cf. Luke's suggestive phrase in this regard, "all that Jesus *began* to do" in Acts 1:1), for example, in the healing of the crippled man at the temple gate called Beautiful (3:6, 12-13, 16; 4:9-10), in the many miracles performed through the apostles among the people (Acts 5:12), in His self-revelation to Stephen as "the Son of Man standing at the right hand of God" in the first martyr's moment of death (7:55-56), and in the so-called "Samaritan Pentecost" (Acts 8:14-17). But, arguably, no post-Pentecost act by the risen Christ has ever rivaled, in the significance of its effect on the on-going worldwide life of the church for all time to come, His postascension appearance to His arch-foe, Saul of Tarsus, on the road to Damascus, occurring sometime between A.D. 32 and A.D. 35 and recorded in Acts 9:3-18; 22:6-16; 26:12-18 (cf. also 1 Cor. 9:1; 15:8).

The Historicity of Paul's Conversion

It is not too much to say that if Paul was not converted as the Acts accounts report, not only is Luke-Acts, taken together as a corporate whole, rendered immediately and directly a false witness to history, but also the Pauline corpus is rendered invalid as a trustworthy rule for faith and practice, because Paul claimed in all of his letters to be a legitimate apostle, meeting all of the requirements of one who would be an apostle, particularly the one Peter mentions in Acts 1:22: "a witness of His resurrection." Paul claimed to have "seen Jesus our Lord" (1 Cor. 9:1). He claimed that Jesus "last of all, . . . appeared unto me also" (1 Cor. 15:8). He claimed that he had received his commission as an apostle "not from men nor by [any] man, but by Jesus Christ" (Gal. 1:1). And he claimed that he neither received his gospel from nor was taught his gospel by any man, but to the contrary, and I quote him, "I received it by revelation from Jesus Christ" (ablative use of the genitive) (Gal. 1:12). So I repeat, it is not overstating the case to say that if Paul was *not* converted as Acts reports his conversion, then the Pauline corpus is no longer a trustworthy guide in matters of faith and practice, and also the church itself, honoring Paul as it so self-consciously does as a true apostle of Jesus Christ, is a false witness to God. But no less certain is it that if Paul *was* converted as Acts reports his conversion, then this single event in a unique way establishes and validates not only the divine character of the Son of God but also the heavenly origination of the entire "Pauline phenomenon"—both the man and his teaching.

It should surprise no one, then, to learn that a vast literature, both pro and con, has grown up around the man Paul and the origin of his message. In fact, the literature on Paul's conversion along with its implications for his ministry is so enormous that I can do little more than recommend a few of the better treatments of the subject.[1] Moreover, I can do little more than mention the kinds of theories that have been advanced to explain on naturalistic grounds this extremely important event in the life of Saul of Tarsus and of the church that reveres his memory, and offer a few remarks by way of rebuttal.

Three extreme rationalizations of the event are that Saul either suffered an epileptic seizure or suffered a sunstroke or, seeing a flash of lightning that blinded him and being thrown from his horse when the horse became startled and bolted at the same flash of lightning, struck his head on the ground and in the daze that followed imagined he had seen the Lord. But these explanations have not commended themselves generally even to the critical mind. More popular is the view that, under the stress of his fanatical persecution of the church, Saul suffered a mental breakdown on the road to Damascus, and in this broken mental state imagined that the Lord of the very ones he was persecuting had called upon him to desist in his persecution and instead to serve Him. But probably the most popular naturalistic explanation is that Saul was subconsciously being conditioned by the logic of the Christian position, plus the dynamic quality of Christians' lives and their fortitude under oppression. Then, it is said, when he underwent that "mood-changing" crisis experience on the road to Damascus, the precise nature of which we are now unable to recover, he became convinced

1. I would recommend Lord Lyttleton's famous book, *Observations on the Conversion and Apostleship of St. Paul* (1774), Stalker's *The Life of St. Paul* (1889), Machen's *The Origin of Paul's Religion* (1925), H. N. Ridderbos's *Paul and Jesus* (1957), Longenecker's *Paul, Apostle of Liberty* (1964) and *The Ministry and Message of Paul* (1971), F. F. Bruce's *Paul and Jesus* (1974) and *Paul: Apostle of the Free Spirit* (1977), and S. Kim's *The Origin of Paul's Gospel* (1981). Those readers interested in further reading are advised to consult the extensive bibliographies provided in most of these works.

because of his prior subconscious preconditioning of mind and psyche that he should become a follower of Christ rather than His persecutor. But such psychologico/psychoanalytic solutions leave too many questions unanswered. In addition to the impossibility of psychoanalyzing a person who lived almost two thousand years ago with any degree of clinical accuracy, what real evidence is there that Saul suffered a mental breakdown? And what was the nature of the crisis experience that triggered it? Such questions as these, and many more besides, must be answered satisfactorily before any credence can be given to these theories.

Then there is Bultmann, who believed that all such depictions of "Biblical supernaturalism" are actually reflections of ancient "mythology." But his own explanation of Saul's conversion is wholly unsatisfactory in that it fails to come to terms with the historical character of the Acts narrative itself: "Not having been a personal disciple of Jesus, *he was won to the Christian faith by the kerygma of the Hellenistic church.'*[2] But neither is Dunn's view any better when he concludes that it is impossible to know for sure whether Jesus was " 'out there,' alive and making himself known to Paul." All that one can say with any certainty, Dunn continues, is that "Paul himself was convinced that what he saw was external to him" but it may have been "after all, all 'in the mind.' "[3]

Such conclusions, as I have said, frankly fail to come to terms with Luke's historical narrative (in the third person) in Acts 9 or with Paul's later accounts (in the first person) in Acts 22 and 26, given on the solemn occasions of defending his office and actions under the auspices of the Roman commander and before high government dignitaries respectively. Pertinent data indicate that his conversion was not merely mentally induced. We are expressly informed that, while Saul alone saw Jesus, the men who were traveling with him both heard a voice (9:7), though they did not understand the words (22:9), and saw the brilliant light (22:9; 26:13-14). And while Paul would later call the event a "vision from heaven" (26:19), which description itself imputes an *ab extra* character to it ("*from* heaven"), the accounts make it clear that his conversion was not subjectively self-induced in the subconscious mind of Saul but, rather, that it resulted from an initiating action external to him (9:3-4; 22:6-7; 26:13-14). Indeed, the ascended Christ represents *Himself* as the initiator in 26:16: "I have appeared to you" (ὤφθην σοι). And Ananias will say later that God had chosen Saul "to see the Righteous One and to hear words from His mouth" (22:14). When all

---

2. Rudolf Bultmann, *Theology of the New Testament*, vol. 1 (London: SCM Press, 1952), p. 187; emphasis original.

3. James D. G. Dunn, *Jesus and the Spirit* (Philadelphia: Westminster Press, 1975), pp. 107-8.

the facts in Acts 9; 22; 26; and 1 Corinthians 15 are taken into account, Longenecker's judgment seems clearly justified:

> Only the Damascus encounter with Christ was powerful enough to cause the young Jewish rabbi to reconsider the death of Jesus; only his meeting with the risen Christ was sufficient to demonstrate that God had vindicated the claims and work of the One he was opposing. Humanly speaking, Paul was immune to the Gospel. Although he was ready to follow evidence to its conclusion, he was sure that no evidence could overturn the verdict of the cross; that is, that Christ died the death of a criminal. But . . . the eternal God "was pleased," as Paul says by way of reminiscence, "to reveal his Son to me" (Gal. 1:16). Thus Paul was arrested by Christ, and made His own (Phil. 3:12).[4]

In support of the "revealedness" and truth-character of his apostleship and the gospel he proclaimed, we can produce no better argument than the one Paul himself adduced in Galatians 1:13–2:10 when he was defending his apostolic calling. The issue we are now facing is, in one sentence, What was the ultimate origin of Paul's gospel and his apostolic commission? It is evident that he could have obtained his gospel and the authority to preach it from only one of three possible sources. Let us look at each of these possibilities in turn.

Did he obtain the gospel he was preaching after his conversion from his previous life in Judaism? To ask the question is to answer it. Certainly not! Paul himself describes that experience in Judaism for us four different times:

> For you have heard of my previous way of life in Judaism, how intensely I

4. Richard N. Longenecker, *The Ministry and Message of Paul* (Grand Rapids: Zondervan, 1971), pp. 34-35. I must add to Longenecker's suggested reason for Saul's immunity to the gospel the additional reason that faith in Christ's obedience for salvation was surely for him incompatible with his Judaistic inclination to rely upon his own obedience to the law for salvation (cf. Jacques Dupont, "The Conversion of St. Paul, and Its Influence on His Understanding of Salvation by Faith," in *Apostolic History and the Gospel*, ed. W. Ward Gasque and Ralph P. Martin (Exeter: Paternoster Press, 1970), pp. 178-94). E. P. Sanders has argued in his *Paul and Palestinian Judaism* (Philadelphia: Fortress Press, 1977) that Palestinian Judaism was not a religion of legalistic works-righteousness wherein right standing before God was earned by good works in a system of strict justice. It is true, of course, as Sanders points out, that one can indeed find references in the literature of the period to God's election of Israel and to His grace and mercy. But Sanders makes too much of these facts, since Palestinian Judaism also taught that the elect man was obligated, even though he would do so imperfectly, to obey the law in order to remain in the covenant. Thus the legalistic principle was still present and ultimately governed the soteric status of the individual. But Paul rightly saw that any obligation to accomplish a "works-righteousness" on the sinner's part would negate the principle of *sola gratia* altogether (Rom. 11:6). For a detailed critical analysis of Sanders's thesis, cf. Karl T. Cooper, "Paul and Rabbinic Soteriology," *Westminster Theological Journal* 44 (1982): 173-39.

persecuted the church of God and tried to destroy it. I was advancing in Judaism beyond many Jews of my own age and was extremely zealous for the tradition of my fathers (Gal. 1:13-14).

I am a Jew, born in Tarsus of Cilicia, brought up in this city at the feet of Gamaliel, thoroughly trained in the law of our fathers, being zealous for God (Acts 22:3).

The Jews all know the way I have lived ever since I was a child, from the beginning of my life in my own country, and also in Jerusalem. They have known me for a long time and can testify, if they are willing, that according to the strictest sect of our religion, I lived as a Pharisee (Acts 26:4-5).

If anyone else thinks he has reasons to put confidence in the flesh, I have more: circumcised on the eighth day, of the people of Israel, of the tribe of Benjamin, a Hebrew of the Hebrews; in regard to the law, a Pharisee; as for zeal, persecuting the church; as for legalistic righteousness, faultless (Phil. 3:4-6).

It is evident from these autobiographical descriptions that Paul was not proclaiming as the Christian apostle what he had learned from his life in Judaism. As the Christian apostle, just to the contrary, he directed men's trust away from personal law-keeping, where his own had resided as a Pharisee, and toward Jesus Christ.

Then, if not at the feet of Gamaliel, did he obtain the gospel he was preaching after his conversion at the feet of the apostles? Listen to Paul again:

When God . . . was pleased to reveal His Son to me . . . I did not consult any man nor did I go up to Jerusalem to see those who were apostles before I was, but I went immediately into Arabia and later returned to Damascus (Gal. 1:15-17).

In this connection, there is separate evidence, if Paul intended by this reference to Arabia to refer to the Nabataean Kingdom, that he did not simply devote himself to a life of quiet contemplation in Arabia after his conversion but in fact immediately began to evangelize the populace there. He informs us in 2 Corinthians 11:32-33 that "the governor under King Aretas guarded the city of Damascus in order to seize me," but one does not stir up the kind of trouble he alludes to in the passage just cited merely by meditation. This would suggest that long before he made any contact with the Jerusalem apostles Paul had already engaged himself in Gentile evangelism.

Then Paul informs us under a self-imposed oath (cf. 1:20: "I assure you before God that what I am writing to you is no lie") that three years passed after his conversion before he finally met any of the apostles, and then it was only Peter and James he met, and only for the space of fifteen days (Gal. 1:18-19). This was doubtless the visit Luke records in Acts 9:26-28, and while it is likely that it was at this time that he "received" the precise details about Jesus' postresurrection appearances, particularly those to Peter and James, that he later "delivered" to the Corinthians in 1 Corinthians 15:5-7, it is evident, since they had no opportunity, that the apostles conferred no authority on him at that time. Furthermore, Paul assures his reader, "I was personally unknown to the churches of Judea" (Gal. 1:22). Then Paul declares that another eleven years passed (I am assuming the correctness of the South Galatia theory here) before he saw the apostles again, this time on the occasion of his so-called "famine-relief" visit to Jerusalem recorded in Acts 11:27-30). On this second occasion, Paul informs us, "I set before [the apostles] the gospel that I preach among the Gentiles" (Gal. 2:2). The outcome of this presentation, which surely would have included his view of Christ Himself, was that the apostles "added nothing to my message" (2:6), but to the contrary, saw "that I had been entrusted with the gospel" (2:7), that "God who was at work in Peter as an apostle to the circumcision was also at work in me [as an apostle] to the Gentiles" (2:8), and "gave me the right hand of fellowship" (2:10). In other words, they again conferred no authority on him but rather only acknowledged the authority that was already his, by virtue of which he had been engaged in his apostolic ministry among the Gentiles for many years. We conclude, then, that throughout this entire fourteen-year period (Gal. 2:1)—during the three-year period preceding his first visit to Jerusalem and during the eleven-year period preceding his second visit to Jerusalem—beginning immediately (Acts 9:20), Paul was "proclaiming Jesus, that this One is the Son of God" (Acts 9:20), "proving that this One is the Messiah" (9:22), and "preaching the faith that he once tried to destroy" (Gal. 1:23)—a ministry that only much later the other apostles personally and directly acknowledged as authentic.

Now if Paul was not preaching what he had learned during his life in Judaism, it is also clear from this review of the first fourteen years of his apostolic ministry that he was not preaching what he had learned from the original apostles either. Nor had they conferred authority on him to execute his ministry as an apostle. But then this means that the gospel he was proclaiming he received neither from his Judaistic training *before* his conversion nor from apostolic indoctrination *after* his conversion. The only remaining alternative is that he was proclaiming a gospel he received, as he says, in and from his conversion experience itself—"by revelation from Jesus Christ" (Gal. 1:12)!

This does not mean, of course, that Paul had known nothing before his conversion about Jesus Christ or about the church's doctrinal teaching concerning Him. He knew some things well enough, for he had confronted them often enough. It does mean that Jesus' postascension appearance to Paul on the Damascus road forced upon him an entirely new interpretive grid or hermeneutical context into which he had to place not only his understanding of Jesus' person and work but also his previous Judaistic instruction concerning law and grace.[5]

Nor does it mean that Paul did not grow in his understanding of Christ during those fourteen years, for indeed, he continued to grow in his knowledge of Christ to the very end of his life (Phil. 3:10-14). It does mean that in all his "growing up" he never "grew away" from that first clear "vision from heaven," as Stalker so poignantly suggests when he writes, "His whole theology is nothing but the explication of his own conversion."[6]

Paul's Christology

Given then the fact and historicity of Jesus' postascension appearance to Paul and the details we have rehearsed regarding his ministry, there is no legitimate reason to question (1) Paul's apostolic calling, which he declared he received "not from men [ἀπ' ἀνθρώπον] nor through man [δι' ἀνθρώπου], but through Jesus Christ and God the Father" (Gal. 1:1)— an expression that many New Testament scholars suggest, because of the contrast Paul draws between "men" and "man" on the one hand and "Jesus Christ and God the Father" on the other, contains an implicit assertion of Christ's divine character; (2) the Lord's continuing leading throughout his ministry (cf. Acts 13:2-3; 16:6-10; 18:9-11; 20:22; 22:17-21 [cf. 9:28-30]; 23:11; 27:23-24; cf. also 2 Cor. 12:1-10); (3) his exercise of the signs of an apostle (2 Cor. 12:11-12; cf. Acts 14:3, 8-10); or (4) his role as a unique organ of revelation in the history of redemption (1 Thess. 2:13; 1 Cor. 2:13; Eph. 3:2-11; 2 Pet. 3:15-16). All this being so, we can assume as we turn to the Pauline corpus that in it we possess a trustworthy mine of information about

5. Cf. J. Gresham Machen, *The Origin of Paul's Religion* (1925; reprint, Grand Rapids: Eerdmans, 1965), pp. 144ff.
6. James Stalker, *The Life of St. Paul* (Edinburgh: T. & T. Clark, 1889), p. 40. Cf. particularly here Margaret E. Thrall, "The Origin of Pauline Christology," in *Apostolic History and the Gospel*, pp. 304-16.

Him who called Paul on his way to Damascus that day out of his life of legalism. Of course, given the restrictions of space, we cannot pretend that we are going to exhaust the wealth of truth to be found therein. We must content ourselves with notices and expositions of only the more apparent lines of evidence that run throughout the great apostle's writings about the supernatural person of Jesus Christ.

As we approach the writings of Paul, we must not allow to slip from our thinking the recognition that Paul was, first and foremost, a missionary and his letters were written for the most part to churches he had founded (Romans is the exception here) and to pastors of those churches (Philemon is the exception here). In these letters Paul affords us a glimpse of the content of the message he proclaimed when first he arrived in a city to evangelize it as the "apostle to the Gentiles." Not surprisingly, we find that his message centered upon Christ. To be specific, the historical events of Christ's death, burial, and resurrection formed the "cutting edge" of his proclamation (1 Cor. 15:3-5). To the Galatians he wrote, "Before your very eyes Jesus Christ was portrayed as crucified" (3:1). To the Thessalonians he declared that he had "shared the gospel of God" with them (1 Thess. 2:8), the content of which concerned "the living and true God" and the coming of "His Son from heaven, whom He raised from the dead—Jesus, who rescues us from the coming wrath" (1:9-10; cf. 2 Thess. 2:5). Among the Corinthians, Paul informs us, he had resolved to know nothing "except Jesus Christ and Him crucified" (1 Cor. 2:2; cf. 1:23), which focus of concentration he then described as his work of "laying a foundation" (3:10-11). Later, in the same letter, he spoke of "the gospel which I preached to you" (15:1), the content of which he spells out in the following terms:

> that Christ died for our sins according to the Scriptures,
>   and that He was buried,
> and that He was raised the third day according to the Scriptures
>   and that He appeared to Cephas, then the Twelve (15:3-5).

In his letter to the Romans he declared that the "gospel of God," having been "promised through His prophets in the holy Scriptures,"

> concerned His Son,
>   who was born of the seed of David according to the flesh,
>   who was powerfully marked out the Son of God according to [His]
>   Spirit of holiness by the resurrection from the dead,
> Jesus Christ our Lord (Rom. 1:1-4).

In the same letter he wrote of "the word of faith which we are proclaiming," and he described that "word" in this fashion: "If you confess with your mouth, 'Jesus is Lord,' and believe in your heart that God raised Him from the dead, you will be saved" (10:9-10). In 2 Corinthians 1:19 Paul declares that he had preached among his readers "the Son of God, Christ Jesus" as God's "Yes" to men, and in 4:5, Paul writes, "We preach . . . Christ Jesus as Lord." In Colossians 1:28, he simply writes, "Christ we proclaim."

Luke, as he had done earlier in Acts with Peter's discourse on the Day of Pentecost, gives us also an account of one of Paul's missionary sermons (13:16-41). In the synagogue at Pisidian Antioch Paul began by rehearsing for his listeners God's care for Israel in times previous (13:16-22) and then quickly focused their attention on the "Savior Jesus," the one whom John the Baptist had served as forerunner (13:23-25). Then, following the format he outlined in 1 Corinthians 15:3-4, he informed them that the rulers of Jerusalem "fulfilled the words of the prophets which are read every Sabbath" (13:27) and "carried out all that had been written concerning Him" (13:29) by condemning Jesus and having Him crucified (under Pilate's orders) and buried. Then Paul declared, "But God raised Him from the dead" (13:30), eliciting as evidence for Christ's resurrection the fact "that for many days He was seen by those who traveled with Him from Galilee to Jerusalem" (13:31) and employing Psalm 2:7; Psalm 16:10; and Isaiah 55:3 to show that His resurrection was "according to the Scriptures." (Note that Paul employed Ps. 16 in precisely the same manner as Peter had done on the Day of Pentecost to make the point that David, when he died, was buried and saw decay with his fathers; David was not writing of himself in Ps. 16 but of Jesus.) Having proclaimed, then, that Jesus died according to the Scriptures, was buried, and rose again according to the Scriptures, Paul applied his proclamation to his audience: "Therefore, I want you to know . . . that through *this One* the forgiveness of sins is proclaimed to you; and from all which you were unable to be justified by the law of Moses, everyone who believes in *this One* is justified" (13:38-39). Here we have the apostolic model of a Christ-centered evangelistic sermon (cf. also 17:2, 22-31; 18:5; 20:21).

It is clear from this biblical data that when we consider Paul's Christology, we are addressing what for him was central to everything else. And he was not silent with regard to who Christ is. We intend to elicit evidence from Paul's letters that will put beyond all legitimate doubt that he regarded Jesus Christ as very God as well as very man.

Jesus as "the Christ"

Beyond all doubt, Jesus was, for Paul, the promised Messiah. This we may assume as a "given." In Paul's writings, "Christ" becomes a proper name for Jesus, indeed Paul's favorite designation for Him, occurring (more often with than without the article) around two hundred and ten times by itself in this sense and many more times in conjunction with other designations.[7] In addition, Paul affirms that the Old Testament Scriptures spoke of Jesus (cf., for example, Acts 13:27-36; 17:2-3; 26:22-23; Rom. 1:1-3; 1 Cor. 15:3-4). And precisely because Paul employs it in conjunction with the term "Lord" ("the Lord Christ" in Rom. 16:18; Col. 3:24; "the [or "our"] Lord Jesus Christ"; "Christ Jesus, the [or "our," or "my"] Lord"; "Jesus Christ, our Lord"), it is clear that for Paul "Christ" was a title of great dignity, compatible in every way with the implicates of deity that are often suggested by the title combinations in which it is found and the predicative statements surrounding it (cf., for example, Col. 3:24: "The Lord Christ you are serving," and Rom. 9:5: "Christ . . . who is over all, God blessed forever").

Jesus as "the Lord"

But it is in his description of Jesus as "the [or "our" or "my"] Lord" (κύριος) that Paul brings out most clearly his assessment of Jesus as divine. That is plain from the following observations: (1) Paul prayed to Christ as "the Lord" (2 Cor. 12:8-9); (2) Paul declared "the name of our Lord Jesus Christ" to be the name to be "called upon" in the church (1 Cor. 1:2; Rom. 10:9-13; cf. Joel 2:32a); (3) Paul coupled "the Lord Jesus Christ" with "God our Father" as the Co-source of those spiritual blessings (grace, mercy, and peace) that God alone has the power to grant (Gal. 1:3; 1 Thess. 1:1; 2 Thess. 1:1-2; Rom. 1:7; 16:20; 1 Cor. 1:3; 2 Cor. 1:2; Eph. 1:2; Phil. 1:2; 1 Tim. 1:2; 2 Tim. 1:2; Titus 1:4; cf. 1 Thess. 3:11; 2 Thess. 1:12; Eph. 6:23); (4) Paul applied to Christ the very term (κύριος) that in the Septuagint is employed to translate the sacred name of Yahweh; and more specifically, (5) Paul applied directly to Jesus Old Testament passages in which God (Yahweh) is the subject (cf. Isa. 8:14 and Rom. 9:32, 33; Joel 2:32 and Rom. 10:12-13; Isa. 40:13 and 1 Cor. 2:16; Ps. 24:1 [LXX, 23:1] and 1 Cor. 10:26 [cf. 10:21-22]; Ps. 68:18 and Eph. 4:8-10; Isa. 45:23 and Phil. 2:10).

Note further that it is as "the Lord" that Paul speaks of Jesus in his "trinitarian" passages (Rom. 15:30; 1 Cor. 12:4-6; 2 Cor. 13:14; Eph. 4:4-6); clearly "Lord" was the christological title Paul used to both equate Jesus with and distinguish Him from the Father and the Spirit, which implies that Paul was presupposing the heavenly triad when he speaks of Jesus as "Lord."[8]

7. Leon Morris (*New Testament Theology* [Grand Rapids: Zondervan, 1986], pp. 39, 41) states that Paul uses "Christ" 379 times in his writings, 72 percent of the New Testament total.

8. Warfield, *The Lord of Glory* (reprint; Grand Rapids: Baker, 1974), p. 231.

Magnificently does Warfield capture the essence of the meaning of "Lord" as a christological title in Paul's writings when he writes:

> "Lord" to [Paul] is not a general term of respect which he naturally applies to Jesus because he recognized Jesus as supreme, and was glad to acknowledge Him as his Master (Eph 6:9, Col 4:), or even in the great words of Col 2:19 as the "Head" of the body which is His Church (cf. Eph 4:15). It is to him the specific title of divinity by which he indicates to himself the relation in which Jesus stands to Deity. Jesus is not "Lord" to him because he has been given dominion over all creation; He has been given this universal dominion because He is "Lord," who with the Father and the Spirit is to be served and worshipped, and from whom all that the Christian longs for is to be expected.[9]

The Preexistence of "the Son"

A further line of evidence suggesting that Jesus Christ, for Paul, was divine is the catena of verses that implies His preexistence as God's Son (cf. 2 Cor. 8:9; Rom. 8:3; Gal. 4:4; Phil. 2:6-7; Col. 1:15-16; Eph. 4:8-9). It has been suggested that such statements need reflect no more than an "ideal" preexistence and do not require Christ's personal preexistence. But such a contention will fail to persuade any but the gullible once the passages have been carefully examined. Consider: The apostle appeals for Christian generosity on the ground that Christ, the Christian's example, "though he was [ὤν] rich, yet for your sakes . . . became poor [ἐπτώχευσεν] (2 Cor. 8:9). He urges Christians to live as sons of God should because "God sent forth [ἐξαπέστειλεν] His Son" to make us His sons (Gal. 4:4). He grounds his argument for Christian self-effacement in the fact that "though [Christ] was in the form of God, . . . He poured Himself out, having taken [λαβών] the form of a servant" (Phil. 2:6-7). He insists that the Colossians must not find in the pagan πλήρωμα ("fullness") their fullness because it is Christ, God's Son (cf. v. 13), who is "before all things" and "by whom and for whom all things were created" (Col. 1:16-17). It is highly doubtful that the apostle would have grounded these pastoral appeals in a merely speculative "ideal" preexistence. Much more likely is it that such appeals were based upon a familiar, treasured, foundational truth central to the Christian faith— namely, that Christ as God's Son had personally preexisted with the Father from eternity and had come to earth on a mission of mercy.

The foregoing material makes it abundantly clear, then, that for Paul the

9. Ibid.

One who apprehended him on the Damascus Road was indeed God in His own right and the proper recipient of man's worship and service. Consequently, Paul can move "easily into a complete linguistic identification of Christ with Yahweh":

> If Yahweh is our sanctifier (Exod. 31:13), is omnipresent (Ps. 139:7-10), is our peace (Judg. 6:24), is our righteousness (Jer. 23:6), is our victory (Exod. 17:8-16), and is our healer (Exod. 15:26), then so is Christ all of these things (1 Cor. 1:30; Col. 1:27; Eph. 2:14). If the gospel is God's (1 Thess. 2:2, 6-9; Gal. 3:8), then that same gospel is also Christ's (1 Thess. 3:2; Gal. 1:7). If the church is God's (Gal. 1:13; 1 Cor. 15:9), then that same church is also Christ's (Rom. 16:16). God's Kingdom (1 Thess. 2:12) is Christ's (Eph. 5:5); God's love (Eph. 1:3-5) is Christ's (Rom. 8:35); God's Word (Col. 1:25; 1 Thess. 2:13) is Christ's (1 Thess. 1:8; 4:15); God's Spirit (1 Thess. 4:8) is Christ's (Phil. 1:19); God's peace (Gal. 5:22; Phil. 4:9) is Christ's (Col. 3:15; cf.Col. 1:2; Phil. 1:2; 4:7); God's "Day" of judgment (Isa. 13:6) is Christ's "Day" of judgment (Phil. 1:6, 10; 2:16; 1 Cor. 1:8); God's grace (Eph. 2:8, 9; Col. 1:6; Gal. 1:15) is Christ's grace (1 Thess. 5:28; Gal. 1:6; 6:18); God's salvation (Col. 1:13) is Christ's salvation (1 Thess. 1:10); and God's will (Eph. 1:11; 1 Thess. 4:3; Gal. 1:4) is Christ's will (Eph. 5:17; cf. 1 Thess. 5:18). So it is no surprise to hear Paul say that he is both God's slave (Rom. 1:9) and Christ's (Rom. 1:1; Gal. 1:10), that he lives for that glory which is both God's (Rom. 5:2; Gal. 1:24) and Christ's (2 Cor. 8:19, 23; cf. 2 Cor. 4:6), that his faith is in God (1 Thess. 1:8, 9; Rom. 4:1-5) and in Christ Jesus (Gal. 3:22), and that to know God, which is salvation (Gal. 4:8; 1 Thess. 4:5), is to know Christ (2 Cor. 4:6).[10]

Such linguistic identification is pervasive throughout Paul's writings and may be observed by ranging freely through the Pauline corpus. But there are eight contexts in particular, in addition to the one we considered in the previous chapter (Rom. 1:3-4), where Paul makes explicit his view of Christ— the great christological passages in Colossians 1:15-20; 2:9; Philippians 2:6-11; Ephesians 4:9-10; 1 Timothy 1:15; 3:16; Romans 9:5; and Titus 2:13.

Colossians 1:15-20: Jesus, as God's Divine Son,
Supreme Over Creation and the Church

Apparently in the Colossian church some teachers, under a kind of Jewish intellectualism resembling if not identical with what some scholars refer to

10. David F. Wells, *The Person of Christ* (Westchester, Ill.: Crossway Books, 1984), pp. 64-65.

as a "pre-Gnostic form of Gnosticism," were teaching the existence of angelic intermediaries (cf. "thrones, powers, rulers, authorities" in 1:16) between the Creator and the material universe, among which intermediaries was Jesus. It was to oppose this christological representation that Paul incorporated this hymn to Christ in his letter to the Colossians.

In this pericope, beginning in 1:15 with the words "who is," the antecedent of which is "the Son of His [that is, "the Father's"; cf. 1:12] love" in 1:13, Paul gives us a magnificent description of the person of our Lord. So sublime is it that it bears quoting in full:

> *Jesus Is Lord of the Natural Creation:*
> Who is the Image of the invisible God,
>> the Firstborn of *all* creation,
>>> because by Him were created *all things* in heaven and upon earth,
>>> things visible and things invisible—
>>> whether thrones or dominions,
>>> whether rulers or authorities—
>>> [because] *all things* through Him and for Him have been created,
>>> and He is before *all things*, and *all things* by Him endure. (emphasis added).

> *Jesus Is Lord of the Spiritual Creation:*
> And He is Head of the body, the church,
>> who is the Beginning,
>>> the Firstborn from the dead, in order that He might come to have first place in *all things*,
>>> because in Him He [God] willed *all* the fullness to dwell, and
>>> [because] through Him [He willed] to reconcile *all things* for Him,
>>>> by making peace through the blood of His cross— through Him,
>>>>> whether things upon earth,
>>>>> or things in heaven (emphasis added).

Paul scales such breathtaking heights in this sublime ascription of divine qualities to Christ that it is not surprising that a vast literature has emerged over the years around this passage of Scripture. Also not surprising, given the spirit of the times in which we live, is the amount of literature devoted to explaining its Christology in terms that eliminate all ontological indications.

It is a virtual "given" today among critical scholars that we have in this section of Colossians a pre-Pauline "hymn" that Paul (or another writer) adapted for his purpose.[11] But there is no consensus among these scholars on how the hymn is to be "strophied," or concerning the nature of its pre-Pauline background. For example, regarding its strophic arrangement, E. Norden urged that the "hymn" should be divided into two strophes of unequal length, each to begin with "who is" (1:15-18a, 18b-30).[12] E. Lohmeyer divided the passage into two strophes of seven lines each (1:15-16e, 18-20), with a connecting section of three lines (1:16f-17).[13] E. Käsemann argues for two strophes of six lines each (1:15-16, 18b-20), connected by 1:17-18a; but in his arrangement he discards the phrase "the church" in 1:18a, and the phrase "through the blood of His cross" in 1:20b as later interpolations.[14] And E. Schweizer divides the material into three strophes (1:15-16, 17-18a, 18b-20); but in order to secure the "original symmetry," with each stanza consisting of three lines, he omits the phrases, "things visible and things invisible—whether thrones or dominions, whether rulers or authorities" in 1:16, the phrases "the church" and "in order that He might come to have first place in all things" in 1:18, and the phrases "by making peace through the blood of His cross—through Him, whether things upon earth or things in heaven" in 1:20.[15]

As for its background, Käsemann argues that it was originally a pre-Christian Gnostic text dealing with the Gnostic Redeemer myth, which the church adapted to form part of a baptismal liturgy.[16] But R. P. Martin has pointed out that the absence of any pre-Christian non-Christian parallel to

11. The word "hymn" does not necessarily denote what we sing today as a congregational song. It is, here, a quasi-technical term, used broadly like that of "creed," to include dogmatic, confessional, liturgical, or doxological material. The criteria employed to identify "hymnic" material in the New Testament are both *stylistic* (rhythm, parallelism of lines, meter, alliteration, antithesis, chiasm) and *linguistic* (unusual vocabulary such as words that occur only once or that seem different from the language of the context). Cf. R. P. Martin, *Carmen Christi* (Cambridge: University Press, 1967), pp. 1-13; cf. also his *Colossians: The Church's Lord and the Christian's Liberty* (Exeter: Paternoster Press, 1972), pp. 39-40.

12. E. Norden, *Agnostos Theos* (Darmstadt: Wissenschaftliche Buchgesellschaft, 1956), pp. 250-54.

13. E. Lohmeyer, *Die Briefe an die Kolosser und an Philemon* (Göttingen: Vandenhoeck and Ruprecht, 1953), pp. 40-68.

14. E. Käsemann, "A Primitive Christian Baptismal Liturgy," *Essays on New Testament Themes*, trans. W. J. Montague (Naperville: Alec R. Allenson, 1964), pp. 149-68.

15. E. Schweizer, *The Churches as the Body of Christ* (Richmond, Va.: John Knox Press, 1964), pp. 64-73; cf. also his "The Church as the Missionary Body of Christ," *New Testament Studies* 8 (1961–62): 1-11, particularly pp. 6-7; and his *The Letter to the Colossians*, trans. Andrew Chester (London: SPCK, 1982), pp. 55-88. In the last work he speaks of "two strophes" but 17-18a still "form a link" between them.

16. Käseman, *Essays on New Testament Themes*, pp. 149-68.

the portrayal of the Redeemer figure as one who achieves reconciliation between God and man raises a serious question concerning the correctness of Käsemann's view.[17]

C. F. Burney and W. D. Davies suggest the pericope should be viewed against the background of Wisdom in Proverbs 8:22 and Genesis 1:1 as the latter is interpreted by Rabbinic Judaism with reference to Wisdom.[18] While this is a more attractive hypothesis than Käsemann's, seeking as it does to locate the hymn's background in the Old Testament, it is based upon the assumption that Paul's opposition at Colossae was mainly from a Jewish source, which is not at all evident.[19]

E. Schweizer urges that its background must be sought in the Wisdom understanding of Hellenistic Judaism. He also believes that the hymn's theology has been corrected, both by later insertions and by the commentary that follows (1:21-23).[20] But P. T. O'Brien, granting Schweizer's understanding of the theology of the author of Colossians for the sake of making his point, has argued that there still seem to remain in the hymn certain elements different from his theology, which fact is, to say the least, strange as long as the author was correcting the hymn's theology anyway. Moreover, it is not at all certain that the author has varied the hymn's theology by his commentary that immediately follows.[21]

While I do not question the possibility that we may well have an early Christian hymn in this passage (there certainly appear to be "hymnic" characteristics in the pericope), I prefer to divide the pericope according to its content into two main sections (1:15-17, 18-20), the former treating Christ's supreme lordship over all of the natural creation and the latter treating His supreme lordship over God's spiritual creation, the church. As for the original composition of the hymn, with O'Brien, I see no reason why Paul himself could not have been the author of an earlier hymn originally written for another occasion and circumstance but here modified and adapted to the situation, "expressing in an exalted hymnic style his beliefs about Christ in view of the situation of his readers."[22] If so, it appears from the

17. Martin, *Colossians*, pp. 41-42.
18. C. F. Burney, "Christ as the ARXH of Creation," *Journal of Theological Studies* 27 (1926): 160-77; W. D. Davies, *Paul and Rabbinic Judaism: Some Rabbinic Elements in Pauline Theology* (London: SPCK, 1955), pp. 150-52.
19. Martin, *Colossians*, p. 43.
20. Schweizer, *Letter to the Colossians*, pp. 55-88.
21. Peter T. O'Brien, *Word Biblical Commentary: Colossians, Philemon*, vol. 44 (Waco Tex.: Word Books, 1982), p. 39. Cf. ibid., pp. 32-42, for an extended discussion of current critical views of Col. 1:15-20. Also Martin (*Colossians*, pp. 40-44) and Donald Guthrie (*New Testament Theology* [Leicester: Inter-Varsity Press, 1981], pp. 352-55) have similar discussions in briefer compass.
22. O'Brien, *Colossians, Philemon*, pp. 41-42. Cf. also C. F. D. Moule (*The Epistles of Paul the*

vocabulary in the hymn (ἀρχή, πλήρωμα) that he made use of some of their language. But whether it was originally Pauline or not does not affect in any way our final exposition, for it is the hymn as it comes to us in *the inspired letter* to the Colossians that is the basis of our remarks.

The first thing that Paul tells us is that Christ, as the Father's Son, is "the Image of the invisible God." What does he mean by this description? Paul equates *"the light of* the gospel of *the glory of Christ,* who is the *Image* of God" (2 Cor. 4:4) with *"the light of the glory of God [imaged] in the face of Jesus Christ"* (2 Cor. 4:6); we may conclude that when Paul called Christ "the Image of God" in both 2 Corinthians 4:4 and Colossians 1:15, he was saying "nothing less than that in him the glory of God, indeed God himself, becomes manifest."[23] In addition, recall that the writer of Hebrews described God's Son as "the radiance of God's glory and the exact representation of His being" (1:3) and that James described "our Lord Jesus Christ" as just "the Glory" of God (2:1; cf. Zech. 2:5). There can be little doubt that Paul, with the New Testament writers in general, by describing Jesus as "the Image of the invisible God," intended to assert that Jesus is "just the invisible God made visible."[24]

This understanding—that Paul intended to assert, among other things, Jesus' divine nature—receives further support by the hymn's accompanying descriptions. Four times Paul employs the phrase τὰ πάντα, once πάσης, once πάντων, once πᾶσιν, and once πᾶν, (all to be translated "all [things]") to express Christ's exaltation over anything that would pretend to be His equal. Paul first declares that Christ is "the Firstborn of *all* creation" (πρωτότοκος πάσης κτίσεως). This should be understood in the Hebraic sense of ascribing priority of rank to the firstborn son, who enjoys a special place in the father's love and who accordingly is the father's primary heir (cf. Heb. 1:2). Clearly, the ὅτι clause of 1:16 and the πρὸ πάντων in 1:17 disallows the Arian insistence that the genitive ("of all creation") should be construed as a partitive genitive.[25] Moreover, with the exception of its occurrence in

---

Apostle to the Colossians and to Philemon [Cambridge: University Press, 1962], pp. 60-62) for his defense of the Pauline authorship of the passage.

23. H. N. Ridderbos, *Paul: An Outline of His Theology,* trans. John R. DeWitt (Grand Rapids: Eerdmans, 1975), p. 70.

24. Warfield, *Lord of Glory,* p. 254. F. F. Bruce comments on "the Image of the invisible God": "What is this but to say that the very nature and being of God have been perfectly revealed in Him—that in Him the invisible has become visible?" (*Commentary on the Epistles to the Ephesians and the Colossians* [London: Marshall, Morgan and Scott, 1957], p. 193). Martin, commenting on "Image," writes, "He is the objectivization of God in human life, a coming into visible expression of the invisible God" (*Colossians,* p. 45).

25. Cf. J. B. Lightfoot, *St. Paul's Epistles to the Colossians and to Philemon,* rev. ed. (1879; reprint, Grand Rapids: Zondervan, 1959), p. 147; Bruce, *Epistles to the Ephesians and Colossians,* p. 194;

Luke 2:7, no special emphasis is placed on the -τοκος element in the word anywhere in the New Testament.

The Son, Paul tells us further, enjoyed preexistence with the Father prior to the creation of the entire universe: He is ("exists") "before *all things*"[26] (1:17; cf. John 1:15, 30; 8:58). Furthermore, God created "*all things* in heaven and on earth—things visible and things invisible—whether thrones or dominions, whether rulers or authorities" by (ἐν) Him, through (διά) Him, and for (εἰς) Him (1:16, τὰ πάντα occurs twice in this verse). Upon the Son all things are dependent for their *continuance* in existence: "*all things* by Him endure [or "hold together"]" (1:17; cf. Heb. 1:3). He was raised from the dead "in order that He might have the preeminence in *all things*" (1:18). And finally—and this has to do with the fact that He carried the responsibilities of the Messianic task—through Him, Paul declares, God has been pleased "to reconcile to Himself *all things*, whether on earth or in heaven" (1:20).

From these clear statements respecting the Son's preexistent and preeminent relationship to the Father and His involvement in the creation, preservation, and reconciliation of all created things, it is apparent that Dunn's recent attempt to empty Paul's description of all references to the Son's *personal* preexistence and to make his words mean nothing more than that the power God exercises in creation is now fully revealed and embodied in Christ falls far short of its full import.[27] Furthermore, Paul's intention behind his description of Jesus as "the Firstborn of all creation" is miles away from the Arian interpretation of the Jehovah's Witnesses, who insist that the word shows that the Son was the "first" of all *other* created things. As we have said, the entire context cries out that the term is to be understood otherwise, namely, in the Hebraic sense as an ascription of priority to the firstborn son who enjoys a special place in the father's love. Sheer theological perversity leads the Jehovah's Witnesses in their *New World Translation* to insert the bracketed word "other" ("all [other] things") throughout the passage in order to justify their Arian view of the Son as being properly part of the created order.

That the Son is also preeminent over the church is stated in Paul's description of Him as "the Head of the body, the church," "the Beginning [of the new humanity]," "the Firstborn from the dead, that He might come to have first place [as the Father's exalted Son] over all things" (1:18a, b, c; cf.

Moule, *Epistles of Paul*, pp. 63-64; Martin, *Colossians*, pp. 45-46; O'Brien, *Colossians, Philemon*, p. 44; Larry R. Helyer, *The Prototokos Title in the New Testament* (dissertation; Fuller Theological Seminary, 1979); Larry R. Helyer, "Arius Revisited: The Firstborn Over All Creation," *Journal of the Evangelical Theological Society* 31, no. 1 (March 1988): 59-67.
26. Cf. Moule, *Epistles of Paul*, pp. 66-67.
27. Cf. Dunn, *Christology in the Making*, pp. 187-94.

Rom. 8:29) and the One through whose peacemaking "cross work" God is finally to reconcile all things for His (Christ's) glory (1:20).

It is difficult to conceive of any biblical passage that more forthrightly affirms the full and unabridged deity of Jesus Christ than Colossians 1:15-20, spelling out as it does on a cosmic scale His role in creating and preserving all things and His divine preeminence over all created things as Creator and Redeemer. Here, in plain, explicit language, Paul declares that Jesus Christ, as God's Son, was existing with the Father prior to the creation of the universe, was Himself God's agent in creation, and as the Image ("glory") of the invisible God, that is, as God Himself, by His incarnation made the invisible God visible to men. Then, as the exalted "Firstborn from the dead," His eschatological preeminence is implied in Paul's assertion that God willed to reconcile all things for His (Christ's) glory (εἰς αὐτόν), which is finally to be fulfilled in the "Eschaton."

Colossians 2:9: Jesus as "the Incarnate Plenitude of Deity"

I purposely postponed the discussion of Paul's phrase in 1:19, "all the fullness" (πᾶν τὸ πλήρωμα), to this point inasmuch as he uses the same phrase in 2:9, with perhaps even greater clarity. The phrase almost certainly means the same thing in both contexts, and to discuss it in connection with 2:9 avoids repetition.

In 1:19, Paul had written, "In Him [God] willed all the fullness to dwell." Here in 2:9 Paul says virtually the same thing, but he specifies the nature of the "fullness" and the manner in which the "fullness" dwells in Jesus. To see this, let us follow his thought. In the last verses of Colossians 1 Paul discussed the "mystery" of God, which, he says, is "Christ in you, the hope of glory" (1:27). A few verses later, Paul affirmed again that God's "mystery," anticipated in the Old Testament revelation but only recently fully revealed, is Christ (2:2) "in whom *all* the treasures of wisdom and knowledge are deposited" (2:3). This is striking enough in that it highlights the uniqueness of Christ as the sole true repository and integrating point of all knowledge. But then a few verses later, Paul excels even himself in his exaltation of his Lord, for in 2:9 he says something even more striking. While he does not describe Christ directly as "God" (θεός), as we shall see him do in Romans 9:5 and Titus 2:13, his statement comes as close to it as is humanly imaginable.[28] Why are his readers to "walk" in Christ and to "be on guard" so that no one should take them captive through the pursuit of knowledge

28. Cf. Oscar Cullmann's remark: "Such a text . . . is just a step from directly designating Jesus 'God' " (*The Christology of the NewTestament* [London: SCM Press, 1959], pp. 311-13).

that springs from human philosophy and tradition? The answer, translated literally, reads as follows: "because [ὅτι] in Him [Christ] dwells all the fullness of deity bodily" (2:9).

To assess Paul's intention here, it will be necessary to give some attention to three of his words. By "fullness" (πλήρωμα) (which is perhaps an example of employing his [Jewish/pre-Gnostic?] opponents' terminology—scholars differ on what precisely was the nature of the Colossian heresy), Paul means plainly and simply "completeness," "totality," or "sum-total."[29] To insure that no one would miss his intention, Paul qualifies this noun with "all" (πᾶν), that is, "all [not just some of] the fullness."

If it is an allusion to his opponents' language, this phrase already carries overtones of "fullness of deity," but Paul clarifies his intention by the following defining genitive "of deity" (θεότητος). The word for "deity" here is θεότης, the "abstract noun from θεός,"[30] meaning "the being as God," or "the being of the very essence of deity." Putting these two words together, Paul is saying something about the "totality of all that is essential to the divine nature."

Concerning this "totality of divine essence" Paul affirms that it "dwells [permanently]" (for this is the force of the preposition κατά prefixed to the verb and the present tense of the verb κατοικέω) in Jesus.

Precisely how it is that this "totality of the very essence of deity" permanently "dwells" in Him, Paul specifies by the Greek adverb σωματικῶς. Some scholars suggest that the word means "essentially" or "really" (as over against "symbolically"; cf. the contrast in 2:17 between "shadow" [σκιά] and "reality" [σῶμα]), but much more likely it means "bodily," that is, "in bodily form," indicating that the mode or manner in which the permanent abode of the full plenitude of deity in Jesus is to be understood is in incarnational terms. In short, Paul intends to say that in Jesus we have to do with the very "embodiment" or incarnation of deity. Christ is God "manifest in the flesh" (1 Tim. 3:16). Here we come very close to a Pauline equivalent to the Johannine ὁ λόγος σάρξ ἐγένετο ("the Word became flesh"). Finally, to underscore Jesus' uniqueness as such, Paul throws the "in Him" forward in the sentence to the position of emphasis, implying by this, against his opponents' claim that "fullness" could be found elsewhere,

29. Cf. Moule, *Epistles of Paul*, p. 164, and his articles, "Pleroma," in *The Interpreter's Dictionary of the Bible*, vol. 3 (Nashville: Abingdon Press, 1962), pp. 826-28; and "'Fullness' and 'Fill' in the New Testament," *Scottish Journal of Theology* 4 (1951): 80. Cf. also Lightfoot, "On the meaning of πλήρωμα," *St. Paul's Epistles to the Colossians and to Philemon*, pp. 252-73.

30. W. F. Arndt and F. W. Gingrich, *A Greek-English Lexicon of the New Testament* (Chicago: University of Chicago Press, 1957), p. 359.

that "in Him [and nowhere else]" permanently resides in bodily form the very essence of deity!

To interpret Paul so is clearly in keeping with his earlier "hymn" to Christ in 1:15-20, as virtually every commentator acknowledges.[31] This view alone coincides with the rich language of the hymn where, as we have already seen, Christ is described as the "Image of the invisible God," who was "before all things" and by, through, and for whom God created all things, and in whom all things "hold together."

Some modern scholars construe Paul's language, both in 1:15-20 and in 2:9, as functional language, but such a construction fails to take seriously the nature of the salvation envisioned in 2:10, its import only being meaningful if the Savior who effects it is the One in whom resides the fullness of deity. As O'Brien remarks, "If the fullness of deity does not reside in him then the Colossians' fullness would not amount to much at all—the very point Paul is making over against the errorists' teaching on fullness."[32]

Philippians 2:6-11: Jesus as the Divine and Exalted Lord

The amount of literature on Philippians 2:6-11 is absolutely staggering.[33] I have no intention, therefore, to interact with it here in a manner approaching comprehensiveness. It is safe to say, however, that on at least one issue all the scholarly literature since Lohmeyer's epochal study *Kyrios Jesus, Eine Untersuchung zu Phil. 2:5-11* in 1928, which is substantially reproduced in his commentary, *Der Brief an die Philipper* (1930), agrees: that in Philippians 2:6-11 we have (at least a fragment of?) an early Christian hymn.[34] Scholars disagree as to whether the hymn is Paul's own composition,[35] or whether it

31. Cf. the commentaries of Olshausen, Endicott, H. A. W. Meyer, J. B. Lightfoot, Abbott (ICC), H. C. J. Moule, A. L. Williams, E. F. Scott, L. B. Radford, K. Wuest, C. F. D. Moule, Carson, Baggott, Hendriksen, Johnston, E. Lohse, R. P. Martin, Rogers, Lucas, O'Brien, and Patzia. Cf. also the writings of such theologians as Liddon, Hodge, Warfield, D. Guthrie, I. H. Marshall, et al.

32. O'Brien, *Colossians, Philemon*, p. 112.

33. For a bibliography on the pericope, cf. Gerald F. Hawthorne, *Word Biblical Commentary: Philippians*, vol. 43 (Waco, Tex.: Word Books, 1983), pp. 71-75; R. P. Martin, *Carmen Christi*, pp. 320-39; cf. Robert B. Strimple ("Philippians 2:5-11 in Recent Studies: Some Exegetical Conclusions," *Westminster Theological Journal* 41 [1979]: 247-68) for a listing and summary of studies since 1963 to the approximate date of his article.

34. Martin, *Carmen Christi*, pp. 21, 28. Martin himself speaks of the hymn specifically as a "piece of early Christian kerygmatic confession" (ibid., p. 21), and devotes Part III of his highly regarded study to supporting this description.

35. I. Howard Marshall ("The Christ-Hymn in Philippians 2:5-11: A Review Article," *Tyndale Bulletin* 19 [1968]: 104-27) and Morna D. Hooker ("Philippians 2:6-11, in *Jesus und Paulus: Festschrift für Werner Georg Kümmel zum 70 Geburtstag*, ed. E. Earle Ellis and Erich Grasser [Göttingen: Vandenhoeck and Ruprecht, 1975], pp. 151-64) both express an openness to Pauline authorship, as does Hawthorne (*Philippians*, p. 78).

was originally pre-Pauline and employed by Paul because it suited his purpose. If it is Pauline, one must acknowledge that he employed some uncustomary language (μορφή, ἁρπαγμός). There is also very little scholarly consensus on how the hymn is to be versified.[36] But, I repeat, they all agree that Philippians 2:6-11 is of "hymnic" literary genre. This may very well be so, for certain stylistic and lexical characteristics usually associated with hymnic material—such as various kinds of parallelism of thought, inversions, unusual vocabulary, and elevated style—are present in the pericope. But I would register mild reservation as to the number of hymns that are present in the passage. Whereas contemporary New Testament scholarship proposes the presence of one hymn that incorporates the whole of the material in these verses, I propose the possibility that what we may actually have are (portions of?) two hymns—the first comprising 2:6-9 and based on Genesis and Isaianic material, the second comprising 2:9-11 and based mainly on Isaianic material. I submit the following structural arrangement of the two proposed hymns as a possibility, preferable, I believe, to arrangements I have seen to date, inasmuch as virtually all of them either eliminate (as interpolation) or rearrange entire lines and phrases in order to bring strophic symmetry to the hymn. My arrangement has in its favor two considerations: it leaves the text as it comes to us in Paul's letter intact, and it allows the content of the material to govern the strophic arrangement and division. I tentatively suggest, then, that the first "hymn" be strophied as follows:

"Who [refers antecedently to "Christ Jesus" in 2:5],

> *Strophe 1:*
> though in the form of God existing,
>> did not regard equality with God a thing to be seized,
>> but Himself He poured out,
> having taken the form of a servant."

Note that by this arrangement there are four lines in this strophe, the first and the fourth being participial clauses, separated by the second and third lines, which set up a contrast ("did not regard" and "but poured"). That the first and fourth lines appear to belong together strophically is evident from

---

36. For four proposed versifications, cf. E. Lohmeyer, *Der Brief an die Philipper*, 12th ed. (Göttingen: Vandenhoeck and Ruprecht, 1964), p. 90; Joachim Jeremias, "Zur Gedankenführung in den paulinischen Briefen: Der Christushymnus, Phil. 2:6-11," in *Studia Paulina*, ed. J. N. Sevenster and W. C. van Unnik (Haarlem: DeErven R. Bohn, 1956), pp. 152-54; Charles H. Talbert, "The Problem of Pre-existence in Philippians 2:6-11," *Journal of Biblical Literature* 86 (1967): 141-53; M. Hooker, in *Jesus und Paulus*. Hooker even comments, "I myself have produced six or seven different analyses—and found each of them convincing at the time!" (ibid., p. 157).

the occurrence of μορφή ("form") in both and the occurrence of participles in both, suggesting also that they are to be viewed as "bracketing" clauses, tying these lines together.

Strophe 2:
"In the precise likeness of men having been born,
    and having been found by external appearance to be a man,
    He humbled Himself,
Having become obedient unto death—

Climactic addendum:
even the death of the cross."

Postponing for the moment any discussion of what I am calling the climactic addendum, which may have been an original short choral refrain at the end of the hymn or Paul's own addendum intended to highlight the shameful character of the death our Lord died, I would point out that again we have a strophic arrangement of four lines, and again the first and the fourth are participial clauses separated by the second and third lines. (These inner lines do not stand in contrast to one another as do the inner lines of the former strophe.) That these four lines appear to form a natural and single strophe is evident from the fact that the participles in both the first and fourth lines are the same (γενόμενος), though their nuance of meaning is different and they appear in inverted word order—in last place in the first line, in first place in the last line. Again, I suggest that these participial clauses serve as "brackets" to set the strophe apart from the preceding strophe and that which follows. Further evidence that these lines are to be construed together strophically is the climactic parallelism of thought between the first and second lines and the occurrences of the word for "man" in the first and second lines (though it is true that they differ in number, being plural in the first line and singular in the second line).

With the two strophes clearly distinguished from each other before us, we may now note the following parallels that suggest that they, taken together, form a single hymn:

1. The two strophes have the same number of lines.
2. Both first lines begin with the preposition ἐν ("in"), which is then followed in each case with a dative noun, then a genitive noun, concluding with a participle.
3. The first lines of the two strophes contain an antithetic parallelism: "form of God" and "likeness of men."
4. The third line in both strophes ascribes to Christ a reflexive action, with the reflexive pronoun ἑαυτὸν ("Himself") appearing in inverted order to the

verb: in the former, *"Himself* He poured out," in the latter, "He humbled
Himself." This striking similarity suggests that the two actions mean essentially the same thing, a possibility that receives further support from the
distinct likelihood that the former phrase has Isaiah 53:12 as its background
while the latter phrase echoes the thought of Isaiah 53:8 (LXX), which is
quoted in Acts 8:33 ("In his *humiliation* He was deprived of justice"), both
Isaianic statements, of course, describing the Suffering Servant.

5. Postponing the reason for my interpretation until later, but assuming
its validity here for the sake of grouping together the several parallels
between the strophes, the hymn moves from the idea of "death" ("poured
Himself out") in strophe 1, line 3, to "servitude" ("He humbled Himself") in
strophe 2, line 3; but it moves in reverse order from the idea of "servitude"
("the form of servant") in strophe 1, line 4, to "death" ("obedient unto
death") in strophe 2, line 4.

6. In strophe 1 the word "God" occurs in the first and second lines; in
strophe 2 the word "man" occurs in the first and second lines, suggesting an
antithetic parallel between these lines of the two strophes.

7. Both strophes deal with the same subject: Jesus' state of humiliation.
The second "hymn" is to be strophied as follows:

Strophe 1:
"Therefore [because of Christ's "servant work"]

God has highly exalted Him,
and He has given to Him the name,
The 'above everything' name."

These lines are separated both from the preceding hymn by the "therefore" (διὸ καὶ, a Pauline connecting phrase) and from the lines that follow
them by the purpose particle ἵνα ("in order that") introducing the
purpose behind the divine action of this strophe. Further evidence that
these lines are to be strophically distinguished from the preceding strophes
is, of course, the shift in the subject of the actions from Christ in the earlier
strophes to the Father here. But the most obvious indication to me that these
lines may be *hymnically* distinguished from the previous two strophes is the
fact that in this strophe we find only three lines, as over against four in the
previous strophes. The three lines here follow the pattern of "independent
line, independent line, dependent line."

As evidence that these lines are to be construed together strophically, we
may cite the undeniable synonymous parallelism in thought between the
first two lines, and the three internal lexical parallels, namely, the repeated
"Him" (αὐτὸν and αὐτῷ) in lines 1 and 2 (in both cases in the emphatic

position), the repeated preposition ὑπέρ ("above") in lines 1 and 3, and the repeated reference to "the name" (τὸ ὄνομα) in lines 2 and 3.

> *Strophe 2:*
> "in order that
>   at the name of Jesus
>   every knee should bow in heaven and on earth and under the earth,
>   and every tongue should confess that Jesus Christ is Lord—
>
> *Climactic addendum:*
> to the glory of God the Father!"

If we postpone for the time being any discussion of the climactic addendum, we have again only three lines to consider. But in strophe 2 the structural arrangement is the precise reverse of strophe 1: where earlier we had the arrangement "independent line, independent line, dependent line," here we find the arrangement "dependent line, independent line, independent line."

Within the strophe itself, again we have an undeniable synonymous parallelism in thought between lines 2 and 3. This parallelism is underscored by the presence of the word "every" in both lines, the aorist subjunctive verb form in both lines, and the adverbial modifying phrase in both lines, the former anticipating the question Where? or Whose? and the latter anticipating the question What? There is also a lexical connection between lines 1 and 3 through the repetition of the proper name "Jesus," found here and nowhere else in the hymn.

Having distinguished between the two strophes, we may now note the following parallels between them:

1. The phrase "the name" is found in the dependent line of both strophes.

2. The word "every" is found in line 3 of both strophes.

3. Both strophes are concerned with the same subject: Jesus' state of exaltation, the former stating the fact itself, and the latter stating the Father's design behind the fact.

We turn now to the climactic addenda: "even the death of the cross" and "to the glory of God the Father." These may have been either original to both hymns or Pauline additions to both. A marked antithesis lies between them, each of them beautifully capturing the mood of its respective hymn: The former, by designating the particular kind of death Christ died, underscores the depth of the humiliation Christ voluntarily underwent; the latter highlights the Father's glory that Christ's exaltation entailed. The former concentrates our attention on the death of Jesus; the latter focuses our attention on the glory of the Father. The former brings the first hymn to a close by focusing on the cross; the latter brings the second hymn to a close by focusing on the glory that followed. These addenda, I submit, neatly summarize for us the essential (one way) flow of the apostle's thought: from humiliation to exaltation, from cross to crown.

This, I suggest, is the likely structural arrangement of the hymns and the relationship between them. Together the two hymns appear as follows:

> Though in the form of God existing,
>> He did not regard equality with God a thing to be seized,[37]
>> but Himself He poured out,[38]
> the form of a servant having taken.[39]

> In the precise likeness of men having been born,
>> and having been found by external appearance to be a man,
>> He humbled Himself,
> having become obedient unto death—even the death of the cross.

> Therefore, God has highly exalted Him,
> and He has given Him the name,
>> the "above everything" name,

> That at the name of Jesus,
> every knee should bow in heaven and on earth and under the earth,
> and every tongue should confess that Jesus Christ is Lord—to the
>> glory of God the Father.

Now it should be obvious that the very first line of the first strophe is directly related to the concern of this present study. What does Paul mean when he declares that Christ Jesus was "existing in the form of God"?[40] Those who are advocates of what is called today the "Adam Christology" insist that it is the equivalent to the Genesis description of Adam as created in the image of God—the meaning here then being that Christ, as was Adam, was truly a man. It is true that the two Greek words εἰκών ("image") and μορφή ("form") are both employed to translate the same Semitic root in the Septuagint, εἰκών translating the Hebrew noun צלם in Genesis 1:26 and μορφή translating the Aramaic noun צלם in Daniel 3:19. But this is

---

37. This translation construes ἁρπαγμὸν as *res rapienda* ("a thing to be seized") rather than *res rapta* ("a thing to be held onto") for reasons that will be forthcoming in the exposition.

38. The reason for this rendering of ἑαυτὸν ἐκένωσεν (literally, "Himself He emptied") will be forthcoming in the exposition.

39. For the reason for this rendering of the aorist participle λαβών as a participle denoting action antecedent to that of the main verb, cf. n. 54.

40. For a summary of the most commonly held views, cf. Hawthorne, *Philippians*, pp. 81-84.

hardly sufficient evidence to warrant the conclusion that εἰκών and μορφή are interchangeable or are synonymous. And the fact must be squarely faced that μορφή is not the word used in the Septuagint to render either "image" (צלם) or "likeness" (דמות) in Genesis 1:26-27. Moreover, this ignores the occurrence of μορφή three lines later, for clearly Jesus did not assume the mere "image" of a servant. To the contrary, He became in very fact the Servant of Yahweh. The connection between Adam as the "image of God" and Christ as the "form of God" simply cannot be made on the basis of such slim linguistic evidence.

Others urge that the meaning of μορφή should be established on the basis of its usage in the Septuagint, but the problem here is that μορφή is only used four times in the Septuagint, and each time it is the translation of a different word (תאר, Judg. 8:18; תמונה, Job 4:16; תבנית, Isa. 44:13; [Aramaic] צלם, Dan. 3:19). At best, taken together, the idea of μορφή as the translation of the four words seems to be that of "visible form," but the number of samples in the Septuagint is just too small and diverse to draw any hard and fast conclusions. Besides, if it means "visible form," it is questionable whether this meets the conditions of the first occurrence in Philippians 2:6, for there Christ is not said to be "*the* μορφή of God" but "*in* the μορφή of God." "In the 'visible form' of God" would be Scripturally inappropriate inasmuch as God is "invisible," as Colossians 1:15 reminds us.

Martin maintains that μορφή in 2:6a is equivalent in meaning to δόξα ("glory"), and he presents a very interesting case for it,[41] but it can hardly be argued that this same equivalency is appropriate for μορφή in the phrase, "form of servant," three lines later.

In light of these problems, I conclude that the weight of linguistic evidence is still on the side of Lightfoot who demonstrated, from a study of both its usage throughout the history of Greek thought and the occurrences of the μορφ- root in the New Testament, that μορφή refers to the "essential attributes" of a thing and that Christ's being in the form of God, while not the linguistic equivalent, is the connotative equivalent to the Pauline description of Christ in 2 Corinthians 4:4 and Colossians 1:15 as the "[essential] image of the [invisible] God."[42] Warfield concurs:

> "Form" is a term which expresses the sum of those characterizing qualities which make a thing the precise thing that it is. Thus, the "form" of a sword (in this case mostly matters of external configuration)

41. Martin, *Carmen Christi*, pp. 108-19.

42. J. B. Lightfoot, *Saint Paul's Epistle to the Philippians* (1868; reprint. Grand Rapids: Zondervan, 1953), p. 110. Cf. also his extended note on "the synonymes μορφή and σχῆμα" (ibid, pp. 127-33).

is all that makes a given piece of metal specifically a sword, rather than, say, a spade. And the "form of God" is the sum of the characteristics which make the being we call "God," specifically God, rather than some other being—an angel, say, or a man. When our Lord is said to be in "the form of God," therefore, He is declared, in the most express manner possible, to be all that God is, to possess the whole fulness of attributes which make God God.[43]

John Murray also concurs, describing Lightfoot's exposition on 2:6a as "yeoman service in the exposition of the first clause of verse 6,"[44] while David Wells declares that it "appears inescapable that by 'form' we are to understand that Paul meant the essence or essential characteristics of a thing."[45] Another fact in its favor, in addition to the evidence from usage, is that this understanding of the term fits both occurrences in 2:6: "form of God" and "form of servant." When we take into account the force of the present participle, which conveys the idea of "continually [beforehand] subsisting"[46] (which in turn excludes any intimation that this mode of subsistence came to an end when He assumed the form of servant), we have here as bold and unqualified an assertion of both the preexistence and the full and unabridged deity of Jesus Christ as one could ever hope to find in the pages of the New Testament.

But having affirmed that here in Philippians 2:6a is yet another indisputable confession by Paul that the incarnate Christ is just God Himself, we are now faced with a difficulty. The classical evangelical interpretation of the entire pericope contends that, when properly understood, these verses depict a great "parabola,"[47] starting with God the Son in the glory of His preexistent condition of sharing the divine essence with God the Father ("in the form of God existing") then tracing His "downward" movement by means of the incarnation ("Himself He emptied") to His "cross work" as the Father's Servant, and then recording His "upward" movement by means of

43. Warfield, *The Person and Work of Christ* (Philadelphia: Presbyterian and Reformed, 1950), p. 39. Cf. *Lord of Glory*, p. 236; and his sermon, "Imitating the Incarnation," in the *Person and Work of Christ*, pp. 566-68.

44. John Murray, *Collected Writings of John Murray*, vol. 3 (Edinburgh: Banner of Truth Trust, 1982), p. 359.

45. Wells, *Person of Christ*, p. 64.

46. Lightfoot, *St. Paul's Epistle to the Philippians*, p. 110; Warfield, *Person and Work of Christ*, p. 40; R. P. Martin, (*An Early Christian Confession* [London: Tyndale, 1970], p. 17) translates ὑπάρχων "was originally possessing." The sharp contrast between the present tense of this participle and the four aorist participles that follow should not go unnoticed.

47. The term is from Emil Brunner, *The Mediator*, trans. Olive Wyon (London: Lutterworth Press, 1934), pp. 561-63.

the Father's exaltation through resurrection and ascension to His present session at His Father's right hand as "Lord." No evangelical, of course, will take exception either to the sentiment behind this or to the high Christology extracted from these verses by such an exposition. Certainly I do not. Nor do I for a moment have any intention of denying to our Lord in the slightest degree His rightful claim to full unqualified deity or to equality with the Father in power and glory. This I have already shown from my exposition of 2:6a. Nor am I unaware of the fact that the New Testament does set forth the work of Christ in precisely these terms of "descent-ascent" (κατάβασις—ἀνάβασις) in some contexts.[48] But this "descent-ascent" motif, purportedly in Philippians 2:6-11, has created for evangelical scholars in this particular context the difficulty of which I spoke earlier. To be more precise, I should speak of two difficulties.

The first difficulty is this: If we understand the beginning point of the "flow" of the passage, as the classical view does, as the preexistent state of the Son of God ("in the form of God being") and take the phrases "Himself He emptied, taking the form of a servant" as the metaphorical allusion to the "downward" event of the incarnation, it is only with the greatest difficulty, because of the intervening clause, that we can avoid the conclusion that the "emptying" involved His surrendering the "form" ("very nature"—NIV) of God. I grant that the verb κενόω may have a metaphorical meaning, as in its other occurrences in the New Testament (Rom. 4:14; 1 Cor. 1:17; 9:15; 2 Cor. 9:3), and that it need not be literally rendered "emptied" in Philippians 2:6. (I too in the end attach a metaphorical meaning to it.) But even a metaphor has a literal meaning when it is divested of its metaphorical "wrapping." What does this metaphor mean literally when it is "unpacked" in the interest of interpretation? The ready answer, of course, is that it refers to the event of the incarnation ("He made Himself of no reputation, by means of taking the form of a servant"). But it is just here that the difficulty arises. For according to the classical view, the intervening clause ("He did not regard . . ."), in the "flow" of the hymn, has to mirror an attitude in the *preexistent Son* that comes on the "prior side" of the event of incarnation. But if this clause describes what the preexistent Son of God as God the Son "thought" (ἡγήσατο) of His equality with God, it does not matter, I suggest, whether ἁρπαγμὸν (from the root ἁρπάζω, meaning "to seize") is construed *res rapta*, that is, "a thing to be held onto," or *res rapienda*, that is, "a thing to be

---

48. Cf. John 3:13; 6:62; Rom. 10:6-7; Eph. 4:8-10; 1 Tim. 3:16; Heb. 4:14–10:8; 1 Pet 3:18-22; cf. also 2 Cor. 8:9. The reader may refer to Richard N. Longenecker (*The Christology of Early Jewish Christianity* [London: SCM Press, 1970], pp. 58-62) for a helpful brief treatment of the theme.

seized"[49]—neither is appropriate as a description of what the Son "thought" with regard to His "equality with God." The former is theologically suspect for it implies that the Son was willing to and did in fact divest Himself of His deity ("the form of God") when He took the "form of a servant," for that is what "equality with God" means lexically, contextually, and according to John 5:18 and 10:28-33.[50] The latter is also suspect theologically for it suggests that the Son did not already possess equality with God; but this introduces confusion into the passage, since it is clearly affirmed in the first clause of 2:6, as we have seen, that the Son was God and was as such "equal with God." If one replies that the Son did not "grasp after" equality with God because He already had it, as the first clause affirms, I would respond that this now introduces a certain theological barrenness, if not an exegetical inanity, into the text at the very point where Paul obviously intends a highly significant insight, for one does not need to be informed of the obvious—that the Son did not seek after something He already possessed. Accordingly, I submit, from the perspective of the classical interpretation of the pericope, that only the *res rapta* interpretation of ἁρπαγμὸν circumvents this barrenness of meaning; but then the evangelical scholar can escape only with the greatest difficulty, if at all, the conclusion that the Son is represented, by the implication in His willingness to forego His "equality with God," that is, His essential divine attributes, as having divested Himself of His "very nature" character of God when He became a man. (And all admit the impossibility of One who is God doing such a thing.) One has only to peruse the evangelical literature on these verses to discover the "hermeneutical gymnastics" that are resorted to to affirm, on the one hand, that the Son did not regard equality with God ("the form of God") a thing to be held onto, and that He accordingly "emptied Himself" (or, "made Himself nothing") by becoming a man, and yet, on the other hand, that He still retained all that He essentially is and was from the beginning. For example, it is said, "He did not divest Himself of His divine attributes, but only the independent use of His attributes." But when did the Son ever exercise His attributes independently? Or, "He did not divest Himself of His deity, but only the glory of His deity." But is not the "divine glory" just the sum and substance of the deity? And how does one square this

---

49. The variation of the *res rapienda* view, known as *res retinenda* ("a thing to be retained") and espoused by Martin (*Carmen Christi*, pp. 143-49), in my opinion is too subtle a distinction to assume that the first-century reader of Paul's letter would have caught it.

50. Cf. G. Stählin: "In [John] 5:18 ἴσος expresses . . . the equality of dignity, will and nature which the later ὁμοούσιος was designed to defend . . . it denotes an equality which is both essential and perfect. This is also the meaning of ἴσα in the famous and difficult verse Phil 2:6" (" ἴσος," *Theological Dictionary of the New Testament*, vol. 3 [Grand Rapids: Eerdmans, 1965], p. 353). Cf. also: "At Phil. 2:6 the ἴσα has all the significance of the concept of equality in Jn. 5:18" (ibid., n. 52).

interpretation with John 1:14 and 2:11 et al.? Or, "He did not divest Himself of His deity, but only His rights as the Deity." But what rights did He forego as God when He became a man? While I do not for a moment agree with the "kenotic" theologians who teach just this—that the Son, according to the teaching of this passage, divested Himself of at least something that was essentially His as God when He became a man—I can appreciate their fearless willingness, given the presumption that the passage begins with the Son in His preexistent state, to take the passage at face value and conclude that here we have a "kenotic Christology," that the Son, in some essential way, divested Himself of His "form of God" in the course of His taking the "form of servant."

The second difficulty is this: If the "flow" of the passage commences, as the classical view maintains, with God the Son in His preexistent state, then He is obviously the primary subject throughout the unfolding drama of the "great parabola." But then we must ask, what can His later exaltation possibly have meant to Him? It seems to me, if exaltation is to have any meaning at all, it must involve elevation to a state not in one's prior possession. But any elevated state is simply nonexistent with regard to God the Son as God. If one replies that His later exalted state involved His being elevated, as the second hymn declares, to the position of *lordship* over all things, I must ask whether the Scripture will permit us to believe that God the Son, often identified by Scripture itself as the God and Yahweh of the Old Testament, was not already *de jure* and *de facto* Lord over creation, nature, religious institutions such as the law and the Sabbath, and, most significant, over the lives of men prior to the exaltation spoken about in Philippians 2:9-11. Does not careful reflection on what is entailed in being God the Son preclude this notion and force the conclusion that the Son as God the Son continued ever, even during the days of His earthly ministry, to be the Lord He was from the beginning? But, if the evangelical scholar insists that the exaltation was still indeed the exaltation of the preexistent Son of God *per se*, then he makes the Son's former state lower in dignity than His latter state and elevates the Son's latter state above that which He enjoyed when "existing in the form of God" prior to His incarnation. But Scripture and right reason simply will not permit such a conclusion. I must ask again then, what meaning can be attached to an exaltation of One who cannot be exalted more highly than He already is?

These two difficulties with the classical interpretation—(1) giving satisfactory meanings to the clauses, "He did not regard equality with God a thing to be held onto" [or, "grasped after"] and "Himself He emptied, taking the form of a servant," while at the same time avoiding a kenotic Christology; and (2) giving intelligible sense to an exaltation of God the Son *per se*—ought to make us willing to consider another interpretation that avoids both problems and at the same time affirms the *vere deus vere homo* doctrine of classical Christology.

The key to the solution of both of these difficulties, and, more important, to the proper interpretation of Paul's intention, in my opinion, is to perceive that it is not God the Son in His preincarnate state as the second person of the holy Trinity *per se* who is the subject throughout the first two strophes and to whom reference is made by the "Him" in verse 9 of the third strophe, but rather, *Christ Jesus* (cf. 2:5 and references to "Jesus" and "Jesus Christ" in 2:10-11 respectively)—God the Son certainly, for this is the meaning of "though in the form of God existing," but God the Son *already incarnately present* with men as Himself the God-man. (I do not deny that in other contexts, for example, 1 Tim. 1:15, "Christ Jesus," as a titular description, does designate the Son of God in His preincarnate state.) The hymn, in other words, does not begin with the Son in His *preexistent* state. It begins with "Christ Jesus," and affirms that, as the God-man, He refused to follow an alternative path to glory than the one His Father had charted for Him. Nor does it refer to the "downward" movement (the κατάβασις) of the incarnation event itself, so vital a part of the classical view, save as an event that had already taken place, presupposing it in its affirmation that He "though existing as God," had "taken the form of servant." By this construction, all that is said of Him is said of Him as the Messiah, the Son-already-dispatched-on-His-mission. (It is possible, and this is only a conjecture, that the first hymn has been "decapitated," and that a previous strophe dealt with His pure preexistent state as God the Son, eternal Son of the eternal Father.)

Now, how does this elimination of the Son's preexistent state and κατάβασις from the hymn's "flow" circumvent the two difficulties earlier highlighted? The answer is that now from the outset in Philippians 2:6 we are no longer interacting with the incarnation as a future or occurring event but as the *God-man's* existing state. Accordingly, the clauses under discussion may now be interpreted within the context of the incarnation as a *fait accompli* rather than a *fait anticipé*. But are meaningful interpretations ready at hand? To this I reply in the affirmative. The clause, "He did not regard equality . . ." may now be meaningfully construed *res rapienda*, that is, "He did not regard equality with God a thing to be seized," and it should be interpreted against the background of His temptation recorded in Matthew 4. We know that Paul is willing to contrast Adam and Christ in Romans 5:12-19 and 1 Corinthians 15:45-49, actually referring to Christ in the latter passage as the Last Adam and the Second Man. I suggest that this phrase in the Philippians hymn draws a further contrast between the respective temptations of Adam and Christ: Adam, the first man, did "regard equality with God [τὸ εἶναι ἴσα θεῷ] a thing to be seized" (cf. Gen. 3:5 where the Serpent's temptation is framed in the words, "you will be like [כ, translated by ἴσα in the LXX at Deut. 13:6; Job 5:14; 10:10; 13:28; 15:16; 24:20; 27:16; 29:14; 40:10; Isa. 51:23] God, knowing good and evil"); Christ, the Last Adam and Second Man, did not. When urged to "seize equality with God" (cf. Matt. 4:3, 6: "Since you are the Son of God . . .") by taking matters into His own hands and asserting His rights as the "Son" *per se* and not as the Son-already-dispatched-on-His-Messianic-mission as the Servant of the Lord, He refused to succumb to the Tempter's suggestion. This "thought" of "seizure of equality," that is, the temptation to walk no longer in the path of the Servant but rather to achieve "lordship" over "all the kingdoms of this world" (Matt. 4:8) by a route (a "self-willed" act of "exaltation") not charted for the Servant in the economy of salvation, Christ Jesus steadfastly resisted.

There is another Old Testament motif, beyond the Adam-Christ contrast that assists us when we address the meaning of "Himself He emptied," and that is the "servant" motif of Isaiah's "Servant Songs." In what I have called the second hymn, lines 1 and 2 of strophe 1 clearly borrow a sentiment from Isaiah 42:1-8, and lines 2 and 3 of strophe 2 directly reflect the language of Isaiah 45:23. And in what I have called the first hymn, Paul's references to the "servant" in strophe 1, line 4, and to Christ's "self-humbling" and "obedience unto death" in lines 3 and 4 of strophe 2 are general allusions to the "servant" motif of Isaiah's songs (cf. Isa. 53:8 [LXX] and Acts 8:33). (By the way, Paul also relates Christ to both Adam and the "servant" motif in Rom. 5:12-19.) We concur with the suggestion of H. Wheeler Robinson, J. Jeremias,[51] and others[52] that the phrase, "Himself He emptied," is the nonliteral Greek dynamic equivalent to the Isaianic phrase, "He poured His soul out [which means, "He poured Himself out"] unto death" (which means, "He voluntarily died") in Isaiah 53:12 and climactically describes the Suffering Servant's self-sacrificing work so often referred to elsewhere in the New Testament (cf., for example, Matt. 8:17; Luke 22:37; Acts 8:32-35; 1 Pet. 2:21-25). The phrase, thus interpreted, derives its meaning from the backdrop of the *high-priestly ministry* of our Lord rather than from the backdrop of His *preexistence;* it refers, as Jeremias writes, "to the sacrifice of His life and not to the self-emptying of His incarnation."[53] I suggest, then,

---

51. H. Wheeler Robinson, *The Cross of the Servant* (London: SCM Press, 1926), pp. 72-74; Jeremias, in *Studia Paulina*, p. 154 n. 3, and his article, "παῖς," in *Theological Dictionary of the New Testament*, vol. 5, pp. 711-12.

52. For example, C. H. Dodd, *According to the Scriptures* (London: Nisbet and Company, 1952), p. 93.

53. Jeremias, in *Studia Paulina*, p. 154 n. 3.

that the aorist participle λαβών in the first hymn, strophe 1, line 4, should be construed as denoting antecedent action ("having taken"),[54] thus placing Christ's "self-emptying" subsequent in time to the "taking." That is to say, the participle does not explain the manner of the "self-emptying" ("emptied, by taking") but rather denotes a prior action that was the necessary precondition to the "self-emptying." A paraphrase of the first strophe will assist the reader in understanding what we are advocating.

> Though Christ Jesus was and is God [now, of course, God incarnate],
>   He [unlike Adam] did not regard equality with God a thing to be seized
>   [at His temptation by a self-willed exercise of power],
> But poured Himself out [unto death],
> Having taken the form of the Servant [of Isaiah 53].

By this construction we have both precluded at the outset a kenotic chris-

---

54. I construe the aorist participle λαβών here as referring to action antecedent to the action denoted in ἐκένωσεν, according to the common rule of Greek syntax that an aorist participle generally denotes action antecedent to that of the main verb.

The fact that the participle follows the main verb in the order does not require that it be construed as denoting coincident or subsequent action. As J. H. Moulton states, "There are a good many NT passages in which exegesis has to decide between antecedent and coincident action, in places where the participle stands second" (A Grammar of New Testament Greek, I: Prolegomena, 3rd ed. [Edinburgh: T. & T. Clark, 1930], p. 132).

Incidentally, while we are on the subject, lest Moulton be quoted against himself, it is imperative that A. T. Robertson's inaccurate citation of Moulton to the effect that "Moulton (Prol., p. 131) observes that when the verb precedes the aorist participle it is *nearly always* the participle of coincident action" (A Grammar of the Greek New Testament in the Light of Historical Research [Nashville: Broadman Press, 1934], p. 1113; emphasis added) be once and for all corrected. What Moulton actually writes is: "The [aorist] participle naturally came to involve past time relative to that of the main verb. Presumably this would happen *less completely* when the participle stood second. . . . In many cases, especially in the NT, the participle and the main verb denote *coincident* or *identical* action" (Prolegomena, p. 131). It should be apparent to all that there is a great deal of difference between what Moulton actually said ("less completely [antecedent action] . . . many") and what Robertson quotes him as saying ("nearly always" [coincident action]). Moulton's final conclusion, as I quoted him previously, is that exegesis must decide in "a good many NT passages" what the writer intended. Frankly, I would modify even Moulton's statement and say that exegesis must finally decide in every case the time relation between the action of the participle and that of the main verb. In other words, one can never merely ascertain the word order (that is, whether the aorist participle appears before or after the main verb) and automatically deduce from this that the participle denotes antecedent, coincident, or subsequent action.

An interesting sidelight to this whole issue, but one that generally supports my construction here, is the fact that C. F. D. Moule suggests as a "principle" that it is still the aorist or present tense of the participle that mainly determines antecedent or coincident action. He says not one word regarding the significance of the position of the participle relative to the main verb (before or after), stating rather, "It often turns out that a Present Participle alludes to an action with which the action of the main verb coincides . . . while an Aorist Participle refers to action previous to what is referred to in the main verb. This 'schoolboy' rule is even safer for N.T. Greek than for the Classical writers (An Idiom Book of New Testament Greek, 2nd ed. [Cambridge: University Press, 1959], pp. 99-100).

tological interpretation and the first difficulty I mentioned earlier and been able to give substantive meaning to 2:6-7b, something the classical view is able to do only with the greatest exegetical ingenuity.

We can now also give substantive meaning to the act of exaltation asserted in the second hymn, for now we may refer it, not directly to God the Son *per se,* but to God the Son in His incarnate state as the Messiah. It is, in other words, the divine-human Messiah, Christ Jesus, who is exalted. And because we are compelled by the historical fact itself to describe the Son, now incarnately existent in Jesus Christ, as "the divine-human Messiah," we can boldly say, without fear of denigrating His divine honor, that the Father's exaltation of Jesus Christ entailed for the Son, *as the Messiah,* a new and genuine experience of exaltation. Precisely because we must use the word "human" as part of our description of Him now, we can also say that something truly new and unique occurred at the resurrection and ascension of Jesus Christ: the man Christ Jesus—the Last Adam and Second Man— assumed *de facto* sovereignty over the universe, over all of the principalities and powers in heavenly places, and over all other men, demanding that they submit to the authority of His scepter. That King's name is Jesus, at the mention of whose name some day every knee will bow and every tongue confess that *Jesus Christ*—the divine-human Messiah—is Lord!

We have completed our consideration of Philippians 2:6-11. Our concluding comments can be brief. Beyond controversy, this pericope, regardless of its precise hymnic structure, when fairly interpreted ascribes deity to "Christ Jesus." It does so in three ways: *first,* by its description of Jesus as "in the form of God [continually] being"; *second,* by its indirect ascription to Him of "equality with God" when it affirmed that He did not "seize" this station, that is, as I have suggested, at the time of His temptation He did not assert Himself or exploit His filial ranking in a self-willed show of power commensurate with His divine station; and *third,* by the very nature of the lordship the Father delegated to Him, the entail of His exaltation. It is true that this lordship was "delegated" to Him, in His role as Messiah, as the result of His labors (cf. the "because" of Isa. 53:12 and the "therefore" of Phil. 2:9), but the specific character of this lordship is described here in terms of Isaiah 45:23, where Yahweh declares such lordship to be His prerogative alone. We must not lose sight of the fact that the conventional or covenantal basis, upon which it was determined that this One should "receive" this specific kind of lordship as the Messiah upon the completion of His suffering, was His own divine sonship, the antecedent condition to the Messianic investiture. Said another way, it is because He was, as the Messiah, "obedient unto death, even the death of the cross" that He was exalted to lordship; but it is also because He is "in the form of God" and "equal with God," as the *divine* Messiah, that the lordship He was delegated could assume the proportions it does and involve the universal obligation of men to worship Him.

In addition to the Pauline passages we have considered (Rom. 1:3-4; Col. 1:15-20; 2:9; Phil. 2:6-11), there are a variety of other Pauline expressions that clearly suggest that Christ was preexistent and therefore the *divine* Son of God. I want to look at three of these briefly, then at two Pauline uses of Θεός as a christological title.

Ephesians 4:9-10: "He descended . . . He ascended"

These verses occur in a context in which Paul asserts Christ's sovereign right to distribute spiritual gifts to His church as He deems fitting and proper. He cites Psalm 68:18 as the explanation of this privilege: "Ascending on high, He led captives in His train, and gave gifts to men." The allusion in this striking metaphor is to Christ's ascension as the vindicating exhibition of His triumph over the spiritual powers of darkness arrayed against Him (Col. 2:15); and being triumphant "in the field" as He was, He now exercises the hard-won privilege of "dividing the booty," that is, "engifting" His own as He deems appropriate.

Now at this point Paul, never one to miss the opportunity to declare again who this Victor is, injects the parenthetical words that are our present interest:

> Now this "He ascended"—what does it mean except that also He descended to the lower, earthly regions.[55] He who descended is also the One who ascended higher than all the heavens, in order that He might fill all the universe [with His kingly power and dominion].

It has been often noted that, insofar as these words actually express it, something is lacking in the Pauline logic: an ascent *per se* neither necessitates nor implies a prior descent. Elijah's ascension to heaven is a case in point (2 Kings 2:11). Paul must be assuming something about the subject of his remarks—a fact so well known and so widely received among the Christians to whom he is writing that it does not need to be spelled out at every turn in

---

55. Cf. Charles Hodge (*A Commentary on the Epistle to the Ephesians* [1856; reprint, Grand Rapids: Eerdmans, 1954], pp. 220-21) for reasons for understanding τὰ κατώτερα [μέρη]τῆς γῆσ as just the earth itself. For the evangelical view that it should also include Christ's death on the cross, cf. William Hendriksen, *New Testament Commentary: Exposition of Ephesians* (Grand Rapids: Baker, 1967), p. 192 n. 111.

his exposition. What is this datum that Paul is so assured his readers will be able to provide? Paul is obviously assuming that the subject of the ascent existed *prior* to His earthly existence and that in order to "ascend" He first would have had to "descend." When this is factored into the Pauline statement—the supposition of Christ's preexistence as the Son of God—what otherwise would be a flaw in his logic is cleared up and seen to be only an enthymeme. And there can be no doubt that if He preexisted as the Son of God (cf. Rom. 8:3; Gal. 4:4), then His "descent" effectively resulted in what classical christologists intend by the doctrine of the incarnation. Even Bultmann, although he traces the "descent–ascent" metaphor here to the Gnostic Redeemer mythology, acknowledges that what Paul had in mind here is "the pre-existent Son's journey to earth."[56]

1 Timothy 1:15: "Christ Jesus came into the world"

In Paul's statement in 1 Timothy 1:15, "Christ Jesus came into the world—sinners to save"—the first of the five "faithful sayings" in his pastoral letters—again Christ's preexistence is implied and, as a corollary to His preexistence, His divine sonship as well.

But just as the "He ascended" in Ephesians 4:8 does not in itself require a prior descent, so the phrase "came into the world" does not necessarily contain within itself the notion of preexistence *per se* (cf. Rom. 5:12; 1 Tim. 6:7). But George Knight trenchantly observes at this point:

> It is one thing to point out that the phrase ἦλθεν (ἔρχεσθαι) εἰς τὸν κόσμον itself does not imply preexistence and it is another to make this evaluation of the phrase when it is used by Christians with Christ Jesus as the subject. Is it not, as a matter of fact, evident that the uniform usage of that phrase *with* reference to Christ Jesus is to both his preexistence and also his incarnation?[57]

He then proceeds to show from an analysis of the six occurrences of the phrase in John's Gospel (1:9; 3:19; 11:27; 12:46; 16:28; 18:37)—the only other book of the New Testament where the expression is found[58]—that when the

---

56. Bultmann, *Theology of the New Testament,* p. 175.

57. George W. Knight III, *The Faithful Sayings in the Pastoral Letters* (Nutley, N.J.: Presbyterian and Reformed, n.d.) pp. 36-37.

58. Warfield writes:

The very language in which [the purpose of the incarnation] is expressed is startling, meeting us here in the midst of one of Paul's letters. For this is not Pauline phraseology that stands before us here; as, indeed, it professes not to be—for does not Paul tell us that he is not speaking in his own person, but is adducing one of the jewels of the Church's faith? At all

phrase is applied to Christ Jesus, it "demands the understanding of pre-existence as well as incarnation."[59] This conclusion enjoys virtually universal support among commentators, and it is only the hyper-critical scholar who refuses to concede the obvious.

1 Timothy 3:16: A Digest of the Christological Mystery

With the aid of a succinct compendium of the great "mystery of Godliness" (that is, the "revealed Secret" of the faith, even Jesus Christ; cf. Col. 1:27; 2:2-3) in the form of a "quotation from an early Christian hymn,"[60] Paul elaborates his Christology—the Great Mystery—in six phrases: "who [61] [that is, Christ Jesus]

> was manifested in the flesh,
>> was vindicated in the spirit,
> was seen by angels,
>> was proclaimed among the nations,
> was believed on in the world,
>> was taken up in glory."

As with the other christological hymns we have considered, this one as well has undergone considerable analysis with regard to its strophic arrangement. Some see strict chronological progression throughout the six lines,

> events, it is the language of John that here confronts us, and whoever first cast the Church's heart-conviction into this compressed sentence had assuredly learned in John's school. For to John only belongs this phrase as applied to Christ; "He came into the world." It is John only who preserves the Master's declarations: "I came forth from the Father, and am come into the world. . . ." It is he only who, adopting, as his wont, the very phraseology of his Master to express his own thought, tells us in his prologue that "the true Light—that lighteth every man—was coming into the world" (*Person and Work of Christ*, pp. 550-51).

Cf. William Hendriksen, who offers the alternative opinion that Paul is not reflecting a "Johannine" phrase as much as he is "simply making use of the Savior's own way of speaking about himself, and is employing language which, having been adopted from his lips by the earliest disciples, had been spread far and wide" (*New Testament Commentary: Exposition of the Pastoral Epistles* [Grand Rapids: Baker, 1957], p. 77). But if Hendriksen is correct, it is strange that John alone of all the Gospel writers retains the phrase. Moreover, Hendriksen seems to ignore the fact that Paul expressly declares that he is citing here a "faithful saying" and not a remark original to himself.

59. Knight, *Faithful Sayings in the Pastoral Epistles*, p. 38.

60. Robert H. Gundry, "The Form, Meaning and Background of the Hymn Quoted in 1 Timothy 3:16," in *Apostolic History and the Gospel*, p. 203.

61. Of the textual variants, there is little doubt that the masculine relative pronoun ὅς is to be preferred to the neuter relative pronoun ὅ and the θεός of the Textus Receptus. For the reasons, cf. Bruce M. Metzger, *A Textual Commentary on the Greek New Testament* (New York: United Bible Societies, 1971), p. 641.

with each line therefore receiving independent treatment. Others see two strophes of three lines each (or two strophes of two lines and a refrain). And still others—the majority view today—divide the quotation into three couplets.

It appears to be a finely crafted piece of poetry with not one but two patterns of internal relationships that bind the six lines together in a remarkable literary unit. There are *first* the six dative nouns—flesh, spirit, angels, nations, world, and glory—that almost certainly are intended to be construed both antithetically and chiastically, that is to say, the hymn moves from that which is earthly ("flesh") to that which is heavenly ("spirit"), then from that which is heavenly ("angels") back to that which is earthly ("nations"), then back again from that which is earthly ("world") to that which is heavenly ("glory"). This being so, it seems that the poet, insofar as the dative nouns are concerned, was thinking in terms of the couplets following an a/b, b/a, a/b pattern, with the hymn's movement being not primarily chronological but spatial, emphasizing the truth that both spheres—the earthly and the heavenly—find their center in Christ as He unites both heaven and earth.[62]

Second, Gundry has observed that when the six lines are considered individually in their entirety, there seems to be a synthetic parallelism between lines 2 and 3—"vindicated, seen"—and lines 4 and 5—"proclaimed, believed on," both of which are framed between line 1 commemorating the Lord's "descent" and line 6 commemorating the Lord's "ascent." The first of these synthetic parallels (lines 2 and 3) takes place in the realm *invisible* to men; the second of these parallels (lines 4 and 5) takes place in the realm *visible* to men, while the third (lines 1 and 6) begins in the *visible* realm and passes into the *invisible*.[63] The pattern here would be a, bb, aa, b.

This strophic analysis or one very similar to it has large currency among most commentators today.[64]

Now we turn to a consideration of the individual lines themselves.

62. Cf. E. Schweizer, *Lordship and Discipleship* (London: SCM Press, 1960), pp. 64-66.

63. Gundry, in *Apostolic History and the Gospel*, pp. 208-9.

64. For example, Hendriksen, *Exposition of the Pastoral Epistles*, pp. 138-39; J. N. D. Kelly, *A Commentary on the Pastoral Letters* (London: Adam and Charles Black, 1963), pp. 90-92. Kelly makes the insightful comment that the parallelism

> makes it practically certain that the hymn is really arranged in three couplets, each containing a carefully designed antithesis. First, Christ incarnate and thus in the form of a servant is seen vindicated at his resurrection. Secondly, Christ receives the worship of angels and is preached to the nations of mankind, i.e., he is brought to the knowledge of all rational beings, celestial and terrestrial. Thirdly, he is accepted both throughout the entire created universe (cf. Col. i.23) and in the heavenly realm itself (ibid., p. 92).

Line 1: "was manifested in the flesh." It is commonly acknowledged that "was manifested in the flesh" refers to the incarnation, and by the constative aorist, speaks of Christ's entire incarnate life as a *revelation* of the divine Son "in the sphere of *human* being." That it has reference to the incarnation, implying as well Christ's preexistence as the Son of God,[65] is evident not only from the fact that we do not speak this way about ordinary man, but also from the fact that the New Testament speaks elsewhere of Jesus' *incarnate* life in terms of "manifestation" (John 1:31; Heb. 9:26; 1 Pet. 1:20; 1 John 1:2; 3:5, 8; cf. John 1:14; Col. 2:9).[66]

Line 2: "was vindicated in the spirit." Opinions vary concerning the meaning of this line. Because σάρξ ("flesh") in the preceding line, as we similarly urged in our exposition of Romans 1:3-4, when applied to Christ has reference to Christ's human nature in its entirety, including His human spirit, it is most unlikely (*contra* Gundry) that His human spirit is the intended referent of πνεῦμα ("spirit") here. The choice, it seems to me, really lies between understanding the referent to be the Holy Spirit or Christ's divine nature. Are there any indications as to which is intended? I think so. If it refers to the Holy Spirit, the preposition ἐν must be construed instrumentally ("by"), and while this is certainly possible, it does violence to the symmetry of the uniform locative sense of all the other ἐν's. Therefore, since Paul has already instructed us in Romans 1:3-4 that Christ was "powerfully marked out the Son of God according to the Spirit of holiness [not the Holy Spirit but His own holy divine Spirit] by the resurrection from the dead," His resurrection there clearly being represented as a *vindicating* event, I would urge that the verb "was vindicated" here refers to the same vindicating event, and that "in the spirit," as the antithesis to "in the flesh," that is, "in the sphere of *human* being," means "in the sphere of *divine* being." A paraphrase of the line would then be "was vindicated [as the Son of God by the resurrection] in the sphere of [His divine] Spirit."[67]

---

65. Walter Lock (*A Critical and Exegetical Commentary on the Pastoral Letters,* International Critical Commentary [Edinburgh: T. & T. Clark, 1936], p. 45) speaks of this "manifestation" as an "unveiling of a previous existence."

66. I. Howard Marshall writes:

> Incarnational language is found in 1 Timothy 3:16 which describes how "he [Jesus] was manifested in the flesh." Although no subject is expressed (the AV "God was manifest" follows a late text), the language is based on that used elsewhere to describe how the Son of God was incarnate. The thought is of an epiphany in human form, and the implication is that a divine or heavenly subject is intended. The reference is certainly to the earthly life of Jesus and not to his resurrection appearances ("Incarnational Christology in the New Testament," in *Christ the Lord,* ed. Harold H. Rowdon [Leicester: Inter-Varsity Press, 1982], p. 10).

67. So also such commentators as Charles Hodge, *Commentary on Romans* (Grand Rapids:

Line 3: "was seen by angels." Since this line contains no ἐν, "angels" is probably to be construed as a true rather than an instrumental dative.[68] This means in turn that ὤφθη, which "nearly always means the self-exhibition of the subject,"[69] quite probably means "appeared" rather than "was seen." The upshot of these two points is that the phrase means something on the order of "appeared to angels," which is not substantively different from the traditional translation.

There is little question that this line refers both to Christ's triumph over the angelic forces of evil by His cross and to His exaltation over all the angelic powers at His ascension (cf. Eph. 1:21; Col. 2:15; Phil. 2:9-11; Heb. 1:4-14; 1 Pet. 3:22; Rev. 5:8-14). It certainly implies His superangelic dignity.[70]

Lines 4, 5, and 6. There is little substantive disagreement among scholars over the meanings of lines 4, 5, and 6. Line 4, "was proclaimed among the nations," reflects the church's conviction that Christ is properly the subject of worldwide proclamation and also the fact that it was proclaiming Him as such. Line 5, "was believed on in the world," reflects the church's confidence in the outcome of that proclamation—the nations of the world will become His disciples. And Line 6, "was taken up in [not "into"] glory," brings the hymn to a close with the imagery of Jesus' ascension to heaven in the glory attendant upon Him on that occasion (cf. the "glory cloud" in Acts 1:9; cf. also Acts 1:11 and Matt. 24:30; 26:64; Mark 14:62).

From beginning to end this hymnic confession of faith (cf. the adverb ὁμολογουμένως in Paul's prefatory introduction to the hymn[71]) extols Christ—the preexistent Son who became "enfleshed," who was then "vindicated" as the divine Son of God by His resurrection from the dead, who, having "ascended," is properly the "acknowledged" Lord among the angels and the "proclaimed" Lord in the world of men. Here is, indeed, a high Christology, found in the confessional framework of an early Christian hymn, that is in accord with that high Christology found throughout the

Eerdmans, 1955 reprint of 1886 edition), on 1:3-4 and Kelly, (Commentary on the Pastoral Epistles, pp. 90-91.

68. Cf. Robertson, Grammar of the Greek New Testament, p. 534; M. R. Vincent, Word Studies in the New Testament, vol. 4 (New York: Charles Scribner's Sons, 1900), p. 241; and Arndt and Gingrich, A Greek-English Lexicon of the New Testament, pp. 581-82, 1, a, δ.

69. Gundry, in Apostolic History and the Gospel, p. 214.

70. Guthrie, only slightly more cautiously, writes: "This [line 3] may well have been a variant way [to that of Heb. 1:4] of expressing the superiority of Christ [to angels]" (New Testament Theology, p. 359).

71. Lock (Commentary on the Pastoral Epistles, p. 44) suggests that it means something on the order of "by common agreement" or "by common profession." Kelly (Commentary on the Pastoral Letters, p. 88) states that it means "by common consent."

Pauline corpus, and it confesses a Messiah who is Deity incarnate!

Two Pauline Usages of θεός as a Christological Title

Romans 9:5. The debate surrounding this verse arises not from a divergence of opinion over textual variants or the meaning of words but rather over the question of punctuation. The most natural way to punctuate the verse is to place commas after both "flesh" and "all" and a period after "forever"—"from whom came the Messiah after the flesh, who is over all, God blessed forever. Amen." This is supported both by the context and by the grammatical and implicatory demands of the verse itself.

No one expresses the significance of the context for the meaning of Romans 9:5 with greater depth of insight than E. H. Gifford:

> St. Paul is expressing the anguish of his heart at the fall of his brethren: that anguish is deepened by the memory of their privileges, most of all, by the thought that their race gave birth to the divine Saviour, whom they have rejected. In this, the usual interpretation, all is most natural: the last and greatest cause of sorrow is the climax of glory from which the chosen race has fallen.[72]

As for the grammatical demand of the verse, it can hardly be denied that the most natural way to handle ὁ ὤν (the definite article and present participle) is to view the phrase as introducing a relative clause and to attach it to the immediately preceding ὁ Χριστός.

The implicatory demand of the verse flows from the presence of the words τὸ κατὰ σάρκα ("insofar as the flesh is concerned"[73]). This expression naturally raises the question, In what sense is the Messiah not from the patriarchs? The second half of the implied antithesis is supplied in the words that follow: "who is over all, God blessed forever." This treatment of the verse, of course, ascribes full, unqualified deity to the Messiah.

James D. G. Dunn, after acknowledging that the "punctuation favours a reference to Christ as 'god,' " immediately blunts the force of his concession by saying: "Even if Paul does bless Christ as 'god' here, the meaning of 'god' remains uncertain. . . . [It] is by no means clear that Paul thinks of Christ here as pre-existent god."[74] Anxious to demonstrate his thesis that early

---

72. E. H. Gifford, *The Epistle of St. Paul to the Romans* (London: John Murray, 1886), pp. 168-69.

73. Cf. F. Blass and A. Debrunner on Romans 9:5: the "addition of the art. [before κατὰ σάρκα] strongly emphasizes the limitation" (*A Greek Grammar of the New Testament and Other Early Christian Literature* [Chicago: University of Chicago Press, 1961], p. 139, para. 266.2).

74. Dunn, *Christology in the Making,* p. 45.

christological thinking developed from a nonincarnational kind to the incarnational Christology of John and maintaining accordingly that Paul could not yet have reached the heights John was later to scale, Dunn fails to take into account the significance of the descriptive phrases on either side of θεὸς: "who is over all" and "blessed forever." The former ascribes supreme lordship over the universe to the Messiah, while the latter acknowledges His right to that everlasting adoration and praise which in other contexts is reserved for God the Creator (Rom. 1:25) and God the Father (2 Cor. 11:31). These striking locutions, once θεὸς is allowed to refer to the Messiah, rule out the possibility of regarding Him as "god" with a lower-case g.

This natural, straightforward rendering of Romans 9:5—which every Greek scholar would unhesitatingly adopt if no question of doctrine were involved—has enjoyed not only the endorsement of "a not inconsiderable number of early Father[s]"[75] and the large majority of commentators,[76] but also the primacy of choice in the AV (1611), RV (1881), ASV (1901), NASB (1971), NIV (1978), and the NKJV (1982).

Some scholars (cf. RSV [1946] and NEB [1970], because they judge it to be an "un-Pauline locution" to refer to Christ as "God," have proposed two alternative punctuations, the first detaching the last expression, θεὸς εὐλογητὸς εἰς τοὺς αἰῶνας (construing it as a doxology), from the preceding and the second detaching the entire expression after σάρκα from the preceding, again construing the clause as a doxology.

It is a clear case of "begging the question" to declare it "un-Pauline" for Paul to refer to Christ as "God" in a Pauline letter where all the syntactical evidence indicates that this may well be the very time that he has done so. Can a writer never express a theological *hapax legomenon* ("said one time")? And to assert that he does so nowhere else requires the additional judgment (which these scholars are willing to make) that Titus 2:13 is at best "deutero-Pauline," that is, non-Pauline in authorship though "Pauline-like" in style and essential substance. Furthermore, it is to ignore the words of Colossians 2:9, not to mention the profusion of exalted terminology throughout Paul's writings that ascribe deity to Jesus.

What about the two alternative proposals? Can their sponsors justify them? The *first*, as we indicated, suggests that the last words of the verse be construed as a disconnected doxology ("May God be blessed forever!"). But Metzger certainly seems to be correct when he writes, "Both logically and

75. Bruce M. Metzger, "The Punctuation of Rom. 9:5," *Christ and Spirit in the New Testament* (Cambridge: University Press, 1973), p. 102.

76. Even John A. T. Robinson admits that "grammatically, there is almost everything to say for [construing θεός in Romans 9:5 as a christological title]" (*Wrestling With Romans* [London: SCM Press, 1979], p. 111).

emotionally such a doxology would interrupt the train of thought as well as be inconsistent with the mood of sadness that pervades the preceding verses."[77] Furthermore, if this detached clause is a doxology to God, it reverses the word order of the subject and the predicate present in every other such doxology in the Bible (over thirty times in the Old Testament and twelve times in the New) where the verbal adjective always *precedes* the noun for God and never follows it as this proposal reputes it to do in Romans 9:5. It is difficult to believe that the apostle, whose ear for proper Hebraic linguistic and syntactical formulae was finely tuned, would violate the established form for expressing praise to God that he himself observes elsewhere (Eph. 1:3; 2 Cor. 1:3). Finally, if this clause is an ascription of praise to God, it differs in another respect from every other occurrence of such in Paul's writings. Invariably, when Paul ascribes blessedness to God, he connects the expression either by some grammatical device or by direct juxtaposition to a word that precedes it. There is, in other words, an antecedent reference to God in the immediately preceding context. For example, he employs ὅ ἐστιν (Rom. 1:25), ὁ ὢν (2 Cor. 11:31), ᾧ (Gal. 1:5; 2 Tim. 4:18), αὐτῷ (Rom. 11:36; Eph. 3:21), and τῷ δὲ θεῷ (Phil. 4:20; 1 Tim. 1:17) to introduce ascriptions of praise to God. In Ephesians 1:3 and 2 Corinthians 1:3, there is an antecedent reference to God in the immediately preceding contexts. Thus all of Paul's doxologies to God are connected either grammatically or juxtapositionally to an immediately preceding antecedent reference to God. Never is there an abrupt change from one subject (in this case, the Messiah in 9:5a) to another (God in 9:5b) as suggested by this proposal. Consequently, this proposal has nothing to commend it and much to oppose it.

The *second* proposal—preferred by most of the scholars who reject the natural view and also commended by the *Greek New Testament* (UBS), the RSV, and the NEB—has even less to commend it, for not only do the objections against the former proposal tell equally against it as well, but an additional objection may be registered. By disconnecting everything after σάρκα and construing the disconnected portion as an independent ascription of praise, it denies to the participle ὢν any real significance. Metzger highlights this failing:

> If . . . the clause [beginning with ὁ ὢν] is taken as an asyndetic [unconnected] doxology to God, . . . the word ὢν becomes superfluous, for "he who is God over all" is most simply represented in Greek by ὁ ἐπὶ πάντων θεός [and "he who is over all" is most simply represented by ὁ ἐπὶ πάντων—RLR]. The presence of the participle suggests that the

<hr>

77. Metzger, *Christ and Spirit in the New Testament*, p. 108.

clause functions as a relative clause (not "he who is . . ." but "who is . . ."), and thus describes ὁ Χριστός as being "God over all."[78]

Nigel Turner also points out that detaching the words beginning with ὁ ὤν from the preceding clause "introduces asyndeton and there is no grammatical reason why a participle agreeing with 'Messiah' should first be divorced from it and than be given the force of a wish, receiving a different person as its subject."[79] One must surely wonder at the strange facility of some scholars to recognize the presence and natural force of the ὁ ὤν in 2 Corinthians 11:31 where we find precisely the same syntactical construction ("God . . . , who is blessed forever") as that here in Romans 9:5 and to fail to recognize its presence and force in Romans 9:5.

I conclude that there can be no justifiable doubt that Paul, by his use of θεός as a christological title—surrounding it with the particular descriptive phrases that he does—ascribes full deity to Jesus Christ who *is and abides as* (the force of the present participle) Lord over the universe and who deserves eternal praise from all.

Titus 2:13. The debate surrounding this verse is whether the apostle Paul[80] intended to refer to one person (Christ) or to two persons (the Father and Christ) when he wrote, "While we wait for the blessed hope, even the appearing of the glory [or, glorious appearing] of the great God and Savior of us, Jesus Christ." The issue, more pointedly put, is this: Are the two words "God" and "Savior" to be construed as referring to one person, or are they to be divorced from one another, because of the demands of exegesis, and referred to two persons? In my opionion, there are five compelling reasons to understand Paul as referring to Christ alone throughout the verse and to translate the relevant phrase as "the appearing of our great God and Savior, Jesus Christ."

First, it is the most natural way to render the Greek sentence, as numerous commentators and grammarians have observed. Indeed, more than one grammarian has noted that there would never have been a question as to

78. Ibid., pp. 105-6. The best brief treatment of Romans 9:5 that I am aware of is Metzger's discussion in his *Textual Commentary on the Greek New Testament*, pp. 520-23.

79. Nigel Turner, *Grammatical Insights Into the New Testament* (Edinburgh: T. & T. Clark, 1965), p. 15.

80. In this section I am assuming that Paul wrote Titus just as the letter claims (1:1). No one in antiquity seems to have questioned Paul's authorship of Titus, it being only in comparatively recent times that his authorship has been called into question. The reader may consult Donald Guthrie (*The Pastoral Epistles* [London: Tyndale, 1957], pp. 212-28), and Everett F. Harrison (*Introduction to the New Testament*, rev. ed. [Grand Rapids: Eerdmans, 1971], pp. 351-63) for general defenses of Paul's authorship of Titus.

whether "God" and "Savior" refer to one person if the sentence had simply ended with "our Savior."[81] *Second,* the two nouns both stand under the regimen of the single definite article preceding "God," indicating (according to the Granville Sharpe rule) that they are to be construed corporately, not separately, or that they have a single referent. If Paul had intended to speak of two persons, he could have expressed this unambiguously by inserting an article before "Savior" or by writing "our Savior" after "Jesus Christ." *Third,* inasmuch as "appearing" is never referred to the Father but is consistently employed to refer to Christ's return in glory, the *prima facie* conclusion is that the "appearing of the glory of our great God" refers to Christ's appearing and not to the Father's appearing. *Fourth,* note has often been made of the fact that the terms θεὸς καὶ σωτήρ ("god and savior") were employed in combination together in the second and first century B.C. secular literature to refer to single recipients of heathen worship. Moulton, for example, writes:

> A curious echo [of Titus 2:13] is found in the Ptolemaic formula applied to the deified kings: thus GH 15 (ii/B.C.), τοῦ μεγάλου θεοῦ . . . καὶ σωτῆρος. . . . The phrase here is, of course, applied to one person.[82]

And Lock writes in the same vein:

> The combination σωτὴρ καὶ θεός had been applied to Ptolemy I, θεὸς ἐπιφανὴς to Antiochus Epiphanes, θεὸν ἐπιφανὴ καὶ . . . σωτῆρα to Julius Caesar [Ephesus, 48 B.C.].[83]

It is difficult to avoid the conclusion in light of this data, as Murray Harris writes, that "one impulse behind this particular verse was the desire to combat the extravagant titular endowment that had been accorded to human rulers."[84] *Fifth,* contrary to the oft-repeated assertion that the use of θεός as a christological title is an "un-Pauline locution" and thus cannot refer to Christ here, our exposition of Romans 9:5 has demonstrated that this simply is not so. Grammatically and biblically, the evidence indicates that Paul intended in Titus 2:13 to describe Christ as "our great God and Savior."[85]

---

81. Murray J. Harris, "Titus 2:13 and the Deity of Christ," in *Pauline Studies: Essays presented to Professor F. F. Bruce on his 70th Birthday,* ed. Donald A. Hagner and Murray J. Harris (Grand Rapids: Eerdmans, 1980), p. 266.

82. James Hope Moulton, *A Grammar of New Testament Greek,* vol. 1, 3rd. ed. (Edinburgh: T. & T. Clark, 1930), p. 84.

83. Lock, *Commentary on the Pastoral Epistles,* p. 145; cf. W. Dittenberger, *Sylloge Inscriptionum Graecarum,* 3rd ed. (Hildesheim: Georg Olms, 1960), 760.6 (=2nd ed., 347.6).

84. Harris, in *Pauline Studies,* p. 267; cf. Turner, *Grammatical Insights,* p. 16.

85. Four alternative translations have been offered for the entire verse. I would refer the reader to Harris's definitive article in *Pauline Studies* for these alternatives and their respective rebuttals.

If we could look no further for Paul's Christology than to these two texts—Romans 9:5 and Titus 2:13—we would have to conclude that his was a Christology of the highest kind. The One who had identified Himself to Paul on the Damascus Road as "Jesus of Nazareth" (Acts 22:8), who as His Lord had called Paul to Himself and whom Paul now served, was "over all things, the ever-blessed God" (Rom. 9:5) and his "great God and Savior" (Titus 2:13). And if this was Paul's christological vision, considering the extensiveness of his missionary travels and the significance of the church (Rome) and the man (Titus) to whom he wrote these letters, we may assume that this same high Christology would have become widely revered and regarded as precious for those for whom Paul's apostolic authority was not a matter of debate. In sum, for Paul and his churches, theirs would have been a high, ontological, incarnational Christology.

We have completed our survey of the Pauline corpus—written over approximately a seventeen-year period during the late fifth, sixth, and seventh decades of the first century—with regard to its Christology. In addition to the scores of verses we have noted in a general way, we have considered in some detail Romans 1:3-4; 9:5; Colossians 1:15-20; 2:9; Philippians 2:6-11; Ephesians 4:9-10; 1 Timothy 1:15; 3:16; and Titus 2:13.

We have seen that from his first days as a Christian, Paul regarded Christ as the Messiah and the incarnate Son of God (Acts 9:20, 22). In his letters he portrays Christ as the preexistent Creator and Yahweh of the Old Testament (Col. 1:15-17) and the Co-source with the Father of all spiritual blessings; His name is to be called upon in the church; at His name every knee is to bow, and every tongue is to confess Him as Lord (Rom. 10:12-13; Phil. 2:9-11). As the Son of God incarnate, He is the visible "Image of the invisible God" (Col. 1:15), who "being in the form of God," possesses all the essential attributes of God and is "equal with God" (Phil. 2:6-7). "In [Christ] dwells all the fullness of deity bodily" (Col. 2:9), the result of the Son of God having become "enfleshed" within the line of David as a man like other men (Rom. 1:3; Phil. 2:7; 1 Tim. 3:16). As a man He died for other men's sins and was buried, but He rose on the third day and ascended some days later to the right hand of God, assuming *de facto* mediatorial sovereignty over the universe. He is, for Paul, Lord "over all, God blessed forever" (Rom. 9:5) and "our great God and Savior" (Titus 2:13).

Now it would appear to be a subterfuge, unbecoming to scholarship, to claim that all of this is only functional language. While it is undoubtedly true that some of Paul's descriptions of Jesus should be viewed as "functional"

(for example, Christ, Servant, Head of the church, even Lord in the mediatorial sense), many are not (for example, Son, Son of God, Lord in the
Yahwistic sense, Image of the invisible God, and God). And we are only
being sensitive to the nuances of Scripture and true to our own deepest
instincts when we acknowledge that even the functional descriptions of
Jesus derive their power to evoke our religious interest and devotion ultimately from the ontological descriptions of Christ that surround them and
lie behind them.

Nor will it satisfy all the data we have considered to acknowledge on the
one hand that Jesus was for Paul both *vere deus* and *vere homo* but assert on the
other that his Christology was an anomaly in the thinking of the first-
century church. What Warfield wrote over three-quarters of a century ago is
still true today:

> Paul is not writing a generation or two [after the generation of those
> who had accompanied Jesus in His life], when the faith of the first
> disciples was a matter only of memory, perhaps of fading memory; and
> when it was possible for him to represent it as other than it was. He is
> writing out of the very bosom of this primitive community and under its
> very eye. His witness to the kind of Jesus this community believed in is
> just as valid and just as compelling, therefore, as his testimony that it
> believed in Jesus at all. In and through him the voice of the primitive
> community itself speaks, proclaiming its assured faith in its divine
> Lord.[86]

If anything has changed since Warfield wrote these words, it is that there
would seem to be even more evidence today than there was in his time that
his insight accords with the actual situation then existing, for, as we have
noted elsewhere, there is a growing consensus today among both critical
and evangelical scholars that in Colossians 1:15-20; Philippians 2:6-11; and
1 Timothy 3:16 we have in hymnic form reflections of the primitive Christology of the early church that may very well antedate the letters of Paul
in which they appear. By these hymns Christ was worshiped. Then in
1 Corinthians 15:3-5 and Romans 1:3-4 we have what may well be reflections
of primitive church confessions, while in 1 Timothy 1:15 we have, beyond
doubt, an early church confession in the form of a "faithful saying" that Paul
endorsed when he declared it to be "worthy of acceptance." When taken at
face value—and there is *no* compelling reason why they should not be—all
of these pericopes reflect the highest kind of Christology in which Jesus is
regarded as the divine, preexistent Son of God who through "descent"

86. Warfield, *Lord of Glory*, p. 257.

became "flesh" for us men and for our salvation and who through "ascent" assumed mediatorial headship over the universe and the church. And in 1 Timothy 1:15 we have the spokesman of the so-called "Pauline community" commending what is now commonly recognized as a piece of teaching framed in the wording of the "Johannine community." So instead of there being competing communities in the early church, each headed up by a specific apostle and each vying with the others for the minds of the masses, here is indication that the primitive church, at least that portion of it that followed the lead of the apostles and for whom the apostles were authoritative teachers in the church, was one in its essential understanding of Christ. One must also take into account that the Jerusalem apostles approved Paul's gospel (which surely would have included an account of who Jesus was for Paul) when he informed them of it on his second visit to Jerusalem (Gal. 2:2, 6-9). Add the fact that for both the (Palestinian?) Aramaic-speaking and (Hellenistic?) Greek-speaking Christians in the primitive church Jesus was "Lord" (cf. the occurrence of both κύριος ["Lord"] and Μαρανα θα [transliterated Aramaic, meaning either "Our *Lord* has [or will] come" or "Our *Lord*, come"] in 1 Cor. 16:22), and we must conclude that such strict distinctions as have been drawn by some modern scholars between an early Christology of the Jewish Palestinian church, a later Christology of the Jewish Hellenistic church (or mission), and a still later Christology of the Hellenistic Gentile church (or mission) (all stages of development before Paul) exist more in the minds of those who espouse the view than in the actual first-century church itself.[87] Paul's testimony, reflected throughout his letters, gives evidence that for Christians generally who lived at that time, Jesus was, as Warfield writes:

> a man indeed and the chosen Messiah who had come to redeem God's people, but in His essential Being just the great God Himself. In the light of [Paul's] testimony it is impossible to believe there ever was a different conception of Jesus prevalent in the Church: the mark of Christians from the beginning was obviously that they looked to Jesus as their "Lord" and "called upon His name" in their worship.[88]

---

87. F. Hahn (*The Titles of Jesus in Christology* [1963, Ger. ed.; reprint, New York: World Publishing, 1969]) and Reginald H. Fuller (*The Foundations of New Testament Christology* [London: Lutterworth Press, 1965]) are two prominent scholars who sponsor such distinctions. But cf. I. Howard Marshall ("Palestinian and Hellenistic Christianity: Some Critical Comments," *New Testament Studies* 19 [1972–73]: 271-87; *The Origins of New Testament Christology* [Downers Grove, Ill.: Inter-Varsity Press, 1976], pp. 24-28, 29, 32-39) for an excellent evangelical response to this theory.

88. Warfield, *Lord of Glory*, pp. 255-56.

THE REMAINING NEW TESTAMENT WITNESS TO JESUS

In this last chapter we propose to listen to the remaining voices of the New Testament concerning the person of Jesus—who He was in Himself and who He was for them. I refer to James, Jude, Peter, the Synoptic Evangelists, and particularly the writer of Hebrews and John.

James's Witness to Jesus

Although Paul would write a large portion of what we know today as the New Testament, he was not the first to write a letter that would become a part of the New Testament canon. That honor goes to James. The Epistle of James, probably written around A.D. 44–45,[1] was almost certainly written by "the Lord's brother" (Gal. 1:19) who bore that name and who most likely had come to faith in Jesus as the Messiah as a result of Jesus' postresurrection appearance to him (1 Cor. 15:7). By virtue of his personal piety and spiritual gifts, he had become the leader of the church in Jerusalem (Gal. 2:9) and presided over the Council in Jerusalem (Acts 15:13-19).

Among modern critical scholars who support a pre-Pauline date for the letter, the opinion is commonly expressed that James's "unobtrusive Christology"—A. M. Fairbairn spoke in 1893 of "the poverty of [James's] Christology"[2]—reflects "an important type of Christianity overshadowed by and misinterpreted through the figure and influence of Paul."[3] The fact that he makes no mention of Jesus' death and resurrection, for example, is interpreted to mean that "the author did not realize the importance of

---

1. Cf. the definitive argument for the early date of James in J. B. Mayor, *The Epistle of St. James*, 3rd ed. (London: Macmillan, 1913), pp. cxliv-clxxvii, clxxviii-ccv. Donald Guthrie (*New Testament Introduction* [London: Inter-Varsity Press, 1970], pp. 736-58, 761-64) may also be consulted for arguments in support of an early date for James.

2. A. M. Fairbairn, *The Place of Christ in Modern Theology*, 10th ed. (London: Hodder and Stoughton, 1902), p. 328.

3. E. M. Sidebottom, *James, Jude and 2 Peter* (Camden, N.J.: Thomas Nelson, 1967), p. 24.

them."[4] Those scholars who urge that James was written contemporaneously with the Pauline corpus interpret the silence respecting Jesus' death and resurrection to mean that its author wrote "to provide a counterblast to Pauline Christianity in the interests of Judaistic Christianity."[5]

But James's Christology is neither "ante-Pauline" nor, as we shall see, "anti-Pauline" in content. Adamson notes:

> Evidence such as that from the Dead Sea and Nag Hammadi has almost miraculously revealed or confirmed . . . the continuity preserved in the distinctive Jewish character, thought, and language of early Christian theology. We can now see that the Jewish first Christians had grown up in a wealth of ancient but lively tradition of messianic Christology, so that James, writing to Jewish converts who had accepted the Christian message, "This is he," was able to give most of his Christian letter not to Christian theology but to Christianity in everyday life.[6]

In other words, we may assume that James took for granted the great events that centered in the historical person of Jesus as he set about the task of writing his guide to Christian behavior. Whatever reasons lay behind his decision not to speak directly of Jesus' death and resurrection (and any number of other things, such as His supernatural conception in Mary's womb, His mighty miracles, His ascension, and His present session at the right hand of His Father), it certainly goes beyond the evidence to conclude that he was unaware of these things and their significance—witness his own response in faith to Jesus' resurrection appearance to him—or that he opposed Paul's Christology—witness his approval of Paul's gospel in Galatians 2:9 and his judgment at the Jerusalem council after listening to the testimonies of Peter and Paul (cf. Acts 15:25). In fact, if we had no more than his one letter to draw upon, we would still have to conclude that James's Christology is in every way consistent with what we learn about Christ from Jesus' self-testimony and from the other New Testament writers.

There is sufficient evidence from parallels between the Sermon on the Mount and verses, clauses, and phrases in James's letter to warrant the assumption that James had heard Jesus preach on numerous occasions (cf. Matt. 5:3 and James 2:5; 5:7 and 2:13; 5:11-12 and 1:2; 5:34-37 and 5:12; 6:11 and 2:15-16; 6:19 and 5:2-3; 6:22 and 4:4, 8; 6:34 and 4:13-14; 7:1 and 4:11-12; 7:7-8 and 1:5; 7:16 and 3:10-13, 18; 7:21-23 and 1:26-27; 7:24 and 1:22-25). And

---

4. Ibid.

5. G. R. Beasley-Murray, *The General Epistles: James, 1 Peter, Jude, 2 Peter* (Nashville: Abingdon Press, 1965), p. 21.

6. James Adamson, *The Epistle of James* (Grand Rapids: Eerdmans, 1976), p. 23.

while he speaks of Jesus by name only twice (1:1; 2:1), on both occasions he specifies Him as "the Lord Jesus Christ"—"designations expressive of marked reverence"[7] signifying both His messiahship and lordship. And in each case this exalted designation is enhanced by a contextual feature that places Him on a par with God the Father. In the former case (1:1), James describes himself as a "servant of God and of the Lord Jesus Christ"—a genitival coordination of God and Jesus that implies the latter's equality with God. In the latter case (2:1), James appositionally describes Jesus as "the Glory,"[8] undoubtedly intending by this term to describe Jesus as the manifested or "Shekinah" ("dwelling") Glory of God (cf. John 1:14; 2 Cor. 4:4; Heb. 1:3; Rev. 21:3). Warfield quite correctly observes:

> The thought of the writer seems to be fixed on those Old Testament passages in which Jehovah is described as the "Glory": e.g., "For I, saith Jehovah, will be unto her a wall of fire round about, and I will be the Glory in the midst of her" (Zech. 2:5). In the Lord Jesus Christ, James sees the fulfillment of these promises: He is Jehovah come to be with His people; and, as He has tabernacled among them, they have seen His glory. He is, in a word, the Glory of God, the Shekinah: God manifest to men. It is thus that James thought and spoke of his own brother who died a violent and shameful death while still in His first youth![9]

James also speaks of Jesus as "the Lord" (which title from New Testament usage elsewhere presupposes His resurrection and ascension) who, as such, is the One in whose name Christians are to pray and who answers their prayers (5:13-14), who heals and forgives (5:14-15), and whose coming Christians are patiently to await (5:7-8). It is true that James also refers to the Father as "the Lord" (cf. 1:7; 4:15; 5:10-11); but precisely because he can pass back and forth between the Father and Jesus in his use of κύριος, applying it now to one, now to the other, he implies the fitness of thinking of Jesus as equal with God. There is even sound reason for believing that it is Jesus who is before his mind when he speaks in 4:12 of the lawgiver and Judge (cf. particularly 5:9).

As Jesus' half-brother, James surely knew of Jesus' death. And inasmuch as he had experienced firsthand an encounter with the glorified Christ, we may be assured that James knew of and believed in Jesus' resurrection. From

---

7. Warfield, *The Lord of Glory* (reprint, Grand Rapids: Baker, 1974), p. 263.

8. Mayor's exposition of τῆς δόξης (2:1), in my opinion, is still the fullest and finest in English; cf. *Epistle of St. James*, pp. 79-82.

9. Warfield, *Lord of Glory*, p. 265.

his references to Christ as "Lord" and to Christ's coming (παρουσία) in 5:7-8, we may surmise that James was also aware of His ascension and present session at the Father's right hand, since such a state is the necessary prerequisite to His return. Therefore, the available data indicates that James knew about and accepted the great objective central events of redemption.

So while James's declared Christology is hardly exhaustive, what he does say about Jesus is explicit and exalting, falling nothing short of implying what would come to be known later as the metaphysical sonship of Jesus.

Jude's Witness to Jesus

The Epistle of Jude was written by Jude, the brother of James (1:1) and so with James a younger half-brother of Jesus Himself (cf. Matt. 13:55; Mark 6:3). When all of the evidence is taken into account, a date for its composition around A.D. 65–80, or perhaps even somewhat earlier, seems appropriate.[10]

In this short letter, only twenty-five verses, Jude refers to Jesus no less than six times by name and always in conjunction with one or more additional titles:"Jesus Christ" (v. 1 [twice]), "our Lord Jesus Christ" (vv. 17, 21), "Jesus Christ, our Lord" (v. 25), and "our only Master and Lord, Jesus Christ" (v. 4). All ascribe to Jesus both the Messianic investiture and lordship, while the contexts in which they occur suggest that for Jude Jesus held a divine station equal to the Father's. For just as in God the Father the called are loved, so also in or for Jesus Christ they are kept (v. 1). Just as they are to keep themselves in the Father's love, so also they are to wait for the mercy of our Lord Jesus Christ to grant them eternal salvation (v. 21). Just as the Father is glorified for the final salvation of the called, so also through Jesus Christ, our Lord, such praise is mediated (v. 25). Just as the Father is the "only God" (v. 25), so also Jesus Christ is "our only Master and Lord" (τὸν μόνον δεσπότην καὶ κύριον) (v. 4). And Jude sees himself as a servant of Jesus Christ (v. 1) precisely because Jesus Christ is "our only Master and Lord" (v. 4).

There is some debate as to whether the full title in verse 4 refers only to Christ ("our only Master and Lord, Jesus Christ") or to both the Father ("the only Master") and Jesus ("our Lord Jesus Christ"). Many commentators argue that the latter is the more likely interpretation, but mainly on *a priori* theological grounds. In my opinion, two facts militate against this view and in favor of the former interpretation. First, both nouns ("Master" and

---

10. Cf. Guthrie (*New Testament Introduction*, pp. 906-12), for a reasoned argument for both the traditional view of the letter's authorship and a first-century rather than a second-century date of composition.

"Lord") stand under the regimen of the single article before "Master," suggesting that they are to be construed together as characterizations of the same person. Certainly κύριος ("Lord") does not require the article; but if Jude intended to refer both to God the Father and to Jesus, he could have made that intention explicit either by placing "our Lord" after "Jesus Christ" as he does in verse 25 or by employing a second article before "our Lord Jesus Christ" as he does in the other two places where he refers singly to Jesus by that title (vv. 17, 21). Second, Peter, modeling 2 Peter 2:1 on the phrase here, evidently understood Jude 4 to refer to Jesus as the Master. These two factors place it beyond all reasonable doubt that Jude intended to describe Jesus as both our Master and our Lord. It is doubtful that the two titles are a pleonasm or tautology; Jude implied by the former title that, in addition to being "our Lord," Jesus is also the "Owner" of Christians by virtue of His Messianic work, with the right that inheres in such ownership to command and to expect His followers' immediate and humble response.

But Jude implied still more about Jesus. For in addition to the six direct references to Jesus by name, there is sound reason to think that he may well have had Jesus in mind when he referred to "the Lord" in verses 5 and 14. Consider the latter context first. Can there really be any doubt, regardless of who the referent is in 1 Enoch 1:4-9, that Jude intended to refer to Jesus in verse 14 when he wrote, "Behold, the Lord will come [ἦλθεν, an aorist with prophetic (future) intention] with His myriad holy ones" (cf. Matt. 16:27; 25:31; Mark 8:38; Luke 9:26; 1 Thess. 3:13; 2 Thess. 1:7-10)? In light of consentient Christian testimony, no other referent will suffice. So then, Jude here ascribed the divine prerogative of eschatological judgment to Jesus.

In the former verse (v. 5), "Jesus" may well be the original reading instead of "Lord";[11] but even with the reading "the Lord," there is every reason to believe that Jesus was still Jude's intended referent. Consider the following: first, Jude employed "Lord" to refer to Jesus four times (vv. 4, 17, 21, 25); second, we have just seen that the almost certain referent of "Lord" in verse

11. Bruce Metzger explains with respect to the reading "[ὁ] κύριος" in the UBS *Greek New Testament* that "a majority of the Committee was of the opinion that the reading ['Ιησοῦς] was difficult to the point of impossibility, and explained its origin in terms of transcriptional oversight" (*A Textual Commentary on the Greek New Testament* [New York: United Bible Societies, 1971] pp. 725-26). But Metzger himself and Allen Wikgren affirm that "critical principles seem to require the adoption of 'Ιησοῦς, which admittedly is the best attested reading among Greek and versional witnesses [e.g., A, B, 33, Vulgate, and some significant church fathers]. Struck by the strange and unparalleled mention of Jesus in a statement about the redemption out of Egypt (yet compare Paul's reference to Χριστός in 1 Cor 10.4), copyists would have substituted (ὁ) κύριος or ὁ θεός" (ibid.). In short, 'Ιησοῦς is both the best supported reading textually and undoubtedly the hardest of the variant readings—canons of criticism which, when both are true of a given reading, normally carry the field.

14 is Jesus; and third, this occurrence of "Lord" in verse 5 comes hard on the heels of Jude's certain reference to Jesus in the immediately preceding verse as "our only Master and Lord, Jesus Christ." So it is virtually certain that Jude ascribes to Jesus, in His preincarnate state as the Yahweh of the Old Testament, first, the deliverance of Israel from Egypt and then the destruction of those within the nation who rebelled; second, the judgment of the angels at the time of their primeval fall; and third, the destruction of Sodom and Gomorrah. And if this is so, Jude was clearly thinking of Jesus Christ in terms that encompass the Old Testament deity. But however one interprets this last verse, it is apparent from the others that, for Jude, Christ was the sovereign Master and Lord of men, He who at His coming will exercise the prerogative to dispense eschatological salvation and judgment as the Savior and Judge of men. There can be no doubt, in light of these facts, that for Jude Christ was divine.

Peter's Witness to Jesus

Peter wrote his two letters most probably during the seventh decade of the first century (the first about A.D. 62–64 during Nero's reign and the second shortly before the end of his life around A.D. 68).[12] As we consider Peter's epistolary witness to Jesus, we should bear in mind that from numerous experiences as one of the original twelve disciples he had gained firsthand insight into the character and work of his Lord. Recall that on the occasion of the first miraculous catch of fish, Peter had expressed a numinous awe of Jesus, calling Him "Lord" and worshiping Him (Luke 5:4-10). Later, moved by Jesus' discourse on the Bread of Life, as the spokesman for the disciples, Peter had confessed that Jesus alone was the wellspring of words of eternal life as the Holy One of God (John 6:68-69). Then after he and Jesus had walked on the Sea of Galilee, he joined the other disciples in the united confession, "You are truly the Son of God" (Matt. 14:33). And, of course, it was Peter who registered the great confession at Caesarea Philippi: "You are the Christ, the Son of the living God" (Matt. 16:16). In addition to seeing the miracles Jesus performed publicly, Peter was among that inner circle of disciples who also witnessed His transfiguration and who heard the Father's attestation to Jesus' unique sonship (Matt. 17:2-6). He was also the private

12. Cf. Guthrie (*New Testament Introduction*, pp. 773-90, 795-96, 820-48, 850-51) for a reasoned defense of the Petrine authorship of both letters and the arguments for placing them in the seventh decade of the first century. Cf. also Gleason L. Archer, Jr., *Encyclopedia of Bible Difficulties* (Grand Rapids: Zondervan, 1982), pp. 425-27, for a brief but substantive defense of the Petrine authorship of 2 Pet.

beneficiary of one of Jesus' postresurrection appearances (he probably was the first apostle to see Him) (Luke 24:34; 1 Cor. 15:5), and he saw Him on several other occasions, specifically hearing Thomas's confession of Jesus as "Lord and God" during one of them (John 20:28). He witnessed Jesus' ascension into heaven and preached the sermon on the Day of Pentecost in which he acclaimed both the messiahship and mediatorial lordship of the divine Jesus. We should not overlook the fact, finally, that Peter was aware of Paul's Christology and approved of it (Gal. 1:19; 2:1-9; 2 Pet 3:15-16). Consequently, one should not be surprised to find Peter espousing the highest kind of Christology "from above" in his letters. Indeed, it would be exceedingly strange to find it in any way otherwise.

First Peter

In his first letter Peter refers to Jesus as "[the] Christ," his most common designation for Him (1:11, 19; 2:21; 3:15, 16, 18; 4:1, 13, 14; 5:1, 10,[13] 14), "Jesus Christ" (1:1, 2, 3, 7, 13; 2:5; 3:21; 4:11), "[the] Lord" (2:3, 13; 3:15; perhaps also in 1:25; 3:12), and "our Lord Jesus Christ" (1:3). What Peter says about Jesus in these contexts reveals a fully developed incarnational Christology. He implies His preexistence with the Father (1:20a),[14] affirming that it was Christ's Spirit who had inspired the prophets in Old Testament times (1:11) and that He had been "manifested" in these last times (1:20b). In accordance with Old Testament prophecy (1:11), as our sinless substitute (2:22, a citation of Isa. 53:9) He suffered death vicariously on the cross (1:2, 11, 19; 2:21, 23, 24; 3:18; 4:1, 13; 5:1),was raised from the dead (1:3, 21; 3:18, 21), ascended to the right hand of God and to glory (1:11, 21; 3:22), and will be revealed in the Eschaton (1:7, 13; 5:1, 4). He is the Mediator between God

---

13. Cf. Metzger (*Textual Commentary on the Greek New Testament*, p. 697), for the reasons for preferring the shorter reading "Christ" over the longer reading "Christ Jesus."

14. Ernest Best declares that "the preexistence of Christ is implied here through the additional words *was manifest*, i.e., at the incarnation" (*1 Peter* [London: Oliphants, 1971], p. 91), and this is, of course, true. But then, if this is so, it would follow that the immediately preceding words, "foreknown before the foundation of the world," *when applied to Christ*, would imply the same as well. James Moffatt says, "In i. 2 . . . Christians are *predestined* [his translation of προγινώσκειν], but here the conception of a personal pre-existence is extended to the personality of Christ" (*The General Epistles: Peter, James and Judas* [London: Hodder and Stoughton, 1928], p. 107). I Howard Marshall observes:

> The writer also speaks of [Christ] as One who was predestined before the foundation of the world, but made manifest at the end of the times (1:20). This appears to be a remnant of incarnational language; Peter does not lay stress on it, but simply makes use of a stereotyped traditional terminology which reflects an existing incarnational theology ("Incarnational Christology in the New Testament," in *Christ the Lord*, ed. Harold H. Rowdon [Leicester: Inter-Varsity Press, 1982], p. 11).

and man (1:21; 2:5; 4:11; 5:10, 14) and the One in whom men must trust for salvation (2:6).

In the course of setting forth his Christology, not only does Peter place Christ in the trinitarian context of the Father and the Spirit (1:2, 3, 11; 4:14), but three times he refers to Old Testament passages in which Yahweh is the subject and uses them of Christ in a way that suggests that Christ is to be equated with the Yahweh of the Old Testament Scriptures. In 2:3, alluding to Psalm 34:8 ("Taste and see that the Lord is good"), he writes with reference to Christ: "if you tasted that the Lord is good."[15] In 2:8, citing Isaiah 8:14b, he equates the Lord of Hosts there, who would become "a stone that causes men to stumble, and a rock that makes them fall" with Christ, the "stone laid in Zion" (2:6, citing Isa. 28:16), and the "stone the builders rejected [who] has become the capstone" (2:7, citing Ps. 118:22). And in 3:14-15, he equates the Lord of Hosts who is to be sanctified in Isaiah 8:12-13 with Christ ("Sanctify Christ as Lord in your hearts").[16]

15. That ὁ κύριος in 2:3 refers to Christ and implies His identity with the Yahweh of Ps. 34:8 is evident from the immediately following phrase in 2:4, "to whom coming, as to a living Stone" (a further echo of Ps. 34:5 [LXX]), where the relative pronoun and the "stone" metaphor clearly refer to Christ as the entire context makes clear. C. E. B. Cranfield comments on 2:3: "[This clause] is a quotation from Ps. 34.8 (slightly modified). That by THE LORD . . . Christ is meant is indicated by the following verse" (*I & II Peter and Jude* [London: SCM Press, 1960], p. 62). He further declares:

> With regard to the significance which the title had for the primitive Church, the following facts are of decisive importance: in the LXX *Kyrios* ("Lord") represents the Divine Name or Tetragrammaton . . . more than six thousand times; the New Testament writers had no scruple about applying Old Testament texts in which *Kyrios* is so used to the exalted Jesus (e.g., Rom. 10.13; I Thess. 5.2; I Peter 2.3; 3.15); and the first Christians, men brought up in Judaism in a religious tradition for which such texts as Ex. 20.3 and Deut. 6.4 were of utterly fundamental importance, prayed to Jesus (e.g., Acts 7.59f.; 9.14; I Cor. 1.2). In view of these facts it can hardly be denied that the confession "Jesus is Lord" was a confession that the exalted Jesus was in the fullest sense divine (ibid., pp. 34-35).

Best likewise comments on 2:3:

> Lord: in Ps. 34:8 the "Lord" is God. Our author in common with the other NT writers regularly understands the "Lord" of the OT to refer to Christ . . . ; this is made clear by the beginning of verse 4 where "him" refers back to "Lord" in verse 3 (*1 Peter*, p. 99).

He even suggests that Peter deliberately substituted "Lord" for "our God" in 1:25, when citing Isa. 40:6-8, to link the word to Christ, who is the "Lord" of 2:3 (ibid., p. 96). Moffatt comments on 2:3:

> Any mention of *the Lord* in the O.T. naturally suggested the divine Christ to an early Christian, and this sent Peter off again . . . to expatiate upon the vital value of Christ to Christians (*Peter, James, and Judas*, p. 114).

Finally, J. N. D. Kelly comments on 2:3: "In the original [Hebrew] 'the Lord' of course denotes Yahweh, but the Christian understanding of the Psalter naturally transferred the title to Christ (*The Epistles of Peter and Jude* [London: Adam & Charles Black, 1969], p. 86).

16. The reading Χριστὸν is textually secure, supported as it is both by "early and diversified external evidence" and by the transcriptional probability that "the more familiar expression (κύριον τὸν θεόν)" replaced "the less usual expression (κύριον τὸν Χριστόν)" (Metzger,

There can be no doubt that Peter regarded Jesus as the Christ, as God's divine Son, and therefore as God incarnate.

Second Peter

In his second letter[17] Peter refers to Jesus as "Jesus Christ" (1:1), "[the] Lord" (3:8, 9, 10, 15; perhaps 2:9), "the Lord and Savior" (3:2), "our Lord and Savior Jesus Christ" (1:11; 2:20; 3:18), and finally, "our God and Savior Jesus Christ" (1:1).

This last reference is very important, for now we find Peter—like Thomas and Paul before him—employing θεός as a christological title. This assertion, of course, has not gone unchallenged, the alternative suggestion being that by θεός Peter intended to refer to the Father. As earlier with Titus 2:13, the issue turns on the question, By the phrase, "the righteousness of our God and Savior Jesus Christ," did Peter intend to refer to two persons (God the Father and Jesus) or to only one person, Jesus alone? It is my opinion, as well as that of the KJV, RV, RSV, NASB, NEB, NIV, and the NKJV, that Peter intended to refer only to Christ, and I offer the following six reasons.

1. It is the most natural way to read the Greek sentence. If Peter had intended to speak of two persons, he could have expressed himself unambiguously to that effect, as he does in the very next verse ("knowledge of God and of Jesus our Lord"), by placing "our Savior" after "Jesus Christ" or by simply inserting an article before "Savior" in the present order. Bigg rightly observes that "if the author intended to distinguish two persons, he has expressed himself with singular inaccuracy."[18]

2. Both "God" and "Savior" stand under the regimen of the single article before "God," linking the two nouns together as referents to a single person.[19] Bigg again rightly states, "It is hardly open for anyone to translate

Textual Commentary on the Greek New Testament, p. 691). On the significance of the verse for Christ's divine nature, Kelly writes, "The verse has a bearing on I Peter's Christology, for as in ii. 3 the title 'the Lord', which in the Hebrew original denotes God, is unhesitatingly attributed to Christ" (*Epistles of Peter and Jude*, p. 142).

17. I am assuming that Simon Peter bar Jonah wrote this letter which bears his name. Cf. E. M. B. Green's *Second Peter Reconsidered* (London: Tyndale, 1960), an admirable monograph of original scholarship, which ably combats today's prevailing liberal contention that 2 Pet. is a spurious "pious forgery."

18. Charles Bigg, *A Critical and Exegetical Commentary on the Epistles of St. Peter and St. Jude*, International Critical Commentary (Edinburgh: T. & T. Clark, 1902), p. 251.

19. Cf. A. T. Robertson, *A Grammar of the Greek New Testament in the Light of Historical Research* (Nashville: Broadman Press, 1934), pp. 785-86; also F. Blass and A. Debrunner, *A Greek Grammar of the New Testament and Other Early Christian Literature* (Chicago: University of Chicago Press, 1961), pp. 144-45, para. 276, and Bruce M. Metzger, "Jehovah's Witnesses and Jesus Christ," *Theology Today* (April 1953): 78-79.

in I Pet. 1.3 ὁ θεὸς καὶ πατὴρ by 'the God and Father,' and yet here decline to translate ὁ θεὸς καὶ σωτήρ by 'the God and Saviour.' "[20]

3. Five times in 2 Peter, including this one, Peter uses the word "Savior." It is always coupled with a preceding noun (the other four times always with κύριος) in precisely the same word order as in 1:1. Here are the last four uses in their precise word order:

1:11: "kingdom of the Lord of us and Savior Jesus Christ"

2:20: "knowledge of the Lord of us and Savior Jesus Christ"

3:4: "commandment of the Lord and Savior"

3:18: "knowledge of the Lord of us and Savior Jesus Christ"

In each of these four cases, "Lord" and "Savior," standing under the regimen of the single article before "Lord," refer to the same person, a fact recognized by all grammarians, commentaries, and Bible versions. If we simply substitute the word θεός for κύριος, we have precisely the word order of verse 1: "righteousness of the God of us and Savior Jesus Christ." In other words, the phrases in these verses are perfectly similar and must stand or fall together. The parallelism of word order between the phrase in 1:1 and the other four phrases, where only one person is intended, puts it beyond all reasonable doubt that one person is intended in 1:1 as well.

E. Käsemann's contrary opinion that "our Lord and Savior" in the four occurrences reflects a "stereotyped" christological formula, and that therefore the employment of θεοῦ in 1:1 stands outside of the stereotype, the phrase thus referring to two persons,[21] is unconvincing. There is no reason why a variant of a stereotyped formula could not occur. And when the grammar clearly indicates that it has occurred, then the interpreter must be led by the grammar.

4. The doxology to "our Lord Jesus Christ" in 3:18 ascribes "glory both now and forever" to Him, suggesting a Christology in which Christ may be glorified as God is glorified. There would be, then, nothing incongruous in describing Christ as God in 1:1.

5. Peter was surely present on the occasion of Thomas's confession of Jesus as both Lord and God (John 20:28), which confession had received Christ's approval. The memory of that confession, not to mention his own confession in Matthew 16:16, would have dissolved any reticence on Peter's part to refer to Jesus as θεός. Such a description of Jesus here as God is simply in line with those earlier confessions and does not go one centimeter beyond them.

---

20. Bigg, *Commentary on the Epistles of St. Peter and St. Jude*, p. 251; cf. Warfield, *Lord of Glory*, p. 270.

21. Ernst Käsemann, "An Apologia for Primitive Christian Eschatology," *Essays on New Testament Themes* (London: SCM Press, 1964), p. 183 n. 2.

6. Peter seems to allude to Paul's letter to the Romans in 2 Peter 2:19 (cf. Rom. 6:16) and 3:15 (cf. Rom. 2:4; 9:22-23; 11:22-23); he would almost certainly have been aware that Paul in Romans 9:5 had referred to Christ as "over all, the ever-blessed God." According "scriptural status" to Paul's letters as he does (3:16), he would have seen nothing inappropriate or "unscriptural" about his own description of Christ as God, just as his "dear brother Paul" had done some years earlier.

We conclude then that 2 Peter 1:1 takes its place alongside John 20:28; Romans 9:5; and Titus 2:13 as a fourth verse in which Jesus is described, by the christological title θεός, as God.

While Peter's Christology in 2 Peter is not as detailed as in his first letter, still we observe the same high Christology "from above." That Jesus is God incarnate Peter attests, as we have just argued, by describing Him as "our God" (1:1) and as being, with the Father, the Co-source of grace and peace (1:2). Divine power (ἡ θεία δύναμις), divine essence (θεία φύσις), and divine majesty (μεγαλειότης) are assigned to Him (1:3, 4, 16).[22] His is an eternal kingdom (1:11), into which Christians will be welcomed when He comes in power (1:16) on His "Day" (3:10), which is "the Day of God" (3:12), to destroy the heavens and earth with fire (3:10-12). He is the Owner (δεσπότης) of men (2:1), whose commands they are to obey (3:2) and through the knowledge of whom all spiritual blessing and Christian virtue come (1:2, 8; 2:20; 3:18). Finally, to Him is directed the doxology in 3:18 ("To Him be the glory both now and forever"), a doxology not unlike those addressed both to Him (2 Tim. 4:18; Heb. 13:20-21; 1 Pet. 4:11; Rev. 1:5b-6) and to the Father (1 Pet. 5:11; Jude 24-25) elsewhere.[23] And yet He is distinct

22. It is exegetically possible that either "God" or "Jesus our Lord" in 1:2 could be the antecedent of the αὐτοῦ ("His") in 1:3, but the preponderance of evidence leans toward the latter. It is the nearest possible antecedent, and having just designated Christ as "our God" in 1:1, it would not be at all strange were Peter to refer to Christ's "divine power." Moreover, inasmuch as Christ is the object of knowledge in 1:2, 8; 2:20; 3:18, it is most likely the case that He is the referent of the phrase "Him who called" in 1:3, although calling is usually assigned to the Father in Scripture (but cf. Matt. 9:13; Mark 2:17; 3:13). (There is no difficulty, considering the rhetorical style of the passage, in referring "His" and "Him who called" to the same person.) If this is so, and I suggest that it is, then both a unique (cf. "His own") glory and the divine nature are ascribed to Him in addition to divine power (so Bigg, Lenski, Barclay, Bauckham). (Note: One last comment is in order: Christians do not become "sharers of His divine nature" in the sense that they are "divinized" but in the sense that they become incorruptible and immortal in Christ's eternal Kingdom.)

23. That the doxology is addressed to Christ in 3:18 is beyond question. That the doxologies in 1 Pet. 4:11 and Heb. 13:21 are also directed to Christ seems apparent from the collocation of words in these respective verses. Bigg (on 1 Pet. 4:11) has rightly pointed out, "It is hardly to be supposed that any serious writer would lay himself open to misunderstanding on so grave a point, when by merely throwing back the words διὰ Ἰησοῦ Χριστοῦ he could have prevented all possibility of mistake" (Commentary on the Epistles of St. Peter and St. Jude, p. 176).

from His Father as the Son of the Father, who in His mediatorial role receives honor and glory from His Father (1:17). All of this comports with what we have seen elsewhere in the Petrine witness to Jesus, and simply adds the weight of its testimony to the New Testament's depiction of the full unabridged deity of Jesus Christ.

The Synoptists' Witness to Jesus

It was most likely during the seventh decade of the first century—the decade in which several of the New Testament letters were written and Peter and Paul were martyred—that the Synoptists wrote their Gospels.[24] In their accounts of Jesus' life and ministry, not only do they report what we have already treated under the topic of Jesus' self-witness (Chapter 2), but also, in doing so, since it can hardly be maintained that they wrote as disinterested biographers,[25] they revealed what they themselves believed regarding Jesus. Thus it can be said at the outset that Jesus' reported *self*-witness reflects also *their* understanding of Him—that is, for all three Jesus was the divine Son of God who, being co-equal and co-essential with the Father in His deity, was dispatched as the Son of the Father on the Messianic errand and thus became man and died for man's sins, but who then rose from the dead the third day after death and now sits at the right hand of God, awaiting the time when He will return in power and great glory to judge the world.

But there are also distinctions between the Evangelists, and these are equally important to note in this study.

Mark's Witness

Matthew and Luke are in some ways more explicit than Mark regarding their views of Christ, but Jesus is for Mark no less divine than He is for the the other two Synoptists (assuming for the time being that He is divine for them). The title "Son of God" as a christological title occurs in 3:11 and 15:39, with the variants "Son of the Most High God" and "Son of the Blessed" occurring in 5:7 and 14:61 respectively.[26] Beside these stand the simple "a

---

24. Cf. D. A. Carson, *Matthew*, pp. 19-21; Walter W. Wessel, *Mark*, pp. 607-8; Walter L. Liefeld, *Luke*, pp. 807-9, all to be found in *The Expositor's Bible Commentary*, vol. 8 (Grand Rapids: Zondervan, 1984) for the reasons for this approximate dating. Donald Guthrie (*New Testament Introduction*, pp. 45-46, 72-76, 110-15) seems to be open to even earlier dates for Matthew and Mark than are Carson and Wessel.

25. This is not to suggest for a moment that because they were, as Jesus' followers, *interested* biographers that their accounts are in any way distortions of His life.

26. Cf. Metzger (*A Textual Commentary on the Greek New Testament*, p. 73) and William L. Lane

son" (12:6), "the Son" (13:22), and "My Son" (1:11; 9:7). In earlier analyses of these passages we demonstrated that in each of these instances the title ascribes to Jesus a unique filial relationship to the Father, this unique sonship being ultimately grounded in His transcendent co-essentiality with the Father.

Mark's "Son of Man" sayings also indicate that, although Jesus as the Danielic "Son of Man" would suffer and be betrayed into the hands of sinners and be killed (8:31; 9:31; 10:33-34; 14:21, 41), He is, as that same Son of Man, also a superhuman, superangelic figure of transcendent dignity who does mighty works, is the Lord of the Sabbath (2:28), has the authority to forgive sins (2:10), and actually *gives* His life as a ransom for many (10:45) in accordance with the prophetic Scriptures (14:21); but who rises from the dead (8:31; 9:9, 31; 10:34), sits on the right hand of the Mighty One (14:62), and will return in clouds with the holy angels and with great power and glory to judge the world (8:38; 13:26-27).

E. Lohmeyer's assessment of Mark's Jesus is clearly on target when he declares that, as the Son of God, Jesus for Mark is "not primarily a human but a divine figure. . . . He is not merely endowed with the power of God, but is himself divine as to his nature; not only are his word and work divine but his essence also."[27] William Lane notes in this same connection that "it is widely recognized that the figure of Jesus in Mark's Gospel is altogether supernatural."[28]

Matthew's Witness

For Matthew, as for Mark, Jesus is the Son of God (2:15; 3:17; 4:3, 6; 11:27; 14:33; 16:16; 17:5; 21:37-38; 22:2; 24:36; 26:63-64; 27:54; 28:19), by which title he intends all that Mark means by it—that Jesus stands in a unique filial relationship to the Father because, as the Father's Son, He is divine. But Matthew makes explicit at some points what Mark takes for granted. Matthew reports Jesus' supernatural entrance into the world as "Immanuel"—"God with us" (1:18-25). In the "embryonic Fourth Gospel" in 11:27 (cf. my discussion, pp. 68-74), he brings out the truth that Jesus' knowledge of the Father is on a par with the Father's reciprocal knowledge of Him, and His sovereign disposition of that knowledge to men is also on a par with the

(*The Gospel According to Mark* [Grand Rapids: Eerdmans, 1974], p. 41 n. 7) for the text-critical arguments respectively for the textual uncertainty and for the presumptive certainty of "the Son of God" in 1:1.

27. E. Lohmeyer, *Das Evangelium des Markus*, 12th ed. (Göttingen: Vandenhoeck and Ruprecht, 1953), p. 4 (my translation).

28. Lane, *Gospel According to Mark*, p. 44 n. 23.

Father's reciprocal sovereign disposition of His knowledge of the Son. And in Matthew's account of the Great Commission we see Jesus placing Himself even in the "awful precincts of the divine Name" (Warfield) as the Co-sharer with the Father and the Spirit in the one ineffable Name or essence of God (28:19).

As the Messianic Son of Man, Matthew's Jesus undergoes a period of humiliation as He serves men (20:28) and suffers all kinds of indignities—even death—at their hands (12:40; 17:12, 22-23; 20:18-19, 28; 26:2, 24, 45). But as the same Son of Man, He possesses the authority to forgive sins (9:6) and is the Lord of the Sabbath (12:8). Although He is killed, according to Matthew His death was a self-sacrifice—"a ransom for many" (20:28)—in accordance with prophetic Scripture (26:24); but He rises from the dead (12:40; 17:9, 23; 20:19), assumes authority at the right hand of the Mighty One (26:64), and will return on the clouds with *His* angels (16:27; 24:31) in power and great glory to judge the nations of the world (19:28; 24:27, 30, 39, 44; 25:31-46; 26:64).

There can be no doubt that Matthew's Jesus—a man surely—is also of supernatural origin, and is superhuman, superangelic, indeed, equal with the Father in essential nature though submissive to the Father's will in His mediatorial role as the Messiah.

Luke's Witness

Luke's witness to Jesus' divine sonship is just as transparent as the other Synoptists' (1:32, 35; 3:22; 4:3, 9, 41; 8:28; 9:35; 10:22; 20:13; 22:70). With Matthew he reports Jesus' supernatural birth, and with Matthew he also records Jesus' claim to a knowledge of the Father equivalent in every way—"complete, exhaustive, and unbrokenly continuous" (Warfield)—with the Father's knowledge of Him, by virtue of which He also is the only adequate Revealer of the Father to men just as the Father is the only adequate Revealer of the Son to men (10:21-22).

With the other Synoptists, Luke's Jesus, as the Danielic Son of Man, suffers for a time at the hands of men "in order to seek and to save that which was lost" (9:22, 44; 18:31-32; 19:10) as it had been predicted in Scripture (18:31; 22:22). But then He rises from the dead (9:22; 18:33; 24:7), ascends to the right hand of the mighty God (22:69), and will return in a cloud with power and great glory (9:26; 21:27) to determine the destinies of men—surely a divine prerogative and function (9:26; 12:8; 21:36). Again, as in the other Synoptic Gospels, Luke's Jesus, as the Son of Man, is a figure of transcendent proportions.

But Luke's Gospel contains a feature absent from the other two Synoptic Gospels. Jesus is for Mark and Matthew "the Lord" (cf. Mark 1:3; Matt. 3:3), but Luke makes this characterization of Jesus explicit through his recurring narrative use of "the Lord" in reference to Jesus (7:13, 19; 10:1, 39, 41; 11:39; 12:42; 13:15; 17:5, 6; 18:6; 19:8; 22:61; 24:3; cf. the numerous occurrences of the same feature in Luke's Acts), no doubt reflecting the postresurrection terminology of the early church and revealing thereby its lofty Christology.[29] As for the significance of Luke's narrative use of "Lord" for Jesus, I. Howard Marshall notes that "what was in the OT [LXX] the name of God has been applied to Jesus"; that ὁ κύριος ("the Lord") "is used of both God and Jesus quite indiscriminately [in Acts], so that it is often hard to determine which Person is meant"; and that in his Gospel Luke employs "Lord" particularly to introduce authoritative statements by Jesus. Marshall concludes from all this that "Jesus . . . is for Luke the Lord [in the Yahwistic sense] during his earthly ministry."[30] Luke, of course, is careful not to place the title with that significance on the lips of the disciples in an indiscriminate, anachronistic way.

The only legitimate judgment that can be passed in view of their united testimony is that for the Synoptic Evangelists Jesus is God incarnate.

The Writer of Hebrews' Witness to Jesus

Most likely in the late sixth or seventh decade of the first century, but almost certainly before the destruction of Jerusalem in A.D. 70, the writer of Hebrews penned his exhortation to Jewish Christians.[31] If Paul wrote it,[32] then it would have had to be written before his martyrdom in Rome around A.D. 64–67.

29. Geerhardus Vos writes on this Lukan feature:

> In [the case of the Evangelist using the title "the Lord" of Jesus] we have, of course, nothing but an instance of the custom which generally prevailed at the time the Gospels were written, of referring to Jesus as "the Lord." The Evangelist must have followed this custom in his daily speech, and no reason can be discovered why he should have refrained from following it in writing, even though it should have been, strictly speaking, an anachronism. For not only the Evangelist, but also the readers for whom he proximately wrote, daily so expressed themselves. Grammatically analyzed . . . the language used means simply this: "He, whom we now call the Lord . . ." (*The Self-Disclosure of Jesus* [1926; reprint, Phillipsburg, N.J.: Presbyterian and Reformed, 1978], p. 119).

30. I. Howard Marshall, *Luke, Historian and Theologian* (Exeter: Paternoster Press, 1970), pp. 166-67.

31. For representative synchronous discussions of the issue of dating, cf. Guthrie, *New Testament Introduction*, pp. 716-18; F. F. Bruce, *Commentary on the Epistle to the Hebrews* (Grand Rapids: Eerdmans, 1964), pp. xlii-xliv; P. E. Hughes, *A Commentary on the Epistle to the Hebrews* (Grand Rapids: Eerdmans, 1977), pp. 30-32.

32. Concerning the authorship of Hebrews, it is regrettable that about the only thing the average intelligent layman knows or hears expressed today is Origen's opinion to the effect that God alone knows the truth of the matter. It is not so commonly recognized that the context of this

The Christ of Hebrews is arguably as fully and truly human as everywhere else in Scripture—He shared our humanity (2:14), was made like His brothers in every way (2:17), was a descendant of Judah (7:14), could sympathize with human weakness, having been tempted in every way like we are (4:15), and "in the days of His flesh" offered up prayers and petitions with loud crying and tears (5:7), as He "learned obedience from the things which He suffered" (5:8).

But the Christ of Hebrews is indisputably divine as well. While the usual New Testament designations of Christ may be found scattered throughout the letter—the simple "Jesus" (2:9; 3:1; 6:20; 7:22; 10:19; 12:2, 24; 13:12), "[the] Christ" (3:6, 14; 5:5; 6:1; 9:11, 14, 24, 28; 11:26), "Jesus Christ" (10:10; 13:8, 21), "[the] Lord" (1:10; 2:3; 7:14; perhaps 12:14; the first two occurrences of which clearly intended in the Yahwistic sense), "Lord Jesus" (13:20), "Jesus, the Son of God" (4:14)—the writer's favorite title for Jesus, above all others is "[the] Son" (1:2, 5 [twice], 8; 3:6; 5:5, 8; 7:28) or its fuller form "[the] Son of God" (4:14; 6:6; 7:3; 10:29). Indeed, it is as God's Son in the preeminent (divine) sense of that title that the writer first introduces Jesus to his readers (1:2).

remark suggests that in Origen's opinion the letter was Pauline—in content if not by the actual pen of Paul. He writes, "If I gave my opinion, I should say that the thoughts are those of the apostle. . . . Therefore, if any church holds that this Epistle is by Paul, let it be commended for this. For not without reason have the ancients handed it down as Paul's" (cited by Eusebius, *Historia Ecclesiastica*, vi, 25, 14).

In my opinion, far too much weight has been given to the statement in 2:3 ("so great salvation, which having first been spoken by the Lord, was confirmed to us by the ones who heard") as being "the most significant point" (Simon J. Kistemaker, *Exposition of the Epistle to the Hebrews* [Grand Rapids: Baker, 1984], p. 7) *against* Pauline authorship. The statement, by this construction, supposedly teaches that the author was a "second-generation" Christian who had heard the gospel from the apostles and was converted as a result of their preaching, thus precluding Paul as the author because he claims in Gal. 1:12 that he received the gospel directly from Christ (cf. Acts. 9:1-9). But Heb. 2:3 does not say what this construction implies that it says. It does not say that the author had first heard the gospel from the apostles and was converted thereby. Rather, it says that the apostles *confirmed* the message of salvation to him, implying thereby that the author was already in possession of it at the time of the act of confirmation, which the apostles could have done for Paul on his second visit to Jerusalem, about which he speaks in Gal. 2:1-10. The actions of the apostles, as described by Paul in Gal. 2, have the appearance of being a "confirming activity." Furthermore, the author's reference to "our brother Timothy" (13:23) surely has a "Pauline ring" about it (cf. 1 Thess. 3:2; 2 Cor. 1:1; Col. 1:1; Philem. 1).

As for its style and grammar (I have translated the entire letter myself) and its doctrinal content, I grant that these matters are different in some ways from Paul's other letters to specific churches and individuals, but its recipients, its very subject matter, and its purpose would have had much to do with determining the style and vocabulary of the letter. There is noting in the content of the letter that Paul could not have written. And it is difficult to comprehend on what other basis the letter would hae been received by the early church as canonical if it had not been recognized as written by an apostle or by some known person standing in direct proximity to the apostolic circle. I recommend that the reader consult R. Laird (*Inspiration and Canonicity of the Bible* [Grand Rapids: Zondervan, 1957], pp. 263-70), who surveys neatly the patristic evidence and concludes that Hebrews is "a genuine Epistle of Paul using Barnabas as his secretary" (ibid., p. 269), though he concedes that another person may well have served Paul as an amanuensis.

As God's "Son" He is the highest and final form of revelation to men, and as God's "Son" He is higher than the greatest representatives of God on earth, that is, the prophets of the Old Testament (1:1-2), higher even than Moses who in comparison was only a servant in God's house (3:5-6). Finally, His name as "Son," whose bearer is (1) the heir of all things, (2) God's cooperating agent in the creation of the world, (3) the radiance of God's glory, (4) the very image of His nature, (5) the sustainer of all things, (6) the purifier from sin, and (7) the Lord (of Ps. 110:1) sitting at the right hand of the majesty on high (1:2-3), is "more excellent" even than that of the highest of creatures, that of "angel" (1:4), whose bearers are only "ministering spirits" (1:14), and whose duty it is to worship Him (1:6).

As explications of the content of that superangelic "more excellent name" of "Son," and *not* simply new names adduced in addition to that of "Son," He is the "God" (θεός) of Psalm 45:6-7 and "the Lord" (κύριος), that is, the Yahweh, of Psalm 102:25-27.[33]

When he wrote, "To the Son, on the other hand, [God says], 'Your throne, O God, will last for ever and ever' " (1:8), the writer of Hebrews became the fourth person in the New Testament to use θεός as a christological title. The controversy surrounding this verse is over whether ὁ θεός is to be construed as a nominative (if so, it may be a subject nominative—"God is your throne for ever and ever"—or a predicate nominative—"Your throne is God for ever and ever") or a vocative, which would yield the translation given above. With the "overwhelming majority of grammarians, commentators, authors of general studies, and English translations,"[34] I believe that the writer applies Psalm 45:6 to Jesus in such a way that He is addressed directly as God in the ontological sense. This position requires (1) that ὁ θεός be interpreted as a vocative and (2) that the theotic character ascribed to Jesus be understood in ontological and not functional terms.

That ὁ θεός is vocatival is apparent for the following reasons: *First,* the fact that the noun appears to be nominative in its inflected form means nothing. The so-called articular nominative with vocative force, as we had occasion to note in connection with our exposition of John 20:28, is a well-established idiom in classical Greek, the Septuagint, and New Testament Greek. The case of the noun in Hebrews 1:8 must be established then on other grounds

---

33. B. B. Warfield, "The Divine Messiah in the Old Testament," *Biblical and Theological Studies* (Philadelphia: Presbyterian and Reformed, 1952), p. 81).

34. Cf. Murray J. Harris, "The Translation and Significance of ὁ θεός in Hebrews 1:8-9," *Tyndale Bulletin* 36 (1985): 146-48; cf. nn. 56, 57, 58, 59. To the sources Harris cites should be added his own definitive article and the one that appeared antecedent to it: "The Translation of אלהים in Psalm 45:7-8," *Tyndale Bulletin* 35 (1984): 65-89.

than its case form. *Second*, the word order in Hebrews 1:8 most naturally suggests that ὁ θεός is vocatival. A vocative immediately after "Your throne" would be perfectly natural. But if ὁ θεός were intended as the subject nominative ("God is your throne"), which Turner regards as a "grotesque interpretation,"[35] it is more likely that ὁ θεός would have appeared before "your throne." If it were intended as a predicate nominative ("Your throne is God"), which Turner regards as "only just conceivable,"[36] it is more likely that ὁ θεός would have been written anarthrously, appearing either before "your throne" or after "for ever and ever." *Third*, in the Septuagint of Psalm 45, which the writer is citing, the king is addressed by the vocative δύνατε ("O Mighty One") in 45:4 and 45:6. This dual vocative heightens the probability, given the word order, that in the next verse ὁ θεός should be rendered "O God."[37] *Fourth*, although "about" or "concerning" is probably the more accurate translation of the preposition πρὸς in Hebrews 1:7 (given the cast of the following quotation), it is more likely that πρὸς introducing the quotation in verse 8 should be translated "to" in light of the second-person character of the quotation itself and on the analogy of the formula (a verb of speaking followed by πρός) in Hebrews 1:13; 5:5; and 7:21. This suggests that ὁ θεός is vocatival. *Fifth*, the following quotation in Hebrews 1:10-12 (from Ps. 102:25-27) is connected by the simple καί to the quotation under discussion in verses 8-9, indicating that it too stands under the regimen of the words introducing verses 8-9. In the latter verses the Son is clearly addressed as κύριε ("O Lord"). These five textual and syntactical features clearly indicate that ὁ θεός should be construed vocatively, meaning that the Son is addressed as "God."

But what is meant by this address? Opinions run the gamut from Vincent Taylor's question-begging comment that "nothing can be built upon this reference, for the author shares the same reluctance of the [other] New Testament writers to speak explicitly of Christ as 'God,' "[38] to Oscar Cullmann's comment that "the psalm is quoted here precisely for the sake of this address,"[39] the chapter in which it occurs leading him to declare that "Jesus' deity is more powerfully asserted in Hebrews than in any other New

35. Nigel Turner, *Grammatical Insights Into the New Testament* (Edinburgh: T. & T. Clark, 1965), p. 461.

36. Nigel Turner, *A Grammar of New Testament Greek* (Edinburgh: T. & T. Clark, 1963), 3:34.

37. Harris, "Translation and Significance of ὁ θεός," p. 142.

38. Vincent Taylor, *The Person of Christ in New Testament Teaching* (London: Macmillan, 1959), p. 96. Raymond E. Brown's comment is quite to the point: "We cannot suppose that the author did not notice that his citation had this effect" of addressing the Son as God ("Does the New Testament Call Jesus God?" *Theological Studies* 26, no. 4 [1965]. 563).

39. Oscar Cullmann, *The Christology of the New Testament* (London: SCM Press, 1980), p. 310.

Testament writing, with the exception of the Gospel of John."[40] What should we conclude? I urge from the context of Hebrews 1 itself that the Son is addressed as God in the ontological sense. As a "Son-revelation," as the final and supreme speech of God to man (v. 2), He is the heir of all things and the Father's agent in creating the universe. He abides as (cf. the timeless ὤν in v. 3) the "perfect Radiance of God's glory" and the "very Image of His nature" (v. 3). As God's Son, He is superior to the angels, such that it is appropriate that they be commanded to worship Him (v. 6). He is the Yahweh and the Elohim of Psalm 102, who eternally existed before He created the heavens and earth (v. 10) and who remains eternally the same though the creation itself should perish (vv. 11-12; cf. Heb. 13:8). It is really adding nothing to what the writer has said to understand him in 1:8 as describing the Son as God in the ontological sense.

E. C. Wickham and others have suggested that if ὁ θεός is really ascribing ontological deity to the Son, the climax of the writer's argument would have come at verse 8 since nothing higher could be said about Him. But, they urge, since in fact the writer goes on in verse 10 to describe the Son as κύριος, this further development of the Son's character becomes the climax, indicating that the former description cannot be construed ontologically. But this objection fails to apprehend the significance of the two terms. While θεός is indeed a term of exalted significance when used titularly of the true God, it speaks only of His divine essence. It is κύριος, coming to us out of the Old Testament citation here, that is God's personal name. In the covenantal sense, it is the more sacred of the two! So actually, the writer's argument, even though it ascribes ontological deity to the Son in 1:8, does not reach its climax until it ascribes the character of Yahweh Himself to the Son, indicating by this ascriptive title that the Son is not only the Creator but the covenant God as well. The writer truly can say nothing higher than this.

Two of the descriptive phrases above deserve further comment. In addi-

40. Ibid., p. 305. I must register a caveat here. Cullmann, of course, must say these things if he is to be exegetically honest. But one must not forget that Cullmann is a "functional christologist." He writes, "We must agree with Melanchthon when he insists that the knowledge of Christ is to be understood only as a knowledge of his work in redemptive history. . . . All speculation concerning his natures is . . . un-Biblical as soon as it ceases to take place in the light of the great historical deeds of redemption" (*Christ and Time*, trans. Floyd V. Filson [Philadelphia: Westminster Press, 1950], p. 128). He says again, "We come to the conclusion that in the few New Testament passages in which Jesus receives the title 'God,' this occurs on the one hand in connection with his exaltation to lordship . . . and on the other hand in connection with the idea that he is himself the divine revelation" (*Christology of the New Testament*, p. 325); and again, "Therefore, in the light of the New Testament, all mere speculation about his natures is an absurdity. Functional Christology is the only kind that exists" (ibid., 326). In other words, after all is said and done, in spite of his splendid exegetical work in Chapter 11 on "the designation of Jesus as 'God,' " for Cullmann Jesus is not God in Himself but only God in self-revelation or *Heilsgeschichte* ("holy-" or "salvation-history").

tion to ascribing to Him the divine work in eternity of creating the world, and the divine work in time of sustaining the universe, the writer describes the Son as "the Radiance [ἀπαύγασμα] of God's glory [δόξα]" and "the very Image [χαρακτήρ] of His nature [ὑπόστασις]." In the former expression, with God's δόξα denoting His nature under the imagery of its splendor, as His ἀπαύγασμα (from ἀπαυγάσειν, "to emit brightness"), one has to do in Jesus with thè personal "outshining" of God's divine glory as "the radiance shining forth from its source of light."[41] In the latter expression, with God's ὑπόστασις denoting His "whole nature, with all its attributes" (Warfield), His "real essence" (F. F. Bruce), or His "very essence" (P. E. Hughes), as His χαρακτήρ (from χαράσσειν, "to engrave, to inscribe, to stamp"), one has to do in Jesus with God's "very image" by which is meant "a correspondence as close as that which an impression gives back to a seal" (Warfield), His "exact representation and embodiment" (Bruce), or the "very stamp" (Hughes) of God. Clearly, such exalted descriptions intend the ascription of divine status to the Son. Accordingly, it is altogether likely inasmuch as the Son is the Yahweh of Psalm 102:25-27 who remains forever the same (1:11-12) and who in the person of Jesus Christ is "the same yesterday, today, and forever" (13:8), that He is the subject of the doxology in 13:21, to whom eternal glory is ascribed. Certainly, the collocation of the relative pronoun and the title "Jesus Christ" in 13:21 favors such an interpretation.

But whatever the case may be with regard to the rather minor matter of the subject of the concluding doxology of the letter, there can be no doubt in view of the content of his first chapter that for the writer of Hebrews all that God is as God, so Jesus is, as the Son, from, to, and throughout eternity.

This conclusion has not gone unchallenged. J. A. T. Robinson, for example, has urged that all of these exalted descriptions are true of Jesus as "God's Man," with only His functional relationship to God as God's "son" being "decisively different" from the relationship that obtains between God and other men.[42] He adduces in support of his view (1) the supposed derivation of the descriptions of 1:3 from Philo and Wisdom 7:26 and (2) what he terms "adoptionist" terminology in 1:2, 4, 9, 13; 2:9, 10, 12f., 16; 3:2f.; 5:1-6, 8, 10; 7:28.[43] James D. G. Dunn also insists (1) that "there is more 'adoptionist' language in Hebrews than in any other NT document,"[44] and (2) that "the element of Hebrews' christology which we think of as ascribing

---

41. Bruce, *Commentary on the Epistle to the Hebrews*, p. 5.
42. John A. T. Robinson, *The Human Face of God* (London: SCM Press, 1973), p. 156.
43. Ibid., p. 156-61.
44. James D. G. Dunn, *Christology in the Making: A New Testament Inquiry Into the Origins of the Doctrine of the Incarnation* (London: SCM Press, 1980), p. 52.

pre-existence to the Son of God has to be set within the context of his indebtedness to Platonic idealism and interpreted with cross-reference to the way in which Philo treats the Logos," that is to say, "what we may have to accept is that the author of Hebrews ultimately has in mind an *ideal* pre-existence [of the Son], the existence of an idea [of the Son] in the mind of God,"[45] and this within a strict monotheism in which the concept of pre-existent sonship is "perhaps more of an idea and purpose in the mind of God than of a personal divine being."[46] In sum, for Dunn, the Christology of Hebrews views Jesus in terms of Wisdom language, so that "the thought of pre-existence is present, but in terms of Wisdom Christology it is the act and power of God which properly speaking is what pre-exists; Christ is not so much the pre-existent act and power of God as its eschatological embodiment."[47]

I concur with I. Howard Marshall's assessment that this impersonal construction of the writer's doctrine of divine sonship is "very alien to the biblical understanding of God as personal, quite apart from imposing a very artificial interpretation upon the biblical text."[48] For while it is true that the Son "was *appointed*" heir of all things (1:2) and "sat down on the right hand of the Majesty on high, *having become* by so much better than the angels, as He has *inherited* a more excellent name than they" (1:4), this need not be "adoptionist" language, but rather, language that envisions the glory that became His upon the conclusion of His humiliation in His role as Messiah and Mediator (cf. Heb. 2:9; Ps. 2:8). Hughes concurs that this is how the so-called "adoptionist" language should be construed, writing on 1:4:

> It is true, of course, that by virtue of his eternal Sonship he has an eternal inheritance and possesses a name which is eternally supreme— *the name* signifying, particularly for the Hebrew mind, the essential character of a person in himself and in his work. But our author at this point is speaking of something other than this: the Son who for our redemption humbled himself for a little while to a position lower than the angels has by his ensuing exaltation *become* superior to the angels (2:9 below), and in doing so has achieved and retains the inheritance of a name which is *more excellent than theirs*.[49]

And if He is said to have "inherited" the name of "Son," as Bruce declares,

45. Ibid., p. 54.
46. Ibid., p. 56.
47. Ibid., p. 209.
48. I. Howard Marshall, in *Christ the Lord*, p. 11 n. 25.
49. Hughes, *Commentary on the Epistle to the Hebrews*, p. 50.

this does not mean that the name was not His before His exaltation. It was clearly His in the days of His humiliation: "Son though He was, He learned obedience by the things which He suffered" (Ch. 5:8). It was His, indeed, ages before His incarnation: this is the plain indication of the statement in Ch. 1:2 that God has spoken to us "in his Son, . . . through whom also he made the worlds."[50]

All of the so-called "adoptionist" language of Robinson and Dunn can be similarly explained; none of it requires that the Son's personal preexistence has to be forfeited in deference to an ideal, impersonal preexistence in the mind of God. And even if the writer's language is that of Philo and the Book of Wisdom, again as Bruce affirms,

> his meaning goes beyond theirs. For them the Logos or Wisdom is the personification of a divine attribute; for him the language is descriptive of a man who had lived and died in Palestine a few decades previously, but who nonetheless was the eternal Son and supreme revelation of God.[51]

Viewed, then, from the Scriptural perspective of the *humiliatio-exaltatio* paradigm, as they rightly should be, the supposed "adoptionist" passages in Hebrews are not "adoptionist" at all. The full unabridged deity of the Son is secure and intact throughout the letter to the Hebrews.

John's Witness to Jesus

Sometime during the last four decades of the first century (it is impossible to be more specific), John the apostle[52] wrote his Gospel, the three letters that bear his name, and finally the Revelation.[53] The Christology found in

---

50. Bruce, *Commentary on the Epistle to the Hebrews*, p. 8.

51. Ibid., p. 5. Citing the opinion of E. Lohmeyer as a correct one, M. Hengel declares that "the divine nature of the 'Son' in Hebrews is . . . established from the beginning. The approach . . . is the same as in the hymn [Phil. 2:6-11] which Paul quotes; the difference is that [in Hebrews] it is made more precise in terms of the metaphysical substantiality of Christ" (*The Son of God* [Philadelphia: Fortress Press, 1976], p. 87).

52. I am assuming that the apostle John rather than Papius' "John the Elder" or someone else was, both in substance and (in the main) literary composition, the author of the Gospel and the Johannine letters. For a full discussion of the question of authorship, cf. Donald Guthrie, *New Testament Introduction*, pp. 241-71, 864-69. Cf. also B. F. Westcott, *The Gospel According to St. John*, vol. 1 (London: John Murray, 1908), pp. ix-lxvii, and Leon Morris, *The Gospel According to John* (Grand Rapids: Eerdmans, 1971), pp. 8-30.

53. Cf. Guthrie (*New Testament Introduction*, pp. 282-87, 883-84, 894, 898, and 949-61) for discussions of the respective dates of each. Leon Morris (*Gospel According to John*, pp. 30-35) suggests a date before A.D. 70 for John's Gospel, a view shared by J. A. T. Robinson (*Redating the*

the Johannine corpus is as explicitly incarnational as is humanly conceivable, a fact even the most radical critics recognize.

The Christology of John's Gospel

We considered in Chapter 4 the John 20:28 occurrence of θεός as a christological title in Thomas's great confession. But precisely because this title occurred in John's reported confession of someone else and was not an affirmation on John's own part, though it would be sheer wrong-headedness to argue so, someone might still insist that Thomas's confession of Christ as θεός does not necessarily reflect John's christological thinking. We are not shut up, however, to this single occurrence of θεός as a christological title in John's Gospel. The title occurs also in John 1:1 and 1:18. These two verses now warrant our closest attention.

John 1:1. The apostle John begins his Gospel with a powerful statement concerning the Logos (ὁ λόγος)—a term, according to his usage, meaning "[the independent, personified] Word [or Wisdom] [of God]."[54] He deliberately repeats the term three times in verse 1 to refer to the Son of God—against the background of the first-century forms of pre-Gnostic and Stoic theology—in order to warn his readers against all of the then-current false forms of the Logos doctrine. Translated literally, verse 1 reads:

> In the beginning was the Word,
> and the Word was with God,
> and God was the Word.

The term occurs in each clause, each time in the nominative case (subjective nominative), and three times ἦν, the imperfect of εἰμί, occurs, "expressive in each case of continuous timeless existence."[55]

In the *first clause*, the phrase "In the beginning," as all commentators observe, is reminiscent of the same phrase in Genesis 1:1. John is saying that "in the beginning," at the time of the creating of the universe, the Word

---

New Testament [London: SCM Press, 1976], pp. 254-84), who places the Johannine letters (as well as the Revelation) also in the general time frame of the seventh decade of the first century. Precise dating of the Johannine corpus is extremely difficult, if not impossible, with the knowledge presently available to us. Suffice it to say, however, that nothing requires that any of the Johannine literature be dated after A.D. 100. All of it can be placed well within the first century A.D.

54. W. F. Arndt and F. W. Gingrich, *A Greek-English Lexicon of the New Testament* (Chicago: University of Chicago Press, 1957), p. 480.

55. J. H. Bernard, *A Critical and Exegetical Commentary on the Gospel According to St. John,* International Critical Commentary (Edinburgh: T. & T. Clark, 1928), 1:2.

"[continuously] was" (not "came to be") already. This is clear not only from the imperfect tense of the verb but also from John's declaring that the Word was in the beginning with God and that "all things were made by Him, and without Him nothing was made which has been made" (v. 3). In short, the Word's preexistent *being* is antecedently set off over against the *becoming* of all created things.

In the *second clause*, the Word is both coordinated *with* God and distinguished in some sense *from* God as possessing an identity of its own. The sense in which the Word is distinguishable from God may be discerned by comparing the phrase in 1:1, ἦν πρὸς τὸν θεόν, with its counterpart in 1 John 1:2 where we read that "the Word," which was "from the beginning" (v. 1), "was with the Father" (ἦν πρὸς τὸν πατέρα). This shows that the "God" in John 1:1b is God the Father. The Word that stands coordinate with and yet distinguishable from God as *Father* is by implication then the preexistent Son, which means that John is thinking of the Word in personal terms. This thought is reminiscent of Hebrews 1:8-9 where, as we have seen, the Son is both identified as Himself God and distinguished from God the Father.

In the *third clause*, John now asserts the obvious: "The Word was God" (KJV, RV, ASV, RSV, NASB, NIV, NKJV). That ὁ λόγος is the subject and θεὸς the predicate nominative is evident from the fact that the former is arthrous while the latter is anarthrous. But the fact that θεός is anarthrous does not mean that it should be construed qualitatively, that is, adjectively ("divine," as Moffatt's translation suggests) or indefinitely ("a god," as the silly schoolboy translation of the Jehovah's Witnesses' *New World Translation* suggests). No standard Greek lexicon offers "divine" as one of the meanings of θεός, nor does the noun become an adjective when it "sheds" its article. If John had intended an adjectival sense, he had an adjective (θεῖος) ready at hand. That the anarthrous noun does not connote indefiniteness as the Jehovah's Witnesses contend is evident from the recurring instances of the anarthrous θεός throughout the Johannine Prologue itself (vv. 6, 12, 13, 18) where in each case it is definite and its referent is God the Father.

That θεός is definite in meaning is suggested by its position in the clause before the copula ἦν, in accordance with E. C. Colwell's observation.[56] But that John wrote θεός anarthrously is due most likely to his desire to keep the Word hypostatically distinct from the Father to whom he had just referred by τὸν θεόν. If John had followed 1:1b by saying, "and ὁ θεός was the Word" or "and the Word was ὁ θεός," he would have implied a retreat from, if not a

---

56. Cf. E. C. Colwell, "A Definite Rule for the Use of the Article in the Greek New Testament," *Journal of Biblical Literature* 52 (1933): 12-21.

contradiction of, the clear distinction he had just drawn in 1:1b, and thus fallen into the error later known as Sabellianism.

Here then John identifies the Word as God (*totus deus*) and by so doing attributes to Him the nature or essence of deity. When John further says in 1:2 that "this One [οὗτος; the One whom he had just designated "God"] was in the beginning with God," and in 1:3 that "through Him all things were created," the only legitimate conclusion is that as God His deity is as ultimate as His distinctiveness as Son, while His distinctiveness as Son is as ultimate as His deity as God.

When John then declares that the Word, whom he had just described as eternally preexistent, uncreated, personal Son and God, "became flesh," he not only goes beyond anything in the first-century pre-Gnostic theology but also ascends to the high ground of incarnational Christology. I. Howard Marshall has observed:

> The prologue of the Gospel comes to a climax in the statement that the Word who had been from the beginning with God and was active in the work of creation and was the light and life of men became flesh and dwelt among us. It is noteworthy that the subject of the passage is the Word or Logos. It is the career of the Logos which is being described, and not until verse 17 is the name Jesus Christ used for the first time, thereby identifying the Word who became flesh with the historical figure of that name. From that time onwards John ceases to use the term Logos and writes about Jesus, using his name and a variety of Jewish messianic titles to refer to him. . . .
>
> For John, then, Jesus is undoubtedly the personal Word of God now adopting a fleshly form of existence. When we talk of incarnation, this is what is meant by it, for it is here that the New Testament offers the closest linguistic equivalent to the term "incarnation": *ho logos sarx egeneto*.[57]

John 1:18. In this verse we face a problem we have not faced before in our appraisal of those verses in which Jesus is either described or addressed as θεός. Here any conclusions we reach must be made on the basis of determining the original reading in the Greek text. Did the original text of John 1:18 read (1) ὁ μονογενής,[58] (2) ὁ μονογενὴς υἱός, (3) μονογενὴς θεός, or (4) ὁ μονογενὴς θεός?

---

57. I. Howard Marshall, in *Christ the Lord*, pp. 2-3.

58. That μονογενής does not mean "only begotten," alluding to some form of generation or to the virginal conception of Jesus, but rather "one and only," "only one of [his] kind," or "unique," enjoys wide consensus today. Warfield writes, 'The adjective 'only begotten' conveys the idea,

The first reading, although it has brevity in its favor, may be dismissed because it has no Greek manuscript support whatsoever. The second reading has in its favor the support of the Greek uncials A, the third corrector of C, K, a later supplement to W, X, Δ, Θ, 063, and many late minuscule manuscripts from the "Byzantine" tradition. It is also found in the Old Latin, the Latin Vulgate, the Curetonian Syriac, the text of the Harclean Syriac, and the Armenian version. It is also found in about twenty church Fathers. In addition, it has in its favor the fact that, apart from John 1:14 where it stands alone, in the other three places where μονογενής occurs in the Johannine literature, it appears in a construction with υἱός (John 3:16, 18; 1 John 4:9). But this reading has three strikes against it. First, on the basis of the text-critical canon that "manuscripts are to be weighed, not counted," the textual support for this reading, in comparison with the two remaining readings, is not impressive, being found mainly in inferior and late manuscripts. Second, the fact that it is found in some significant church Fathers is not a substantive argument in its favor, inasmuch as the Ante-Nicene Fathers tended to "follow the analogy of the versions," υἱός being "one of the numerous Ante-Nicene readings of the 'Western type' . . . [which fail to] approve themselves as original in comparison with the alternative readings."[59] Third, while it can be readily understood, if θεός were the original reading, how υἱός could have arisen, namely, through the scribal tendency to conform a strange reading to a more common one (in this case, to the formula in John 3:16, 18; and 1 John 4:9), it is difficult to explain, if υἱός were the original reading, why a scribe would have changed it to θεός.

The two remaining readings, both supporting an original θεός, differ only in that the former omits the article while the latter retains it before μονογενής. The manuscript support for the former is Bodmer Papyrus 66, the original hand of ℵ, B, the original hand of C, and L, plus the Syriac Peshitta, the

not of derivation and subordination, but of uniqueness and consubstantiality: Jesus is all that God is" (*Biblical Doctrines* [New York: Oxford University Press], p. 194). Cf. Dale Moody, "God's Only Son: The Translation of John 3:16 in the Revised Standard Version," *Journal of Biblical Literature* 72 (1953): 213-19, and Karl-Heinz Bartel, μονογενής, in *The New International Dictionary of New Testament Theology*, vol. 2, ed. Colin Brown (Grand Rapids: Zondervan, 1976), p. 725. Cf. also Arndt and Gingrich, *A Greek-English Lexicon of the New Testament*, p. 529.

59. F. J. A. Hort, *Two Dissertations* (Cambridge: Macmillan, 1876), pp. 7-8. Hort's dissertation laid the groundwork for virtually all subsequent text-critical work on John 1:18, and provided the single greatest impulse toward the conclusion that θεός is the original reading. What is most telling as an indication of his careful scholarship is that Hort did his work without the advantage of having the two great Bodmer Papyri 66 and 75, the later discovery of which vindicated his conclusion. Metzger writes, "With the acquisition of P66 and 75, both of which read θεός, the external support of this reading has been notably stengthened" (*Textual Commentary on the Greek New Testament*, p. 198). Cf. J. Finnegan (*Encountering New Testament Manuscripts* [London: SPCK, 1975], pp. 111-77 [summarized pp. 174-77]) for a textual history of John 1:18.

marginal reading of the Harclean Syriac, the Roman Ethiopic, the Diatesseron, and about seventeen church Fathers, including the heretical Valentinians and Arius. The manuscript evidence for the latter is Bodmer Papyrus 75, the third hand of ℵ, the Greek minuscule 33 (the best of the cursives), and the Coptic Bohairic. Of these two, the former has the better manuscript support. But the *combined* weight of both, speaking purely from the perspective of manuscript support, lends exceedingly strong support for the originality of θεός in John 1:18. Also in its favor is that it is the harder reading (the *lectio difficilior*). The reputable textual critic must admit that the evidence points rather decisively in favor of an original θεός. Of course, because the nature of the problem calls for a judgment of evidence, the final decision will always have an element of uncertainty about it, but the evidence is so weighty in one direction that it puts θεός as the original reading beyond reasonable doubt. Indeed, if it were not for the christological implications in the reading itself ("[the] only [Son], [Himself] God"), one suspects that such combined manuscript support and the fact that it is the harder reading would be sufficient under less doctrinally pregnant circumstances to carry the field of scholarly opinion. Even so, there is a trend in modern translations to adopt θεός as the original reading (NASB, NIV). Therefore, I suggest that John 1:18 be translated as follows:

> God no man has seen at any time;
> The only [Son], [Himself] God, who is [continually][60] in the bosom of
> the Father—
> That One revealed Him.

Here then in John 1:1 and (quite probably) in 1:18 we have two more uses of θεός as a christological title, the contexts of which place beyond question that John regards Jesus as God the Son incarnate.

We consulted John's Gospel earlier when we were considering Jesus' self-understanding borne to us particularly in His "Son of God" sayings (cf., for example, 5:17-26; 10:30, 36), His "Son of Man" sayings (cf., for example, 3:13; 6:62), and His "I am" sayings (cf., for example, 8:24, 58).

And we sought its counsel also in Chapter 3 when we were amassing the preresurrection corroborative evidence in support of His deity in, for example, His recorded "works" and His disciples' testimonies respecting Him (cf., for example, 1:34, 49; 6:69; 11:27; 16:30).

---

60. Warfield underscores the truth, on the basis of ὤν, the present participle, in 1:18, that the divine state of the Logos "is not one which has been left behind at the incarnation, but one which continues uninterrupted and unmodified" (*The Person and Work of Christ* [Philadelphia: Presbyterian and Reformed, 1950], pp. 55-56).

Since John incorporated these data in his Gospel, we may assume that they reflect his Christology as well, for he expressly declares that he wrote what he did in order to bring his readers to faith in Jesus as "the Christ, the Son of God" (20:31). Surely, for example, the high incarnational Christology in his Prologue reflects his personal Christology as well. But three other features in John's Gospel that we have not yet treated in any direct way afford still further insight into his personal Christology.

I refer, *first*, to the two paragraphs in 3:16-21 and 3:31-36 which may be in their contexts continuing remarks by Jesus and by John the Baptist respectively (the NIV seems to construe them as such), but which may also, in fact, be reflections by John the Evangelist himself on the themes touched upon by Jesus and the Baptist.[61] If the latter case is the correct reading of the matter, we have in both instances discourses by John upon the transcendent nature and origin of Jesus. In 3:16-21, he speaks of Jesus as God's "unique Son" (ὁ υἱὸς μονογενής) (3:16, 18), whom God "sent into the world" (3:17), who Himself, as the Light, "has come into the world" (3:19), and through faith in whom eternal life is mediated (3:16, 18). In 3:31-36, the same themes are advanced: Jesus is God's Son, whom God "sent" (3:34), and who may be thus characterized as Himself "the One who comes from above" (3:31a) and "the One who comes from heaven" (3:31b). What Jesus declares is what He Himself has seen and heard in heaven (3:32). He is "over all" (3:31) in that His Father "has given all things into His hand" (3:35), including the Spirit without limit (3:34). And, as in the former paragraph, the destiny of men turns upon their relation to Him (3:36). These features—"the descent of Christ from the supernal world, the experiential character of His knowledge of the things of heaven, His identification with God, so that to hear Him is to seal the veracity of God, His all-comprehensive authority in the sphere of revelation, the function of faith [in Him] as mediating eternal life . . . whilst unbelief with reference to Him results in exclusion from life and permanent abiding under the wrath of God"[62]—these features, I say, as a piece of John's Christology all serve to underscore both the preexistence and the absolutely transcendent character of the One who occupies center stage throughout his Gospel.

I highlight, *second*, John's citation of Isaiah 6:10 in 12:40, which brings out the divine sovereignty in salvation and reprobation. Concerning this cita-

---

61. Morris (*Gospel According to John*, pp. 228, 242) regards both pericopes as Johannine reflections. While Vos comments only on the latter passage, he too suggsts that the evidence, when all of it is taken into account, "slightly favors attribution of the words to the Evangelist" (*Biblical Theology* [Grand Rapids: Eerdmans, 1948], p. 352). So also Westcott, Lagrange, and Lightfoot.

62. Vos, *Biblical Theology*, pp. 352-53.

tion John declares, "These things Isaiah said because he saw His [the preincarnate Son's] glory, and spoke concerning Him"; one must conclude that the transcendent character of Jesus Christ is just the transcendence of Yahweh Himself, for it was "Yahweh, seated on a throne, high and exalted" (Isa. 6:1; cf. 57:15) whom Isaiah reports that he saw in vision when he spoke these words. Morris quite properly remarks:

> John sees in the words of the prophet primarily a reference to the glory of Christ. Isaiah spoke these things "because he saw his glory". The words of Isaiah 6:3 refer to the glory of Yahweh, but John puts no hard and fast distinction between the two. To him it is plain that Isaiah had in mind the glory revealed in Christ.[63]

This being so, it should not go unnoticed that it was the preincarnate Christ who commissioned and sent Isaiah on his prophetic mission, which Jesus Himself noted in Matthew 23:34 (cf. Luke 11:49) and which Peter alludes to in 1 Peter 1:11.

I point out, *third*, that since for John the glory of Christ is equivalent to the glory of Yahweh Himself, it is highly probable that, when John refers to Christ as "the Lord" (ὁ κύριος) in his Gospel narrative (cf. 4:1; 6:23; 11:2; 20:20; 21:12), he intends the title, used as it is in the Septuagint to translate the divine name Yahweh, in its most eminent, that is to say, in its divine, Yahwistic sense.[64]

There can be no doubt that John's Christology is incarnational in the highest conceivable sense, Jesus Christ being true God and true man. No view of John's Christology that claims otherwise is exegetically respectable.

The Christology of 1 and 2 John

The *Sitz im Leben* behind these two letters seems to be a situation in which certain teachers (precursors or followers of Cerinthus?) were denying the possibility of a real incarnation, quite possibly insisting rather that Jesus began His earthly life as a mere man and that "the Christ" or "the Son of God," a higher divine power or emanation, came upon Him at His baptism

---

63. Morris, *Gospel According to John*, p. 605.

64. I remind the reader once again of Cullmann's trenchant insight: "If . . . the whole Gospel culminates in [Thomas's] confession, and, on the other hand, the author writes in the first verse of the first chapter, 'And the Logos *was* God,' then there can be no doubt that for him all the other titles for Jesus which are prominent in his work ('Son of Man,' 'Son of God,' 'Lord,' and in the prologue, 'Logos') ultimately point toward this final expression of his Christological faith" (*Christology of the New Testament*, p. 308).

and departed from Him just prior to His crucifixion. It is likely that this is the view John was combating in 1 John 5:6 when he wrote that Jesus Christ, the Son of God, is "the One who came through water [that is, the event of baptism] and blood [that is, the event of crucifixion]." Alexander, with admirable clarity, explains:

> The Greek [aorist participle, ἐλθὼν, meaning "came"] makes the "coming" refer to a definite historical event, [showing that] *came by water and blood* must refer to specific events in Christ's Incarnate experience. . . . This is not quite all. John adds: *not by water only, but by water and blood.* Great weight is thus thrown on the words *and blood.* Some must have been saying that Jesus Christ *did* come by water but not by *blood*. What heresy is this? Probably Cerinthianism. Cerinthus taught as follows. At the baptism the Divine Christ came into the man Jesus. Jesus, allied now to the Divine Christ, brought news of the hitherto unknown God and lived and ministered in perfect virtue. Just before the Crucifixion the Christ left Jesus and returned to glory. The man Jesus was crucified and resurrected. This view accepted Christ's coming "by water"; it denied (since for no Gnostic could the Divine suffer) Christ's coming "by blood," the blood of the Cross. John's seceding teachers seem to have been tarred with this Cerinthian brush.[65]

Accordingly, to combat this specific form of docetic or adoptionist Christology John wrote his letters.

It will be immediately evident from even a cursory reading of these letters that "the same concept of incarnation as in the Gospel is present in 1 and 2 John, and indeed it is the principal Christological idea in these Epistles."[66] This is plain from the fact that John defends (1) the dual confession that Jesus is both the Christ (1 John 2:22; 5:1) and the Son of God (1 John 2:22-23; 4:15; 5:5; cf. 1:3, 7; 2:24; 3:8, 23; 4:9, 14; 5:9, 11, 12, 13, 20), and (2) the incarnational prerequisite that God the Father "sent" His Son into the world (1 John 4:9, 10, 14), and that, having been "sent," the Son was "sent" in such a way that He "came in the flesh" (1 John 4:2; 2 John 7; cf. 1 John 5:6, 20) and thus was "manifested" to men (1 John 1:2 [twice]; 3:8) in such a way that, while still "the Eternal Life, which was with the Father" from the beginning (1 John 1:1-2), He could be heard, seen with the human eye, gazed upon, and touched by human hands. So intense is John's conviction as to the necessity

---

65. Neil Alexander, *The Epistles of John: Introduction and Commentary* (London: SCM Press, 1962), pp. 118-19; cf. F. F. Bruce, *The Epistles of John: Introduction, Exposition and Notes* (London: Pickering and Inglis, 1970), pp. 118-19; cf. also I. Howard Marshall, "Incarnational Christology in the New Testament," in *Christ the Lord*, pp. 4-5.

66. Marshall, in *Christ the Lord*, p. 5.

of a real incarnation that he makes the confession, "Jesus Christ has come in the flesh," a test of orthodoxy—to confess the same is to be "of God"; to deny it is to be "not of God" but "of Antichrist" (1 John 4:2-3).

1 John 5:20. In this verse John quite likely intends to employ θεός once again as a christological title.[67] Translated literally, the verse reads:

> And we know that the Son of God has come, and He has given us understanding in order that we may know the True One. And we are in the True One in His Son Jesus Christ. This is the true God and life eternal.

The issue is to determine whom John had in mind when he wrote, "This is the true God." We must choose between the Father and the Son. A case can be made for either, but I am personally persuaded that a better case can be made for understanding θεός as referring to the Son.

The case for the Father being the referent of "the true God" highlights the following features in the verse. First, reference to the Father is indirectly but clearly present in the verse in the genitives τοῦ θεοῦ and αὐτοῦ following the two occurrences of "the Son." This makes it evident that the Father is a bonafide possibility as the referent. Second, it is likely that the two occurrences of "true One" (τὸν ἀληθινόν, τῷ ἀληθινῷ) both refer to the Father rather than to the Son for the following reasons: (1) It would be a harsh rendering to interpret John as saying that "He [the Son] has given us understanding that we may know the true One [that is, Himself]"; if this is what he had intended, John would more likely have written "the Son" than the "true One." (2) The Father clearly seems to be the referent of the second occurrence of "true One" (and by forward extension to the first occurrence as well) because of the αὐτοῦ in the phrase immediately following it: "in *His* Son" (the NIV rendering, "even in His Son," implies the presence of a καί before the prepositional phrase, but there is no καί in the Greek text). (3) It is truer to Johannine thought to represent the Son's Messianic mission as a revelation of the Father than as a revelation of Himself (cf. John 1:18; 17:3-4). Since it is highly unlikely that John would have referred to two different persons so closely in the same verse by the one adjective "true," these features point to the Father as the referent of John's phrase "the true God."

---

67. I have examined the remaining passages that are often cited as ascribing deity to Jesus by the application of θεός as a title to Him and have concluded that Acts 20:28 *quite possibly* does so (cf. Turner, *Grammatical Insights,* pp. 14-15), that 2 Thess. 1:12 *only possibly* does so, that Eph. 5:5 *probably does not,* and that Gal. 2:20; 1 Thess. 4:9; Col. 2:2; 1 Tim. 1:17; 3:16; 5:21; James 1:1; and John 17:3 *positively do not.*

Furthermore, this would accord with John's clear reference to the Father as "the only true God" in John 17:3. Both exegetically and theologically, this interpretation is possible, and it has been espoused by such notable expositors as Brooke (ICC), Westcott, and Dodd.

But, in my opinion, four grammatical or exegetical considerations tell against it, favoring as a result the greater likelihood that the last clause refers to Jesus Christ. *First*, the nearest possible antecedent to οὗτός ("This One") is the immediately preceding phrase "Jesus Christ," and it is an exegetically sound principle to find the antecedent of demonstrative pronouns in the nearest possible noun unless there are compelling reasons for not doing so. There are no such reasons here, as there are in the oft-cited counter examples of 1 John 2:22 or 2 John 7, which require that one go further forward in the sentence to "His" or to "true One" or to "God." (The suggestion of some critics that "in His Son, Jesus Christ" is a gloss and should therefore be omitted, this being suggested in order to make "the true One" the nearest antecedent, has no manuscript support and must be judged for what it is—a mere expediency.) *Second*, to choose the more distant antecedent—that is, the Father—injects a tautology, if not an inanity, into the verse, for one does not need to be informed that the Father, who admittedly has just been twice identified already as the "true One," is "the true God," whereas John advances the thought and avoids the tautology if he is saying that Jesus Christ is "the true God." It is true that Jesus describes the Father as "the only true God" in John 17:3, but there the Father has not been previously identified as the "true One." *Third*, the singular οὗτός and the fact that "true God" and "eternal life" both stand under the regimen of the single article before "God," thereby binding the two predicates closely together on the pattern, for example, of "the true God who is (for us) eternal life" (unless both are *titles* of a person, which seems preferable for this avoids placing a person and an abstract concept under the regimen of a single article) indicate that *one* person is before the mind of the apostle. This eliminates the suggestion of some that the first title refers to the Father and the second refers to the Son. And while the Father has life in Himself (John 5:26; 6:57) and gives to men eternal life (1 John 5:11), He is nowhere designated "the Eternal Life" as is Jesus in 1 John 1:2 (cf. also John 1:4; 6:57; 11:25; 14:6). "This predicate fits Jesus better than it fits God," writes Brown.[68] But then if Jesus Christ is the referent of "Eternal Life," and if both titles refer to one person, it would follow that He is also the referent of "the true God." *Fourth*, while

---

68. Raymond E. Brown, *The Epistles of John,* Anchor Bible Series (Garden City, N.Y. · Doubleday, 1982), p. 626.

John reports that Jesus describes the Father as "the only true God" (John 17:3), he himself either describes Jesus as or records that Jesus describes Himself as "the true Light" (John 1:9; 1 John 2:8; cf. John 1:14, 17), "the true Bread" (John 6:32), "the true Vine" (John 15:1), "the true One" (Rev. 3:7; 19:11), "the true Witness" (Rev. 3:14), and "the true Sovereign" (Rev. 6:10). We have already established that John is not at all reticent about designating Christ as "God" (cf. John 1:1; 1:18; 20:28). So just as "the true One" can refer as a title both to the Father (1 John 5:20) and to the Son (Rev. 3:7), nothing would preclude John from bringing the adjective "true," which is used of Jesus elsewhere, and the noun "God" which he himself has used of Jesus, together here and applying both in their combined form as "the true God" to Jesus Christ. I am persuaded that these considerations make it highly probable that 1 John 5:20 is another occurrence of θεός as a christological title. Athanasius, Cyril of Alexandria, Jerome, Bede, Luther, and Calvin in earlier times, and Bengel, Warfield, Brown, Bruce, (even) Bultmann, Marshall, Murray, Olshausen, Schnackenburg, and the recent translators of the NIV, to name only a few in more modern times, have so interpreted John here.

Portraying Jesus Christ, the Son of the Father, then, as just "the true God and Eternal Life" (1 John 5:20) and the Co-source with the Father of the blessings of grace, mercy, and peace (2 John 3), who came "in the flesh" and "through water and blood, not with water only but with the water and with the blood," John asserts a "real and lasting union between the Son of God and the flesh of Jesus"[69] from the very beginning of Jesus' life and throughout His ministry, including even the event of His death. Presupposing the same concept of incarnation as is found in John 1:1-3, 14, John leaves no room for a docetic or an adoptionist Christology. Only the real incarnation of the Son of God satisfies all the doctrinal affirmations of these letters.[70]

The Christology of the Revelation

When one analyzes the "Revelation of Jesus Christ" (1:1) for its Christology, its nature as "apocalyptic" being unique within the New Testament corpus itself, one should not be surprised if he finds the Christology contained therein to be more "marvelous," if not more "other worldly," than

69. Marshall, in *Christ the Lord*, p. 5.

70. There is no explicit Christology in 3 John, the only allusion to Christ being the reference to "the Name" in v. 7. But about this term Westcott writes: "From the contexts it is evident that 'the Name' is 'Jesus Christ' . . . or, as it is written at length, 'Jesus Christ, the Son of God' (John xx.31; I John iv.15). This 'Name' is in essence the sum of the Christian creed. . . . When analyzed it reveals the triune 'Name' into which the Christian is baptized, Matt. xxviii.19" (*The Epistles of St. John*, 3rd ed. [London: Macmillan, 1892], pp. 238-39). Cf. also Warfield, *Lord of Glory*, p. 274.

elsewhere in the New Testament. Indeed, this is what one does find. But this is not to suggest that its representation of Christ differs in any essential way from the Christology of Paul, or of the Synoptic Evangelists, or of the writers of the general epistles, or of Hebrews, or of the rest of the Johannine corpus. But it must be acknowledged that its Christology is more consistently "advanced," to use Beasley-Murray's term,[71] in that it portrays Christ almost singularly from the perspective of His state of exaltation. The customary names and titles for Jesus are still present—"Jesus" (1:9 [twice]; 12:17; 14:12; 17:6; 19:10 [twice]; 20:4; 22:16), "Christ" (20:4, 6; cf. also "His [the Lord's] Christ," 11:15; "His [God's] Christ," 12:10), "Jesus Christ" (1:1, 2, 5), "Lord" (11:8; probably 14:13; cf. also "the Lord of lords," 17:14; 19:16; and "the Lord's Day, 1:10), "Lord Jesus" (22:20, 21), "a son of man," meaning "a man" (1:13; 14:14; cf. Dan. 7:13-14), "the Son of God" (once, in 2:18, but cf. "My Father," 2:27; 3:5, 21; and "His God and Father," 1:6), and "the Word of God" (19:13). But by far, the most common (twenty-eight times) is the almost personal, "new" name John (1:1, 9; 22:8), as the Apocalyptist, uses for the glorified Christ—"the Lamb"(ἀρνίον, 5:6, 8, 12, 13; 6:1, 16; 7:9, 10, 14, 17; 12:11; 13:8; 14:1, 4 [twice], 10; 15:3; 17:14 [twice]; 19:7, 9; 21:9, 14, 22, 23, 27; 22:1, 3), a representation found elsewhere in the New Testament only at John 1:29, 36; and 1 Peter 1:19 (cf. Acts 8:32) where the word is ἀμνός. What is truly remarkable about this title in the Revelation is that, while "the Lamb" is identified as "the Lamb that was slain" (5:6, 9, 12; 13:8), with allusions to His death in expressions such as "the blood of the Lamb" (7:14; 12:11), and while the term itself, as Warfield notes, always carries the "implied reference to the actual sacrifice,"[72] *never is the One now so designated a figure of meekness in a state or condition of humility.* Beckwith observes:

> [Lamb] is the name given to him in the most august scenes. As the object of the worship offered by the hosts of heaven and earth, chapts. 4-5; as the unveiler of the destinies of the ages, chapts. 5-6; as one enthroned, before whom and to whom the redeemed render the praise of their salvation, 7:9ff.; as the controller of the book of life, 13:8; as the Lord of the hosts on mount Zion, 14:1; as the victor over the hosts of Antichrist, 17:14; as the spouse of the glorified Church, 19:7; as the temple and light of the new Jerusalem, 21:22f.; as the sharer in the throne of God, 22:1,—Christ is called the Lamb. Nowhere in the occurrence of the name is there evident allusion to the figure of *meekness and gentleness* in suffering.[73]

71. G. R. Beasley-Murray, *The Book of Revelation* (London: Oliphants, 1974), p. 24.
72. Warfield, *Lord of Glory,* p. 290.
73. Isbon T. Beckwith, *The Apocalypse of John* (1919; reprint, Grand Rapids: Baker, 1967), p. 315.

In other words, if Jesus is "the Lamb" in the Revelation, He is the "Lamb glorified." And this depiction of Christ as the glorified Lamb is dominant throughout the Apocalypse.

Of course, He is certainly a *human* Messiah still, as the "male child" (12:5, 13), the "Lion of the tribe of Judah" (5:5), and the "Root and Offspring of David" (5:5; 22:16) who is capable of dying, but who by His exaltation is the "Firstborn from the dead" (1:5) and thus the "Ruler of the kings of the earth" (1:5), indeed, the "King of kings and Lord of lords" (19:16; cf. 17:14). And while He is set off over against God in that He is the Son of God (2:18) and the Word of God (19:13) and in that God is His Father (1:6; 2:27; 3:5, 21; 14:1), indeed, even in that God is His God (1:6; 3:2, 12; cf. 11:15; 12:10) who gives to Him both the authority to rule (2:27) and the Revelation itself to show to His servants (1:1), He is represented as being Himself divine. Beckwith observes again in this connection:

> Nowhere else are found these wonderful scenes revealing to the eye and ear the majesty of Christ's ascended state, and these numerous utterances expressing in terms applicable to God alone the truth of his divine nature and power. He is seen in the first vision in a form having the semblance of a man, yet glorified with attributes by which the Old Testament writers have sought to portray the glory of God; his hair is white as snow, his face shines with the dazzling light of the sun, his eyes are a flame of fire, his voice as the thunder of many waters; he announces himself as eternal, as the one who though he died is the essentially living One, having all power over death, 1:13-18. He appears in the court of heaven as coequal with God in the adoration offered by the highest hosts of heaven and by all the world, 5:6-14. He is seen coming forth on the clouds as the judge and arbiter of the world, 14:14-16. Wearing crowns and insignia which mark him as King of kings and Lord of lords, he leads out the armies of heaven to the great battle with Antichrist, 19:11-21. In keeping with these scenes, attributes and prerogatives understood to belong to God only are assigned to him either alone or as joined with God; he is the Alpha and Omega, the first and the last, the beginning and the end, 22:13, 1:17, 2:8—a designation which God also utters of himself, 1:8, cf. Is. 44:6, 48:12; worship is offered to him in common with God, 7:10, 5:13—a worship which angelic beings are forbidden to receive, 19:10; doxologies are raised to him as to God, 1:6; the throne of God is his throne, the priests of God are his priests, 3:21, 22:1, 20:6; life belongs essentially to him as to God, compare 1:18 with 4:9, 10.[74]

74. Ibid., pp. 312-13. In this same regard, H. B. Swete writes:

What is the relation of Christ, in His glorified state, to God? (i) He has the prerogatives of

Beasley-Murray likewise affirms:

> Constantly the attributes of God are ascribed to Christ, as in the opening vision of the first chapter, which is significantly a vision of Christ and not of God. The lineaments of the risen Lord are those of the Ancient of Days and of his angel in the book of Daniel (chs. 7 and 10). Christ is confessed as Alpha and Omega (22:13), as God is also (1:8). The implications of the claim are drawn out in the book as a whole. . . . In the closing vision of the city of God . . . God and the Lamb are united as Lord of the kingdom and source of its blessedness. It is especially noteworthy that John depicts the throne of God and the Lamb as the source of the river of water of life in the city, thereby conveying the notion of a single throne, a single rule, and a single source of life. He adds, "his servants shall worship him; they shall see his face, and his name shall be on their foreheads" (22:3f.). In the context it is difficult to interpret the pronoun "his" as meaning anything other than "God and the Lamb" as a unity. The Lamb remains as the mediator . . . yet he is inseparable from the God who enacts his works . . . through him.[75]

In light of these facts, we may fairly bring this brief overview of the Revelation to a close by concluding that any reader who will take the time to check for himself will discover that the Revelation sets before its reader an awe-inspiring divine Christ, and thus unites its witness, and that in a singularly marvelous way, to the consentient testimony of the New Testament as a whole in support of the full and unabridged deity of the Son of God.

In this chapter we reviewed the remaining New Testament witness to Jesus as that witness is set forth in the Christologies of James, Jude, Peter, the Synoptic Evangelists, and particularly the writer of Hebrews and John. It was our intention throughout to discern as clearly and as accurately as possible the Jesus in whom these New Testament writers believed and

---

God. He searches men's hearts (2:23); He can kill and restore to life (1:18; 2:23); He receives a worship which is rendered without distinction to God (5:13); His priests are also priests of God (20:6); He occupies one throne with God (22:1, 3), and shares one sovereignty (11:15); (ii) Christ receives the titles of God. He is the Living One (1:18), the Holy and the True (3:7), the Alpha and the Omega, the First and the Last, the Beginning and the End (22:13). (iii) Passages which in the Old Testament relate to God are without hesitation applied to Christ, e.g., Deut. 10:17 (Apoc. 17:14), Prov. 3:12 (Apoc. 3:19), Dan. 7:9 (Apoc. 1:14), Zech. 4:10 (Apoc. 5:6). Thus the writer seems either to coordinate or to identify Christ with God. Yet he is certainly not conscious of any tendency to ditheism, for his book . . . is rigidly monotheistic; nor, on the other hand, is he guilty of confusing the two Persons (*The Apocalypse of St. John*, 3rd ed. [London: Macmillan, 1911], p. clxii).

75. Beasley-Murray, *Book of Revelation*, pp. 24-25. Cf. also Donald Guthrie (*The Relevance of John's Apocalypse* [Grand Rapids: Eerdmans, 1987], pp. 37-64) for a recent defense against Dodd, Bultmann, and others who contend that the Christology of Revelation is "so far below that of the rest of the New Testament as to be negligible."

whom they proclaimed to others. I think it a fair deduction that Jesus was for all of them,[76] as well as for the entire early Christian community that followed the teaching of the apostles, the promised Messiah of Old Testament hope and expectation who, while being certainly human in every sense of the word, exhibited by His life, His words, and His works that He was also the divine Son of God and thus God incarnate. *Theirs, in a phrase, was an incarnational Christology.* This is not to suggest that one can find anywhere in their writings christological formulae that set forth their views with the later *formulaic* precision of the Fathers at Nicaea or Chalcedon. Such later formulae came as the hard-won systematized responses to specific, sometimes bizarre, doctrinal errors that circulated in later times about Christ. But I urge that these New Testament writers provide such an all-pervasive and singularly united witness to a Christ who is both true God and true man that only christological formulae such as those that came forth from Nicaea in A.D. 325 and from Chalcedon in A.D. 451 do full justice to all of the biblical data.

Having surveyed the whole of the New Testament for its Christology, with the necessary data now at hand, I want to deal with one final, very significant issue. One finds it often said in critical circles today that if Jesus had really believed He was God, such an explicit claim would be found on His lips. Moreover, critical scholars say, if Jesus had really been regarded by the New Testament witness as God manifest in the flesh, one would find the New Testament filled with explicit statements to that effect and not just the eight occurrences of θεός we have culled from the New Testament record (in their historical order of occurrence, John 20:28; Rom. 9:5; Titus 2:13; 2 Pet. 1:1; Heb. 1:8; John 1:1; John 1:18; and 1 John 5:20). What shall we say to these observations?

First, even if we had needed to conclude from our investigation that Jesus was never called "God" in the New Testament, His deity is still solidly evidenced to us, as we have seen, on the New Testament grounds that He is portrayed therein as possessing divine attributes, as exercising divine functions, as the recipient of both angelic and human worship, as the respondent to the petitionary prayers of the saints, and as the object of saving trust. *Second*, while one never finds Jesus in any Gospel making the explicit claim in so many words, Ἐγώ εἰμι θεός (Greek) or אֲנָה אֱלָהָא (Aramaic) (just as He did not regularly go around claiming in so many words to be the "Christ"), one may understand, given His *Sitz im Leben*, why Jesus deemed

---

76. The reader is urged to read Gerald Bray's brief but brilliant defense of the doctrinal unity of the apostles and the New Testament writings in his *Creeds, Councils and Christ* ([Downers Grove, Ill.: Inter-Varsity Press, 1984], pp. 55-61).

it wise, before His hearers' minds and hearts had been prepared for such and before His own ministry had been completed, not to travel around in the intensely monotheistic setting of pre-Christian Palestine claiming in so many words to be God. *Third*, as for the relatively few occurrences of θεός as a christological title throughout the New Testament, Murray Harris has quite properly noted that

> in all strands of the NT θεός generally signifies the Father. Short of coining a new theological term to denote deity, writers who believed in the divinity of Jesus were forced to employ current terminology and run the risk of being branded ditheistic. One reason for the relative infrequency of the NT use of θεός in reference to Jesus may in fact have been the danger recognized by the early church that if θεός were applied to Jesus as regularly as to the Father, Jews would have tended to regard Christianity as incurably deuterotheological, and Gentiles would probably have viewed it as polytheistic.[77]

So faced with the fact that "the Old Testament heritage dominated the use of the title God [for the Father],"[78] and yet having the need to address not only the Father but also the Son as God and needing at the same time to distinguish between them, the church, under the wise guidance of the apostles, adopted the practice that is observed to this very day of addressing primarily the Father as θεός and addressing primarily the Son as κύριος. The latter, however, certainly intends deity as fully as the former, but it also contains the suggestion of the exalted status that became His as the God-man by virtue of His incarnational work as Messiah and Savior (cf. Acts 2:36; Phil. 2:6-11). The fact that the references to Jesus as θεός are few in number is no argument, therefore, against His being deity. The sparse number simply reflects the exigencies that obtained under the given circumstances and needs of the time.

While it is still in vogue in some quarters to argue that none of the eight occurrences of θεός as a christological title are themselves indisputably clear references to Jesus, justifying Nigel Turner's comment that "the simple grammarian may be forgiven for suspecting that special pleading has contributed to the debilitation of tremendous affirmations in the New Testament" respecting the deity of Jesus Christ,[79] it is increasingly being urged

77. Murray J. Harris, "Titus 2:13 and the Deity of Christ," in *Pauline Studies: Essays Presented to Professor F. F. Bruce on His 70th Birthday*, ed. Donald A. Hagner and Murray J. Harris (Grand Rapids: Eerdmans, 1980), pp. 265-66.

78. Brown, "Does the New Testament Call Jesus God?" p. 569.

79. Turner, *Grammatical Insights*, p. 16.

that the New Testament employment of θεός as a christological title had its origin, not in apostolic teaching, but in the liturgy and prayers of the worshiping community. As evidence of this theory, Brown points out that the occurrences in Romans, Titus, 2 Peter, and 1 John are doxological in character, that the occurrences in Hebrews and John's Prologue appear respectively in the citation of a psalm and in a hymn, and that Thomas's confession occurred on Sunday (!), suggesting that "My Lord and my God", was a "confessional formula used in liturgy."[80] He also asserts that "the usage of calling Jesus God was a liturgical usage and had its origin in the worship and prayers of the Christian community."[81] A. W. Wainwright, agreeing that some if not all of these uses have a "liturgical background," explains that the apostles and the early church could only express in worship what they, in their inmost feelings, surmised but were unable to adjust to their monotheism:

> The writers of the New Testament seem to have been reluctant to commit to writing the confession that Jesus is God. The reluctance of St. Paul and the author of the Epistle to the Hebrews may have been caused by their inability to give an account of the relationship of this belief to the Jewish monotheism to which they continued to subscribe. Their faith outstripped their reason, and they were able to give joyful utterance to a belief which they felt incapable of expounding. But each of these writers, on one occasion [sic], allowed himself to give expression to this deep-seated belief, and to include in the text of an epistle language which he used more frequently in private and public worship. [How does Wainwright know that these writers used this language more frequently in their private worship?]
> The author of the Fourth Gospel interwove this belief into his thought. . . . St. John too was in contact with a liturgical tradition in which Jesus was hailed as Lord and God. Perhaps, by placing the confession of Thomas at the very end of the Gospel, he was suggesting that it was only in the moment of worship that men were able to comprehend that Jesus was God.[82]

This theory must be roundly rejected. It is the offspring of a form-critical approach that will not permit teachings or events in the New Testament

80. Brown, "Does the New Testament Call Jesus God?" pp. 570-71.

81. Ibid. Brown declares that "the title 'God' was applied to Jesus more quickly in the liturgical formulae than in narrative and epistolary literature" (*The Gospel According to John I-XII* [Garden City, N.J.: Doubleday, 1966], p. 24).

82. A. W. Wainwright, "The Confession Jesus Is 'God' in the New Testament," *Scottish Journal of Theology* 10 (1957): 295.

documents to be untouched history, but rather views them as the result of theological reshaping by an early Christian community. It is a mere expediency to declare that the occurrences of θεός in Titus, 2 Peter, and 1 John are doxological in character, as Brown does. And it is surely a case of special pleading to say, because the writer of Hebrews is quoting a psalm, that Hebrews 1:8 is liturgical. But even if it were, is not Psalm 45 part of Scripture and "profitable for doctrine"? To make John 1:1 fit the theory, Brown must argue that the Prologue of John is "an early Christian hymn, probably stemming from Johannine circles, which has been adapted to serve as an overture to the Gospel narrative."[83] But this view of John's Prologue is not shared by all, by any means. Morris, for example, describes the language of the Prologue as being, at most, "elevated prose" and not hymnic.[84] And to suggest, as Wainwright does, that the early church could confess in worship what it neither could conceptualize nor dare to express in nonliturgical prose or narrative is to impute an uncommonly low level of reflective capability to the first-century Christians and their leaders and to suggest that it was not their primary concern that their worship be in accordance with truth and fact. Worship must be grounded in sound doctrine. Any confession of faith must be sound likewise. Are we to suppose that the early church did not understand this? The biblical evidence would indicate that they understood this better than Wainwright gives them credit for doing. The apostles and the early church were deeply concerned with sound doctrine, and aberrations were not tolerated (cf. 1 Cor. 1:10-13; 3:4-9; Rom. 16:17; Gal. 1:6-9; Eph. 4:3-6; 2 Tim. 1:13-14; 2:2; 4:1-4; Titus 1:9-11; 2:1; 1 John 4:1-3; 2 John 7-11; Jude 3-4). They would not have expressed in their liturgy what they could not express in their prose.

These scholars have misread the facts governing the situation. The early church did worship Jesus as God, and the apostles upon occasion, as we have seen, actually expressed Jesus' *theotic* character in their writings by the explicit use of θεός as a christological title. But it was not the church's worship that induced the apostles to include such expressions in their writings. Rather, it was the apostles' teaching that grounded for Christians the appropriateness of worshiping Christ as God.

It is also incorrect to insist, with Raymond E. Brown and many others, that "although the Johannine description and acceptance of the divinity of Jesus has ontological implications . . . in itself this description remains primarily

83. Brown, *Gospel According to John I-XII*, p. 1.
84. Leon Morris, *Gospel According to John*, p. 72. Morris further comments, "[The prologue] is written in a meditative strain. . . . This lends a musing air to the passage. But it does not make it poetry" (ibid.).

functional" because "the Johannine acceptance of Jesus as divine or equal to God . . . is not divorced from the fact that Jesus was sent by God and acted in God's name and in God's stead."[85] Brown goes even farther in another place and states categorically that "none of the instances [where Jesus is called God] attempts to define Jesus essentially."[86] Even apart from the fact that John the Baptist also claimed to have been sent from God and in fact acted in God's name and in His stead (John 1:6) with no charge of blasphemy ever being levelled at him for claiming such, in both John 1:1 and 1:18 θεός is used of the Father, unquestionably designating what He essentially is. It is difficult to believe that θεός means something entirely different in these same two verses when applied to Jesus. A tough-minded reading of the three occurrences of the title in the Fourth Gospel will reveal that its first usage in 1:1 as a description of the preexistent Logos provides the governing control over the meaning of its description of Him in 1:18 as the incarnate Logos and the later description of Him in John 20:28 as the risen Christ. In each case the term "does not describe [Jesus'] function, but indicates who he is."[87]

These unmistakably clear New Testament attributions of deity to Christ explain a phenomenon in early patristic literature. Ignatius, third bishop of Antioch (Syria) who was martyred in Rome in A.D. 108 is, along with Clement of Rome, the earliest of the extrabiblical Christian writers. In his letter to the Ephesians Ignatius speaks of the "blood of God" (αἵματι θεοῦ, 1:1; cf. Acts 20:28) and says that "our God, Jesus the Christ" (ὁ θεός ἡμῶν Ἰησοῦς ὁ Χριστός) was conceived by Mary (18:2), and that "God was manifest as man" (θεοῦ ἀνθρωπίνως φανερουμένου, 19:3). In his letter to the Smyrnaeans he glorifies "Jesus Christ, the God" (Ἰησοῦν Χριστὸν τὸν θεόν) who had given them wisdom (1:1). In his letter to the Romans, twice in the salutation he refers to "Jesus Christ, our God" (Ἰησοῦ Χριστοῦ τοῦ θεοῦ ἡμῶν; Ἰησοῦ Χριστῷ τῷ θεῷ ἡμῶν), and later to "the passion of my God" (τοῦ πάθους τοῦ θεοῦ μου, 6:3). In his letter to Polycarp he bids Polycarp farewell "in our God, Jesus Christ" (ἐν θεῷ ἡμῶν Ἰησοῦ Χριστῷ), 8:3). In the mid-second century, in so-called 2 Clement 1:1, Clement informs his Christian brothers that it is necessary to think "of Jesus Christ as God" (περὶ Ἰησοῦ Χριστοῦ ὡς περὶ θεοῦ). The pagan Pliny the Younger (A.D. 61–112), governor of Bithynia in Asia Minor, in Letter 10.96.7 reports that Christians of his day were chanting verses "to Christ as if to a god" (Christo quasi deo).

85. Brown, Gospel According to John I-XII, p. 408.
86. Brown, "Does the New Testament Call Jesus God?" p. 572.
87. Cf. B. A. Mastin, "A Neglected Feature of the Christology of the Fourth Gospel," New Testament Studies 22 (1976): 43-46.

Without these clear New Testament titular descriptions of Jesus as θεός we could still always assert that the early Fathers had deduced, and rightly so, the propriety of their use of the title from all the other New Testament data that treats Him as divine. But it could also be argued that the church has deduced too much. As it is, with these references to Jesus as "God" embedded in the New Testament literature, we stand on the "concrete" that bridges the age of the apostles and the age of the earliest Fathers and the later church beyond. Here—in what the New Testament reports that He taught about Himself and in what He led the apostles to affirm about Him—is the exegetical grounding for the church's freedom today to speak of Jesus as the divine-human God-man, to worship Him as the Son of God, and to serve Him as its Lord.

EPILOGUE

A PERSONAL WITNESS

Throughout the foregoing chapters we have been seeking to answer the perennial question: Who is Jesus Christ? Jesus Himself forced this question on every man with His penetrating questions: "What do you think of the Christ? Whose Son is He?" Both the New Testament and the historic Christian church have declared that He is the divine Son of God who, as God's ordained Messiah, became flesh for us men and for our salvation and paid the penalty for sin on the cross.

Jesus' question, interestingly, has to do with *thoughts:* "What do you *think* of the Christ?" Thoughts are all-important in this world. They determine every human action, either directly or indirectly. And thoughts about Christ, I suggest, are of paramount significance. Whatever else one may think of Karl Barth's total theological edifice (and I find much in it with which I must disagree), he was absolutely right when he declared that what a man thinks about Christ will determine what he ultimately thinks about everything else. Jesus even declared that a man's eternal destiny would be determined by his thoughts about Him (John 8:24).

Jesus' question is also eminently *existential:* "What do *you* think of the Christ?" It is very easy for one to immerse himself so deeply in the "community of men" that he lets that "community" think for him without realizing it. But when it comes to thoughts about Christ, this is a perilous path. It is very tempting for one to "feel out" which way the theological wind is blowing in the modern church and to conclude that, enlightened as the modern church must be, surely the numerous voices within her venue must be right in urging upon men a "modern Christ" different in kind from the two-natured Christ that the New Testament and the Christian church have confessed. Here I would urge enormous caution, but since I have given many reasons already for such counsel, I will let someone else explain why this approach is not wise. While I was researching this book at Tyndale House, Cambridge, the editor of the London newspaper, *The Daily Tele-*

graph, in his lead editorial for the Christmas Eve edition 1985, entitled "God Bless Us, Everyone," wrote:

> The aspect of the [Christmas] festival which most continues to fascinate modern industrialised man (. . . flying in the face of the conventional wisdom) has to do with its miraculous character. Those who crowd the churches tonight . . . will not be celebrating the birth of a good man simply. The wonder of Christmas is precisely that God himself, by whom the heavens and earth were made, was born as a tiny child, humbling himself to share in our humanity. . . . *The Bishop of Durham describes the biblical narrative of Christ's birth as "unlikely." But the entire point of the story is that it is not only unlikely but wholly unique;* quite impossible to accept without the belief that God can and does intervene in the affairs of men. *It may be that our culture has a deeper instinct than many within the Church have realised that this belief is actually true. And it needs to be said that until this realisation sinks home, the crisis within the Church . . . will grow increasingly grave.*
>
> That the Church is in deep crisis becomes increasingly clear. . . . At a time when industrialised man [is] weary of being the plaything of large-scale processes, and hungry for a resacralised understanding of human existence, *the Church is becoming more and more committed to . . . a non-supernatural version of traditional Christian doctrine. . . .*
>
> The only way the Church can become again a vehicle for divine truth is to understand once more how ephemeral and how worthless is all the wisdom of the rulers of this world. . . . *A first step would be to understand that the Church has put its money on a liberal secularist biblical criticism to the point of intellectual collapse* (emphasis added).

The editor concluded,

> When [this] reality [of the supernatural Christ] has thus been faced [by the Church] the Church may be in a position to kneel before the Christ child, and to say in all humility, in the words of THOMAS the Doubter, "My Lord and my God."

This editorial reveals uncommon insight into the intellectual currents of the church today. Its author with exceptionally clear vision understands where the modern church is intellectually and spiritually—in deep crisis. The modern church has lost its way precisely for the reason he indicates: insensitivity to the worthlessness of the wisdom of this world. A large segment of the church's educators and ministers in their intellectual life has "put its money" on a liberal secularist biblical criticism to the point that the church faces not only intellectual collapse but also wholesale loss of the respect of the man on the street who still believes or would like to believe that the biblical message is true. I urge the reader not to listen to these modern "doctors of the church" who would deliver the church from its "bondage to the New Testament's arcane model of vertical transcendence," but rather to "search the Scriptures" for himself as the Beraeans did (Acts 17:11).

Occasionally, one hears the admonition to "face reality," to "wake up and begin to live in the real world." I would urge that to enter believingly into the world of the New Testament's witness concerning Jesus Christ *is* to enter into the real world, and to begin to understand things as they really are. At the end of the first chapter, I invited my reader to continue with me on an investigative pilgrimage through the evidences from Scripture for Jesus Christ as God incarnate. I suggested then that there was more at stake than just an intellectually satisfying faith. That journey has now reached its end. Now I invite my reader, if he has not already done so, to face squarely the fact that Jesus Christ is God incarnate, and that as God's Son He came into the world because His Father in heaven "so loved the world that He gave His one and only Son that whoever believes in Him shall not perish but have eternal life" (John 3:16). If the reader has been convinced from the biblical data that all of this is true, I invite him to submit by faith to Christ's saving scepter.

SCRIPTURE INDEX

327

GENERAL INDEX

Abbott, T. K., 251n
Adamson, James, 281
Alexander, J. A., 124n
Alexander, Neil, 309
Alford, Henry, 94, 205, 207n
American Scientific Affiliation, 23
Archer, Gleason, L., Jr., 285n
Arndt, W. F., and Gingrich, F. W., 146, 171n, 205, 250, 271n, 302, 305n
Ascension account, exposition of, 216-22
Baird, J. A., 55n
Baptism accounts, exposition of, 143-53
Barrett, C. K., 60n, 166, 174n, 180-81, 183, 184
Bartel, Karl-Heinz, 305n
Barth, Karl, 16-17, 323
Beasley-Murray, G. R., 281, 313, 315
Becker, J., 87
Beckwith, Isbon T., 313, 314
Bengel, J. A., 207n, 312
Berger, K., 37
Berkhof, L., 137n
Berkouwer, G. C., 14, 78n, 93n, 191, 218, 219
Bernard, J. H., 168n, 174n, 302
Best, Ernest, 286n, 287n
Betz, O., 200n
Bigg, Charles, 288-89, 290n
Blass, F., 123, 272n, 288n
Blomberg, Craig, 116
Boobyer, G. H., 159
Bornkamm, Günther, 28, 53, 195n, 196, 197-98

Borsch, F. H., 59
Bousset, W., 31, 34
Bowden, John, 28, 36
Bray, Gerald, 14n, 316n
Brooke, A. E., 311
Brown, Raymond E., 4, 7, 48, 93n, 102n, 109n, 110n, 146, 147, 165, 166, 180, 213, 214, 297n, 311, 312, 317, 318-19, 319-20
Bruce, A. B., 75n
Bruce, F. F., 54, 60n, 61n, 229-30, 233n, 247n, 294n, 299, 300-301, 309n, 312
Brunner, E., 132, 258n
Bultmann, Rudolf, 3, 9, 21-23, 28, 33, 34, 48, 50, 53, 55n, 57, 82, 87, 99, 116, 144, 159, 168, 169, 176, 195-96, 200n, 217, 234, 267, 312, 315n
Burge, G. M., 54n
Burney, C. F., 137n, 246
Burton, E. D., 30
Buswell, J. Oliver, Jr., 135n, 139n
Caird, G. B., 69n, 70
Calvin, John, 122, 134
Carson, Donald A., 52n, 53n, 56, 60, 61, 62, 69, 75, 76n, 86, 87, 88, 93, 94, 101, 119-20, 291n
Catchpole, D. R., 52
Chapman, John, 69
"Christ," title of, 45-52
Clark, Gordon H., 217n
Colpe, C., 59
Colwell, E. C., 53, 154n, 185, 303
Conzelmann, H., 28, 37, 38
Cooper, Karl T., 235n

343